ISRAEL

GOVERNMENT SYSTEM HANDBOOK

STRATEGIC INFORMATION AND DEVELOPMENTS

International Business Publications, USA
Washington DC, USA - Israel

ISRAEL

GOVERNMENT SYSTEM HANDBOOK

STRATEGIC INFORMATION AND DEVELOPMENTS

UPDATED ANNUALLY

We express our sincere appreciation to all government agencies and international organizations which provided information and other materials for this handbook

Cover Design: International Business Publications, USA

2018 Updated Reprint International Business Publications, USA
ISBN 1-4330-2581-7

Printed in the USA

For additional analytical, business and investment opportunities information, please contact Global Investment & Business Center, USA at (703) 370-8082. Fax: (703) 370-8083. E-mail: ibpusa3@gmail.com Global Business and Investment Info Databank - www.ibpus.com

ISRAEL

GOVERNMENT SYSTEM HANDBOOK

STRATEGIC INFORMATION AND DEVELOPMENTS

TABLE OF CONTENTS

STRATEGIC AND DEVELOPMENT PROFILES **11**

STRATEGIC PROFILE 11
Geography *12*
People *14*
Government *16*
Economy *18*
Energy *22*
Communications *24*
Transportation *25*
Military *26*
Transnational Issues *26*
TERRORISM 26

IMPORTANT INFORMATION FOR UNDERSTANDING ISRAEL **28**

BASIC DATA 28
Geography *28*
People *28*
Government *28*
Economy *28*
PEOPLE 29
GOVERNMENT 30
POLITICAL CONDITIONS 30
ECONOMY 31
FOREIGN RELATIONS 32
DEFENSE 32
U.S.-ISRAELI RELATIONS 33
Principal U.S. Officials *33*
ADMINISTRATIVE DIVISIONS 34
Israeli-occupied territories *36*
POPULATION AND DEMOGRAPHICS 38
Cities *39*
ETHNIC AND RELIGIOUS GROUPS 40
Jews *40*
Arabs *41*
Bedouin 42
Other Arabic-speaking groups *42*
Druze 42
Maronites 42
Copts 42
Other citizens *42*

Samaritans ... 42
Armenians ... 42
Circassians ... 43
Assyrians ... 43
People from post-Soviet states ... 43
Finns ... 43
Romani ... 43
Vietnamese ... 44
African Hebrew Israelites of Jerusalem ... 44
Naturalized foreign workers ... 44
Non-citizens ... *44*
African refugees ... 44
Foreign workers ... 44
Other refugees ... 45
LANGUAGES ... 45
RELIGION ... 45
EDUCATION ... 45
POLICY AND IMMIGRATION ... 45
Citizenship and Entry Law ... *46*
Russian immigration ... *47*
The increase in the number of emigrants ... *48*
Factors for the emigration ... *48*
The absorption of the emigration wave ... *49*

ISRAEL: STRATEGIC INFORMATION AND US POLICY ... 50

COUNTRY BACKGROUND ... 53
Historical Overview ... *53*
GOVERNMENT, POLITICS, AND SOCIETY ... 54
Israeli Electoral Process and Government-Building ... *54*
Political and Societal Evolution ... *55*
Current Government ... *56*
Corruption Allegations Involving Netanyahu ... *56*
Major Domestic Issues ... *57*
ECONOMY AND DEVELOPMENTS ... *58*
ISRAELI SECURITY AND CHALLENGES ... 59
Strategic and Military Profile ... *59*
Military Superiority and Homeland Security Measures ... 59
Undeclared Nuclear Weapons Capability ... 60
U.S. Cooperation ... 60
Iran and the Region ... *60*
Iranian Nuclear Agreement and the U.S. Withdrawal ... 60
Iran in Syria: Cross-Border Attacks with Israel45 ... *61*
Russia ... *62*
Hezbollah in Lebanon ... *62*
Hamas and Gaza ... *63*
ISRAEL AND KEY U.S. POLICY ISSUES ... 65
Security Cooperation74 ... *65*
Preserving Israel's Qualitative Military Edge (QME) ... 65
U.S. Aid and Arms Sales to Israel ... *66*
Aid ... 66
Arms Sales ... 67
End-Use Monitoring and Leahy Law Vetting ... 67
Missile Defense Cooperation ... *68*
Pending Security Cooperation Legislation ... *68*

Sensitive Technology and Intelligence *69*
BILATERAL TRADE 70
ISRAELI-PALESTINIAN ISSUES 70
Peace Process and International Involvement *70*
Jerusalem *72*
Settlements *75*
U.S. Policy 77

GOVERNMENT AND POLITICAL SYSTEM - STRATEGIC INFORMATION 79

SYSTEM OF GOVERNMENT BASICS 79
EXECUTIVE BRANCH *79*
PRESIDENT 80
PRIME MINISTER 82
Political positions 84
LEGISLATIVE BRANCH 85
KNESSET - BASIC INFORMATION *86*
Political Parties in Israel 87
Israeli Knesset Parties and Their Leaders *88*
Electoral system *91*
Organisation of the Knesset *91*
SPEAKER AND THE DEPUTY SPEAKERS 91
ELECTION AND APPOINTMENT OF POSITION HOLDERS *95*
ELECTION OF REPRESENTATIVES TO APPOINTMENTS COMMITTEES BY THE KNESSET 95
ELECTION OF REPRESENTATIVES BY A COMMITTEE OF THE KNEESSET 99
DETERMINING THE NUMBER OF SUPREME COURT JUSTICES 100
KNESSET ORGANIZATION AND ADMINISTRATIVE PROCEDURES *101*
SITTINGS 101
AGENDA 104
DEBATE PROCEDURES 105
VOTING IN THE KNESSET PLENUM 108
Committee chairs *109*
EXECUTIVE BRANCH - CABINET OF MINISTERS 111
Thirty-fourth government of Israe *111*
Policy guidelines 112
Cabinet members 112
Security cabinet 113
Government agencies and special committees *114*
GOVERNMENT MINISTRIES 114
The Office of the President *114*
The Knesset *114*
Prime Minister's Office *114*
Ministry of Agriculture *115*
Ministry of Communication *115*
Ministry of Construction and Housing *115*
Ministry of Defense *115*
Ministry for the Development of the Negev and the Galilee *115*
Ministry of Education, Culture and Sports *116*
Ministry of Energy and Water Resources *116*
Ministry of Environmental Protection *116*
Ministry of Finance *116*
Ministry of Foreign Affairs *116*
Ministry of Health *117*
Ministry of Immigrant Absorption *117*

Ministry of Industry and Trade *117*
Ministry of the Interior *117*
Ministry of Justice *118*
Ministry of Labor and Social Welfare *118*
Ministry of Public Security *118*
Ministry of Science and Technology *118*
Ministry of Tourism *119*
Bank of Israel *119*
National Authority of Religious Services *119*
Chief Rabbinate of Israel *120*
State Comptroller and Ombudsman *120*
MINISTERSS - NAMES AND CONTACTS 120
Israeli security forces *121*
Military 121
Police 121
Intelligence 121
Emergency services 122
Other organizations 122
LOCAL GOV ERNMENT 123
BASIC INFORMATION *123*
POLITICS AND DEVELOPMENTS 127
Political conditions *127*
Political issues *127*
JUDICIAL SYSTEM 128
Secular courts *128*
Supreme Court 128
District courts 128
Magistrate courts 129
Labor courts *129*
Military courts *129*
Criminal procedure *129*
Judicial selection *130*
Religious courts *130*
Jewish religious courts 130
Non-Jewish religious courts 130
Legal practice *131*
LOCAL GOVERNMENT IN ISRAEL 131
ROLES 131
Other abilities and responsibilities *132*

GOVERNMENT, ELECTIONS AND POLITICAL DEVELOPMENTS 133

THE ELECTORAL SYSTEM 134
POLITICAL FRAMEWORK: ELITE, VALUES, AND ORIENTATIONS 134
MULTIPARTY SYSTEM *139*
CIVIL-MILITARY RELATIONS *141*
Voting method *141*
ISRAELI LEGISLATIVE ELECTION, 2015 142

FOREIGN POLICY AND NATIONAL SECURITY 143

MINISTRY OF FOREIGN AFFAIRS (ISRAEL) 145
MINISTER *146*
The Iranian Threat: Overview *147*

ELECTORAL SYSTEM AND POLITICAL DEVELOPMENTS 148

BASIC INFORMATION ... 148
Electoral procedure ... *148*
ISRAEL FOREIGN POLICY STRATEGY AND DEVELOPMENTS ... 150
No recognition or diplomatic relations ... *150*
Partial recognition or trade agreements ... *151*
RELATIONS WITH MIDDLE EASTERN STATES ... 151
Egypt ... *151*
Jordan ... *151*
Morocco ... *152*
Iran ... *152*
RELATIONS WITH THE UNITED STATES ... 153
RELATIONS WITH AFRICAN STATES ... 156
RELATIONS WITH LATIN AMERICA ... 157
RELATIONS WITH WESTERN EUROPE ... 158
US ASSISTANCE TO ISRAEL - STRATEGIC INFORMATION ... 159
Background ... *159*
Qualitative Military Edge (QME) ... *160*
QME and U.S. Arms Sales to the Gulf ... *162*
U.S. Bilateral Military Aid to Israel ... *163*
The Current 10-Year Security Assistance Memorandum of Understanding (MOU) ... 163
Foreign Military Financing (FMF) and Arms Sales ... *165*
Cash Flow Financing26 ... 165
Early Transfer and Interest Bearing Account ... 166
F-35 Joint Strike Fighter ... 166
Excess Defense Articles ... 167
Defense Budget Appropriations for U.S.-Israeli Missile Defense Programs ... *167*
Iron Dome ... 168
Iron Dome's Performance ... *168*
Coproduction and U.S. Funding ... *168*
David's Sling ... 169
Coproduction and U.S. Funding ... 170
The Arrow and Arrow II ... 170
High Altitude Missile Defense System (Arrow III) ... *171*
Coproduction and U.S. Funding ... 171
Emergency U.S. Stockpile in Israel ... *173*
Defense Budget Appropriations/Authorization for Anti-Tunnel Defense ... 174
Aid Restrictions and Possible Violations ... *174*
Arms Sales and Use of U.S.-Supplied Equipment ... 175
Human Rights Vetting (Leahy Law)62 ... 175
Use of U.S. Funds within Israel's Pre-June 1967 Borders ... 176
Other Ongoing Assistance and Cooperative Programs ... *176*
Migration & Refugee Assistance ... 176
Loan Guarantees ... *177*
Loan Guarantees for Economic Recovery ... 177
American Schools and Hospitals Abroad Program (ASHA)74 ... 179
U.S.-Israeli Scientific & Business Cooperation ... *179*
U.S.-Israeli Energy Cooperation (BIRD Energy) ... 181
U.S.-Israeli Water Cooperation ... 181
U.S.-Israeli Cybersecurity Cooperation ... 181
EU ISRAEL COOPERATION ... 182
1. Political Background ... *182*
2. Economic Background ... *182*
3. The Association Agreement ... *182*
Trade Relations ... *185*

Co-operation ... 185
Euro-Mediterranean Partnership ... *187*
Support to the Middle East Peace Process ... *189*
Peace and tolerance ... 189

BASIC LAWS AND REGULATIONS DETERMINIGN THE FUNCTIONS OF THE STATE OF ISRAEL ... 191

ISRAEL AS THE NATION-STATE OF THE JEWISH PEOPLE ... 191
THE GOVERNMENT ... 192
THE PRESIDENT OF THE STATE ... 207
THE JUDICIARY ... 212
Basic Provisions ... *212*
Judges ... *212*
The Courts ... *214*
Miscellaneous Provisions ... *215*
THE STATE COMPTROLLER ... 216
THE ARMY ... 217
JERUSALEM, CAPITAL OF ISRAEL ... 217
ISRAEL LANDS ... 218
THE STATE ECONOMY ... 218
The State Economy (Amendment) ... *219*
HUMAN DIGNITY AND LIBERTY* ... 219
FREEDOM OF OCCUPATION* ... 220

ISRAEL MILITARY AND NATIONAL SECURITY STRATEGY ... 222

INTERNATIONAL AND DOMESTIC SECURITY ... 224
NATIONAL SECURITY ... 226
Historical Background ... *227*
CONCEPTS OF NATIONAL SECURITY ... 229
The Dahiyah Doctrine ... *229*
Doctrine Characteristics ... *229*
IDF Principles of War ... *231*
ISRAEL DEFENSE FORCES ... 233
ISRAEL'S NUCLEAR WEAPONS ... 235
The Sinai Crisis ... *236*
U.S. Spies On Dimona ... *237*
Israel's First Bomb ... *237*
Vanunu Reveals Secrets ... *238*
Sources and Resources ... *239*
ISRAEL'S SECURITY DOCTRINE ... 241
Basic Points ... *241*
THE OPERATIONAL LEVEL ... *241*
Defensive Strategy - Offensive Tactics ... 241
Capabilities ... 241
Main Areas of Activity ... 242
ISRAELI CASUALTIES IN BATTLE ... 242
THE ISRAELI DEFENSE INDUSTRY ... 243
Born Of Necessity ... *243*
Industry Players ... *244*
The Government Sector ... *244*
The Private Sector ... *245*
Civilian Markets ... *246*
Chariot of Fire ... *246*
ISRAEL HAS 17TH LARGEST DEFENSE BUDGET ... 247

THE ISRAELI NAVY 248
Mission 248
Modernization 249
WOMEN OF THE IDF 249
Women in Israeli Combat Units 249
"Chen"-The Women's Corps 250
History 250
Women's Service in the IDF 250
Structure and Objectives 251
The Corps Disbands 252
WOMAN & SPECIAL FORCES 252
ISRAEL AND WEAPONS OF MASS DESTRUCTION 254
Nuclear weapons 254
Chemical weapons 254
Biological weapons 254
DEVELOPMENT HISTORY 255
Pre-Dimona 1949-1956 255
NEGEV NUCLEAR RESEARCH CENTER 256
Negotiation 257
Excavation 258
Rupture with France 258
British aid 258
Costs 259
Weapons production 1967-present 259
NUCLEAR CAPACITY 260
NUCLEAR TESTING 263
IMPORTANT INFORMATION AND EVALUATIONS 263
Dimona 263
Weapons production 263
Stockpile ESTIMATES 264
DELIVERY SYSTEMS 265
Missiles 265
Aircraft 266
Marine 267
Other 268
POLICY AND DEVELOPMENTS 269
Possession 269
Doctrine 269
Use 270
Maintaining nuclear superiority 271
Nuclear Non-Proliferation Treaty and United Nations' Resolutions 271

ECONOMY AND ECONOMIC DEVELOPMENTS 273

ECONOMY: BASIC INFORMATION 273
OECD membership 277
Challenges 277
MAFOR SECTORS 277
Agriculture 277
Financial sector 277
Technology sector 278
Energy 279
Natural gas 279
Gas discoveries 279
Electricity 280

Solar power ... 281
Industrial sector ... *281*
Diamond industry ... 281
Defense industry ... *281*
Tourism ... *282*
External trade ... *282*
Rankings ... *283*

SUPPLEMENTS ... 285

MUNICIPAL GOVERNMENT CONTACTS ... 285
Municipal government : Cities of Israel ... *285*
Regional Councils in Israel ... *286*
EMBASSIES OF ISRAEL ... 288
ECONOMIC & TRADE REPRESENTATIVES ABROAD ... 291
BASIC TITLES ON ISRAEL ... 304

STRATEGIC AND DEVELOPMENT PROFILES

STRATEGIC PROFILE

Capital (and largest city)	Jerusalem 31°47′N 35°13′E31.783°N 35.217°E
Official language(s)	Hebrew, Arabic
Ethnic groups	75.4% Jewish, 20.6% Arab, 4% other
Demonym	Israeli
Government	Parliamentary democracy
- President	Shimon Peres
- Prime Minister	Benjamin Netanyahu
- Knesset Speaker	Reuven Rivlin
- Supreme Court President	Dorit Beinisch
Independence	from British Mandate of Palestine
- Declaration	May 14, 1948
	Area
- Total [1]	20,770 / 22,072 km^2 (151st) 8,019 / 8,522 sq mi
- Water (%)	~2%
	Population
- 2010 estimate	7,602,400 (95th)
- 2008 census	7,406,900
- Density	365.3/km^2 (30th) 946.1/sq mi
GDP (PPP)	2009 estimate
- Total	$206.430 billion (49th)
- Per capita	$28,393 (29th)
GDP (nominal)	2009 estimate
- Total	$194.825 billion (40th)
- Per capita	$26,796 (28th)
Gini (2008)	39.2
HDI (2007)	▲ 0.935 (very high) (27th)
Currency	Shekel (₪) (ILS or NIS)
Time zone	IST (UTC+2)
- Summer (DST)	IDT (UTC+3)
Drives on the	right
Internet TLD	.il
Calling code	972

[1] Excluding / Including the Golan Heights and East Jerusalem; see below.
Includes all permanent residents in Israel proper, the Golan Heights and East Jerusalem.
[2] Also includes Israeli population in the West Bank. Excludes non-Israeli population in the West Bank and the Gaza Strip.

Israel officially the **State of Israel** is a parliamentary democracy in the Middle East, on the south-eastern shore of the Mediterranean Sea. It borders Lebanon in the north, Syria in the northeast, Jordan and the West Bank in the east, Egypt and the Gaza Strip on the southwest, and the Gulf of Aqaba in the Red Sea to the south, and it contains geographically diverse features within its relatively small area. In its Basic Laws Israel defines itself as a Jewish and Democratic State; it is the world's only Jewish-majority state.

On 29 November 1947, the United Nations General Assembly recommended the adoption and implementation of the partition plan of Mandatory Palestine. On 14 May 1948, David Ben-Gurion, the Executive Head of the World Zionist Organization and president of the Jewish Agency for Palestine, declared "the establishment of a Jewish state in Eretz Israel, to be known as the State of Israel," a state independent upon the termination of the British Mandate for Palestine, 15 May 1948. Neighboring Arab armies invaded Palestine on the next day and fought the Israeli forces. Israel has since fought several wars with neighboring Arab states, in the course of which it has occupied the West Bank, Sinai Peninsula (between 1967 and 1982), Gaza Strip and the Golan Heights. Portions of these territories, including East Jerusalem, have been annexed by Israel, but the border with the neighboring West Bank has not yet been permanently defined has signed peace treaties with Egypt and Jordan, but efforts to resolve the Israeli–Palestinian conflict have so far not resulted in peace.

Israel's financial center is Tel Aviv, while Jerusalem is the country's most populous city and its capital (although not recognized internationally as such). The population of Israel, as defined by the Israel Central Bureau of Statistics, was estimated in 2013 to be 8,002,300 people, of whom 6,030,100 are Jewish. Arabs form the country's second-largest ethnic group with 1,653,900 people (including Druze and Bedouins). The great majority of Israeli Arabs are settled-Muslims, with smaller but significant numbers of semi-settled Negev Bedouins and Christians. Other minorities include various ethnic and ethno-religious denominations such as Druze, Maronites, Samaritans, Black Hebrew Israelites, Armenians, Circassians and others.

Israel is a representative democracy with a parliamentary system, proportional representation and universal suffrage. The Prime Minister serves as head of government and the Knesset serves as Israel's unicameral legislative body. Israel has one of the highest life expectancies in the world. It is a developed country, an OECD member, and its economy, based on the nominal gross domestic product, was the 43rd-largest in the world in 2012. Israel has the highest standard of living in the Middle East and the third highest in Asia

Background: Following World War II, the British withdrew from their mandate of Palestine, and the UN partitioned the area into Arab and Jewish states, an arrangement rejected by the Arabs. Subsequently, the Israelis defeated the Arabs in a series of wars without ending the deep tensions between the two sides. The territories occupied by Israel since the 1967 war are not included in the Isreal country profile, unless otherwise noted. In keeping with the framework established at the Madrid Conference in October 1991, bilateral negotiations are being conducted between Israel and Palestinian representatives (from the Israeli-occupied West Bank and Gaza Strip) and Israel and Syria, to achieve a permanent settlement. On 25 April 1982, Israel withdrew from the Sinai pursuant to the 1979 Israel-Egypt Peace Treaty. Outstanding territorial and other disputes with Jordan were resolved in the 26 October 1994 Israel-Jordan Treaty of Peace.

GEOGRAPHY

Location: Middle East, bordering the Mediterranean Sea, between Egypt and Lebanon

Geographic coordinates: 31 30 N, 34 45 E

Map references: Middle East

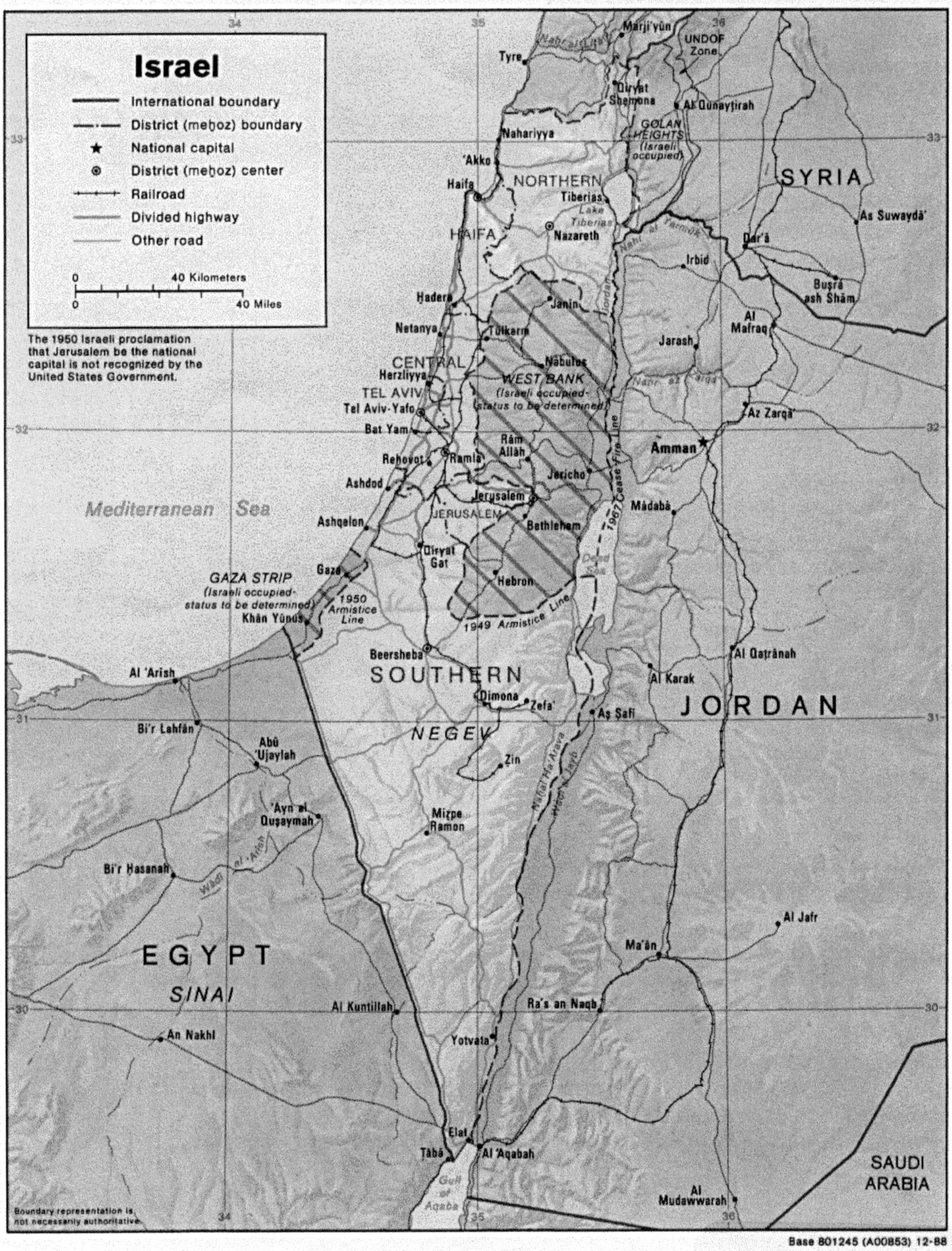

Area:
total: 20,770 sq km
land: 20,330 sq km
water: 440 sq km

Area - comparative: slightly smaller than New Jersey

Land boundaries:
total: 1,006 km
border countries: Egypt 255 km, Gaza Strip 51 km, Jordan 238 km, Lebanon 79 km, Syria 76 km, West Bank 307 km

Coastline: 273 km

Maritime claims:
continental shelf: to depth of exploitation
territorial sea: 12 nm

Climate: temperate; hot and dry in southern and eastern desert areas

Terrain: Negev desert in the south; low coastal plain; central mountains; Jordan Rift Valley

Elevation extremes:
lowest point: Dead Sea -408 m *highest point:* Har Meron 1,208 m

Natural resources: copper, phosphates, bromide, potash, clay, sand, sulfur, asphalt, manganese, small amounts of natural gas and crude oil

Land use:
arable land: 17%
permanent crops: 4%
permanent pastures: 7%
forests and woodland: 6%
other: 66%

Irrigated land: 1,800 sq km

Natural hazards: sandstorms may occur during spring and summer

Environment - current issues: limited arable land and natural fresh water resources pose serious constraints; desertification; air pollution from industrial and vehicle emissions; groundwater pollution from industrial and domestic waste, chemical fertilizers, and pesticides

Environment - international agreements:
party to: Biodiversity, Climate Change, Desertification, Endangered Species, Hazardous Wastes, Nuclear Test Ban, Ozone Layer Protection, Ship Pollution, Wetlands
signed, but not ratified: Climate Change-Kyoto Protocol, Marine Life Conservation

42 in the Israeli-occupied Golan Heights, 24 in the Gaza Strip, and 29 in East Jerusalem

PEOPLE

Population: 5,842,454
note: includes about 171,000 Israeli settlers in the West Bank, about 20,000 in the Israeli-occupied Golan Heights, about 6,500 in the Gaza Strip, and about 172,000 in East Jerusalem

Age structure:
0-14 years: 28% (male 825,443; female 787,159)
15-64 years: 63% (male 1,831,142; female 1,820,424)
65 years and over: 9% (male 248,695; female 329,591)

Geography - note: there are 231 Israeli settlements and civilian land use sites in the West Bank,

Population growth rate: 1.67%

Birth rate: 19.32 births/1,000 population

Death rate: 6.22 deaths/1,000 population

Net migration rate: 3.63 migrant(s)/1,000 population

Sex ratio:
at birth: 1.05 male(s)/female
under 15 years: 1.05 male(s)/female
15-64 years: 1.01 male(s)/female
65 years and over: 0.75 male(s)/female
total population: 0.99 male(s)/female

Infant mortality rate: 7.9 deaths/1,000 live births

Life expectancy at birth:
total population: 78.57 years

male: 76.57 years
female: 80.67 years

Total fertility rate: 2.6 children born/woman

Nationality:
noun: Israeli(s)
adjective: Israeli

Ethnic groups: Jewish 80.1% (Europe/America-born 32.1%, Israel-born 20.8%, Africa-born 14.6%, Asia-born 12.6%), non-Jewish 19.9% (mostly Arab) (1996 est.)

Religions: Jewish 80.1%, Muslim 14.6% (mostly Sunni Muslim), Christian 2.1%, other 3.2% (1996 est.)

Languages: Hebrew (official), Arabic used officially for Arab minority, English most commonly used foreign language

Literacy:
definition: age 15 and over can read and write
total population: 95%
male: 97%
female: 93%

GOVERNMENT

Country name:
conventional long form: State of Israel
conventional short form: Israel
local long form: Medinat Yisra'el
local short form: Yisra'el

Data code: IS

Government type: parliamentary democracy

Capital: Jerusalem
note: Israel proclaimed Jerusalem as its capital in 1950, but the US, like nearly all other countries, maintains its Embassy in Tel Aviv

Administrative divisions: 6 districts (mehozot, singular - mehoz); Central, Haifa, Jerusalem, Northern, Southern, Tel Aviv

Independence: 14 May 1948 (from League of Nations mandate under British administration)

National holiday: Independence Day, 14 May 1948; note - Israel declared independence on 14 May 1948, but the Jewish calendar is lunar and the holiday may occur in April or May

Constitution: no formal constitution; some of the functions of a constitution are filled by the Declaration of Establishment (1948), the Basic Laws of the parliament (Knesset), and the Israeli citizenship law

Legal system: mixture of English common law, British Mandate regulations, and, in personal matters, Jewish, Christian, and Muslim legal systems; in December 1985, Israel informed the UN Secretariat that it would no longer accept compulsory ICJ jurisdiction

Suffrage: 18 years of age; universal

Executive branch:

chief of state: President Reuven RIVLIN (since 27 July 2014)
head of government: Prime Minister Binyamin NETANYAHU (since 31 March 2009, most recently reformed on 15 May 2015)
cabinet: Cabinet selected by prime minister and approved by the Knesset
elections/appointments: president indirectly elected by the Knesset for a 7-year term (limited to 1 term); election last held on 10 June 2014 (next to be held in 2021 but can be called earlier); following legislative elections, the president, in consultation with party leaders, tasks a Knesset member (usually the member of the largest party) with forming a government
election results: Reuven RIVLIN elected president in second round; Knesset vote - Reuven RIVLIN (Likud) 63, Meir SHEETRIT (The Movement) 53, other/invalid 4

Legislative branch:
description: unicameral Knesset (120 seats; members directly elected in a single nationwide constituency by proportional representation vote; members serve 4-year terms)

elections: last held on 17 March 2015 (next to be held by 5 November 2019 but can be called earlier)

election results: percent of vote by party - Likud 23.4%, Zionist Union 18.7%, Joint List 10.5%, Yesh Atid 8.8%, Kulanu 7.5%, The Jewish Home 6.7%, Shas, 5.7%, Yisrael Beitenu 5.1%, UTJ 5%, Meretz 3.9%, Yachad 3%, other 1.7%; seats by party - Likud 30, Zionist Union 24, Joint List 13, Yesh Atid 11, Kulanu 10, The Jewish Home 8, Shas 7, Yisrael Beitenu 6, UTJ 6, Meretz 5; composition - men 91, women 29, percent of women 24.2%

Judicial branch:
highest court(s): Supreme Court (consists of the chief justice and 14 judges)
judge selection and term of office: judges selected by the Judicial Selection Committee consisting of 3 Supreme Court judges, 2 Cabinet members including the Minister of Justice as chairman, 2 Knesset members, and 2 representatives from the Israel Bar Association; judges can serve up to mandatory retirement at age 70
subordinate courts: Court for Administrative Matters; district and magistrate courts; national and regional labor courts; special and religious courts

Political parties and leaders:
Balad [Jamal ZAHALKA]
Democratic Front for Peace and Equality or HADASH [Ayman ODEH]
Israeli Labor Party [Avi GABBAY]
Joint List [Ayman ODEH] (coalition includes Balad, HADASH, United Arab List, Ta'al))
Kulanu [Moshe KAHLON]
Likud [Binyamin NETANYAHU]
Meretz [Tamar ZANDBERG]
SHAS [Arye DERI]
Ta'al (Arab Movement for Renewal) [Ahmad TIBI]
Tekumah/National Union (Ichud Leumi) [Uri ARIEL]
The Jewish Home (Habayit Hayehudi) [Naftali BENNETT]
The Movement (Hatnuah) [Tzipora "Tzipi" LIVNI]
United Arab List [Masud GANAIM]
United Torah Judaism or UTJ [Yaakov LITZMAN] (an alliance of three parties)
Yachad [Eli YISHAI]
Yesh Atid [Yair LAPID]
Yisrael Beiteinu [Avigdor LIEBERMAN]
Zionist Union or Zionist Camp [Avi GABBAY] (alliance includes Israeli Labor Party, The Movement)

International organization participation:
BIS, BSEC (observer), CE (observer), CERN, CICA, EBRD, FAO, IADB, IAEA, IBRD, ICAO, ICC (national committees), ICRM, IDA, IFAD, IFC, IFRCS, ILO, IMF, IMO, IMSO, Interpol, IOC, IOM, IPU, ISO, ITSO, ITU, ITUC (NGOs), MIGA, OAS (observer), OECD, OPCW (signatory), OSCE (partner), Pacific Alliance (observer), Paris Club, PCA, SELEC (observer), UN, UNCTAD, UNESCO, UNHCR, UNIDO, UNWTO, UPU, WCO, WHO, WIPO, WMO, WTO

Diplomatic representation in the US:
chief of mission: Ambassador Ron DERMER (since 3 December 2013)
chancery: 3514 International Drive NW, Washington, DC 20008
telephone: [1] (202) 364-5500
FAX: [1] (202) 364-5607

consulate(s) general: Atlanta, Boston, Chicago, Houston, Los Angeles, Miami, New York, Philadelphia, San Francisco

Diplomatic representation from the US:
note: on 14 May 2018, the US Embassy relocated to Jerusalem from Tel Aviv, replacing the site of the Jerusalem Consulate General
chief of mission: Ambassador David M. FRIEDMAN (since 23 May 2017)
embassy: David Flusser St.14, Jerusalem, 9378322
telephone: [972] (2) 630-4000
consular agent: Haifa

Flag description: white with a blue hexagram (six-pointed linear star) known as the Magen David (Shield of David) centered between two equal horizontal blue bands near the top and bottom edges of the flag

ECONOMY

Israel has a technologically advanced free market economy. Cut diamonds, high-technology equipment, and pharmaceuticals are among its leading exports. Its major imports include crude oil, grains, raw materials, and military equipment. Israel usually posts sizable trade deficits, which are offset by tourism and other service exports, as well as significant foreign investment inflows.

Between 2004 and 2013, growth averaged nearly 5% per year, led by exports. The global financial crisis of 2008-09 spurred a brief recession in Israel, but the country entered the crisis with solid fundamentals, following years of prudent fiscal policy and a resilient banking sector. Israel's economy also weathered the 2011 Arab Spring because strong trade ties outside the Middle East insulated the economy from spillover effects.

Slowing domestic and international demand and decreased investment resulting from Israel's uncertain security situation reduced GDP growth to an average of roughly 2.8% per year during the period 2014-17. Natural gas fields discovered off Israel's coast since 2009 have brightened Israel's energy security outlook. The Tamar and Leviathan fields were some of the world's largest offshore natural gas finds in the last decade. Political and regulatory issues have delayed the development of the massive Leviathan field, but production from Tamar provided a 0.8% boost to Israel's GDP in 2013 and a 0.3% boost in 2014. One of the most carbon intense OECD countries, Israel generates about 57% of its power from coal and only 2.6% from renewable sources.

Income inequality and high housing and commodity prices continue to be a concern for many Israelis. Israel's income inequality and poverty rates are among the highest of OECD countries, and there is a broad perception among the public that a small number of "tycoons" have a cartel-like grip over the major parts of the economy. Government officials have called for reforms to boost the housing supply and to increase competition in the banking sector to address these public grievances. Despite calls for reforms, the restricted housing supply continues to impact younger Israelis seeking to purchase homes. Tariffs and non-tariff barriers, coupled with guaranteed prices and customs tariffs for farmers kept food prices high in 2016. Private consumption is expected to drive growth through 2018, with consumers benefitting from low inflation and a strong currency.

In the long term, Israel faces structural issues including low labor participation rates for its fastest growing social segments - the ultraorthodox and Arab-Israeli communities. Also, Israel's progressive, globally competitive, knowledge-based technology sector employs only about 8% of the workforce, with the rest mostly employed in manufacturing and services - sectors which face downward wage pressures from global competition. Expenditures on educational institutions remain low compared to most other OECD countries with similar GDP per capita.

GDP (purchasing power parity):

$316.5 billion (2017 est.)
$304.4 billion (est.)
$296.6 billion (est.)
note: data are in 2017 dollars
country comparison to the world: 55

GDP (official exchange rate):
$350.6 billion (2017 est.)
GDP - real growth rate:
3.3% (2017 est.)
4% (est.)
2.6% (est.)
country comparison to the world: 100

GDP - per capita (PPP):
$36,300 (2017 est.)
$35,600 (est.)
$35,400 (est.)
note: data are in 2017 dollars
country comparison to the world: 54

Gross national saving:
23.7% of GDP (2017 est.)
24% of GDP (est.)
24.7% of GDP (est.)
country comparison to the world: 67

GDP - composition, by end use:
household consumption: 55.4%
government consumption: 22%
investment in fixed capital: 20.5%
investment in inventories: 0.2%
exports of goods and services: 29.8%
imports of goods and services: -27.9% (2017 est.)

GDP - composition, by sector of origin:
agriculture: 2.3%
industry: 26.6%
services: 69.5% (2017 est.)

Agriculture - products:
citrus, vegetables, cotton; beef, poultry, dairy products

Industries:
high-technology products (including aviation, communications, computer-aided design and manufactures, medical electronics, fiber optics), wood and paper products, potash and

phosphates, food, beverages, and tobacco, caustic soda, cement, pharmaceuticals, construction, metal products, chemical products, plastics, cut diamonds, textiles, footwear

Industrial production growth rate:
4% (2017 est.)
country comparison to the world: 68

Labor force:
4.021 million (2017 est.)
country comparison to the world: 94

Labor force - by occupation:
agriculture: 1.1%
industry: 17.3%
services: 81.6% (est.)

Unemployment rate:
4.3% (2017 est.)
4.8% (est.)
country comparison to the world: 57

Population below poverty line:
22% (2014 est.)
note: Israel's poverty line is $7.30 per person per day

Household income or consumption by percentage share:
lowest 10%: 1.7%
highest 10%: 31.3% (2010)

Distribution of family income - Gini index:
42.8 (2013)
39.2 (2008)
country comparison to the world: 48

Budget:
revenues: $92.82 billion
expenditures: $102.1 billion (2017 est.)

Taxes and other revenues:
26.7% of GDP (2017 est.)
country comparison to the world: 109

Budget surplus (+) or deficit (-):
-2.7% of GDP (2017 est.)
country comparison to the world: 110

Public debt:
61% of GDP (2017 est.)
62.3% of GDP (est.)
country comparison to the world: 70

Fiscal year:
calendar year

Inflation rate (consumer prices):
0.2% (2017 est.)
-0.5% (est.)
country comparison to the world: 16

Central bank discount rate:
0.1% (15 December 2015)
0.25% (31 December 2014)
country comparison to the world: 140

Commercial bank prime lending rate:
3.3% (31 December 2017 est.)
3.42% (31 December 2016 est.)
country comparison to the world: 168

Stock of narrow money:
$98.28 billion (31 December 2017 est.)
$79.58 billion (31 December 2016 est.)
country comparison to the world: 40

Stock of broad money:
$223.1 billion (31 December 2017 est.)
$189 billion (31 December 2016 est.)
country comparison to the world: 37

Stock of domestic credit:
$280.8 billion (31 December 2017 est.)
$257.5 billion (31 December 2016 est.)
country comparison to the world: 39

Market value of publicly traded shares:
$243.9 billion (31 December 2015 est.)
$200.5 billion (31 December 2014 est.)
$203.3 billion (31 December 2013 est.)
country comparison to the world: 32

Current account balance:
$10.39 billion (2017 est.)
$11.17 billion (est.)
country comparison to the world: 22

Exports:
$60.6 billion (2017 est.)
$56.17 billion (est.)
country comparison to the world: 46

Exports - commodities:
machinery and equipment, software, cut diamonds, agricultural products, chemicals, textiles and apparel
Exports - partners:
US 28.8%, UK 8.2%, Hong Kong 7%, China 5.4%, Belgium 4.5% (2017)
Imports:
$66.76 billion (2017 est.)
$63.54 billion (est.)

country comparison to the world: 44

Imports - commodities:
raw materials, military equipment, investment goods, rough diamonds, fuels, grain, consumer goods

Imports - partners:
US 11.7%, China 9.5%, Switzerland 8%, Germany 6.8%, UK 6.2%, Belgium 5.9%, Netherlands 4.2%, Turkey 4.2%, Italy 4% (2017)

Reserves of foreign exchange and gold:
$113 billion (31 December 2017 est.)
$95.45 billion (31 December 2016 est.)
country comparison to the world: 24

Debt - external:
$93.02 billion (31 December 2017 est.)
$87.96 billion (31 December 2016 est.)
country comparison to the world: 51

Stock of direct foreign investment - at home:
$119.4 billion (31 December 2017 est.)
$107.3 billion (31 December 2016 est.)
country comparison to the world: 43

Stock of direct foreign investment - abroad:
$106.9 billion (31 December 2017 est.)
$98.11 billion (31 December 2016 est.)
country comparison to the world: 35

Exchange rates:
new Israeli shekels (ILS) per US dollar -
3.61 (2017 est.)
3.84 (est.)
3.84 (est.)
3.89 (2014 est.)
3.58 (2013 est.)

ENERGY

Electricity access:
electrification - total population: 100%

Electricity - production:
60.44 billion kWh (est.)
country comparison to the world: 49

Electricity - consumption:
52.78 billion kWh (est.)
country comparison to the world: 49

Electricity - exports:
5.2 billion kWh (est.)
country comparison to the world: 36

Electricity - imports:
0 kWh (est.)
country comparison to the world: 161

Electricity - installed generating capacity:
17.22 million kW (est.)
country comparison to the world: 47

Electricity - from fossil fuels:
95.5% of total installed capacity (est.)
country comparison to the world: 50

Electricity - from nuclear fuels:
0% of total installed capacity (est.)
country comparison to the world: 112

Electricity - from hydroelectric plants:
0% of total installed capacity (est.)
country comparison to the world: 181

Electricity - from other renewable sources:
4.9% of total installed capacity (est.)
country comparison to the world: 97

Crude oil - production:
390 bbl/day (est.)
country comparison to the world: 94

Crude oil - exports:
0 bbl/day (est.)
country comparison to the world: 139

Crude oil - imports:
215,600 bbl/day (est.)
country comparison to the world: 28

Crude oil - proved reserves:
12.73 million bbl (1 January 2017 est.)
country comparison to the world: 91

Refined petroleum products - production:
278,300 bbl/day (est.)
country comparison to the world: 44

Refined petroleum products - consumption:
199,900 bbl/day (est.)
country comparison to the world: 56

Refined petroleum products - exports:
115,700 bbl/day (est.)
country comparison to the world: 41

Refined petroleum products - imports:
98,020 bbl/day (est.)

country comparison to the world: 57

Natural gas - production:
8.5 billion cu m (est.)
country comparison to the world: 45

Natural gas - consumption:
8.66 billion cu m (est.)
country comparison to the world: 50

Natural gas - exports:
2.605 billion cu m (2011 est.)
country comparison to the world: 36

Natural gas - imports:
160 million cu m (est.)
country comparison to the world: 71

Natural gas - proved reserves:
176 billion cu m (1 January 2017 est.)
country comparison to the world: 47

Carbon dioxide emissions from consumption of energy:
62.5 million Mt (2014 est.)
country comparison to the world: 51

COMMUNICATIONS

Telephones - fixed lines:
total subscriptions: 3.24 million
subscriptions per 100 inhabitants: 39 (2017 est.)
country comparison to the world: 42

Telephones - mobile cellular:
total subscriptions: 10.54 million
subscriptions per 100 inhabitants: 127 (2017 est.)
country comparison to the world: 82

Telephone system:
general assessment: most highly developed system in the Middle East
domestic: good system of coaxial cable and microwave radio relay; all systems are digital; competition among both fixed-line and mobile cellular providers results in good coverage countrywide; Israeli cellular providers upgraded to 4G in 2014
international: country code - 972; submarine cables provide links to Europe, Cyprus, and parts of the Middle East; satellite earth stations - 3 Intelsat (2 Atlantic Ocean and 1 Indian Ocean) (2018)

Broadcast media:
state broadcasting network, operated by the Israel Broadcasting Authority (IBA), broadcasts on 2 channels, one in Hebrew and the other in Arabic; 5 commercial channels including a channel broadcasting in Russian, a channel broadcasting Knesset proceedings, and a music channel supervised by a public body; multi-channel satellite and cable TV packages provide access to foreign channels; IBA broadcasts on 8 radio networks with multiple repeaters and Israel Defense Forces Radio broadcasts over

multiple stations; about 15 privately owned radio stations; overall more than 100 stations and repeater stations

Internet country code:
.il

Internet users:
total: 6,521,539
percent of population: 79.8% (July 2016 est.)
country comparison to the world: 65

Broadband - fixed line subscriptions:
total: 2.342 million
subscriptions per 100 inhabitants: 28 (2017 est.)
country comparison to the world: 49

TRANSPORTATION

Railways:
total: 610 km
standard gauge: 610 km 1.435-m gauge

Highways:
total: 15,965 km
paved: 15,965 km (including 56 km of expressways)
unpaved: 0 km

Pipelines: crude oil 708 km; petroleum products 290 km; natural gas 89 km

Ports and harbors: Ashdod, Ashqelon, Elat (Eilat), Hadera, Haifa, Tel Aviv-Yafo

Merchant marine:
total: 20 ships (1,000 GRT or over) totaling 711,831 GRT/823,929 DWT
ships by type: container 19, roll-on/roll-off 1

Airports: 58

Airports - with paved runways:
total: 33
over 3,047 m: 2
2,438 to 3,047 m: 7
1,524 to 2,437 m: 7
914 to 1,523 m: 10
under 914 m: 7

Airports - with unpaved runways:
total: 25
2,438 to 3,047 m: 1
1,524 to 2,437 m: 2
914 to 1,523 m: 2
under 914 m: 20

Heliports: 2

MILITARY

Military branches: Israel Defense Forces (includes ground, naval, and air components), Pioneer Fighting Youth (Nahal), Frontier Guard, Chen (women); note - historically there have been no separate Israeli military services

Military manpower - military age: 18 years of age

Military manpower - availability:
males age 15-49: 1,499,186
females age 15-49: 1,462,063

Military manpower - fit for military service:
males age 15-49: 1,226,903
females age 15-49: 1,192,319

Military manpower - reaching military age annually:
males: 50,348
females: 47,996

Military expenditures - dollar figure: $8.7 billion

Military expenditures - percent of GDP: 9.4%

TRANSNATIONAL ISSUES

Disputes - international: West Bank and Gaza Strip are Israeli-occupied with current status subject to the Israeli-Palestinian Interim Agreement - permanent status to be determined through further negotiation; Golan Heights is Israeli-occupied; Israeli troops in southern Lebanon since June 1982 **Illicit drugs:** increasingly concerned about cocaine and heroin abuse; drugs arrive in country from Lebanon and increasingly Jordan

TERRORISM

Terrorist groups - home based:
Kahane Chai (Kach):
aim(s): expel Arabs from Israel's biblical lands and, ultimately, restore the biblical state of Israel
area(s) of operation: Israel and West Bank settlements
note(s): considered to be operationally inactive in recent years (April 2018)

Terrorist groups - foreign based:
Hizballah:
aim(s): destroy the state of Israel
area(s) of operation: has been operational across Israel in the past, especially in the north; has in the past launched numerous rockets and other airborne projectiles and devices into Israeli towns in many regions; has the capability to launch rockets and missiles (April 2018)

Israel, the West Bank, and the Gaza Strip

Violence and terrorism by Palestinian groups opposed to the peace process continued in 1999. Throughout the year, HAMAS and the PIJ were responsible for numerous small-scale attacks, such as shootings and stabbings, although the number of incidents continued to decline from previous years. Among the more notable attacks were two failed bombing attempts in Haifa and Tiberias on 5 September carried out by Israeli Arabs working on behalf of HAMAS's military wing. The bombs--intended for Israeli buses--exploded prematurely, killing three of the perpetrators and injuring two Israelis.

Other terrorist incidents included a shooting in early August in Hebron that injured two Israeli settlers; a double murder of a young Israeli couple hiking near Megiddo in late August; and several explosions of homemade pipe bombs in Netanya in August, November, and December, one of which injured more than 30 Israelis. In mid-August a West Bank Palestinian, who was reported to have been inspired by literature on HAMAS, rammed his car into a group of hitchhiking Israeli soldiers, injuring at least 11. In late October a shooting attack on a bus near the Tarqumiya junction wounded five Israelis.

Israel continued vigorous counterterrorist operations, including numerous arrests and seizures of weapons and explosives. In early May, Israeli officials uncovered a plan to smuggle several wanted Palestinians--who were carrying paraphernalia for manufacturing bombs--from Gaza into Israel. In mid-August, Israeli authorities apprehended seven members of a PIJ cell near Janin who admitted to perpetrating four attacks on Israelis dating back to 1998. Israeli authorities also captured a four-man PIJ squad in late August as the men tried to infiltrate into Israel to carry out a suicide mission. In mid-December an undercover unit of the Israeli Defense Force killed two HAMAS members--one of whom was a leader of the group's military wing--in a shootout near Hebron. Authorities detained three other HAMAS militants in the incident.

The Palestinian Authority (PA), which was responsible for security in Gaza and most major West Bank cities, continued to act against Palestinian perpetrators of violence against Israel. The PA's security forces preempted several terrorist attacks over the year, including the arrests in mid-May of two close associates of a senior HAMAS military leader and, in early June, of 10 HAMAS members who planned to carry out anti-Israeli bombings. Israeli Prime Minister Ehud Barak and other senior officials publicly acknowledged the continuing improvement in Israeli-PA security cooperation. Israeli security officials publicly credited the Palestinian security services for foiling a terrorist bombing in Tel Aviv in March and for preventing at least two attacks against Israeli civilians in October. The PA also sought more actively to develop leads about HAMAS and PIJ activity and acted--in some cases--in cooperation with Israel to disrupt the groups' activities. While the PA's counterterrorist campaign showed improvement, it continued to face challenges from the resilient terrorist infrastructure of groups opposed to the peace process.

In early September the PA and Israel signed a follow-on accord to the Wye agreement at Sharm el-Sheikh, which reaffirmed a number of provisions regarding security cooperation.

IMPORTANT INFORMATION FOR UNDERSTANDING ISRAEL

Official Name: State of Israel

BASIC DATA

GEOGRAPHY

Area: 20,325 sq. km.[1] (7,850 sq. mi.); about the size of New Jersey.
Cities: *Capital*--Jerusalem.[2] *Other cities*--Tel Aviv, Haifa.
Terrain: Plains, mountains, desert, and coast.
Climate: Temperate, except in desert areas.

[1]Including Jerusalem
[2]Israel proclaimed Jerusalem as its capital in 1950. The United States, like nearly all other countries, maintains its embassy in Tel Aviv.

PEOPLE

Population : 5.9 million.
Annual growth rate : 1.9%.
Ethnic groups : Jewish 4.7 million; non-Jewish 1.2 million.
Religions: Judaism, Islam, Christianity, Druze.
Languages: Hebrew, Arabic, Russian, English.
Education: *Years compulsory*--11; *Literacy*--Jewish 97%, Arab 90%.
Health : *Infant mortality rate*--7.4/1000. *Life expectancy*-- 79.5 years (female), 75.5 years (male).
Work force (2.1 million): *Manufacturing*--20%. *Commerce*--13%. *Education*--12%. *Other business services*--10%. *Health and social services*--9%. *Construction*--7%. *Other*--6%. *Transportation*--6%. *Public Administration*--6%. *Hotels and restaurants*--4%. *Banking and finance*--4%. *Agriculture*--2%. *Electricity and water*--1%.

GOVERNMENT

Type: Parliamentary democracy.
Independence: May 14, 1948.
Constitution: None.
Branches: *Executive*--president (chief of state); prime minister (head of government). *Legislative*--unicameral, Knesset. *Judicial*--Supreme Court.
Political parties: Likud-led bloc, Labor Party, and various other secular and religious parties, including some wholly or predominantly supported by Israel's Arab citizens. A total of 13 parties--constituting blocs of smaller parties--are represented in the 14th Knesset, elected May 29, 1996.
Suffrage: Universal at 18.

ECONOMY

Natural resources: Copper, phosphate, bromide, potash, clay, sand, sulfur, bitumen, manganese.
Agriculture: *Products*--citrus and other fruits, vegetables, beef, dairy, poultry products.
Industry: *Types*--food processing, diamond cutting and polishing, textiles and clothing, chemicals, metal products, transport equipment, electrical equipment, high technology electronics.
Trade: *Exports*--$22.5 billion: polished diamonds, citrus and other fruits, chemical and oil

products, electrical and electronic products, textiles and clothing, processed foods. Tourism is also an important foreign exchange earner. *Imports*--$29.0 billion: military equipment, rough diamonds, oil, chemicals, machinery, iron and steel, textiles, vehicles, ships and aircraft. *Major partners*--U.S., EU, India, Hong Kong, Japan, South Korea.

PEOPLE

Of the approximately 5.9 million Israelis in 1997, about 4.7 million were Jewish. While the non-Jewish minority grows at an average rate of 4.9% per year, the Jewish population has increased by more than 27% since 1989 as a result of massive immigration to Israel, primarily from the republics of the former Soviet Union. Since 1989, nearly 841,000 such immigrants have arrived in Israel, making this the largest wave of immigration since independence. In addition, almost 20,000 members of the Ethiopian Jewish community have immigrated to Israel, 14,000 of them during the dramatic May 1991 Operation Solomon airlift.

The three broad Jewish groupings are: the Ashkenazim, or Jews who came to Israel mainly from Europe, North and South America, South Africa, and Australia; the Sephardim, who trace their origin to Spain, Portugal, and North Africa; and Eastern or Oriental Jews, who descend from ancient communities in Islamic lands. Of the non-Jewish population, about 75% are Muslims, 16% are Christian, and about 9% are Druze and others.

Education between ages 5 and 16 is free and compulsory. The school system is organized into kindergartens, 6-year primary schools, 3-year junior secondary schools, and 3-year senior secondary schools, after which a comprehensive examination is offered for university admissions. There are seven university-level institutions in Israel.

With a population drawn from more than 100 countries on 5 continents, Israeli society is rich in cultural diversity and artistic creativity. The arts are actively encouraged and supported by the government. The Israeli Philharmonic Orchestra performs throughout the country and frequently tours abroad. The Jerusalem Symphony, the orchestra of the Israeli Broadcasting Authority, also tours frequently as do other musical ensembles. Almost every municipality has a chamber orchestra or ensemble, many boasting the talents of gifted performers recently arrived from the countries of the former Soviet Union.

Folk dancing, which draws upon the cultural heritage of many immigrant groups, is very popular. Israel also has several professional ballet and modern dance companies. There is great public interest in the theater; the repertoire covers the entire range of classical and contemporary drama in translation, as well as plays by Israeli authors. Of the three major repertory companies, the most famous, Habimah, was founded in 1917.

Active artist colonies thrive in Safed, Jaffa, and Ein Hod, and Israeli painters and sculptors exhibit and sell their works worldwide. Haifa, Tel Aviv, and Jerusalem have excellent art museums, and many towns and kibbutzim have smaller high-quality museums. The Israel Museum in Jerusalem houses the Dead Sea Scrolls along with an extensive collection of Jewish religious and folk art. The Museum of the Diaspora is located on the campus of Tel Aviv University. Israelis are avid newspaper readers. Israeli papers have an average daily circulation of 600,000 copies. Major daily papers are in Hebrew; others are in Arabic, English, French, Polish, Yiddish, Russian, Hungarian, and German.

GOVERNMENT

Israel is a parliamentary democracy. Its governmental system is based on several basic laws enacted by its unicameral parliament, the Knesset. The president (chief of state) is elected by the Knesset for a 5-year term.

The prime minister (head of government) exercises executive power and has in the past been selected by the president as the party leader most able to form a government. In the May 1996 elections, Israelis for the first time voted for the prime minister directly, in accordance with recent legislation. The members of the cabinet must be collectively approved by the Knesset.

The Knesset's 120 members are elected by secret ballot to 4-year terms, although the prime minister may decide to call for new elections before the end of the 4-year term. Voting is for party lists rather than for individual candidates, and the total number of seats assigned each party reflects that party's percentage of the vote. Successful Knesset candidates are drawn from the lists in order of party-assigned rank. Under the present electoral system, all members of the Knesset are elected at large.

The independent judicial system includes secular and religious courts. The courts' right of judicial review of the Knesset's legislation is limited. Judicial interpretation is restricted to problems of execution of laws and validity of subsidiary legislation. The highest court in Israel is the Supreme Court, whose judges are approved by the president.

Israel is divided into six districts, administration of which is coordinated by the Ministry of Interior. The Ministry of Defense is responsible for the administration of the occupied territories.

POLITICAL CONDITIONS

From the founding of Israel in 1948 until the election of May 1977, Israel was ruled by successive coalition governments led by the Labor alignment or its constituent parties. From 1967-70, the coalition government included all of Israel's parties except the communist party. After the 1977 election, the Likud bloc, then composed of Herut, the Liberals, and the smaller La'am Party, came to power forming a coalition with the National Religious Party, Agudat Israel, and others.

Politics in Israel is dominated by Zionist parties. They traditionally fall into three camps, the first two being the largest: Labor Zionism (social democrat), Revisionist Zionism (conservative) and Religious Zionism. There are also several non-Zionist Orthodox religious parties, non-Zionist left-wing groups as well as non-Zionist and anti-Zionist Israeli Arab parties.

Golda Meir, Prime Minister of Israel from 1969 to 1974, once joked that "in Israel, there are 3 million prime ministers".The particular version of proportional representation used, in which the whole country is a single constituency, encourages the formation of a large number of political parties, many with very specialized platforms, and often advocating the tenets of particular interest-groups. The prevalent balance between the largest parties means that the smaller parties can have strong influence disproportionate to their size. Due to their ability to act as tie breakers, they often use this status to block legislation or promote their own agenda, even contrary to the manifesto of the larger party in office.

From the founding of Israel in 1948 until the election of May 1977, Israel was ruled by successive coalition governments led by the Labor Alignment (or Mapai prior to 1967). From 1967 to 1970, a national unity government included all of Israel's parties except for the two factions of the

Communist Party of Israel. After the 1977 election, the Revisionist Zionist Likud bloc (then composed of Herut, the Liberals, and the smaller La'am Party) came to power, forming a coalition with the National Religious Party, Agudat Israel, and with others.

The 2013 Freedom in the World annual survey and report by U.S.-based Freedom House, which attempts to measure the degree of democracy and political freedom in every nation, ranked Israel as the Middle East and North Africa's only free country. In 2016 the Economist Intelligence Unit has rated Israel as "flawed democracy"

On 31 March 2009 the Knesset approved the appointment of Benjamin Netanyahu as Prime Minister, despite Kadima having won slightly more votes than Netanyahu's Likud. Netanyahu's government took office the following day, 1 April 2009.

On 19 March 2013 Netanyahu was designated Prime Minister again after Likud Yisrael Beiteinu won the most seats in the January elections. The new coalition included the Yesh Atid, the Jewish Home and Hatnuah parties, and excluded ultra-Orthodox parties. Netanyahu achieved reelection to the national post on 18 March 2015, and subsequently formed a governing coalition with Likud at the forefront, which included the Jewish Home, Kulanu, Shas and United Torah Judaism.

ECONOMY

Israel has a diversified modern economy with substantial government ownership and a rapidly developing high-tech sector. Poor in natural resources, Israel depends on imports of oil, coal, food, uncut diamonds, other production inputs, and military equipment. Its GDP in 1997 reached $98 billion, or $16,800 per person. The major industrial sectors include metal products, electronic and biomedical equipment, processed foods, chemicals, and transport equipment. Israel possesses a substantial service sector and is one of the world's centers for diamond cutting and polishing. It is also a world leader in software development and is a major tourist destination.

Israel's strong commitment to economic development and its talented work force led to economic growth rates during the nation's first two decades that frequently exceeded 10% annually. The years after the 1973 Yom Kippur War were a lost decade economically, as growth stalled and inflation reached triple-digit levels. The successful economic stabilization plan implemented in 1985 and the subsequent introduction of market-oriented structural reforms reinvigorated the economy and paved the way for its rapid growth in the 1990s.

Two developments have helped to transform Israel's economy since the beginning of the decade. The first is the wave of Jewish immigration, predominantly from the countries of the former U.S.S.R., that has brought some 841,000 new citizens to Israel. These new immigrants, many of them highly educated, now constitute some 16% of Israel's 5.9 million population. Their successful absorption into Israeli society and its labor force forms a remarkable chapter in Israeli history. The skills brought by the new immigrants and their added demand as consumers have given the Israeli economy a strong upward push.

The second development benefiting the Israeli economy is the Mideast peace process begun at the Madrid conference of October 1991, which led to the signing of accords between Israel and the Palestinians and a peace treaty between Israel and Jordan. The peace process has helped to erode Israel's economic isolation from its neighbors and has begun a process of regional economic integration that will help to stabilize the region. It has also opened up new markets to Israeli exporters farther afield, such as in the rapidly growing countries of East Asia. The peace process has stimulated an unprecedented inflow of foreign investment in Israel, as companies that formerly shunned the Israeli market now see its potential contribution to their global strategies.

Israeli companies, particularly in the high-tech area, have recently enjoyed considerable success raising money on Wall Street and other world financial markets; Israel now ranks second among foreign countries in the number of its companies listed on U.S. stock exchanges.

Economic growth slowed considerably over the last 2 years, to 4.4% in 1996 and only 1.9% in 1997. Per capita income fell slightly in 1997 for the first time in the previous 10 years. The slowdown is generally attributed to setbacks in the peace process, the waning of the beneficial effects of immigration, labor shortages in high-tech industries, tighter fiscal and monetary policy, and the Asian financial crisis which began in late 1997.

The United States is Israel's largest trading partner; two-way trade totaled some $12.6 billion in 1997. The principal U.S. exports to Israel include computers, integrated circuits, aircraft parts and other defense equipment, wheat, and automobiles. Israel's chief exports to the U.S. include diamonds, jewelry, integrated circuits, printing machinery, and telecommunications equipment. The two countries signed a free trade agreement (FTA) in 1985 that progressively eliminated tariffs on most goods traded between the two countries over the following ten years. An agricultural trade accord was signed in November 1996, which addressed the remaining goods not covered in the FTA. Some non-tariff barriers and tariffs on goods remain, however. Israel also has trade and cooperation agreements in place with the European Union and Canada, and is seeking to conclude such agreements with a number of other countries, including Turkey and several countries in Eastern Europe.

FOREIGN RELATIONS

In addition to seeking an end to hostilities with Arab forces, against which it has fought five wars since 1948, Israel has given high priority to gaining wide acceptance as a sovereign state with an important international role. Before 1967, it had established diplomatic relations with a majority of the world's nations, except for the Arab states and most other Muslim countries. While the Soviet Union and the communist states of Eastern Europe (except Romania) broke diplomatic relations with Israel in the 1967 war, those relations were restored by 1991.

Today, Israel has diplomatic relations with some 153 states. Following the Madrid conference in 1991, and as a direct result of the peace process, Israel established or renewed diplomatic relations with 62 countries. Most important are its ties with Arab states. In addition to full diplomatic relations with Egypt and Jordan, Israel now has ties of one kind or another with Morocco, Tunisia, Oman, Qatar, and Bahrain.

On October 1, 1994, the Gulf States publicly announced their support for a review of the Arab boycott, in effect abolishing the secondary and tertiary boycotts against Israel. Israel has diplomatic relations with 9 non-Arab Muslim states and with 32 of the 43 Sub-Saharan states that are not members of the Arab League. Israel established relations with China and India in 1992.

DEFENSE

Israel's ground, air, and naval forces, known as the Israel Defense Force (IDF), fall under the command of a single general staff. Conscription is universal for Jewish men and women over the age of 18, although exemptions may be made on religious grounds. Druze, members of a small Islamic sect living in Israel's mountains, also serve in the IDF. Israeli Arabs, with few exceptions, do not serve. During 1950-66, Israel spent an average of 9% of GDP on defense. Real defense expenditures increased dramatically after both the 1967 and 1973 wars. In 1996, the military budget reached 10.6% of GDP and represented about 21.5% of the total 1996 budget.

In 1983, the United States and Israel established the Joint Political Military Group, which meets twice a year. Both the U.S. and Israel participate in joint military planning and combined exercises, and have collaborated on military research and weapons development.

U.S.-ISRAELI RELATIONS

Commitment to Israel's security and well-being has been a cornerstone of U.S. policy in the Middle East since Israel's creation in 1948, in which the United States played a key supporting role. Israel and the United States are bound closely by historic and cultural ties as well as by mutual interests. Continuing U.S. economic and security assistance to Israel acknowledges these ties and signals U.S. commitment. The broad issues of Arab-Israeli peace have been a major focus in the U.S.-Israeli relationship. U.S. efforts to reach a Middle East peace settlement are based on UN Security Council Resolutions 242 and 338 and, under the Clinton Administration, have been based on the premise that as Israel takes calculated risks for peace, it is the role of the United States to help minimize those risks.

UNSC resolutions provided the basis for cease-fire and disengagement agreements concerning the Sinai and the Golan Heights between Israel, Egypt, and Syria and for promoting the Camp David accords and the Egyptian-Israeli Peace Treaty. They were also the foundation for President Reagan's September 1982 peace initiative and Secretary Shultz's January 1988 initiative aimed at stimulating conditions to bring Jordan and representative Palestinians into the Middle East peace process.

The landmark October 1991 Madrid conference also recognized the importance of Security Council Resolutions 242 and 338 in resolving regional disputes, and brought together for the first time Israel, the Palestinians, and the neighboring Arab countries, launching a series of direct bilateral and multilateral negotiations. These talks were designed to finally resolve outstanding security, border, and other issues between the parties while providing a basis for mutual cooperation on issues of general concern, including the status of refugees, arms control and regional security, water and environmental concerns, and economic development.

On a bilateral level, relations between the United States and Israel have been strengthened in recent years by the establishment of cooperative institutions in many fields. Bilateral foundations in the fields of science and technology include the Binational Science Foundation and the Binational Agricultural Research and Development Foundation. The U.S.-Israeli Education Foundation sponsors educational and cultural programs.

In addition, the Joint Economic Development Group maintains a high-level dialogue on economic issues. In early 1993, the United States and Israel agreed to establish a Joint Science and Technology Commission. In 1983, the United States and Israel established the Joint Political Military Group, which includes joint military planning and combined exercises. In 1996, reflecting heightened concern about terrorism, the United States and Israel established a Joint Counterterrorism Group designed to enhance cooperation in fighting terrorism.

PRINCIPAL U.S. OFFICIALS

U.S. Embassy
chief of mission: Ambassador David M. FRIEDMAN (since 23 May 2017)

Deputy Chief of Mission--Luis Moreno
Political Affairs--Marc Sievers
Economic Affairs--David Burnett
Management-- Elizabeth Moore, Acting
Consular Affairs--Andrew Parker
Public Affairs--Bonnie Gutman, Acting
Commercial Affairs--Jonathan Heimer
Science Attaché--Paul Rohrlich
Defense Attaché-- Col. Richard Burgess
Legal Attaché-- Jeff Walker

The **U.S. Embassy** in Israel is located at 71 Hayarkon Street, Tel Aviv (tel. 03-519-7575).

U.S. Consulate General
Consul General--Daniel Rubinstein
Deputy Principal Officer--Gregory Marchese

ADMINISTRATIVE DIVISIONS

The State of Israel is divided into six main administrative districts, known as *mehozot* (מחוזות; singular: *mahoz*) – Center, Haifa, Jerusalem, North, Southern, and Tel Aviv Districts, as well as the Judea and Samaria Area in the West Bank. Districts are further divided into fifteen sub-districts known as *nafot* (נפות; singular: *nafa*), which are themselves partitioned into fifty natural regions

District	Main city	Sub-district	Population
North	Nazareth	Kinneret, Safed, Acre, Golan, Jezreel Valley	1,242,100
Haifa	Haifa	Haifa, Hadera	880,000
Center	Ramla	Rishon LeZion, Sharon (Netanya), Petah Tikva, Ramla, Rehovot	1,770,200
Tel Aviv	Tel Aviv	Bat Yam, Bnei Brak, Giv'atayim, Holon, Ramat Gan, Tel Aviv	1,227,000
Jerusalem	Jerusalem	Jerusalem	910,300
South	Beersheba	Ashkelon, Beersheba	1,053,600
Judea and Samaria	Modi'in Illit	Judea and Samaria	2,592,555 (350,143 Jewish settlers)

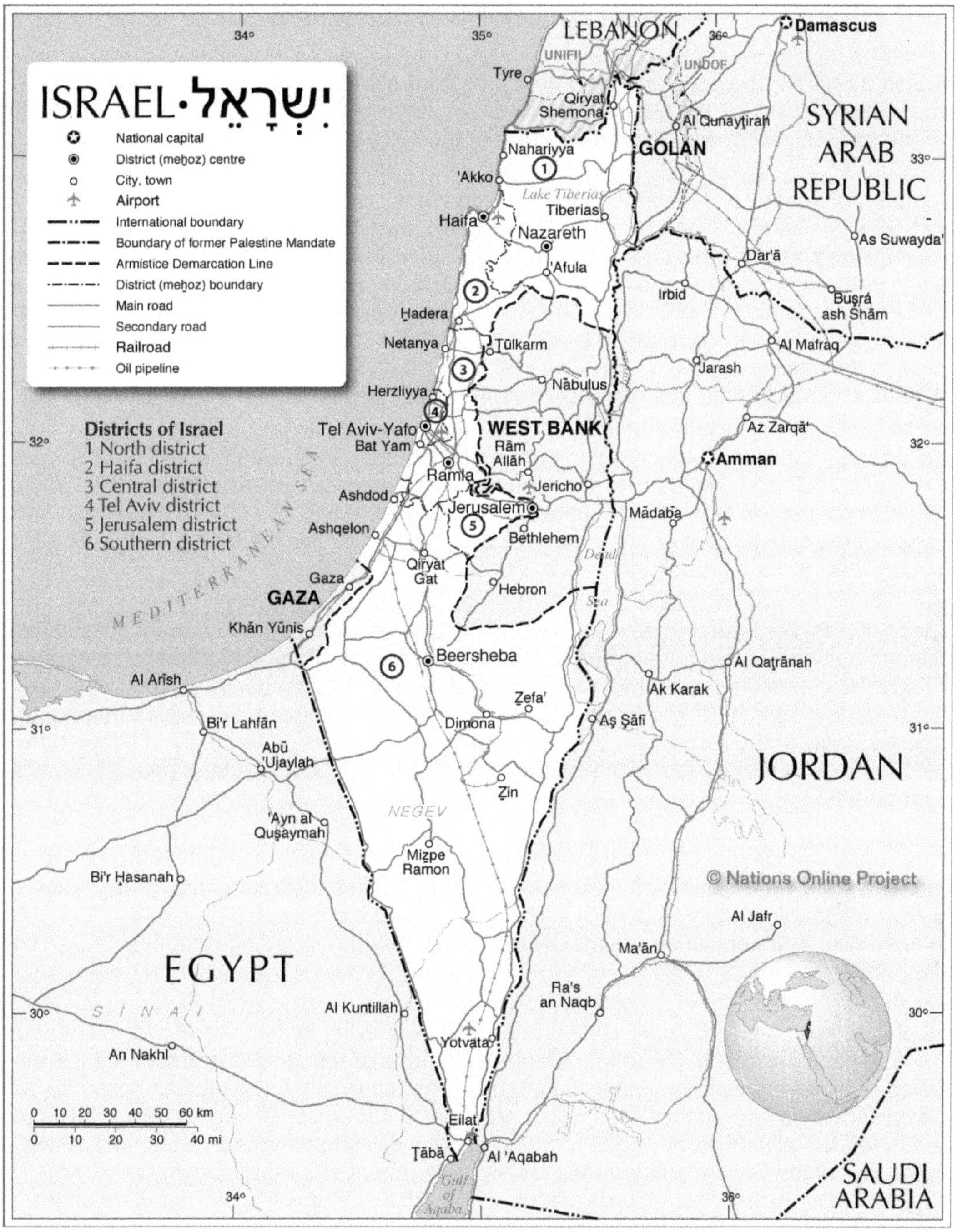

For statistical purposes, the country is divided into three metropolitan areas: Tel Aviv metropolitan area (population 3,206,400), Haifa metropolitan area (population 1,021,000), and Beer Sheva metropolitan area (population 559,700).

Israel's largest municipality, both in population and area, is Jerusalem with 773,800 residents in an area of 126 square kilometers (49 sq mi) (in 2009). Israeli government statistics on Jerusalem include the population and area of East Jerusalem, which is widely recognized as part of the Palestinian territories under Israeli occupation. Tel Aviv, Haifa, and Rishon LeZion rank as Israel's next most populous cities, with populations of 393,900, 265,600, and 227,600 respectively.

ISRAELI-OCCUPIED TERRITORIES

In 1967, as a result of the Six-Day War, Israel took control of the West Bank (Judaea and Samaria), East Jerusalem, the Gaza strip and the Golan Heights. Israel also took control of the Sinai Peninsula, but returned it to Egypt as part of the 1979 Israel–Egypt Peace Treaty

Following Israel's capture of these territories, settlements consisting of Israeli citizens were established within each of them. Israel applied civilian law to the Golan Heights and East Jerusalem, incorporating them into its sovereign territory and granting their inhabitants permanent residency status and the choice to apply for citizenship. In contrast, the West Bank has remained under military occupation, and Palestinians in this area cannot become citizens. The Gaza Strip is independent of Israel with no Israeli military or civilian presence, but Israel continues to maintain control of its airspace and waters. The Gaza Strip and the West Bank are seen by the Palestinians and most of the international community as the site of a future Palestinian state.

The UN Security Council has declared the annexation of the Golan Heights and East Jerusalem to be "null and void" and continues to view the territories as occupied. The International Court of Justice, principal judicial organ of the United Nations, asserted, in its 2004 advisory opinion on the legality of the construction of the Israeli West Bank barrier, that the lands captured by Israel in the Six-Day War, including East Jerusalem, are occupied territory.

The status of East Jerusalem in any future peace settlement has at times been a difficult hurdle in negotiations between Israeli governments and representatives of the Palestinians, as Israel views it as its sovereign territory, as well as part of its capital. Most negotiations relating to the territories have been on the basis of United Nations Security Council Resolution 242, which emphasises "the inadmissibility of the acquisition of territory by war", and calls on Israel to withdraw from occupied territories in return for normalization of relations with Arab states, a principle known as "Land for peace".

The West Bank was annexed by Jordan in 1948, following the Arab rejection of the UN decision to create two states in Palestine. Only Britain recognized this annexation and Jordan has since ceded its claim to the territory to the PLO. The West Bank was occupied by Israel in 1967 during the Six-Day War. The population are mainly Arab Palestinians, including refugees of the 1948 Arab-Israeli War.

From their occupation in 1967 until 1993, the Palestinians living in these territories were under Israeli military administration. Since the Israel–PLO letters of recognition, most of the Palestinian population and cities have been under the internal jurisdiction of the Palestinian Authority, and only partial Israeli military control, although Israel has on several occasions redeployed its troops and reinstated full military administration during periods of unrest. In response to increasing attacks as part of the Second Intifada, the Israeli government started to construct the Israeli West Bank barrier. When completed, approximately 13% of the Barrier will be constructed on the Green Line or in Israel with 87% inside the West Bank.

The Gaza Strip was occupied by Egypt from 1948 to 1967 and then by Israel after 1967. In 2005, as part of Israel's unilateral disengagement plan, Israel removed all of its settlers and forces from the territory. Israel does not consider the Gaza Strip to be occupied territory and declared it a "foreign territory". That view has been disputed by numerous international humanitarian organizations and various bodies of the United Nations.

Following June 2007, when Hamas assumed power in the Gaza Strip, Israel tightened its control of the Gaza crossings along its border, as well as by sea and air, and prevented persons from entering and exiting the area except for isolated cases it deemed humanitarian. Gaza has a border with Egypt and an agreement between Israel, the European Union and the PA governed how border crossing would take place (it was monitored by European observers). Egypt adhered to this agreement under Mubarak and prevented access to Gaza until April 2011 when it announced it was opening its border with Gaza.

POPULATION AND DEMOGRAPHICS

As of 2013, the population of Israel is 8 million, 6,015,000 of them Jewish. For statistical purposes, the country has three metropolitan areas; Gush Dan-Tel Aviv (population 3,150,000), Haifa (population 996,000), and Beersheba (population 531,600). Some argue that Jerusalem, Israel's largest city with a population of 763,600, and Nazareth, should also be classified as metropolitan areas. In total, Israel has 74 cities, 14 of which have populations of over 100,000. Other forms of local government in Israel are local councils of which there are 144 governing small municipalities generally over 2,000 in population, and regional councils of which there are 53, governing a group of small communities over a relatively large geographical area.

Israel's population is diverse demographically; 76% Jewish, 20% Arab, and 4% unaffiliated. In terms of religion, 76% are Jewish, 16% Muslim, 2% Christian, 2% Druze, and 4% are unclassified by choice. 8% of Israeli Jews are haredi; 9% are "religious", 12% "religious-traditionalists", 27% are "non-religious traditionalists", and 43% are "secular". Other small, but notable groups in Israel, include Circassians of whom there are approximately 3,000 living mostly in two northern villages, 2,500 Lebanese, and 5,000 Armenians predominantly in Jerusalem

The **demography of Israel** is monitored by the Israel Central Bureau of Statistics. The State of Israel has a population of approximately 8,012,400 inhabitants as of 31 March 2013. 75.4 percent of them are Jewish (about 6,037,700 individuals), 20.6 percent are Arabs (about 1,656,600 individuals), while the remaining 4 percent (about 318,100 individuals) are defined as "others" (family members of Jewish immigrants who are not registered at the Ministry of Interior as Jews, non-Arab Christians, non-Arab Muslims and residents who do not have an ethnic or religious classification).

The territory of Israel can be defined in a number of ways as a result of a complex and unresolved political situation (see table below). For example, whilst the Israel Central Bureau of Statistics defines the area of Israel to include the annexed East Jerusalem and Golan Heights and to exclude the militarily controlled regions of the West Bank and Gaza Strip, it defines the population of Israel to also include Israeli settlers living in the West Bank.

		Population (thousands)				Area (km^2)	
Name	Status Description	Israeli Citizens (Including Jews and Arabs)	Cumulative Total	Non-Israeli Palestinians	Cumulative Total	Area	Cumulative Total
Israel (Green Line)	Area sovereign to Israel since 1948	6,674	6,674	0	0	20,582	20,582
East	Occupied since	455	7,129	225 (double	225	336	20,918

Jerusalem	1967, subject to Israeli law since 1980 (see Jerusalem Law)			counted)			
Golan Heights	Occupied since 1967, subject to Israeli law since 1981 (see Golan Heights Law)	42	7,172	n.a.	n.a. (Syrians)	1,154	22,072
Seam Zone (West Bank)	Area between the Green Line and the Israeli West Bank barrier. Occupied in 1967	188	7,359	35	260	200	22,272
Other Israeli settlements and IDF Military Areas (West Bank Area C)	Other Israeli settlements (not in East Jerusalem or the Seam Zone) and areas in the West Bank directly controlled by the IDF . Occupied in 1967	57	7,473	115	375	2,961	25,233
Palestinian civil control (West Bank Areas A+B)	Palestinian National Authority civil controlled area. Subject to "joint" military control with the IDF. Occupied in 1967	0	7,473	2,311	2,686	2,143	27,376
Gaza Strip	Palestinian governed area. Israel controls airspace, maritime border and 80% of land border. Occupied in 1967, unilaterally disengaged in 2005, declared a foreign entity in 2007.	0	7,473	1,552	4,238	360	27,736

CITIES

Within Israel's system of local government, an urban municipality can be granted a city council by the Israeli Interior Ministry when its population exceeds 20,000. The term "city" does not generally refer to local councils or urban agglomerations, even though a defined city often contains only a small portion of an urban area or metropolitan area's population.

Largest cities or towns of Israel

Rank	City name	District	Pop.
1	Jerusalem	Jerusalem	796,200
2	Tel Aviv	Tel Aviv	404,500

3	Haifa	Haifa	269,300
4	Rishon LeZion	Central	231,700
5	Ashdod	Southern	211,400
6	Petah Tikva	Central	210,800
7	Beersheba	Southern	195,800
8	Netanya	Central	188,200
9	Holon	Tel Aviv	182,000
10	Bnei Brak	Tel Aviv	161,100

ETHNIC AND RELIGIOUS GROUPS

The most prominent ethnic and religious groups, who live in Israel at present and who are Israeli citizens or nationals, are as follows:

JEWS

According to Israel's Central Bureau of Statistics, in 2008, of Israel's 7.3 million people, 75.6 percent were Jews of any background. Among them, 70.3 percent were Sabras (Israeli-born), mostly second- or third-generation Israelis, and the rest are olim (Jewish immigrants to Israel) – 20.5 percent from Europe and the Americas, and 9.2 percent from Asia and Africa, including the Arab countries.

The ethnic division of The Jewish population of Israel (including non Halackic Russians) as of 2009 is as follows.

Ethnic Makeup of Jewish Population of Israel		
TOTAL	5,818,000	100%
Mizrahi Jews and Sephardic Jews	2,921,000	50.2%
Morocco	800,000	15.2%
Iraq	404,000	7.7%
Yemen	295,000	4.9%
Iran	236,000	4.0%
Algeria/Tunisia	224,000	3.8%
Other Asia	150,000	2.5%
Turkey	147,000	2.5%
Libya	136,000	2.3%
Egypt	112,000	1.9%
Other Asia	200,000	1.7%
India/Pakistan	76,000	1.3%
Latin America	25,000	0.04%
Other Africa (Not South Africa)	3,000	0.05%
Beta Israel (Ethiopia)	130,000	2.2%
Ashkenazi Jews	2,767,000	47.5%
Russia	1,018,000	20.9%
Poland	400,000	8.3%
Romania	351,000	7.6%
Other Europe	168,000	3.7%
North America (Including 4,000 African American Black Hebrews)	165,000	2.8%

Germany/Austria	160,000	2.7%
Bulgaria/Greece	97,000	1.9%
Latin America	82,000	1.4%
Hungary	63,000	1.3%
Czechoslovakia	60,000	1.2%
South Africa	20,000	0.4%

The errors occurring due to these calculations were:

- There was no distinction made between Sephardim and Ashkenazim. (If the Sephardim, Mountain Jews and other non-Ashkenazi groups are included in Mizrachim, then Mizrachim will outnumber Ashkenazim by a margin of 52 to 48).
- Many Sephardim from Turkey were counted as Mizrachim.
- Mountain Jews, Georgian Jews and Bukharan Jews who together constitute ~15% of FSU Jews counted as Ashkenazim until 1996 (until 1996, Central Asia and the Caucasian Republics were counted as part of Europe. After 1996, from 1997 onwards they were counted as part of Asia).
- The Harbin Jews (~1,000) from China counted as Mizrachim, although they were Russian speaking Ashkenazim.
- After 1996, Russian speaking Ashkenazim from Kazakhstan, Kyrghizia and Armenia counted as Mizrachim.
- Close to 20,000 South African Jews were classified as Mizrachim, although almost all of them are Ashkenazim (Lithuanian, English and Afrikaans speaking).
- A few hundred Black Hebrews from the United States were classified as Ashkenazim.
- All Jews from Latin America were classified as Ashkenazim, although significant numbers are Sephardim (15–20% in Argentina and Mexico, 20%+ in Brazil, similar percentages in other countries). Close to three fifths of the Latin American Jews in Israel are Argentine, with one tenth each from Uruguay and Brazil.
- 86,000 Bulgarian/Greek Jews are classified as Ashkenazim, although the majority are Sephardim/Romaniotes.
- Jews whose Jewishness was not recognized were not counted; almost all of them were Ashkenazim (~275,000 in 2007).

ARABS

Arab citizens of Israel are those Arab residents of Mandatory Palestine, who remained within Israel's borders following the 1948 Arab-Israeli War, and the establishment of the state of Israel. It is including those born within the state borders subsequent to this time, as well as those who had left during the exodus (or their descendants), who have since re-entered by means accepted as lawful residence by the Israeli state (primarily family reunifications).

In 2006, the official number of Arab residents in Israel was 1,413,500 people, about 20 percent of Israel's population. This figure includes 209,000 Arabs (14% of the Israeli-Arab population) in east Jerusalem, also counted in the Palestinian statistics, although 98 percent of East Jerusalem Palestinians have either Israeli residency or Israeli citizenship. Most Arab citizens of Israel are Muslim, particularly of the Sunni branch of Islam, and there is a significant Arab Christian minority from various denominations, numbering 122,000 - a majority group of Christians in Israel. As of 2008, Arab citizens of Israel comprise just over 20 percent of the country's total population. About 82.6 percent of the Arab population in Israel is Sunni Muslim (with a very small minority of Shia), another 9 percent is Druze, and around 9 percent is Christian (mostly Oriental Orthodox and Catholic denominations).

Bedouin

The Arab Muslim citizens of Israel include also the Bedouins, who are divided into two main groups: the Bedouin in the north of Israel, who live in villages and towns for the most part, and the Bedouin in the Negev, who include half-nomadic and inhabitants of towns and Unrecognized villages. According to the Israeli Ministry of Foreign Affairs, as of 1999, 110,000 Bedouins live in the Negev, 50,000 in the Galilee and 10,000 in the central region of Israel.

OTHER ARABIC-SPEAKING GROUPS

Druze

The Arab citizens of Israel include also the Druze who were numbered at an estimated 129,800 at the end of 2011. All of the Druze living in what was then British Mandate Palestine became Israeli citizens after the declaration of the State of Israel. Though some individuals identify themselves as "Palestinian Druze", most Druze do not consider themselves to be 'Palestinian', and consider their Israeli identity stronger than their Arab identity. Druze serve prominently in the Israel Defense Forces, and are represented in mainstream Israeli politics and business as well, unlike Muslim Arabs who are not required to and choose not to serve in the Israeli army.

Maronites

The Maronite Christian community in Israel of around 7,000 resides mostly in the Galilee, with a presence in Haifa, Nazareth and Jerusalem. It is largely composed of families that lived in Palestine in villages such as Jish long before the establishment of Israel in 1948. In recent years, the community was joined by some former pro-Israeli Lebanese militia members and their families, who fled Lebanon after 2000 withdrawal of IDF from South Lebanon.

Copts

Some 1,000 Israeli citizens belong to the Coptic community, originated in Egypt.

OTHER CITIZENS

Samaritans

The Samaritans are an ethnoreligious group of the Levant. Ancestrally, they claim descent from a group of Israelite inhabitants who have connections to ancient Samaria from the beginning of the Babylonian Exile up to the beginning of the Common Era. 2007 population estimates show that 712 Samaritans live half in Holon, Israel and half at Mount Gerizim in the West Bank. The Holon community holds Israeli citizenship, while the Gerizim community resides at an Israeli controlled enclave, holding dual Israeli-Palestinian citizenship.

Armenians

About 4,000 Armenians reside in Israel mostly in Jerusalem (including in the Armenian Quarter), but also in Tel Aviv, Haifa and Jaffa. Armenians have a Patriarchate in Jerusalem and churches in Jerusalem, Haifa and Jaffa. Although Armenians of Old Jerusalem have Israeli identity cards, they are officially holders of Jordanian passports.

CIRCASSIANS

In Israel, there are also a few thousand Circassians, living mostly in Kfar Kama (2,000) and Reyhaniye (1,000). These two villages were a part of a greater group of Circassian villages around the Golan Heights. The Circassians in Israel enjoy, like Druzes, a *status aparte*. Male Circassians (at their leader's request) are mandated for military service, while females are not.

ASSYRIANS

There are around 1,000 ethnic Assyrians living in Israel, mostly in Jerusalem and Nazareth. Assyrians are an Aramaic speaking, Eastern Rite Christian minority who are descended from the ancient Mesopotamians. The old Syriac Orthodox monastery of Saint Mark lies in Jerusalem. Other than followers of the Syriac Orthodox Church, there are also followers of the Assyrian Church of the East and the Chaldean Catholic Church living in Israel.

PEOPLE FROM POST-SOVIET STATES

Non-Jewish immigrants from the former Soviet Union many of whom are ethnic Russians, Ukrainians, and Belarusians, who were eligible to immigrate due to having, or being married to somebody who has, at least one Jewish grandparent. A very small number of these immigrants also belong to various non-Slavic ethnic groups from the Former Soviet Union such as Moldovans, Tatars, Germans and Siberian Yupiks (Siberian Eskimos) among others. In addition, a certain number of former Soviet citizens, primarily women of Russian and Ukrainian ethnicity, immigrated to Israel, after marrying Muslim or Christian Arab citizens of Israel, who went to study in the former Soviet Union in the 1970s and 1980s. The total number of those primarily Slavic ancestry people among Israeli citizens is around 40,000.

FINNS

Although most Finns in Israel are either Finnish Jews or their decedents, a small number of Finnish Christians moved to Israel in the 1940s before the independence and have since then gained citizenship following the independence, for the most part many of the original Finnish settlers intermarried with the other Israeli communities in the country, and therefore remain very small in number, A moshav near Jerusalem named "Yad Ha'Shmona"" meaning the Memorial for the eight or the hand for the eight was established in 1971 by a group of Finnish Christian-Israelis although today most members are Israeli and are predominantly Hebrew speakers.

ROMANI

Some Eastern European Roma are known to have arrived in Israel in the late 1940s and early 1950s, being from Bulgaria or having intermarried with Jews in the post-WWII displaced persons camps or, in some cases, having pretended to be Jews when Zionist representatives arrived in those camps. The exact numbers of these Romanies living in Israel are unknown, since such individuals tended to assimilate into the Israeli Jewish environment. According to several recent accounts in the Israeli press, some families preserve traditional Romani lullabies and a small number of Romani expressions and curse words, and pass them on to generations born in Israel who, for the most part, are Jews and speak Hebrew. The Romani community in Israel has grown since the 1990s, as some Roma immigrated there from the former Soviet Union. A community related to the Romanies and living in Israel and the Palestinian territories and in neighboring countries are known as Dom people.

VIETNAMESE

The number of Vietnamese people in Israel is estimated at 200-400. Most of them came to Israel in between 1976–1979, after prime minister Menachem Begin authorized their admission to Israel and granted them political asylum. The Vietnamese people living in Israel are Israeli citizens who also serve in the Israel Defense Forces. Today, the majority of the community lives in the Gush Dan area in the center of Tel Aviv but also a few dozen Vietnamese-Israelis or Israelis of Vietnamese origin live in Haifa, Jerusalem and Ofakim.

AFRICAN HEBREW ISRAELITES OF JERUSALEM

The African Hebrew Israelite Nation of Jerusalem is a small spiritual group whose members believe they are descended from the Ten Lost Tribes of Israel. With a population of over 5,000, most members live in their own community in Dimona, Israel, with additional families in Arad, Mitzpe Ramon, and the Tiberias area. At least some of them consider themselves to be Jewish, but mainstream scholarship does not consider them to be of Israelite but of subsaharan African origin. Their ancestors were African Americans who after several years in Liberia migrated to Israel in the late 1960s and demanded that Israel give them citizenship in the state. When Israel refused they relinquished their United States citizenship and de facto became stateless. After some deliberation the Israeli government granted them citizenship. The African Hebrew Israelites like the Haredim and Israeli Arabs are not required to serve in the military however they do receive social benefits from the state including free healthcare. Most believe in Jesus and the New Testament however one member of the community underwent a conversion to Orthodox Judaism and served in the Israeli army.

NATURALIZED FOREIGN WORKERS

Some naturalized foreign workers and their Israeli born children, predominantly from the Philippines, Nepal, Nigeria, Senegal, Romania, China, Cyprus, Turkey, Thailand and Latin America.

NON-CITIZENS

AFRICAN REFUGEES

The number and status of African refugees in Israel is disputed and controversial but it is estimated that at least 16,000 refugees mainly from Eritrea, Sudan, South Sudan, Ethiopia and the Ivory Coast reside and work in Israel. A recent check (late 2011) published in Ynet pointed out the Number only in Tel Aviv is 40,000 which represents 10 percent of the city's population. The vast majority is living at the southern parts of the city. There is a significant population in the southern Israeli cities of Eilat, Arad and BeerSheva.

FOREIGN WORKERS

There are around 300,000 foreign workers, residing in Israel under temporary work visas. Most of those foreign workers engage in agriculture and construction. The main groups of those foreign workers include the Chinese, Thai, Filipino, Nigerian, Romanian and Latin Americans.

OTHER REFUGEES

Approximately 100-200 refugees from Bosnia, Kosovo, Kurdistan and North Korea who were absorbed in Israel as refugees, most of them were also given Israeli resident status and currently reside in Israel.

LANGUAGES

Due to its immigrant nature, Israel is one of the most multicultural and multilingual societies in the world. Hebrew and Arabic are the official languages in the country, while English and Russian are the two most widely spoken non official languages. Georgian, Yiddish, Romanian, Ukrainian, Amharic, Armenian, Bulgarian, Ladino, French, Persian, Hungarian, Spanish, German, Vietnamese, Thai, Tagalog and Polish are the most commonly used other foreign languages A certain degree of English is spoken widely, and is the language of choice for many Israeli businesses. Courses of Hebrew and English language are mandatory in the Israeli school system, and most schools offer either Arabic, Spanish, German or French.

RELIGION

According to a 2010 Israel Central Bureau of Statistics study on Israelis aged over 18, 8% of Israeli Jews define themselves as *haredim* (or Ultra-Orthodox); an additional 12% are "religious" (non-haredi orthodox, also known as: dati leumi/national-religious or religious zionist); 13% consider themselves "religious-traditionalists" (mostly adhering to Jewish Halakha); 25% are "non-religious traditionalists" (only partly respecting the Jewish Halakha), and 43% are "secular". Among the seculars, 53% say they believe in God. Due to the higher birth rate of religious and traditionalists over seculars, the share of religious and traditionalists among the overall population is even higher.

Religious makeup

Group	Population	%
Jews	5,907,500	75.4%
Muslims	1,354,300	17.3%
Christians	155,100	2.0%
Druze	129,800	1.6%
Other	289,900	3.7%

EDUCATION

Education between ages 5 and 15 is compulsory. It is not free, but it is subsidized by the government, individual organizations (such as the Beit Yaakov System) or a combination. Parents are expected to participate in costs as well. The school system is organized into kindergartens, 6-year primary schools, and either 6-year secondary schools or 3-year junior secondary schools + 3-year senior secondary schools (depending on region), after which a comprehensive examination is offered for university admissions.

POLICY AND IMMIGRATION

As Israel's continued existence as a Jewish state relies upon maintenance of a Jewish demographic majority, Israeli demographers, politicians and bureaucrats have treated Jewish population growth promotion as a central question in their research and policymaking. Non-Jewish population growth and immigration is regarded as a threat to the Jewish demographic majority and to Israel's security, as detailed in the Koenig Memorandum.

Israel is the thirty-fourth most-densely crowded country in the world. In an academic article, Jewish National Fund Board member Daniel Orenstein, argues that, as elsewhere, overpopulation is a stressor on the environment in Israel; he shows that environmentalists have conspicuously failed to consider the impact of population on the environment and argues that overpopulation in Israel has not been appropriately addressed for ideological reasons.

In the 1950s Shoham Melamad found that the high fertility rate of Arabs was viewed as a demographic threat to the Jewish nation. Rabbi Menachem M. Schneerson however stated, that Arabs in Israel should be treated equally to any other Israeli citizens, and be allowed to have children just like any other citizen.

A 1967 Maariv editorial suggested that Jews should be encouraged to have large families, while Palestinians in the West Bank & Gaza Srip and in Israel should be encouraged to adopt birth control measures. Schnitzer also advocated for the adoption of an open policy encouraging Arabs to emigrate overseas. In 2003 Benjamin Netanyahu opined that if the percentage of Arab citizens of Israel rises above its current level of about 20 percent, Israel would not be able to retain a Jewish demographic majority, the basis of Israel's self-definition as a "Jewish democratic state".

Netanyahu's comments were criticized as racist by Arab Knesset members and the Association for Civil Rights in Israel. In May 2009, Michael Oren, the current Israeli Ambassador to the USA, wrote an article in Commentary Magazine in which he discussed the "Arab Demographic Threat" as one of "Seven Existential Threats" facing Israel. Shimon Peres and Benjamin Netanyahu both warned that Bedouin population growth in the Negev was a "demographic" or "palpable" threat to a Jewish majority.

CITIZENSHIP AND ENTRY LAW

The Citizenship and Entry into Israel Law (Temporary Order) 5763 was first passed on 31 July 2003 and has since been extended until 31 July 2008. The law places age restrictions for the automatic granting of Israeli citizenship and residency permits to spouses of Israeli citizens, such that spouses who are inhabitants of the West Bank and Gaza Strip are ineligible. On 8 May 2005, The Israeli ministerial committee for issues of legislation once again amended the Citizenship and Entry into Israel Law, to restrict citizenship and residence in Israel only to Palestinian men over the age of 35, and Palestinian women over the age of 25. Those in favor of the law say the law not only limits the possibility of the entrance of terrorists into Israel, but, as Ze'ev Boim asserts, allows Israel "to maintain the state's democratic nature, but also its Jewish nature" (i.e. its Jewish demographic majority). Critics, including the United Nations Committee on the Elimination of Racial Discrimination, say the law disproportionately affects Arab citizens of Israel, since Arabs in Israel are far more likely to have spouses from the West Bank and Gaza Strip than other Israeli citizens.

The law originated in a 2002 Cabinet order freezing the issuance of citizenship on family reunification grounds between Israeli citizens and residents of Iran, Afghanistan, Lebanon, Libya, Sudan, Syria, Iraq, Pakistan, Yemen and areas governed by the Palestinian Authority. Renewal of the law's effect in mid-2005 relaxed some of its condition by restricting its scope to those families where the husband is under 35 years of age and the wife is under 25 years old. In the interim the law was tested against Israel's Basic Laws, which operate in a manner similar to a constitution, when the Association for Civil Rights in Israel, filed a 2003 petition to have the law struck down.

The law was upheld in a split 6-5 High Court decision rendered in 2006, but the decision criticized a number of aspects of the law. In particular, the minority judgement, written by Chief Justice Aharon Barak, emphasized the temporary nature of the law's effect, arguing that "the appropriate goal of increasing security is not justifying severe harm to many thousands of Israeli citizens."

A draft bill to replace the law rather than seek a second renewal following the expiry of its application in January, 2007, sought to expand the areas targeted by the law beyond Palestinian Authority-controlled areas to include other regions with which Israel is in a state of military conflict

Those in favor of the law, such as Ze'ev Boim, say it is aimed at preventing terrorist attacks and that "We have to maintain the state's democratic nature, but also its Jewish nature."

Critics argue that the law is discriminatory because it disproportionately affects Israeli Arabs, since Israeli Arabs are far more likely to have spouses from the West Bank and Gaza Strip than other Israeli citizens. Such critics have included the United Nations Committee on the Elimination of Racial Discrimination, which unanimously approved a resolution stating that the Israeli law violated an international human rights treaty against racism; and Amnesty International, which has argued that "[in its current form the law is discriminatory and violates fundamental principles of equality, human dignity, personal freedom and privacy, enshrined in the Basic Law: Human Dignity and Liberty, as well as the right of children to live with both parents, and other fundamental rights enshrined in international human rights treaties to which Israel is a party and which it is obliged to uphold." When the law was renewed in June 2008, the publisher of the Israeli daily Ha'aretz argued that its existence makes Israel into an apartheid state.

In January 2012, Arab Knesset member Jamal Zahalka expressed concern that the law would lead to large-scale emigration of Arab-Israelis from Israel into Palestinian Authority areas, and claimed that Israel was taking advantage of the Supreme Court's decision to bring about an exodus of Arabs from Israel.

The suspect in custody of the November 21, 2012 Tel Aviv bus bombing, was originally from the Palestinian town of Beit Liqya but had been granted residence in Israel under the law, and was living with his family in Tayibe. The man used his employer's car to gain access to Tel Aviv

RUSSIAN IMMIGRATION

In the 1970s a major immigration wave of Soviet Union Jews went to Israel.

A mass emigration was politically undesirable for the Soviet regime. In the wake of Israel's victory in the Six-Day War in 1967, the USSR broke off diplomatic relations with the Jewish state. Anti-Zionist propaganda campaign in the state-controlled mass media and the rise of Zionology were accompanied by harsher discrimination of the Soviet Jews. By the end of 1960s, Jewish cultural and religious life in the Soviet Union had become practically impossible, and the majority of Soviet Jews were assimilated and non-religious.

The sense of pride for the victorious Jewish nation over Soviet-armed Arab armies stirred up Zionist feelings.

Many were formally refused permission to leave. A typical excuse given by the *OVIR* (ОВиР), the MVD department responsible for provisioning of exit visas was that the persons who had been given access at some point in their careers to information vital to Soviet national security could not be allowed to leave the country.

THE INCREASE IN THE NUMBER OF EMIGRANTS

After the Dymshits–Kuznetsov hijacking affair in 1970 and the crackdown that followed, strong international condemnations caused the Soviet authorities to increase the emigration quota. In the years 1960-1970, only 4,000 people left the USSR; in the following decade, the number rose to 250,000.

In 1972 the USSR imposed the so-called "diploma tax" on would-be emigrants who received higher education in the USSR. In some cases, the fee was as high as twenty annual salaries. This measure was apparently designed to combat the brain drain caused by the growing emigration of Soviet Jews and other members of the intelligentsia to the West. Following international protests, the Kremlin soon revoked the tax, but continued to sporadically impose various limitations. Many of those allowed to leave to Israel chose other destinations, most notably the United States.

Whoever requested to leave the USSR had to apply for a visa, which would have a request letter from a family member living in the same country which they were interested in emigrating to. The person sending of the visa, would be obligated to support his family member. The request of the family member should be notarized in the country of origin, and then sent to the family member that lives in the USSR. The person requesting the visa would then need to go to the department of the Ministry of the Interior, which was called "Ovir" (the office of visas and to registrations of the Ministry of the Interior). In the Ministry of the Interior he had to fill all sorts of documents, which partly included filling up intrusive questions. One then had to bring a "karakteristika" – a sort of a recommendation letter from his manager in his workplace. To obtain a visa he also had to get approvals from any children's schools and from the local community where he was living. An approval that one did not have any economic debts inside the USSR, an approval from ones parents and even an approval from one's divorcee if the person requesting the visa was divorced. If the emigrant was a party member, he had to obtain an approval from the offices of the local party and from the professional union that they had agreed he could leave. After all the approvals were handed in and everyone affiliated with the person requesting the visa was notified of his intention to leave the country, all the documents were handed to the "Ovir", with an additional payment of forty Russian rubles. Typically, an official response to the request would arrive after half a year. If the answer was positive, then one had to hand in confirmations attesting that any children had left their schools, and that one had left the workplace and that the apartment had been sold. During the six day war, the emigration wave from the USSR almost stopped completely, and in addition to that the authorities did not accept any requests for emigration visas. The reason was that the USSR supported the Arab states during the war, and due to a dissociation with Israel. In 1971 the anti-Zionist wave reached a record, and even so, during this year a decision was made by the senior decision makers regarding the granting of exit-visas to emigrating Jews.

FACTORS FOR THE EMIGRATION

The overwhelming victory of Israel during the Six-Day War changed the opinion of many of the Jews in the USSR. The victory increased the feeling of Jewish pride amongst them. Furthermore, it increased their feeling of alienation with the USSR, which had a pact with the Arab states during the course of the war. After the war the Soviet Jews started to send letters to the Soviet authorities in demand of letting them immigrate to Israel. Except for the arousal of the national emotions amongst the Jews of the USSR, there were also additional reasons for them to choose to emigrate:

Jews were discriminated against in higher education institutions (in a policy known as Numerus clausus), by government institutions, and in professional advancement.

1. Anti-Zionistic propaganda was common in the Soviet media.
2. Many Jews were dissatisfied with the political and economic situation.
3. Increased nationalism among Soviet nations made some Jews consider their right for a national identity.
4. There was increased communication between Soviet Jews and Jews worldwide.

THE ABSORPTION OF THE EMIGRATION WAVE

During the late 1960s and 1970s, about 163,000 Soviet Jews emigrated to Israel; the majority of the emigration wave happened between 1969 and 1973. In comparison with the other emigrants who emigrated to Israel during the same period of time, it is reported that the emigrants of the USSR felt a strong connection with Israel, and most intended to remain in the country.

In comparison to the emigrants who arrived from the western countries, a smaller percentage of the USSR emigrants reported that they were unsatisfied with their jobs. In the aspect of finding a job, only one third from the workers claimed that the state helped them finding work.

The USSR emigrants during those years felt that the acquisition of the Hebrew language was important almost as finding housing and employment, and therefore they considered it a high priority. Language schools ("Ulpan") were set up by the country and available for free for the immigrants, which helped them acquire the Hebrew language.

An increasing number of Soviet Jews began choosing to emigrate to the United States instead. Known as "dropouts", they would apply for US refugee visas while waiting at transit centers in Europe. In March 1976, the dropout rate reached above 50%. Most of the Soviet Jews who wanted to immigrate to Israel for religious, ideological, or family reasons had already done so by 1973; the majority of immigrants in the late 1970s were motivated to leave the Soviet Union for economic reasons and due to antisemitism, and saw more opportunities in the United States. However, a smaller number continued arriving in Israel. In 1979, a record 71,000 Jews were granted permission to leave, of whom only 12,117 immigrated to Israel.

Most of the Soviet Jews who continued emigrating to Israel were those with stronger Jewish identities from the Baltics, Moldova, and Georgia, while the dropouts were mainly assimilated Jews from the Russian heartland

ISRAEL: STRATEGIC INFORMATION AND US POLICY[1]

Since Israel's founding in 1948, successive U.S. Presidents and many Members of Congress have demonstrated a commitment to Israel's security and to close U.S.-Israel cooperation. Strong bilateral ties influence U.S. policy in the Middle East, and Congress provides active oversight of the executive branch's actions. Israel is a leading recipient of U.S. foreign aid and a frequent purchaser of major U.S. weapons systems. By law, U.S. arms sales cannot adversely affect Israel's "qualitative military edge" over other countries in its region. The two countries signed a free trade agreement in 1985, and the United States is Israel's largest trading partner.

Israel regularly seeks help from the United States to bolster its regional security and defense capabilities. Legislation in Congress frequently includes proposals to strengthen U.S.-Israel cooperation, such as the U.S.-Israel Security Assistance Authorization Act of 2018 (S. 2497 and H.R. 5141).

Concerns about Iran dominate Israel's strategic calculations. Prime Minister Binyamin Netanyahu influenced President Trump's May 2018 decision to withdraw from the 2015 Iranian nuclear agreement and to reimpose sanctions on Iran, and Israel has made common cause with several Arab states to counter Iran's regional activities. During 2018, Israel and Iran have clashed over Iran's presence in Syria, fueling speculation about the possibility of broader conflict between the two countries and how Russia's presence in Syria might affect the situation. A serious threat persists from Hezbollah's rocket arsenal in Lebanon, adding to the uncertainty along Israel's northern border.

Hamas and other militant groups in Gaza may present less of an immediate threat to Israeli population centers. Nevertheless, various forms of conflict have taken place around the Gaza-Israel frontier in 2018. Improving difficult living conditions for Palestinians in Gaza while also ensuring Israel's security presents a challenge, given: Hamas' control of Gaza, Israeli and Egyptian control of its access points, and recent reductions in U.S. and Palestinian Authority (PA) funding.

Israel's political impasse with the Palestinians continues. Israel has militarily occupied the West Bank since the 1967 Arab-Israeli war, with the PA exercising limited self-rule in some areas since the mid-1990s. The Trump Administration's recognition of Jerusalem as Israel's capital in December 2017 and its relocation of the U.S. embassy there in May 2018 were greeted warmly by Israel but rejected by Palestinians and many other international actors. The success of an anticipated U.S. diplomatic proposal may depend on a number of factors, including whether Israel embraces it and can persuade Palestinians or Arab state leaders to do so. Approximately 590,000 Israelis live in residential neighborhoods or "settlements" in the West Bank and East Jerusalem. These settlements are of disputed legality under international law.

Israel has a robust economy and an active democracy. Prime Minister Netanyahu's governing coalition includes various right-of-center and religious parties. Domestic debates continue about the government's commitment to rule of law and freedom of expression, and how to balance market-friendly economic policies with individuals' concerns about cost of living. The role and status of Arab citizens presents challenges for the state and society. Netanyahu is facing a number of corruption allegations, and some political commentators anticipate that Netanyahu will call national elections ahead of the attorney general's decision on whether to indict him.

[1] ISRAEL: Background and U.S. Relations Jim Zanotti Specialist in Middle Eastern Affairs July 31, 2018 Congressional Research Service

U.S.-Israel defense, diplomatic, and economic cooperation has been close for decades, based on common democratic values, religious affinities, and security interests. On May 14, 1948, the United States was the first country to extend de facto recognition to the state of Israel. Subsequently, relations have evolved through legislation, bilateral agreements, and trade.

U.S. officials and lawmakers often consider Israel's security as they make policy choices in the Middle East. Congress provides military assistance to Israel and has enacted other legislation in explicit support of its security. Such support is part of a regional security order—largely based on U.S. arms sales to Israel and Arab countries—that has avoided major Arab-Israeli interstate conflict for about 45 years. Some Members of Congress have occasionally authorized and appropriated funding for programs benefitting Israel at a level exceeding that requested by the executive branch. Other Members have sought greater scrutiny of some of Israel's actions.

Iran continues to be a top Israeli security concern. Israel has sought to influence U.S. policy on Iran, and supported the Trump Administration's May 2018 withdrawal from the Iranian nuclear agreement. In recent years, Israel and Arab Gulf states have discreetly cultivated closer relations with one another in efforts to counter Iran.1 As Iran-backed groups have been successful in helping Syria's government regain effective control of the country, Israel has conducted a number of airstrikes targeting these groups. Israeli officials consider an indefinite Iranian presence in Syria to be a serious security threat exacerbating the threat already posed by Hezbollah in Lebanon, and have vowed to prevent it. As a result, Israel's relationship with Russia, which cooperates with Iran in Syria and hosts advanced air defense systems there, has become more important. Israel also remains threatened by Hamas and other terrorist groups in the Gaza Strip while considering ways to work on Gaza's difficult humanitarian and security situation with neighboring Egypt and a wide range of actors.

1 See, e.g., Adam Entous, "Donald Trump's New World Order," *New Yorker*, June 18, 2018; Neri Zilber, "Israel's secret Arab allies," *New York Times*, July 15, 2017.
2 See, e.g., Tamar Hermann and Ephraim Yaar, "Will Trump's Peace Plan Gain Traction?" Israel Democracy Institute, July 2, 2018.
3 "Abbas illness sparks succession race for Palestinian presidency," Middle East Eye, May 23, 2018; CRS In Focus IF10644, *The Palestinians: Overview and Key Issues for U.S. Policy*, by Jim Zanotti; Adnan Abu Amer, "US, Palestinian political fallout hasn't hampered security ties," *Al-Monitor Palestine Pulse*, June 6, 2018; Avi Issacharoff, "If you're asking about Abbas's successor, you're not paying attention," *Times of Israel*, May 25, 2018.

In the Israeli-Palestinian conflict, political disputes persist over key issues including security parameters, Israel-West Bank borders, Jewish settlements, Palestinian refugees, and the status of Jerusalem. Polls suggest wide skepticism among the Israeli public about prospects for a negotiated end to the conflict.2 Contentious domestic politics for both Israelis and Palestinians make it difficult for them to make diplomatic concessions, particularly in a climate where questions surround the continued leadership of Prime Minister Netanyahu (see " Corruption Allegations Involving Netanyahu " below) and Palestine Liberation Organization (PLO) Chairman and Palestinian Authority (PA) President Abbas.3 Possibly complicating the situation further, President Trump recognized Jerusalem as Israel's capital in December 2017 and the Administration moved the U.S. embassy from Tel Aviv to Jerusalem in May 2018. The Trump Administration may be contemplating a diplomatic proposal aimed at restarting Israeli-Palestinian negotiations with the support of the Arab states that Israel has been discreetly cooperating with against Iran. Israelis debate how their leaders should prioritize options such as participating in

diplomatic initiatives, preserving the current facts on the ground, and acting unilaterally to influence outcomes.

Israeli leaders and significant segments of Israeli civil society regularly emphasize the importance of closeness with the United States. Yet, a number of geopolitical factors distinguish Israel from other developed countries, including the regional threats it faces, its unique historical experience, and its population's relatively higher level of direct military service.4

4 Military service remains compulsory for most Jewish Israeli young men and women, and most Jewish Israeli men remain on reserve duty until the age of 40 (for soldiers) or 45 (for officers).

Figure 1. Israel: Map and Basic Facts

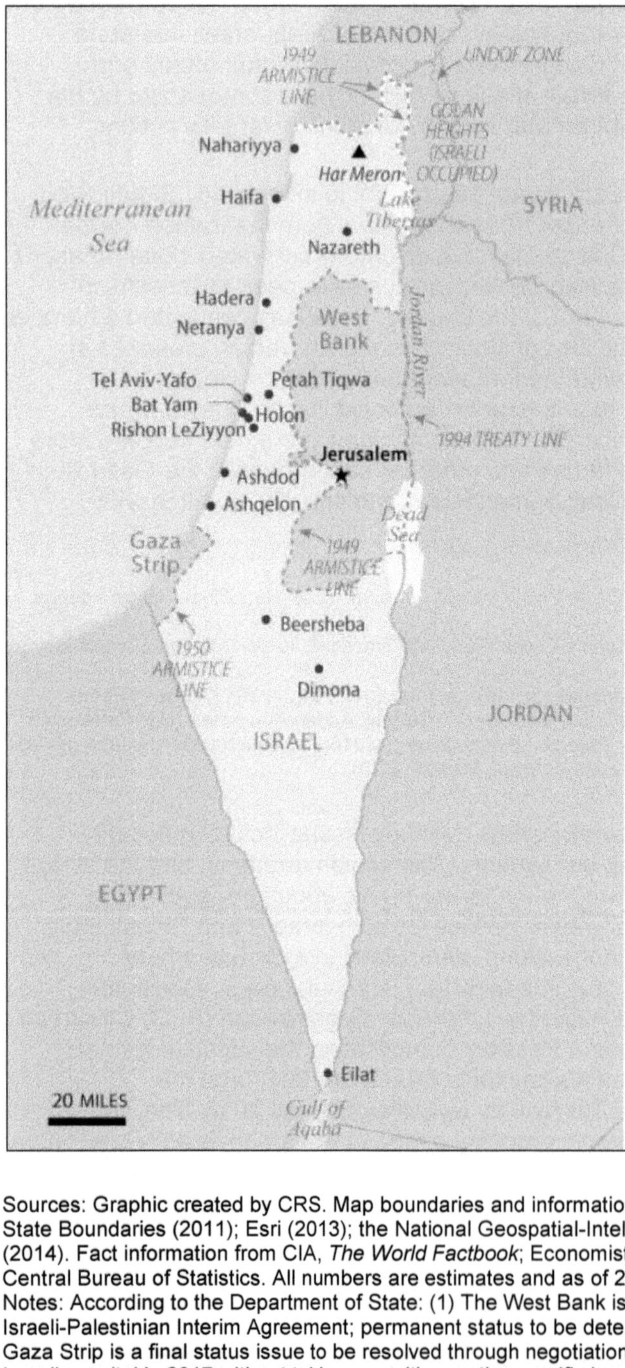

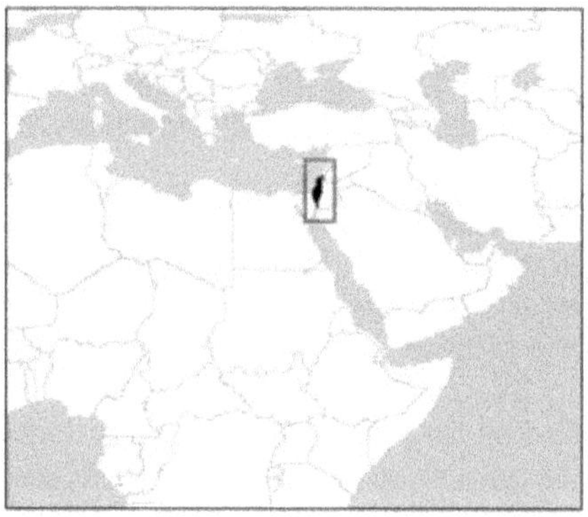

Israel

Population: 8.8 million
Includes an estimated 391,000 settlers in the West Bank (2016), 201,000 in East Jerusalem (2014), and 22,000 in the Golan Heights (2016)

Jews: 75%; **Arabs:** 21%; **Other:** 4% (2016)

Real GDP growth rate/per capita (at PPP): 3.3%/$36,340

Unemployment rate: 4.2%

Population below poverty line: 22% (2014)

Inflation rate: 0.2%

Budget deficit as % of GDP: 2.2%

Public debt as % of GDP: 61.0%

Foreign exchange and gold reserves: $113 billion

Current account surplus as % of GDP: 3.0%

Export partners: U.S. 29.3%, Hong Kong 7.4%, United Kingdom 6.5%, China 5.5%, Belgium 4.2 (2016)

Import partners: U.S. 12.2%, China 8.9%, Switzerland 6.4%, Germany 6.1%, Belgium 5.9% (2016)

Sources: Graphic created by CRS. Map boundaries and information generated by Hannah Fischer using Department of State Boundaries (2011); Esri (2013); the National Geospatial-Intelligence Agency GeoNames Database (2015); DeLorme (2014). Fact information from CIA, *The World Factbook*; Economist Intelligence Unit; IMF World Outlook Database; Israel Central Bureau of Statistics. All numbers are estimates and as of 2017 unless specified.
Notes: According to the Department of State: (1) The West Bank is Israeli occupied with current status subject to the 1995 Israeli-Palestinian Interim Agreement; permanent status to be determined through further negotiation. (2) The status of the Gaza Strip is a final status issue to be resolved through negotiations. (3) The United States recognized Jerusalem as Israel's capital in 2017 without taking a position on the specific boundaries of Israeli sovereignty. (4) Boundary representation is not necessarily authoritative. See https://www.state.gov/p/nea/ci/is/.

COUNTRY BACKGROUND

HISTORICAL OVERVIEW

The quest for a modern Jewish homeland can be traced to the publication of Theodor Herzl's *The Jewish State* in 1896. Herzl was inspired by the concept of nationalism that had become popular among various European peoples in the 19th century, and was also motivated by European anti-Semitism. The following year, Herzl described his vision at the first Zionist Congress, which encouraged Jewish settlement in Palestine, the territory that had included the Biblical home of the Jews and was then part of the Ottoman Empire.

During World War I, the British government issued the Balfour Declaration, supporting the "establishment in Palestine of a national home for the Jewish people." Palestine became a British Mandate after the war and British officials simultaneously encouraged the national aspirations of the Arab majority in Palestine, insisting that its promises to Jews and Arabs did not conflict. Jews immigrated to Palestine in ever greater numbers during the Mandate period, and tension between Arabs and Jews and between each group and the British increased, leading to periodic clashes. Following World War II, the plight of Jewish survivors of the Holocaust gave the demand for a Jewish home added urgency, while Arabs across the Middle East concurrently demanded self-determination and independence from European colonial powers.

In 1947, the United Nations General Assembly developed a partition plan (Resolution 181) to divide Palestine into Jewish and Arab states, proposing U.N. trusteeship for Jerusalem and some surrounding areas. The leadership of the Jewish Yishuv (or polity) welcomed the plan because it appeared to confer legitimacy on the Jews' claims in Palestine despite their small numbers. The Palestinian Arab leadership and the League of Arab States (Arab League) rejected the plan, insisting both that the specific partition proposed and the entire concept of partition were unfair given Palestine's Arab majority. Debate on this question prefigured current debate about whether it is possible to have a state that both provides a secure Jewish homeland and is governed in accordance with democratic values and the principle of self-determination.

After several months of civil conflict between Jews and Arabs, Britain officially ended its Mandate on May 14, 1948, at which point the state of Israel proclaimed its independence and was immediately invaded by Arab armies. During and after the conflict, roughly 700,000 Palestinians were driven or fled from their homes, an occurrence Palestinians call the *nakba* ("catastrophe").5 Many became internationally designated refugees after ending up in areas of Mandate-era Palestine controlled by Jordan (the West Bank) or Egypt (the Gaza Strip), or in nearby Arab states. Palestinians who remained in Israel became Israeli citizens.

5 CRS Report RL34074, *The Palestinians: Background and U.S. Relations*, by Jim Zanotti.

The conflict ended with armistice agreements between Israel and its neighboring Arab states: Egypt, Jordan, Lebanon, and Syria. The territory controlled by Israel within these 1949-1950 armistice lines is roughly the size of New Jersey. Israel has engaged in further armed conflict with neighbors on a number of occasions since then—most notably in 1956, 1967, 1973, and 1982. Since the 1950s, Israel also has dealt with the threat of Palestinian guerrilla or terrorist attacks. In 1979, Israel concluded a peace treaty with Egypt, followed in 1994 by a peace treaty with Jordan, thus making another multi-front war less likely. Nevertheless, as discussed throughout the report, security challenges persist from Iran and groups allied with it, and from other developments in the Arab world.

GOVERNMENT, POLITICS, AND SOCIETY

Israel is a parliamentary democracy in which the prime minister is head of government (see textbox below for more information) and the president is a largely ceremonial head of state. The unicameral parliament (the Knesset) elects a president for a seven-year term. The current president, Reuven Rivlin, took office in July 2014. Israel does not have a written constitution. Instead, Basic Laws lay down the rules of government and enumerate fundamental rights. Israel has an independent judiciary, with a system of magistrates' courts and district courts headed by a Supreme Court.

The political spectrum is highly fragmented, with small parties exercising disproportionate power due to the relatively low vote threshold for entry into the Knesset (3.25%), and larger parties needing small-party support to form and maintain coalition governments. Since Israel's founding, the average lifespan of an Israeli government has been about 23 months. In 2014, however, the Knesset somewhat tightened the conditions for bringing down a government.

ISRAELI ELECTORAL PROCESS AND GOVERNMENT-BUILDING

Elections to Israel's 120-seat Knesset are direct, secret, and proportional based on a party list system, with the entire country constituting a single electoral district. All Israeli citizens age 18 and older may vote. Turnout in elections since 2001 has ranged between 62% and 72% of registered voters (before that it generally ranged between 77% and 80%). Elections must be held at least every four years, but are often held earlier due to difficulties in holding coalitions together. A Central Elections Committee is responsible for conducting and supervising the elections. The committee includes representatives from parties in the current Knesset and is headed by a Supreme Court justice.

National laws provide parameters for candidate eligibility, general elections, and party primaries—including specific conditions and limitations on campaign contributions and public financing for parties.6 Since 2007, a "cooling-off law" requires that senior Israeli military officers wait at least three years before entering civilian politics.7

Following elections, the task of forming a government is given by Israel's president to the Knesset member the president believes has the best chance to form a government as prime minister. The would-be prime minister has 28 days to assemble a majority coalition, and the president can extend this period for an additional 14 days. The government and its ministers are installed following a vote of confidence by at least 61 Knesset members. Thereafter, the ministers determine the government's course of action on domestic issues, while military and national security actions are largely directed through a "security cabinet" (formally known as the Ministerial Committee on Defense) consisting of a group of key ministers—some whose membership is set by law, others who are appointed by the prime minister—who number no more than half of all cabinet ministers.8

6 For additional details on Israel's campaign finance laws, see Ruth Levush, "Campaign Finance: Israel," Law Library of Congress, July 25, 2012.
7 The law was reportedly intended to counter Israeli military officers' cultivation of civilian political connections and influence in anticipation of their possible career transitions.
8 See, e.g., Isabel Kershner, "Israeli Law Vesting War Power in 2 Top Leaders Faces Criticism," *New York Times*, May 3, 2018; Dan Williams, "Netanyahu's new security cabinet may hesitate on any Iran war," Reuters, March 19, 2013.

Table 1. Israeli Security Cabinet Members

Member	Party	Ministerial Position(s)	Previous Knesset Terms

Binyamin Netanyahu	Likud	Prime Minister Minister of Foreign Affairs	8
Avigdor Lieberman	Yisrael Beiteinu	Minister of Defense	5 (resigned Knesset seat in May 2016)
Moshe Kahlon	Kulanu	Minister of Finance	3
Naftali Bennett	Ha'bayit Ha'Yehudi	Minister of Education	1
Ayelet Shaked	Ha'bayit Ha'Yehudi	Minister of Justice	1
Gilad Erdan	Likud	Minister of Public Security Minister of Strategic Affairs Minister of Information	4
Aryeh Deri	Shas	Minister of Interior	3
Yisrael Katz	Likud	Minister of Transportation Minister of Intelligence and Atomic Energy	6
Yoav Galant	Kulanu	Minister of Construction and Housing	0
Sofa Landver	Yisrael Beiteinu	Minister of Immigrant Absorption	6

POLITICAL AND SOCIETAL EVOLUTION

Israeli society and politics have evolved. In the first decades following its founding, Israeli society was dominated by secular Ashkenazi (Eastern European) Jews who constituted the large majority of 19th- and early 20th-century Zionist immigrants. Many leaders from these immigrant communities sought to build a country dedicated to Western liberal and communitarian values. From 1948 to 1977, the social democratic Mapai/Labor movement led Israeli governing coalitions.

The 1977 electoral victory of Menachem Begin's more nationalistic Likud party helped boost the influence of previously marginalized groups, particularly Mizrahi (Eastern) Jews who had immigrated to Israel from Arab countries and Iran. This electoral result came at a time when debate in Israel was intensifying over settlement in the territories occupied during the 1967 Arab-Israeli War. Begin and his successor in Likud, Yitzhak Shamir, helped drive the political agenda over the following 15 years. Although Labor under Yitzhak Rabin later initiated the Oslo peace process with the Palestinians, its political momentum slowed and reversed after Rabin's assassination in 1995.

Despite Labor's setbacks, its warnings that high Arab birth rates could eventually make it difficult for Israel to remain both a Jewish and a democratic state while ruling over the Palestinians gained traction among many Israelis. In this context, Prime Minister Ariel Sharon, a longtime champion of the Israeli right and the settlement movement, split from Likud and established Kadima as a more centrist alternative in 2005. He was succeeded as Kadima's leader and prime minister by Ehud Olmert in 2006. Likud returned to power in 2009 with Netanyahu as prime minister (he had previously served in the position from 1996 to 1999). Since then Netanyahu has led two additional coalitions following elections in 2013 and 2015.9

9 For a figure showing the various strains in Israeli politics over time, see a table in "The evolution of Israeli politics," economist.com, March 15, 2015.
10 See, e.g., Hirsh Goodman and Alan Baker, "The Dangers of a Unilateral Israeli Withdrawal from the West Bank and Eastern Jerusalem," Jerusalem Center for Public Affairs, January 22, 2017.

The enduring appeal of Netanyahu and right-of-center parties to Israeli voters in recent years may stem from a number of factors, including

· Arguments by some that Palestinians have rejected peace and that Israeli military withdrawals from southern Lebanon (in 2000) and the Gaza Strip (in 2005) emboldened Hezbollah and Hamas and contributed to subsequent conflict.10

· The influence of distinct religious, ethnic, or ideological groups, such as Russian speakers who emigrated from the former Soviet Union in the 1990s, and citizens aligned with the "national religious" (modern Orthodox) movement. Both groups skew toward the political right and include many of the biggest supporters of settlements.

Given the fragmentation of Israeli political parties under its electoral system, compromise among diverse groups is a necessity for forming and maintaining a governing coalition. As mentioned above, the system generally gives smaller parties disproportionate influence on key positions they espouse. For example, Netanyahu relies on support from two Haredi (ultra-Orthodox Jewish) parties that are generally aligned with the other right-of-center parties on national security issues, but make specific demands (i.e., subsidies and military exemptions to support traditional lifestyles) in exchange for their backing. Such support is largely anathema to secular Israeli middle class voters, many of whom would prefer that government resources be used to benefit a broader cross-section of Israelis.

Also, many Arab Israelis, who make up nearly 20% of the population, are largely separate from Jewish Israeli citizens in where and how they live, are educated, and otherwise socialize. Arab Israeli citizens generally identify more closely with left-of-center parties. However, left-of-center parties face increased difficulty in forming governing coalitions because no Arab party has ever been part of a one.

CURRENT GOVERNMENT

Israeli Prime Minister Binyamin Netanyahu presides over a coalition government that includes six parties generally characterized as right of center (see Appendix A). The varying interests of the coalition's members and some intra-party rifts contribute to difficulties in building consensus on several issues, including

· How to strengthen Israel's security and protect its Jewish character while preserving rule of law and freedom of expression for all citizens.

· How to promote general economic strength while addressing popular concerns regarding economic inequality and cost of living.

CORRUPTION ALLEGATIONS INVOLVING NETANYAHU

The Israeli police recommended in February 2018 that Attorney General Avichai Mandelblit indict Prime Minister Netanyahu for bribery, fraud, and breach of trust.11 Mandelblit may decide in 2019 whether to press charges.12 In response to the police recommendations, Netanyahu—who has consistently denied the allegations—said that the recommendations "will end with nothing" and that he will stay in office to pursue Israel's well-being.13 However, they could threaten Netanyahu's position as prime minister.

11 Rory Jones, "Israeli Police Recommend Charges Against Netanyahu," *Wall Street Journal*, February 14, 2018. Netanyahu appointed Mandelblit to his post in 2016. Mandelblit earlier served as a cabinet secretary. Isabel Kershner, "Promoted by Netanyahu, Israel's Attorney General Must Now Scrutinize Him," *New York Times*, February 14, 2018. Separate investigations or reports implicate other figures from Netanyahu's Likud party or the government coalition, including former Knesset Coalition Chairman David Bitan, Welfare Minister Haim Katz, Interior Minister Aryeh Deri, and Israel's U.N. Ambassador Danny Danon. Mazal Mualem, "Israelis not ready to topple Netanyahu over corruption," *Al-Monitor Israel Pulse*, December 15, 2017.
12 Ben Caspit, "Netanyahu seemingly unfazed by wife's fraud indictment," *Al-Monitor Israel Pulse*, June 25, 2018.
13 "The Latest: Israel PM: Recommendations to indict 'nothing,'" *Times of Israel*, February 13, 2018.
14 "Poll: Netanyahu's Likud would remain biggest party despite corruption probes," *Times of Israel*, February 21, 2018.
15 David M. Halbfinger and Isabel Kershner, "New Netanyahu Corruption Allegations: The Details," *New York Times*, February 21, 2018.
16 "Sara Netanyahu indicted for misusing $100,000 in state funds to buy gourmet food," *Times of Israel*, June 21, 2018.
17 Ian Deitch, "Israel's ex-PM Ehud Olmert released from prison," Associated Press, July 2, 2017. For information on previous allegations against Netanyahu and other Israeli prime ministers, see Irit Pazner Garshowitz and Jonah Engel Bromwich, "Prime Ministers' History of Run-Ins with the Law," *New York Times*, February 15, 2018.

The recommendations cover two specific cases. One Israeli media source has summarized them as follows:

In Case 1000, Netanyahu and his wife are alleged to have received illicit gifts from billionaire benefactors, most notably the Israeli-born Hollywood producer Arnon Milchan, totaling NIS 1 million ($282,000). In return, Netanyahu is alleged by police to have intervened on Milchan's behalf in matters relating to legislation, business dealings, and visa arrangements.

Case 2000 involves a suspected illicit quid pro quo deal between Netanyahu and Yedioth Ahronoth publisher Arnon Mozes that would have seen the prime minister weaken a rival daily, the Sheldon Adelson-backed Israel Hayom, in return for more favorable coverage from Yedioth.14

Later in February, developments in ongoing investigations appeared to implicate Netanyahu or his close associates in additional instances of alleged corruption. One case deals with possible overtures made to a judge about quashing an investigation of Netanyahu's wife Sara in exchange for the judge's appointment as attorney general, and another deals with possible actions to enrich a telecom magnate in expectation of favorable media coverage.15 In June 2018, Sara Netanyahu was indicted, along with a former staffer from Netanyahu's office, for the fraudulent use of state funds.16

Legally, Netanyahu could continue in office if indicted, but he could face public pressure to resign, and his coalition partners could face public pressure to withdraw their support for the government. Israel's previous prime minister, Ehud Olmert, announced his decision to resign in July 2008 amid corruption-related allegations, two months before the police recommended charges against him.17

MAJOR DOMESTIC ISSUES

The Knesset has recently passed some notable legislation. In July 2018, it passed a Basic Law defining Israel as the national homeland of the Jewish people.18 Also in July, the Knesset voted to withhold funds from the Palestinian Authority to "penalize it for paying stipends to Palestinian prisoners in Israel, their families and the families of Palestinians killed or wounded in confrontations with Israelis."19 Another bill passed in July permits single women to be surrogate parents, but does not extend the same permission to single men or same-sex couples.20

18 Some observers are concerned that the law might further undermine the place of Arabs in Israeli society, while others view its effect as mainly symbolic. See, e.g., Ruth Eglash, "Jewish or democratic? Israel debates its founding principles," *Washington Post*, July 12, 2018; Dov Lieber, "Law Sets Israel as 'Jewish State,'" *Wall Street Journal*, July 20, 2018. Before the law passed, lawmakers removed a clause that would have permitted the state to authorize "a community composed of people having the same faith and nationality to maintain the exclusive character of that community." "Israel adopts controversial Jewish nation-state law," Agence France Presse, July 19, 2018.
19 Isabel Kershner, "Israelis Vote to Penalize Payments for 'Martyrs,'" *New York Times*, July 4, 2018. Israel is obligated to transfer said tax revenues to the PA per the Paris Protocol of 1994. Congress has enacted legislation (Taylor Force Act, Title X of P.L. 115-141) that places restrictions on U.S. economic aid to the Palestinians because of Palestinian payments "for acts of terrorism." CRS Report RS22967, *U.S. Foreign Aid to the Palestinians*, by Jim Zanotti.
20 Bar Peleg, "Hundreds Protest in Tel Aviv After Netanyahu Flip-flops on Surrogacy Bill," haaretz.com, July 18, 2018.
21 Tovah Lazaroff, "In 'annexation' push, Knesset limits Palestinian access to high court," jpost.com, July 17, 2018.
22 Jeffrey Heller, "Israeli Legislation Reining in Supreme Court Wins Preliminary Approval," Reuters, May 6, 2018.
23 See, e.g., Chaim Levinson, "Netanyahu Pushes to Expand Western Wall Egalitarian Prayer Space," haaretz.com, June 19, 2018.
24 Amnesty International, *Forced and Unlawful: Israel's Deportation of Eritrean and Sudanese Asylum-Seekers to Uganda*, June 2018.

Additionally, controversial legislation has passed to apply some aspects of Israeli law to settlements in the West Bank,21 and is pending to limit the Supreme Court's power of judicial review over legislation.22 Several of the government's opponents and critics have voiced warnings that these and other initiatives may stifle dissent or undermine the independence of key Israeli institutions such as the media, the judiciary, and the military.

Some government policies in the domestic sphere are the subject of contention. For example, in 2017, the government suspended a decision it had previously made to allow for a mixed-gender prayer space in the Western Wall plaza in Jerusalem's Old City. According to Netanyahu, the government is reviewing the issue and plans to suggest another approach.23 Another issue has been Israeli government policy regarding African migrants who have reached Israel. The policy has fluctuated, partly based on rulings from Israel's Supreme Court. Considerable international criticism had centered on government proposals—which have since been scrapped—to forcibly deport some migrants to third countries (Rwanda and Uganda).24

Early elections could happen (legally, elections are required in the second half of 2019) if the governing coalition splits over the cases against Prime Minister Netanyahu or some other issue. If early elections take place, Netanyahu (if he runs) could face challenges from figures on the right of the political spectrum (including Education Minister Naftali Bennett and Defense Minister Avigdor Lieberman), or nearer the center or left (former finance minister Yair Lapid, Labor Party leader Avi Gabbay, and retired generals Gabi Ashkenazi and Benny Gantz). Reportedly, Netanyahu may call for elections before the attorney general decides on whether to bring criminal charges against him, in hopes of claiming a popular mandate to continue in office even if he is indicted.25

ECONOMY AND DEVELOPMENTS

Israel has an advanced industrial, market economy in which the government plays a substantial role. Despite limited natural resources, the agricultural and industrial sectors are well developed. The engine of the economy is an advanced high-tech sector, including aviation, communications, computer-aided design and manufactures, medical electronics, and fiber optics. Israel still benefits from loans, contributions, and capital investments from the Jewish diaspora, but economic strength has lessened its dependence on external financing.

25 Caspit, op. cit.
26 Based on data from the International Monetary Fund's World Economic Outlook Database, April 2018.
27 Ibid.
28 Economist Intelligence Unit, *Country Report: Israel*, generated June 28, 2018.

29 OECD Economic Surveys: Israel, March 2018.
30 Ibid.

Israel's economy is experiencing a period of moderate growth (between 2.5% and 4% annually since 2014).26 While International Monetary Fund (IMF) growth projections for Israel remain close to 3% over the next five years,27 the Economist Intelligence Unit projects average growth of 3.8% through 2022 over much of that time due to expectations of greater domestic consumption and exports.28 For information on prospective natural gas exports, see CRS Report R44591, *Natural Gas Discoveries in the Eastern Mediterranean*, by Michael Ratner.

Although Israel's overall macroeconomic profile and fiscal position appears positive, the country has the highest relative poverty level and the sixth-highest income inequality level within the 37-country Organisation of Economic Cooperation and Development (OECD).29 Poverty and inequality particularly disadvantage Arab Israelis and Israeli Haredim (ultra-Orthodox Jews).30

ISRAELI SECURITY AND CHALLENGES

STRATEGIC AND MILITARY PROFILE

Israel relies on a number of strengths, along with discreet coordination with Arab states, to manage potential threats to its security and existence.

MILITARY SUPERIORITY AND HOMELAND SECURITY MEASURES

Israel maintains conventional military superiority relative to its neighbors and the Palestinians. Shifts in regional order and evolving asymmetric threats have led Israel to update its efforts to project military strength, deter attack, and defend its population and borders. Israel appears to have reduced some unconventional threats via missile defense systems, reported cyber defense and warfare capabilities, and heightened security measures vis-à-vis Palestinians.

According to estimates from *IHS Jane's*, Israel's military features total active duty manpower across the army, navy, and air force of approximately 180,000, plus 445,000 in reserve—numbers aided by mandatory conscription for most young Jewish Israeli men and women, followed by extended reserve duty. Israel's overall annual defense budget is approximately $16.4 billion, constituting about 4.6% of its total gross domestic product (GDP).31

31 "Israel Defence Budget," *Jane's Defence Budgets*, April 12, 2018. For purposes of comparison, *IHS Jane's* reports that the U.S. defense budget totals close to $657 billion annually, constituting approximately 3.3% of total GDP. The World Bank, citing data from the Stockholm International Peace Research Institute, states the following figures for defense spending as a percentage of GDP in other key Middle Eastern countries as of 2017: Egypt-1.4%, Iran-3.2%, Iraq-3.8%, Jordan-4.8%, Lebanon-4.7%, Saudi Arabia-10.2%, Turkey-2.1%.
https://data.worldbank.org/indicator/MS.MIL.XPND.GD.ZS.
32 Gad Lior, "Cost of border fences, underground barrier, reaches NIS 6bn," Ynetnews, January 30, 2018.
33 Hans M. Kristensen and Robert S. Norris, "Worldwide deployment of nuclear weapons, 2017," *Bulletin of the Atomic Scientists*, vol. 73(5), 2017, pp. 289-297.
34 Eli Lake, "Secret U.S.-Israel Nuclear Accord in Jeopardy," *Washington Times*, May 6, 2009.
35 Kristensen and Norris, op. cit.; "Strategic Weapon Systems," *Jane's Sentinel Security Assessment – Eastern Mediterranean*, June 26, 2018; "Operation Samson: Israel's Deployment of Nuclear Missiles on Subs from Germany," *Der Spiegel*, June 4, 2012.
36 Joshua S. Block, "An ally reminds us of its value," jpost.com, May 8, 2018; Marty Oliner, "US-Israel relationship: More critical than ever," *The Hill*, May 3, 2017.
37 The United States and Israel do, however, have a Mutual Defense Assistance Agreement (TIAS 2675, dated July 23, 1952) in effect regarding the provision of U.S. military equipment to Israel, and have entered into a range of stand-alone agreements, memoranda of understanding, and other arrangements varying in their formality.

Israel has a robust homeland security system featuring sophisticated early warning practices, thorough border and airport security controls, and reinforced rooms or shelters that are engineered to withstand explosions in most of the country's buildings. Israel also has proposed and partially constructed a national border fence network of steel barricades (accompanied at various points by watch towers, patrol roads, intelligence centers, and military brigades) designed to minimize militant infiltration, illegal immigration, and smuggling from Egypt, Syria, Lebanon, Jordan, and the Gaza Strip.32

Undeclared Nuclear Weapons Capability

Israel is not a party to the Nuclear Nonproliferation Treaty (NPT) and maintains a policy of "nuclear opacity" or *amimut*. A 2017 report estimated that Israel possesses a nuclear arsenal of around 80-85 warheads.33 The United States has countenanced Israel's nuclear ambiguity since 1969, when Israeli Prime Minister Golda Meir and U.S. President Richard Nixon reportedly reached an accord whereby both sides agreed never to acknowledge Israel's nuclear arsenal in public.34 Israel might have nuclear weapons deployable via aircraft, submarine, and ground-based missiles.35 No other Middle Eastern country is generally thought to possess nuclear weapons.

U.S. Cooperation

Israeli officials closely consult with U.S. counterparts in an effort to influence U.S. decisionmaking on key regional issues. Israel's leaders and supporters routinely make the case to U.S. officials that Israel's security and the broader stability of the region remain critically important for U.S. interests. They also argue that Israel has multifaceted worth as a U.S. ally and that the Israeli and American peoples share core values.36 See Appendix B for selected U.S.-based interest groups relating to Israel. The United States and Israel do not have a mutual defense treaty or agreement that provides formal U.S. security guarantees.37

IRAN AND THE REGION

Iran remains of primary concern to Israeli officials largely because of (1) Iran's antipathy toward Israel, (2) Iran's broad regional influence, and (3) the possibility that Iran will be free of nuclear program constraints in the future. As mentioned above, in recent years Israel and Arab Gulf states have discreetly cultivated closer relations with one another in efforts to counter Iran.

Iranian Nuclear Agreement and the U.S. Withdrawal

Prime Minister Netanyahu has sought to influence U.S. decisions on the international agreement on Iran's nuclear program (known as the Joint Comprehensive Plan of Action, or JCPOA). He argued against the JCPOA when it was negotiated in 2015, and welcomed President Trump's May 2018 withdrawal of the United States from the JCPOA and accompanying reimposition of U.S. sanctions on Iran's oil and central bank transactions. In a September 2017 speech before the U.N. General Assembly, Netanyahu had called on the signatories of the JCPOA to "fix it or nix it."38 Then, a few days before President Trump's May announcement, Netanyahu presented information that Israeli intelligence operatives apparently seized in early 2018 from an Iranian archive. Netanyahu used the information, which purportedly describes past work by Iran on a nuclear weapons program, to express concerns about Iran's credibility and its potential to parlay existing know-how into nuclear-weapons breakthroughs after the JCPOA expires.39

38 Israeli Prime Minister's Office, PM Netanyahu's Speech at the United Nations General Assembly, September 19, 2017.

39 Israeli Prime Minister's Office, PM Netanyahu reveals the Iranian secret nuclear program, April 30, 2018.
40 See, e.g., Israeli Prime Minister's Office, Statement by PM Netanyahu, May 8, 2018; Jonathan Ferziger and Udi Segal, "Netanyahu's Challenge: Help Trump Fix or Scrap the Iran Deal," Bloomberg, October 18, 2017.
41 David E. Sanger and David D. Kirkpatrick, "A Risky Bet on Breaking Tehran's Will," *New York Times*, May 9, 2018; Amos Harel and Yaniv Kubovich, "Despite Faults, Iran Nuclear Deal Works, Israeli Military Chief Tells Haaretz," *Ha'aretz*, March 30, 2018; Bernard Avishai, "Why Israeli Nuclear Experts Disagree with Netanyahu about the Iran Deal," newyorker.com, October 24, 2017.
42 See, e.g., Halbfinger, op. cit., citing former Israeli military intelligence chief Amos Yadlin.
43 Ofer Zalzberg of the International Crisis Group, cited in David M. Halbfinger, "For Israel's Prime Minister, Vindication and New Threats to Confront," *New York Times*, May 9, 2018.
44 James Masters, "Israeli PM Benjamin Netanyahu defends Iran nuclear claims in face of criticism," CNN, May 1,

Although concern about Iran and its nuclear program is widespread among Israelis, their views on the JCPOA vary. Netanyahu and his supporters in government have routinely complained that the JCPOA fails to address matters not directly connected to Iran's nuclear program, such as Iran's development of ballistic missiles and its sponsorship of terrorist groups.40 Media reports suggest that a number of current and former Israeli officials have favored preserving the JCPOA because of the limits it placed on Iranian nuclear activities for some time or these officials' doubts about achieving international consensus for anything stricter.41

Commentators speculate on the possibility that Israel might act militarily against Iranian nuclear facilities if Iran resumes certain activities currently stopped under the JCPOA.42 According to one analyst, one group of Israeli officials have preferred to keep the nuclear deal in place while focusing on pressing challenges in Syria, while another group (including Netanyahu) have favored seizing the opportunity to make common cause with the Trump Administration to pressure Iran economically and militarily.43 However, shortly after Netanyahu publicly presented the Iranian nuclear archive, he said in an interview that he was not seeking a military confrontation with Iran.44

45 For more information on this issue, see CRS In Focus IF10858, *Iran and Israel: Growing Tensions Over Syria*, by Carla E. Humud, Kenneth Katzman, and Jim Zanotti.
46 Thomas L. Friedman, "The Real Next War in Syria: Iran vs. Israel," *New York Times*, April 15, 2018.
47 Israeli Prime Minister's Office, PM Netanyahu's Remarks at the Start of the Cabinet Meeting, May 6, 2018.
48 "Israel strikes Iranian targets in Syria in response to rocket fire," BBC, May 10, 2018. Iran denied firing at Israeli positions in the Golan. "Iran denies attacking Israeli positions," Deutsche Welle, May 11, 2018. Syrian media claimed that Syria was involved in the attacks on the Golan. Josef Federman, "Israel accuses Iranian forces of rocket attack on Golan," Associated Press, May 9, 2018.
49 "IDF: Overnight raids set back Iranian military in Syria by 'many months,'" *Times of Israel*, May 10, 2018.
50 Israel Defense Forces statement, IDF shoots down a Syrian fighter jet, July 24, 2018; "Israel 'shoots down' Syrian fighter over Golan Heights," BBC News, July 24, 2018.

IRAN IN SYRIA: CROSS-BORDER ATTACKS WITH ISRAEL45

A "shadow war" has developed between Israel and Iran over Iran's presence in Syria. In the early years of the Syria conflict, Israel primarily employed airstrikes to prevent Iranian weapons shipments destined for Hezbollah in Lebanon. Since 2017, with the government of Bashar al Asad increasingly in control of large portions of Syria's territory, Israeli leaders have expressed intentions to prevent Iran from constructing and operating bases or advanced weapons manufacturing facilities in Syria. The focus of Israeli military operations in Syria has expanded in line with an increasing number of Iran-related concerns there. Further exacerbating Israeli sensitivities, Iran-backed forces (particularly Hezbollah) have moved closer to the Israeli-occupied Golan Heights since late 2017 via actions against Syrian opposition groups.

On February 10, 2018, Iranian personnel based at Tiyas air base in central Syria apparently sent an armed drone into Israeli airspace. A senior Israeli military source was quoted as saying, "This is the first time we saw Iran do something against Israel—not by proxy. This opened a new period."46

In May 2018, Prime Minister Netanyahu asserted that Iran had transferred advanced weaponry to Syria (weaponized drones, ground-to-ground missiles, anti-aircraft batteries) in recent months. He stated that Israel was "determined to block Iran's aggression" and that "we do not want escalation, but we are prepared for any scenario."47

Since the February 10 incident, Israel has reportedly struck Iranian targets on multiple occasions. The resulting exchanges of fire (including the downing of an Israeli F-16 during the February incident) and subsequent official statements from Israel, Iran, Syria, and Russia have highlighted the possibility that limited Israeli strikes to enforce "redlines" against Iran-backed forces could expand into wider conflict, particularly in cases of miscalculation by one or both sides.

On May 10, according to the Israeli military, Iran's Islamic Revolutionary Guard Corps-Quds Force fired rockets at Israeli military positions in the Golan Heights, as retaliation against earlier Israeli strikes against Iranian targets in Syria.48 This triggered Israeli strikes in Syria on a larger scale than any Israeli operations there since the 1973 Yom Kippur War.49 Reportedly, Israel has since conducted some additional airstrikes in Syria, and on two separate occasions in July its military claimed that it shot down a Syrian drone and a fighter jet over the Golan Heights using Patriot missiles.50

RUSSIA

Russia's advanced air defense systems in Syria could affect Israeli operations.52 To date, Russia does not appear to have acted militarily to thwart Israeli airstrikes against Iranian or Syrian targets. However, Russian officials' statements in response to Israeli actions in Syria since February have fueled speculation about Russia's position vis-à-vis Israel and Iran,53 given that Russia's military presence in Syria is protected by Iran-backed ground forces.

Israeli officials reportedly continue to consult with Russian officials about deconflicting Israeli military operations in Syria and discussing ways to limit Iran's presence there.54 In May 2018, Russian Foreign Minister Sergei Lavrov called for the withdrawal of all non-Syrian forces from the southern border area "on a reciprocal basis."55 However, as of July, Hezbollah reportedly has been helping lead an offensive against rebels in southern Syria.56 In a press conference following his July 16 summit with President Trump, Russian President Vladimir Putin stated a desire to have the situation between Israel and Syria in the Golan Heights return to what it had been before Syria's civil war.57

HEZBOLLAH IN LEBANON

Hezbollah has challenged Israel's security near the Lebanese border for decades—with the antagonism at times contained near the border, and at times escalating into broader conflict.58 Speculation persists about the potential for wider conflict and its regional implications.59 In recent years, Israeli officials have sought to draw attention to Hezbollah's weapons buildup—including reported upgrades to the range, precision, and power of its projectiles—and its alleged use of Lebanese civilian areas as strongholds.60 Previously during Syria's civil war, Israel reportedly provided various means of support to rebel groups in the vicinity of the Syria-Israel border in order to prevent Hezbollah or other Iran-linked groups from controlling the area.61

61 Rory Jones, et al., "Israel Gives Cash, Aid to Rebels in Syria," *Wall Street Journal*, June 19, 2017.
62 "Nasrallah: Israel Targeting Syria Air Base Was 'a Historic Mistake,'" jpost.com, April 13, 2018.
63 John Duchak, "With Iran and Israel at the Brink, Where Does Hezbollah Stand?" Atlantic Council, May 8, 2018.
64 Ibid.; Martin Indyk and Natan Sachs of the Brookings Institution, cited in Sewell Chan, "The Bigger Conflict Behind the Cross-Border Clashes in Syria," *New York Times*, May 11, 2018.
Increased conflict between Israel and Iran over Iran's presence in Syria raises questions about the potential for Hezbollah's Lebanon-based forces to open another front against Israel. In April 2018, Hezbollah leader Hassan Nasrallah

said that an Israeli strike on Iranian targets at Tiyas air base was a "pivotal incident in the history of the region that can't be ignored" and a "historic mistake." Earlier that same day, Hezbollah's deputy leader Naim Qassem said that Hezbollah would not open a front against Israel from Lebanon, but that it was ready for "surprises."62 One May analysis expressed doubt that either Israel or Iran would seek to expand the scope of their emerging conflict in Syria to Lebanon.63 However, the same analysis and some others speculated that if Israel-Iran conflict in Syria worsens and Iran feels cornered, it could look to gain leverage over Israel by having Hezbollah launch attacks from Lebanon.64

HAMAS AND GAZA

Major Israel-Hamas Conflicts Since 2008

December 2008-January 2009: Israeli code name "Operation Cast Lead"

· Three-week duration, first meaningful display of Palestinians' Iranian-origin rockets, Israeli air strikes and ground offensive

· Political context: Impending leadership transitions in Israel and United States; struggling Israeli-Palestinian peace talks (Annapolis process)

· Fatalities: More than 1,100 (possibly more than 1,400) Palestinians; 13 Israelis (3 civilians)

November 2012: "Operation Pillar of Defense (or Cloud)"

· Eight-day duration, Palestinian projectiles of greater range and variety, Israeli airstrikes, prominent role for Iron Dome

· Political context: Widespread Arab political change, including rise of Muslim Brotherhood to power in Egypt; three months before Israeli elections

· Fatalities: More than 100 Palestinians, 6 Israelis (4 civilians)

July-August 2014: "Operation Protective Edge/Mighty Cliff"

· About 50-day duration, Palestinian projectiles of greater range and variety, Israeli air strikes and ground offensive, extensive Palestinian use of and Israeli countermeasures against tunnels, prominent role for Iron Dome

· Political context: Shortly after (1) unsuccessful round of Israeli-Palestinian peace talks, (2) PA consensus government formation and end of Hamas's formal responsibilities for governing Gaza, (3) prominent youth killings

· Fatalities: More than 2,100 Palestinians, 71 Israelis (5 civilians), and 1 foreign worker

Israel faces a threat from the Gaza Strip (via Hamas and other militant groups).65 Although Palestinian militants maintain rocket and mortar arsenals, the threat from projectiles has reportedly been diminished by Israel's Iron Dome defense system.66 Tunnels that Palestinian militants used somewhat effectively in a 2014 conflict with Israel have been largely neutralized by systematic Israeli efforts, with some financial and technological assistance from the United States.67 Under President Abdel Fattah al Sisi, Egyptian military efforts have significantly reduced smuggling over land into Gaza.

65 For information on Palestinian militants' capabilities in Gaza, see CRS Report RL34074, *The Palestinians: Background and U.S. Relations*, by Jim Zanotti.

66 Neri Zilber, "Israel and Hamas: Negotiating With Rockets and Bombs," Daily Beast, May 31, 2018.
67 CRS Report RL33222, *U.S. Foreign Aid to Israel*, by Jeremy M. Sharp.
68 U.N. General Assembly, Resolution adopted by the Human Rights Council on 18 May 2018, A/HRC/RES/S-28/1.
69 http://www.un.org/en/ga/search/view_doc.asp?symbol=A/ES-10/L.23.
70 Mark Weiss, "Fighting kite terror," *Jerusalem Report*, July 9, 2018; "IDF strikes 2 Hamas posts in Gaza as firefighters tackle balloon blazes," *Times of Israel*, July 16, 2018; Ben Caspit, "Netanyahu feeling the heat from Gaza," *Al-Monitor Israel Pulse*, July 16, 2018; Mark Landler, "As Violence Flares, Kushner Threatens to Abandon Plan to Rebuild Gaza," *New York Times*, July 23, 2018.

In 2018, protests and violence along security fences dividing Gaza from Israel have attracted international attention. Israel's use of live fire and the death of more than 120 Palestinians in the spring (including several deaths on May 14, the day that the U.S. embassy opened in Jerusalem) led the U.N. Human Rights Council to call in May for an "independent, international commission of inquiry" to produce a report.68 A June U.N. General Assembly resolution condemned both Israeli actions against Palestinian civilians and the firing of rockets from Gaza against Israeli civilians.69 Subsequently, some Israel-Gaza violence has ensued over Palestinians' use of incendiary kites or balloons to set fires in southern Israel and a sniper's killing of an Israeli soldier in July, fueling speculation about possible escalation.70

U.S. and PA funding reductions have added to questions about humanitarian assistance for Gaza's population, who remain largely dependent on external donor funding and face chronic economic difficulties and shortages of electricity and safe drinking water.71 Since 2007, as part of a larger regime of Israeli-Egyptian control over access to and from Gaza, Israel has limited the shipment of building materials into Gaza because of concerns that Hamas might divert materials for reconstruction toward military infrastructure. The possibility that humanitarian crisis could destabilize Gaza has prompted discussions among U.S., Israeli, and Arab leaders aimed at improving living conditions and reducing spillover threats.72 These discussions have sparked public debate about how closely humanitarian concerns should be linked with political outcomes involving Israel, Hamas, and the PA, or with an anticipated U.S. diplomatic initiative (see " Peace Process and International Involvement ").73

71 Fares Akram and Mohammed Daraghmeh, "As U.S. aid dries up, Gaza families pushed deeper into poverty: 'Death is better than this life,'" Associated Press, June 7, 2018; World Bank, Economic Monitoring Report to the Ad Hoc Liaison Committee, March 19, 2018; CRS Report RS22967, *U.S. Foreign Aid to the Palestinians*, by Jim Zanotti.
72 White House, Readout of the Gaza Conference at the White House, March 14, 2018; Amos Harel, "Abbas Is Key Obstacle to Gaza Rehabilitation, Top Israeli Security Brass Warns," haaretz.com, July 3, 2018.
73 Ben Caspit, "Why is Israel propping up Hamas in Gaza?" *Al-Monitor Israel Pulse*, June 27, 2018; Ilan Goldenberg, "Kushner's Peace Plan Is a Disaster Waiting to Happen," foreignpolicy.com, June 25, 2018; Adnan Abu Amer, "Palestinians skeptical of humanitarian efforts in Gaza," *Al-Monitor Palestine Pulse*, June 19, 2018; Jared Kushner, Jason Greenblatt, and David Friedman, "Help is at hand for Palestinians. It's all up to Hamas," *Washington Post*, July 19, 2018; Shlomi Eldar, "Abbas appears set to compromise for Fatah-Hamas reconciliation," *Al-Monitor Israel Pulse*, July 30, 2018.
74 The Jewish Virtual Library maintains a page that contains hyperlinked documents, speeches, and reports under the heading "U.S.-Israel Relations: Strategic & Military Cooperation," available at http://www.jewishvirtuallibrary.org/jsource/US-Israel/strattoc.html.
75 See, e.g., Saar Haas, "Israel is 7th largest arms exporter in the world," Ynetnews, March 17, 2018. According to this article, 49% of Israeli weapons exported from 2013 to 2017 went to India, 13% to Azerbaijan, and 6% to Vietnam.

ISRAEL AND KEY U.S. POLICY ISSUES

SECURITY COOPERATION74

Strong bilateral relations have reinforced significant U.S.-Israel cooperation on defense, including military aid, arms sales, joint exercises, and information sharing. It also has included periodic U.S.-Israel cooperation in developing military technology.

U.S. military aid has helped transform Israel's armed forces into one of the most technologically sophisticated militaries in the world. This aid for Israel has been designed to maintain Israel's "qualitative military edge" (QME) over neighboring militaries, since Israel must rely on better equipment and training to compensate for a manpower deficit in a conflict against one or more regional states. U.S. military aid, a portion of which may be spent on procurement from Israeli defense companies, also has helped Israel build a domestic defense industry, and Israel in turn is one of the top exporters of arms worldwide.75

On November 30, 1981, the United States and Israel signed a memorandum of understanding (MOU) establishing a framework for consultation and cooperation to enhance the national security of both countries. In 1983, the two sides formed a Joint Political Military Group to implement provisions of the MOU. Joint air and sea military exercises began in 1984, and the United States has constructed facilities to stockpile military equipment in Israel. In 1986, Israel

and the United States signed an MOU—the contents of which are classified—for Israeli participation in the Strategic Defense Initiative (SDI/"Star Wars"), under which U.S.-Israel co-development of the Arrow ballistic missile defense system has proceeded. In 1987, Israel was designated a "major non-NATO ally" by the Reagan Administration, and in 1996, under the terms of Section 517 of the Foreign Assistance Act of 1961, as amended, Congress codified this status, affording Israel preferential treatment in bidding for U.S. defense contracts and expanding its access to weapons systems at lower prices. In 2001, an annual interagency strategic dialogue, including representatives of diplomatic, defense, and intelligence establishments, was created to discuss long-term issues.

The U.S.-Israel Enhanced Security Cooperation Act (P.L. 112-150) of 2012 and U.S.-Israel Strategic Partnership Act (P.L. 113-296) of 2014 encouraged continued and expanded U.S.-Israel cooperation in a number of areas, including defense, homeland security, cyber issues, energy, and trade. The latter act designated Israel as a "major strategic partner" of the United States—a designation whose meaning has not been further defined in U.S. law or by the executive branch.

PRESERVING ISRAEL'S QUALITATIVE MILITARY EDGE (QME)

Since the late 1970s, successive Administrations have argued that U.S. arms sales are an important mechanism for addressing the security concerns of Israel and other regional countries. During this period, some Members of Congress have argued that sales of sophisticated weaponry to Arab countries may erode Israel's QME over its neighbors. However, successive Administrations have maintained that Arab countries are too dependent on U.S. training, spare parts, and support to be in a position to use sophisticated U.S.-made arms against the United States, Israel, or any other U.S. ally in a sustained campaign. Arab critics routinely charge that Israeli officials exaggerate the threat they pose. The threat of a nuclear-armed or regionally bolstered Iran, though it has partially aligned Israeli and Sunni Arab interests in deterring a shared rival, may be exacerbating Israeli fears of a deteriorated QME, as Saudi Arabia and other Gulf states dramatically increase defense procurements from U.S. and other foreign suppliers.

In 2008, Congress enacted legislation requiring that any proposed U.S. arms sale to "any country in the Middle East other than Israel" must include a notification to Congress with a "determination that the sale or export of such would not adversely affect Israel's qualitative military edge over military threats to Israel."76 In parallel with this legal requirement, U.S. and Israeli officials frequently signal their shared understanding of the U.S. commitment to maintaining Israel's QME. However, the codified definition focuses on preventing arms sales to potential regional Israeli adversaries based on a calculation of conventional military threats, raising questions about the definition's applicability to evolving unconventional threats to Israel's security.

76 §36(h) of the Arms Export Control Act, which contains the "qualitative military edge" requirement, was added by §201(d) of the Naval Vessel Transfer Act of 2008 (P.L. 110-429). The act defines QME as "the ability to counter and defeat any credible conventional military threat from any individual state or possible coalition of states or from nonstate actors, while sustaining minimal damages and casualties, through the use of superior military means, possessed in sufficient quantity, including weapons, command, control, communication, intelligence, surveillance, and reconnaissance capabilities that in their technical characteristics are superior in capability to those of such other individual or possible coalition of states or nonstate actors." The details of official U.S. assessments of QME are generally classified.

What might constitute a legally defined adverse effect to QME is not clarified in U.S. legislation. After the passage of the 2008 legislation, a bilateral QME working group was created allowing

Israel to argue its case against proposed U.S. arms sales in the region.77 For example, former Secretary of Defense Robert Gates wrote that, in 2010, the Obama Administration addressed concerns that Israel's leaders had about the possible effect on QME of a large U.S. sale of F-15 aircraft to Saudi Arabia by agreeing to sell Israel additional F-35 aircraft.78

77 Barbara Opall-Rome, "Israeli Brass Decry U.S. Arms Sales to Arab States," *Defense News*, January 23, 2012. According to this article, the U.S. side of the working group is led by the Under Secretary of Defense for Policy and Assistant Secretary of State for Political-Military Affairs, while the Israeli side is led by the Defense Ministry's policy chief and the Israel Defense Forces director of planning.
78 Eli Lake (citing *Duty* by Robert Gates), "In Gates Book, Details of Israel's Hard Bargaining Over Saudi Arms," *Daily Beast*, January 10, 2014. A former senior Pentagon official was cited as saying that Israel's concerns were based on "worries about what might happen if the House of Saud lost power to a more radical regime." Ibid.
79 Anna Ahronheim, "Israel receives three more F-35 Adir jets," jpost.com, June 25, 2018.

The U.S.-Israel Strategic Partnership Act (P.L. 113-296) enacted in December 2014 requires more frequent QME assessments and executive-legislative consultations. It also requires that QME determinations include evaluations of how potential arms sales would change the regional balance, while identifying measures Israel may need to take in response to the potential sales, and assurances or possible assurances from the United States to Israel as a result of the potential sales.

U.S. AID AND ARMS SALES TO ISRAEL

Specific figures and comprehensive detail regarding various aspects of U.S. aid and arms sales to Israel are discussed in CRS Report RL33222, *U.S. Foreign Aid to Israel*, by Jeremy M. Sharp. That report includes information on conditions that, in each fiscal year, generally allow Israel to use its military aid earlier and more flexibly than other countries.

AID

Israel is the largest cumulative recipient of U.S. foreign assistance since World War II. Since 1976, Israel has generally been the largest annual recipient of U.S. foreign assistance, with occasional exception of Iraq and Afghanistan after 2004. Since 1985, the United States has provided approximately $3 billion in grants annually to Israel. In the past, Israel received significant economic assistance, but now almost all U.S. bilateral aid to Israel is in the form of

Foreign Military Financing (FMF). U.S. FMF to Israel represents approximately one-half of total FMF and between 15-20% of Israel's defense budget. The new 10-year bilateral military aid MOU commits the United States to $3.3 billion annually from FY2019 to FY2028, subject to congressional appropriations. The United States also generally provides some annual American Schools and Hospitals Abroad (ASHA) funding and funding to Israel for migration assistance.

Arms Sales

Israel uses approximately 74% of its FMF to purchase arms from the United States, in addition to receiving U.S. Excess Defense Articles (EDA). Given the new MOU's phase-out of Israeli use of FMF for domestic arms producers, by FY2028 all of Israel's FMF will go toward U.S.-origin arms.

Israel's procurement of the F-35 Joint Strike Fighter from the United States has been underway since 2016. To date, Israel has received 12 F-35s, and it is under contract to receive a total of 50 by 2024.79 In late 2017, Israel was the first non-U.S. country to declare operational capability for the F-35, and it has reportedly used the aircraft in combat over Israel's northern border. Under the terms of its arrangements with the United States, Israel has had domestic contractors install customized equipment and weaponry, and it is the only F-35 recipient to date with the right to perform depot-level aircraft maintenance within its own borders.80

80 Ibid.
81 Sean McCormack, U.S. Department of State Spokesman, Daily Press Briefing, Washington, DC, January 29, 2007. The Consolidated Appropriations Act, 2008 (P.L. 110-161) significantly restricted the export of U.S.-manufactured cluster munitions. Restrictions on cluster munitions exports have been carried forward to apply to appropriations in subsequent years as well. Since 2008, Israel has been acquiring domestically manufactured cluster munitions.
82 For background on the Leahy Law, see CRS Report R43361, *"Leahy Law" Human Rights Provisions and Security Assistance: Issue Overview*, coordinated by Nina M. Serafino.
83 See the text of the Members' February 17, 2016, letter to Secretary of State John Kerry at http://www.politico.com/f/?id=00000153-c56c-d662-a75b-cfecc6be0000.
84 See the text of Assistant Secretary of State for Legislative Affairs Julia Frifield's April 18, 2016, response letter to Representative Henry C. Johnson at http://www.politico.com/f/?id=00000154-7c2f-d905-a357-7c7f04750000.

End-Use Monitoring and Leahy Law Vetting

Sales of U.S. defense articles and services to Israel are made subject to the terms of both the Arms Export Control Act (AECA) and the July 23, 1952, Mutual Defense Assistance Agreement between the United States and Israel (TIAS 2675). The 1952 agreement states:

The Government of Israel assures the United States Government that such equipment, materials, or services as may be acquired from the United States ... are required for and will be used solely to maintain its internal security, its legitimate self-defense ... and that it will not undertake any act of aggression against any other state.

Past Administrations have acknowledged that some Israeli uses of U.S. defense articles may have failed to meet the requirements under the AECA and the 1952 agreement that Israel only use such articles for self-defense and internal security purposes. These past Administrations have transmitted reports to Congress stating that "substantial violations" of agreements between the United States and Israel regarding arms sales "may have occurred." The most recent report of this type was transmitted in January 2007 in relation to concerns about Israel's use of U.S.-supplied cluster munitions during military operations against Hezbollah in Lebanon during 2006.81 Other examples include findings issued in 1978, 1979, and 1982 with regard to Israel's military operations in Lebanon and Israel's air strike on Iraq's nuclear reactor complex at Osirak in 1981.

Additionally, Section 620M of the Foreign Assistance Act of 1961 (FAA), as amended (commonly known as the Leahy Law),82 prohibits the furnishing of assistance authorized by the FAA and the AECA to any foreign security force unit where there is credible information that the unit has committed a gross violation of human rights. The State Department implements Leahy vetting to determine which foreign security force units (and individuals within the units) are eligible to receive U.S. assistance or training.

In 2016, Senator Patrick Leahy and 10 other Members of Congress corresponded with the State Department on the application of the Leahy Law to some specifically alleged instances of possible extrajudicial killings or torture by Israeli personnel.83 The State Department assured the Members of Congress that it was properly conducting Leahy vetting and monitoring the instances that were mentioned in their letter.84 In November 2017, Representative Betty McCollum introduced the Promoting Human Rights by Ending Israeli Military Detention of Palestinian Children Act (H.R. 4391), which would prohibit the use of aid for Israel in support of various types of ill-treatment of Palestinian children.

MISSILE DEFENSE COOPERATION

Congress provides hundreds of millions of dollars in annual assistance beyond Administration-requested amounts for Israel's Iron Dome anti-rocket system and joint U.S.-Israel missile defense programs such as Arrow and David's Sling. The new MOU provides for $500 million in annual funding from FY2019 to FY2028, with possibly more in exceptional circumstances. In July 2016, the United States and Israel announced that they had successfully conducted a special trial—the first of its kind in eight years—to test the connectivity of U.S.- and Israeli-controlled missile defense systems that are based in and around Israel.85

85 Yuval Azulai, "Israel, US conduct joint missile defense trial," *Globes*, July 6, 2016. The trial reportedly included such Israeli missile defense assets as David's Sling, Arrow 2, and Arrow 3; and such U.S. assets as Patriot (of which, some batteries have been acquired by Israel), Terminal High Altitude Air Defense (THAAD), Aegis, and the radar station located in Israel's Negev Desert. The trial was a follow-up to the biennial bilateral "Juniper Cobra" joint military exercise.
86 Text of letter available at https://roskam.house.gov/media-center/press-releases/roskam-and-meng-lead-over-40-members-congress-bipartisan-letter-urging.
87 Yuval Azulai, "Rafael set for Iron Dome sale to Romania," *Globes*, May 17, 2018.
88 Michael Bachner, "Israel Aerospace Industries earned $2 billion in Iron Dome radar sales—report," *Times of Israel*, February 22, 2018.

Some countries have sought to acquire elements used in Israeli missile defense systems. In April 2018, 40 Members of Congress sent a letter to the Chair and Ranking Member of the House Appropriations Subcommittee on Defense asking the Subcommittee to "carefully study" whether the U.S. Army might immediately acquire Iron Dome.86 A 2018 report stated that Rafael Advanced Defense Systems Ltd.—the primary Israeli contractor for Iron Dome—has entered into a cooperation agreement with Romania that would be the first to involve the export of Iron Dome's interception system.87 Israel Aerospace Industries reportedly has sold the radar used in the Iron Dome and David's Sling systems to a number of countries, including Canada and India.88

PENDING SECURITY COOPERATION LEGISLATION

U.S.-Israel Security Assistance Authorization Act of 2018 (S. 2497 and H.R. 5141). This bill includes the following provisions:

· *FMF authorization.* Would authorize FMF of at least $3.3 billion per year from FY2019 to FY2028 (the duration of the new MOU).

· *Extension of war reserves stockpile authority and access to loan guarantees.* Would extend this authority and access through FY2023.

· *Precision guided munitions (PGMs).* Would (1) authorize a joint U.S.-Israel assessment of how the United States can help provide PGMs to help with potential conflicts with Hezbollah and Hamas; (2) authorize the President to utilize the Special Defense Acquisition Fund to transfer PGMs to reserve stocks for Israel; and (3) authorize the modification of rapid acquisition and deployment procedures to aid U.S. production of PGMs under circumstances of urgent need.

· *Report on Israel's eligibility for strategic trade authorization exception.* Would require the President to report to Congress on Israel's status regarding this exception.

· *Cybersecurity cooperation* (H.R. 5141 only). Would direct the Homeland Security Department to establish a grant program to support cybersecurity research, development, demonstration, and commercialization in accordance with a 2008 bilateral agreement.

· *Worldwide foreign assistance, space exploration, and countering drone aircraft.* Would encourage and authorize cooperative U.S.-Israel efforts on these issues.

· *Additional reporting on Israel's QME and security posture.* Would require the periodic reports on Israel's QME that are already legally mandated to include additional information about threats to Israel and countermeasures available to it.

2019 National Defense Authorization Act (NDAA, H.R. 5515). The conference version of H.R. 5515 (found in H.Rept. 115-874) includes the following provisions:

· *Section 1272.* Would authorize the funding currently authorized for anti-tunneling efforts to also be used for countering drone aircraft (unmanned aerial systems).

· *Section 1273.* Provisions from S. 2497/H.R. 5141 on the extension of war reserves stockpile authority and the joint U.S.-Israel assessment on PGMs.

SENSITIVE TECHNOLOGY AND INTELLIGENCE

Arms sales, information sharing, and technical collaboration between the United States and Israel raise questions about what Israel might do with capabilities or information it acquires. The United States and Israel have regularly discussed Israel's dealings on sensitive security equipment and technology with various countries, especially China.89 Sources have reported that the United States has established de facto veto power over Israeli third-party arms sales.90 And since the 1980s there have been at least three cases in which U.S. government employees were convicted of disclosing classified information to Israel or of conspiracy to act as an Israeli agent.91

89 Office of Naval Intelligence, *Worldwide Challenges to Naval Strike Warfare*, 1996. The 1997 edition of this report said that the design for China's J-10 fighter (also known as the F-10—the designation used in the report) "had been undertaken with substantial direct assistance, primarily from Israel and Russia, and with indirect assistance through access to U.S. technologies." ONI, *Worldwide Challenges to Naval Strike Warfare*, 1997. See also Robert Hewson, "Chinese J-10 'benefited from the Lavi project,'" *Jane's Defence Weekly*, May 16, 2008; Duncan L. Clarke and Robert J. Johnston, "U.S. Dual-Use Exports to China, Chinese Behavior, and the Israel Factor: Effective Controls?" *Asian Survey*, Vol. 39, No. 2, March-April 1999. The Lavi fighter (roughly comparable to the U.S. F-16) was developed in Israel during the 1980s with approximately $1.5 billion in U.S. assistance, but did not get past the prototype stage. In 2000, a planned Israeli sale to China of the Phalcon airborne radar system was canceled under U.S. pressure.
90 Barbara Opall-Rome, "U.S. OKs Israel-China Spy Sat Deal," *Defense News*, October 12, 2007. This article quotes a U.S. official as saying, "We don't officially acknowledge our supervisory role or our de facto veto right over their exports.... It's a matter of courtesy to our Israeli friends, who are very serious about their sovereignty and in guarding their reputation on the world market."

91 The most prominent espionage case is that of Jonathan Pollard, who pled guilty in 1986 with his then wife Anne to selling classified documents to Israel. Israel later acknowledged that Pollard had been its agent, granted him citizenship, and began petitioning the United States for his release. Pollard was released on parole in November 2015. The second case is that of Department of Defense analyst Lawrence Franklin, who pled guilty in 2006 to disclosing classified information to an Israeli diplomat and to two lobbyists from the American Israel Public Affairs Committee (AIPAC). The third case is that of Ben-Ami Kadish, who had worked at the U.S. Army's Armament Research, Development, and Engineering Center in Dover, New Jersey. Kadish pled guilty in 2009 to one count of conspiracy to act as an unregistered agent of Israel.
92 According to the European Commission's Directorate-General for Trade, for 2017 the countries of the European

BILATERAL TRADE

The United States is Israel's largest single-country trading partner,92 and—according to data from the U.S. International Trade Commission—Israel is the United States's 24th-largest trading Union accounted for 35.8% of Israel's total trade volume, while the United States accounted for 19.6%. Document available at http://trade.ec.europa.eu/doclib/docs/2006/september/tradoc_113402.pdf.

93 Statistics on Israel's status relative to other U.S. trading partners compiled by the U.S. International Trade Commission, available at http://dataweb.usitc.gov/SCRIPTS/cy_m3_run.asp.
94 Statistics compiled by Foreign Trade Division, U.S. Census Bureau, available at http://www.census.gov/foreign-trade/balance/c5081.html.
95 CRS Report RL33222, *U.S. Foreign Aid to Israel*, by Jeremy M. Sharp.
96 For example, statements by President Trump fueled public speculation about the level of his commitment to a negotiated "two-state solution," a conflict-ending outcome that U.S. policy has largely advocated since the Israeli-Palestinian peace process began in the 1990s.
Additionally, some media reports suggested that Israel was coordinating its West Bank settlement construction plans with U.S. officials. Danny Zaken, "Israel, US coordinated on settlement construction," *Al-Monitor Israel Pulse*, October 23, 2017.
97 Adam Rasgon, "Abbas Slams Trump Jerusalem Move as 'Condemned, Unacceptable,'" jpost.com, December 6, 2017.
98 On December 18, the United States vetoed a draft Security Council resolution that was backed by all other 14 members of the Council. The resolution would have reaffirmed past Security Council resolutions on Jerusalem, nullified actions purporting to alter "the character, status or demographic composition of the Holy City of Jerusalem," and called upon all states to refrain from establishing diplomatic missions in Jerusalem. U.N. document S/2017/1060, "Egypt: Draft Resolution." On December 21, the U.N. General Assembly adopted a nonbinding resolution (by a vote of 128 for, nine against, and 35 abstaining) that contained language similar to the draft Security Council resolution.
99 Ahmad Melham, "Abbas reaches out to Europeans to help rebuild negotiations framework," *Al-Monitor Palestine*
partner.93 The two countries concluded a Free Trade Agreement (FTA) in 1985, and all customs duties between the two trading partners have since been eliminated. The FTA includes provisions that protect both countries' more sensitive agricultural sub-sectors with nontariff barriers, including import bans, quotas, and fees. Israeli exports to the United States have grown since the FTA became effective. Qualified Industrial Zones (QIZs) in Jordan and Egypt are considered part of the U.S.-Israel free trade area. In 2017, Israel imported approximately $12.6 billion in goods from and exported $21.9 billion in goods to the United States.94 The United States and Israel have launched several programs to stimulate Israeli industrial and scientific research, for which Congress has authorized and appropriated funds on several occasions.95

ISRAELI-PALESTINIAN ISSUES

For historical background on these issues, see CRS Report RL34074, *The Palestinians: Background and U.S. Relations*, by Jim Zanotti.

PEACE PROCESS AND INTERNATIONAL INVOLVEMENT

The prospects for an Israeli-Palestinian peace process are complicated by many factors. Since President Trump took office, he and officials from his Administration have expressed interest in brokering a final-status Israeli-Palestinian agreement. Many of their statements and policies, however, have raised questions about the timing and viability of any new U.S.-backed diplomatic initiative.96 The change in U.S. policy on Jerusalem in December 2017 has complicated the U.S. role (see " Jerusalem ," below). Israeli leaders generally celebrated the change, but PLO Chairman Abbas strongly objected.97 Many other countries opposed President Trump's statements on Jerusalem. This opposition was reflected in December action at the United Nations.98

Citing alleged U.S. bias favoring Israel, Palestinian leaders have broken off high-level political contacts with the United States and have sought support from other international actors and organizations to improve their negotiating position with Israel.99 However, the PA continues *Pulse*, January 31, 2018; Khaled Abu Toameh and Stuart Winer, "Palestinians court Russia as new broker in peace process," *Times of Israel*, February 2, 2018; "US weighs UN funding cuts after Palestinians join agencies," Agence France Presse, May 23, 2018; International Criminal Court statement, "Statement by ICC Prosecutor, Mrs Fatou Bensouda, on the referral submitted by Palestine," May 22, 2018.

100 See Neri Zilber and Ghaith al-Omari, *State with No Army, Army with No State: Evolution of the Palestinian Authority Security Forces: 1994-2018*, Washington Institute for Near East Policy, March 2018; Abu Amer, op. cit.
101 CRS Report RS22967, *U.S. Foreign Aid to the Palestinians*, by Jim Zanotti.
102 Boaz Bismuth, "Trump to Israel Hayom: The Palestinians are not looking to make peace," *Israel Hayom*, February 11, 2018.
103 Entous, op. cit.; "Kushner: Peace Deal to Benefit Both Sides in Mideast Conflict," Reuters, May 14, 2018; Daniel Siryoti, et al., "Amid PA rejectionism, Arab nations threaten to 'go over Abbas' head,'" *Israel Hayom*, June 25, 2018; Jonathan Cook, "Sisi key to Trump's Sinai plan to kill Palestinian state," Middle East Eye, July 5, 2018; Jack Khoury, "Arab Leaders Asked U.S. Not to Reveal Mideast Peace Plan, Palestinians Say," haaretz.com, June 29, 2018.
104 "Transcript: Jared Kushner's Interview with a Palestinian Newspaper," *New York Times*, June 24, 2018.
105 Dennis Ross, "The Next Mideast Explosion," *New York Daily News*, May 20, 2018; Goldenberg, op. cit.; Phil Gordon and Prem Kumar, "Jared Kushner's Middle East Fantasy," theatlantic.com, June 25, 2018.
106 "President Abbas calls for three days of mourning, describes US embassy in Jerusalem as settlement outpost," WAFA, May 14, 2018.
107 See, e.g., Amir Tibon, "Saudi King Tells U.S. That Peace Plan Must Include East Jerusalem as Palestinian Capital," *Ha'aretz*, July 29, 2018.
108 Entous, op. cit.; Aiden Pink, "Palestinians Should 'Shut Up' Or Make Peace, Saudi Prince Told Jewish Groups," *Jewish Daily Forward*, April 29, 2018; Dexter Filkins, "The Ascent," *New Yorker*, April 9, 2018; James S. Robbins, "An Emerging Arab Israeli Thaw," nationalinterest.org, April 3, 2018; Jeffrey Goldberg, "Saudi Crown Prince: Iran's Supreme Leader 'Makes Hitler Look Good,'" theatlantic.com, April 2, 2018.
109 The Arab Peace Initiative offers a comprehensive Arab peace with Israel if Israel were to withdraw fully from the territories it occupied in 1967, agree to the establishment of a Palestinian state with a capital in East Jerusalem, and provide for the "[a]chievement of a just solution to the Palestinian Refugee problem in accordance with UN General Assembly Resolution 194." The initiative was proposed by Saudi Arabia, adopted by the 22-member Arab League (which includes the PLO), and later accepted by the 56-member Organization of the Islamic Conference (now the Organization of Islamic Cooperation) at its 2005 Mecca summit. The text of the initiative is available at security coordination with Israel.100 Tensions over Jerusalem appear to have influenced Administration decisions to reduce or delay certain types of aid to the Palestinians,101 and have made prospects for restarting Israeli-Palestinian talks in 2018 less certain.102

Reports suggest that the Administration is preparing a detailed document on the peace process that it may share in an attempt to overcome obstacles to progress.103 At the end of a June 2018 trip to meet with various Middle Eastern leaders, senior White House advisor Jared Kushner (the President's son-in-law) said that the Administration's plan was almost done. Kushner also said, "If President Abbas is willing to come back to the table, we are ready to engage; if he is not, we will likely air the plan publicly."104 Some former U.S. officials have cautioned against presenting a plan given current Palestinian opposition.105 In May, Abbas characterized the possible removal of core issues of the Israeli-Palestinian conflict—namely, Jerusalem's status and Palestinian refugee claims—from the negotiating table as "an American slap."106

The Administration seeks support from some Arab states, including Saudi Arabia, the United Arab Emirates, Jordan, and Egypt, for the anticipated U.S. initiative. While these Arab states have criticized the U.S. stance on Jerusalem,107 there are also signs that the shared goal of countering Iranian influence in the region is leading some of them to interact more overtly with Israeli counterparts and to dissuade the Palestinians from abandoning U.S.-backed diplomacy.108 The 2002 Arab Peace Initiative remains a key reference point for Arab positions on issues of Israeli-Palestinian dispute.109

110 Anne Barnard, et al., "Talk of a Peace Plan That Snubs Palestinians Roils Middle East," *New York Times*, December 3, 2017; Goldenberg, op. cit.
111 Siryoti, op. cit.
112 Jack Khoury and Amir Tibon, "Abbas Rejects Trump's Plan for Gaza: An Attempt to Divide Palestinians," haaretz.com, June 18, 2018.
113 See, e.g., Scott R. Anderson and Yishai Schwartz, "How to Move the U.S. Embassy to Jerusalem," November 30, 2017.
114 In 1980, under the first Likud Party government, the Israeli Knesset passed the Basic Law: Jerusalem—Capital of Israel, which declares "Jerusalem, complete and united, is the capital of Israel." See http://www.mfa.gov.il for the complete text of the Basic Law. Israel had first declared Jerusalem to be its capital in 1950.
115 White House, Office of the Press Secretary, Statement by President Trump on Jerusalem, December 6, 2017.
116 Bismuth, op. cit. The President previously said that "we took Jerusalem off the table." White House, Remarks by President Trump and Prime Minister Netanyahu of Israel Before Bilateral Meeting, Davos, Switzerland, January 25, 2018. This fueled media speculation about whether the President was simply referring to what he had already done (i.e., recognize some unspecified portion of Jerusalem as Israel's capital), or whether his policy on Jerusalem might more broadly foreclose Palestinian claims to East Jerusalem and its holy sites.

Speculation surrounds the particulars of the possible Trump Administration proposal. Dating back to unconfirmed reports from late 2017, some observers anticipate that a proposal could favor Israeli positions that call for limited Palestinian sovereignty, maintaining most West Bank settlements, locating a Palestinian capital on the outer fringes of Jerusalem, and dismissing refugee claims to a right of return.110 Palestinian officials have complained that the United States is trying to undermine Abbas and dictate a solution.111 In June, Abbas's spokesperson accused the Administration and Israel of seeking to separate Gaza from the West Bank under the guise of humanitarian aid.112

JERUSALEM

In December 2017, President Trump recognized Jerusalem as Israel's capital and pledged to move the U.S. embassy from Tel Aviv to Jerusalem. These actions represented a departure from the decades-long U.S. executive branch practice of not recognizing Israeli sovereignty over Jerusalem or any part of it.113 The President pointed to the Jerusalem Embassy Act of 1995 (P.L. 104-45) as a significant factor in the policy change. The western part of Jerusalem that Israel has controlled since 1948 has served as the official seat of its government since shortly after its founding as a state. Israel officially considers Jerusalem (including the eastern part it unilaterally annexed after the 1967 Arab-Israeli war, while also expanding the city's municipal boundaries) to be its capital (see Figure 2 below).114

In his December remarks, President Trump stated that he was not taking a position on "specific boundaries of the Israeli sovereignty in Jerusalem," and would continue to consider the city's final status to be subject to Israeli-Palestinian negotiations.115 However, he did not explicitly mention Palestinian aspirations regarding Jerusalem; Palestinians envisage East Jerusalem as the capital of their future state. In a February 2018 interview, the President said that he would support specific boundaries as agreed upon by both sides.116 He also has called on all parties to maintain the "status quo" arrangement at Jerusalem's holy sites (see textbox below).

The "Status Quo" at the Temple Mount/Haram al Sharif

The status of Jerusalem and its holy sites has been a long-standing issue of political and religious contention between Jews and Muslims. A number of violent episodes occurred in Jerusalem during the 1920s and 1930s, and control over the city and key areas in and around it was a major strategic consideration in the Arab-Israeli wars of 1948 and 1967.

Notwithstanding Israel's 1967 takeover and subsequent annexation of East Jerusalem, it allowed the Jordanian *waqf* (or Islamic custodial trust) that had been administering the Temple Mount/Haram al Sharif (the "Mount/Haram") and its holy sites before the war to continue doing so, and established a "status quo" arrangement that has been Israel's proclaimed policy since then. Under the arrangement (largely based on past practices dating from the 16th century until the 1948 war), Muslims can access the Mount/Haram and worship there, while Jews and other non-Muslims are permitted limited access but not permitted to worship. Jewish worship is permitted at the Western Wall at the base of the Mount/Haram. Occasional access restrictions applied to Muslim patrons, such as those based on gender or age, have contributed to allegations that Israeli implementation of the status quo has been "piecemeal."117

The status quo is criticized and challenged by some individuals and groups who assert that Israel should advance Jewish historical and religious claims to the Mount/Haram, despite rulings from government-appointed rabbis proscribing Jewish visits there.118 Various events arguably fueling concerns among Palestinians about possible Israeli attempts to change the status quo have included:

· September 1996 clashes (during Netanyahu's first term as prime minister) leading to the deaths of 54 Palestinians and 14 Israeli security personnel after Israel opened a passage leading to/from the Western Wall esplanade through a tunnel (known as the Hasmonean or Kotel Tunnel) that archeologists had uncovered and restored.119

· A September 2000 Mount/Haram visit by Likud Party leader (and future prime minister) Ariel Sharon just prior to the outbreak of the second Palestinian intifada.

· Changes in 2003 where Israel ended coordination with the Jordanian waqf over non-Muslim visits to the Mount/Haram and the waqf began restricting non-Muslims from entering the Dome of the Rock and Al Aqsa Mosque.120

· A series of incidents since fall 2014 featuring visits by Israeli political figures to the Mount/Haram, protests, violence, and periodic access closures.121

These tensions exist within a larger context of competing national and religious narratives regarding Jerusalem. Israelis have routinely used their influence with municipal and national authorities to advance Jewish objectives in the city, while Palestinians with little or no influence over Jerusalem's formal administration have resorted to protests and occasional violence.

Netanyahu has insisted that the status quo access arrangements for the Mount/Haram will continue. However, upholding these arrangements is periodically challenged by Israeli-Palestinian tensions from some Israeli Jews' actions to increase their presence at the Mount/Haram (especially during Jewish holidays), or from some Palestinians' anticipation that such actions might be imminent.

117 Wendy Pullan, *et al.*, *The Struggle for Jerusalem's Holy Places*, Routledge: New York, 2013, p. 15; Ir Amim and Keshev, *Dangerous Liaison: The Dynamics of the Rise of the Temple Movements and Their Implications*, March 1, 2013, pp. 12-15.
118 State Department, International Religious Freedom Report for 2017, Israel, Golan Heights, West Bank, and Gaza.
119 Pullan, op. cit., p. 37.
120 State Department 2015 Report on International Religious Freedom, Israel and the Occupied Territories; Tova Dvorin, "Jordan Pushes Full Control Over Temple Mount, Israel Rejects," *Arutz Sheva*, October 19, 2015.
121 See, e.g., State Department, International Religious Freedom Report for 2017, Israel, Golan Heights, West Bank, and Gaza; International Crisis Group, "How to Preserve the Fragile Calm at Jerusalem's Holy Esplanade," Middle East Briefing No. 48, April 7, 2016.

On February 23, the State Department spokesperson issued the following press statement announcing that the embassy would open in May 2018, to coincide with Israel's 70th anniversary:

Figure 2. Greater Jerusalem

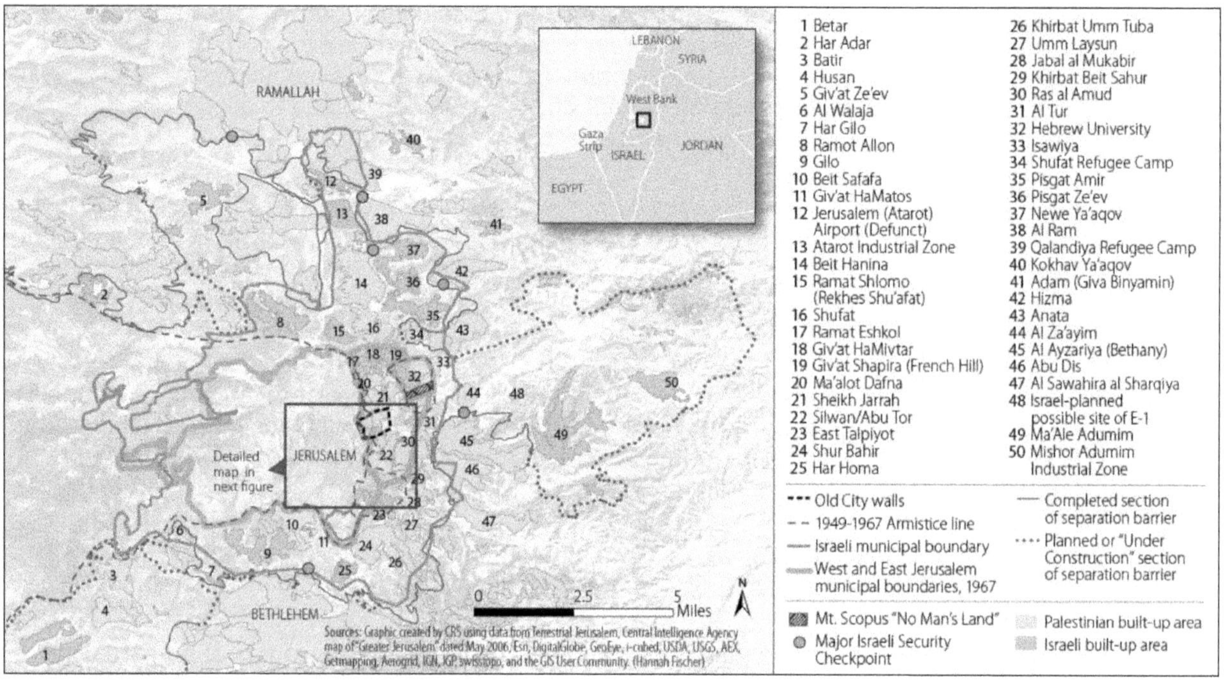

Note: All locations and lines are approximate.

Figure 3. Jerusalem: Some Key Sites

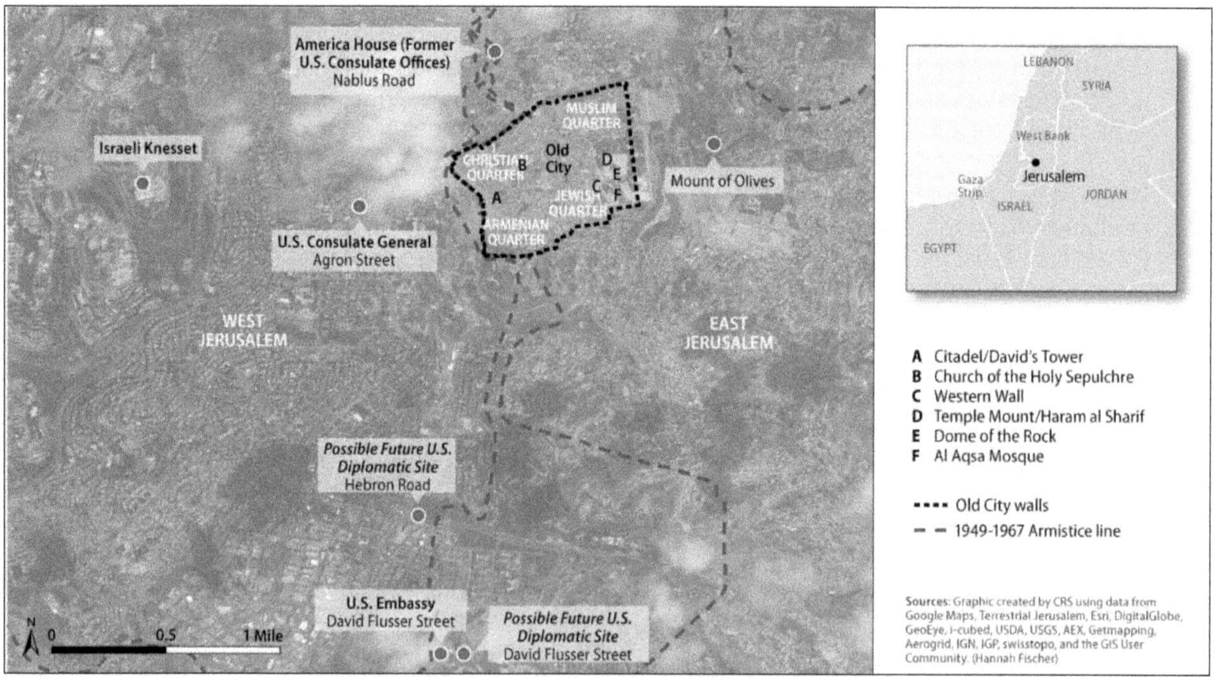

Note: All locations and lines are approximate.

The Embassy will initially be located in the Arnona neighborhood, in a modern building that now houses consular operations of U.S. Consulate General Jerusalem. Those consular operations, including American citizen and visa services, will continue at the Arnona facility without interruption, as part of the Embassy. Consulate General Jerusalem will continue to operate as an independent mission with an unchanged mandate, from its historic

Agron Road location. Initially, the interim Embassy in Arnona will contain office space for the Ambassador and a small staff. By the end of next year, we intend to open a new Embassy Jerusalem annex on the Arnona compound that will provide the Ambassador and his team with expanded interim office space. In parallel, we have started the search for a site for our permanent Embassy to Israel, the planning and construction of which will be a longer-term undertaking.

The embassy opened on May 14 at the Arnona facility (see **Figure 3** below) amid criticism from several international actors and violence on the same day at the Gaza-Israel frontier (see " Hamas and Gaza " above). According to the State Department spokesperson, the site is located "partly in West Jerusalem and partly in what's considered no man's land," as it lies "between the 1949 armistice lines" in a zone that was demilitarized between 1949 and 1967.122 The White House stated that it cost $400,000 to modify the facility to function as an embassy.123 The ambassador's official residence is to transition to Jerusalem at a later date.124

122 State Department Press Briefing, February 27, 2018. One article describing the various issues involved with the site's location said that a U.N. official "described the site as 'occupied territory' but not 'Occupied Palestinian Territory (OPT),'" as No Man's Land had not been under the formal control of either the Israeli or the Jordanian side after the 1948 Arab-Israeli war. The article also said, "The continuous Israeli use of the western part of the no man's land makes putting the U.S. embassy there uncontroversial for Israelis from both the right and left of the political spectrum." Michael Lipin, "Why New US Embassy Isn't Entirely in Israel," Voice of America, May 14, 2018.
123 White House, President Donald J. Trump Keeps His Promise To Open U.S. Embassy In Jerusalem, Israel, May 14, 2018.
124 State Department, Briefing on the Opening of the U.S. Embassy in Jerusalem, May 11, 2018.
125 Gardiner Harris and Isabel Kershner, "Casino Mogul Offers to Fund Israel Embassy," *New York Times*, February 24, 2018.

Congress could consider a number of legislative and oversight options with regard to the plans mentioned above to expand the embassy at the Arnona site, and later to plan and construct a permanent embassy. These options could focus on funding, timeframe and logistics, progress reports, and security for embassy facilities and staff. A State Department official said in February that a new embassy building would take 7 to 10 years to construct, and a former official estimated that building a new embassy in Jerusalem may cost about $500 million.125

SETTLEMENTS

Israel has approximately 130 official residential communities (known internationally and by significant segments of Israeli society as "settlements") in the West Bank, and approximately 100 additional settlement outposts unauthorized under Israeli law.126 It also maintains other military and civilian land-use sites in the West Bank. In addition, Israeli authorities and Jewish Israeli citizens have established roughly 14 main residential areas (referred to variously as "settlements" or "neighborhoods") in East Jerusalem.127 All of these residential communities are located beyond the 1949-1967 armistice line (the "Green Line") in areas that Palestinians assert are rightfully part of their envisioned future state.

126 http://peacenow.org.il/en/settlements-watch/settlements-data/population.
127 For information on the planning and permitting process for settlement construction, see http://peacenow.org.il/wp-content/uploads/2017/10/Planning-Process-Chart.pdf.
128 For more information on the history of the settlements and their impact on Israeli society, see Idith Zertal and Akiva Eldar, *Lords of the Land: The War for Israel's Settlements in the Occupied Territories, 1967-2007*, New York: Nation

Books, 2007; Gershom Gorenberg, *The Accidental Empire: Israel and the Birth of the Settlements, 1967-1977*, New York: Times Books, 2006.

129 The most-cited international law pertaining to Israeli settlements is the Fourth Geneva Convention, Part III, Section

The first West Bank settlements were constructed following the 1967 war, and were initially justified as residential areas connected to personnel involved with Israel's military occupation. Major West Bank residential settlement building began in the late 1970s with the advent of the pro-settler Gush Emunim ("Bloc of the Faithful") movement and the 1977 electoral victory of Menachem Begin and the Likud Party. Subsequently, Israelis have expanded existing settlements and established new ones. Israelis who defend the settlements' legitimacy generally use some combination of legal, historical, strategic, nationalistic, or religious justifications.128

The international community generally considers Israeli construction on territory beyond the Green Line to be illegal.129 In 2015, an Israeli anti-settlement advocacy group said that a two-tier III, Article 49 *Relative to the Protection of Civilian Persons in Time of War*, August 12, 1949, which states in its last sentence, "The Occupying Power shall not deport or transfer parts of its own civilian population into the territory it occupies." Israel insists that the West Bank does not fall under the international law definition of "occupied territory," but is rather "disputed territory" because the previous occupying power (Jordan) did not have an internationally recognized claim to it, and given the demise of the Ottoman Empire at the end of World War I and the end of the British Mandate in 1948, Israel claims that no international actor has superior legal claim to it.

130 "Israel's West Bank housing policy by numbers," Agence France Presse, May 10, 2015, quoting Rabbis for Human Rights. The two agreements that define respective Israeli and PA zones of control in the West Bank (including Areas A, B, and C) are (1) the Israeli-Palestinian Interim Agreement on the West Bank and the Gaza Strip, dated September 28, 1995; and (2) the Protocol Concerning the Redeployment in Hebron, dated January 17, 1997.

131 In a July 2004 International Court of Justice advisory opinion, the barrier's construction was deemed illegal. The text of the opinion is available at http://www.icj-cij.org/docket/index.php?pr=71&code=mwp&p1=3&p2=4&p3=6.

132 Information as of 2017 accessed from Washington Institute of Near East Policy's "Settlements and Solutions" interactive map at http://www.washingtoninstitute.org/westbankinteractivemap/#.

133 Ibid.

134 See, e.g., Joel Greenberg, "Israeli settlers evacuated from West Bank outpost following court order," *Washington Post*, September 2, 2012.

Israel retains military control over the West Bank and has largely completed a separation barrier that roughly tracks the Green Line, but departs from it in a number of areas that include significant settlement populations.131 Israeli officials state that the barrier's purpose is to separate Israelis and Palestinians and prevent terrorists from entering Israel. Palestinians object to the barrier being built on their territory because it cuts Palestinians off from East Jerusalem and, in some places, bisects their landholdings and communities. It also is seen by many as an Israeli device to unilaterally determine borders between Israel and a future Palestinian state. Not counting East Jerusalem, one source states that 77% of Israeli settlers live within the barrier's perimeter.132 Counting East Jerusalem, the figure grows to 85%.133

Settlers affect the political and diplomatic calculus in various ways. They influence key voting blocs in Israel's coalition-based parliamentary system (although they do not all share the same background or interests, settlers constitute about 6% of the Israeli population). Additionally, some initiate public protest and even violent resistance against government efforts to limit or regulate their actions. Also, they have a significant symbolic role in a country whose initial survival depended on pioneering spirit in the face of adversity.

Some Israelis caution that the demand to provide security to settlers and their transportation links to Israel could perpetuate Israeli military control in the West Bank even if other rationales for maintaining such control eventually recede. Protecting settlers is made more difficult by altercations between some settlers and Palestinian West Bank residents, and some settlers' defiance of Israeli military authorities.

When ordered by Israel's court system to dismantle outposts, the government has complied. In some cases, the government placated settlers by relocating displaced outpost residents within the boundaries of settlements permitted under Israeli law.134

U.S. Policy

U.S. policy on settlements has varied since 1967. Until the 1980s, multiple Administrations either stated or implied that settlements were "contrary to international law," with President Carter's

Secretary of State Cyrus Vance stating explicitly that settlements were "illegal" in 1980.135 President Reagan later stated that settlements were "not illegal," but "ill-advised" and "unnecessarily provocative."136 Since then, the executive branch has generally refrained from pronouncements on the settlements' legality.137 Rather, a common U.S. stance has been that settlements are an "obstacle to peace." Additionally, loan guarantees to Israel currently authorized by U.S. law are subject to possible reduction by an amount equal to the amount Israel spends on settlements in the occupied territories.138

135 Daniel Kurtzer, "Do Settlements Matter? An American Perspective," *Middle East Policy*, vol. 16, issue 3, fall 2009.
136 Nicholas Rostow, "Are the Settlements Illegal?" *The American Interest*, March/April 2010.
137 Ibid.
138 For more information on this issue, see CRS Report RL33222, *U.S. Foreign Aid to Israel*, by Jeremy M. Sharp.
139 Aaron David Miller, "The Inside Story of U.S. Meddling in Israel's Elections," *Daily Beast*, December 4, 2014.
140 U.S. and Israeli leaders publicly differed on whether Obama's expectations of Israel contradicted statements that the George W. Bush Administration had made. Glenn Kessler and Howard Schneider, "U.S. Presses Israel to End Expansion," *Washington Post*, May 24, 2009; Ethan Bronner, "Israelis Say Bush Agreed to West Bank Growth," *New York Times*, June 3, 2009.
141 See, e.g., a presidential signing statement for P.L. 114-125 (H.R. 644) at https://www.whitehouse.gov/the-press-office/2016/02/25/signing-statement-hr-644. For more information, see CRS Report R44281, *Israel and the Boycott, Divestment, and Sanctions (BDS) Movement*, coordinated by Jim Zanotti.
142 In response, the House adopted H.Res. 11, condemning Resolution 2334 and the Obama Administration's abstaining vote, on January 5, 2017, by a 340-80 vote (with four voting "present").

A former U.S. official wrote in 2014 that U.S. Administrations are "not entirely sure what to do with the fact that Israeli prime ministers of all political stripes have continued Israeli settlement building on the West Bank and construction in parts of east Jerusalem that we'd like to see become the capital of a Palestinian state."139 An April 2004 letter from President George W. Bush to then Israeli Prime Minister Ariel Sharon explicitly acknowledged that "in light of new realities on the ground, including already existing major Israeli populations (sic) centers, it is unrealistic to expect that the outcome of final status negotiations will be a full and complete return to the armistice lines of 1949."

The Obama Administration generally opposed Israeli settlement activity, but took differing approaches at various points. During the Administration's first term, it sought to freeze all settlement activity, including in East Jerusalem.140 Israel responded with a partial 10-month moratorium. In February 2011, the United States vetoed a draft U.N. Security Council resolution that would have characterized Israeli settlements in the West Bank and East Jerusalem as illegal. During President Obama's second term, he signed trade and customs legislation (P.L. 114-26 and P.L. 114-125) opposing punitive economic measures against Israel (such as measures advocated by a non-governmental boycott, divestment, and sanctions [BDS] movement). However, he asserted in a presidential signing statement for P.L. 114-125 that certain provisions treating "Israeli-controlled territories" (i.e., West Bank settlements) beyond the Green Line in the same manner as Israel itself were not in line with U.S. policy.141 Finally, in December 2016, the Obama Administration decided to abstain from (rather than veto) a U.N. Security Council resolution (Resolution 2334) similar to the one it vetoed in 2011.142

To date, the Trump Administration has been less critical than the Obama Administration of Israeli settlement-related announcements and construction activity. In February 2017, the White House press secretary released a statement with the following passage:

While we don't believe the existence of settlements is an impediment to peace, the construction of new settlements or the expansion of existing settlements beyond their current borders may not be helpful in achieving that goal. As the President has expressed many times, he hopes to achieve peace throughout the Middle East region.143

143 White House Office of the Press Secretary, Statement by the Press Secretary, February 2, 2017.
144 Danny Zaken, "Israel, US coordinated on settlement construction," *Al-Monitor Israel Pulse*, October 23, 2017.
145 Jeffrey Heller, "White House dismisses idea of U.S.-Israel discussing settlement annexation," Reuters, February 12, 2018.

Some reports suggest that Israel at some point coordinated settlement construction plans with Trump Administration officials.144 However, in February 2018 a White House spokesperson denied reports that U.S. officials may have discussed the possible annexation of some settlements with Prime Minister Netanyahu.145

GOVERNMENT AND POLITICAL SYSTEM - STRATEGIC INFORMATION

SYSTEM OF GOVERNMENT BASICS

The **Israeli system of government** is based on parliamentary democracy. The Prime Minister of Israel is the head of government and leader of a multi-party system. Executive power is exercised by the government. Legislative power is vested in the Knesset. The Judiciary is independent of the executive and the legislature. The political system of the State of Israel and its main principles are set out in 11 Basic Laws. Israel does not have a written constitution

EXECUTIVE BRANCH

The Prime Minister is the chief executive of Israel, and the most powerful political figure in the country. The Prime Minister is elected by the Knesset, and makes foreign and domestic policy decisions which are voted on by the cabinet. The cabinet is composed of ministers, most of whom are the heads of government departments, though some are deputy ministers and ministers without portfolio. Cabinet ministers are appointed by the Prime Minister, who must appoint members based on the distribution of votes to political parties. The cabinet's composition must also be approved by the Knesset.

The Prime Minister may dismiss cabinet members, but any replacements must be approved by the Knesset. Most ministers are members of the Knesset, though only the Prime Minister is required to be one. The cabinet meets weekly on Sundays, and there may be additional meetings if circumstances require it. Each cabinet meeting is chaired by the Prime Minister.

A select group of ministers led by the Prime Minister forms the security cabinet, responsible for outlining and implementing a foreign and defense policy. This forum is designed to coordinate diplomatic negotiations, and to make quick and effective decisions in times of crisis and war.

The Israeli government has 28 ministries, each of them responsible for a sector of public administration. Many Ministries are located in the Kiryat Ben Gurion Government complex in the area of Givat Ram in Jerusalem. Each ministry is led by a minister, who is also a member of the cabinet and is usually a member of the Knesset. The Office of the Prime Minister coordinates the actions of the work of all government ministries, and serving and assisting the Prime Minister in his daily work.

The President of the State is the *de jure* head of state of Israel, but the position is largely an apolitical and ceremonial role, with real executive powers lying in the hands of the Prime Minister. The President's ceremonial roles include signing every law (except those pertaining to the President's powers) and international or bilateral treaty, ceremonially appointing the Prime Minister, confirms and endorses the credentials of ambassadors, and receives the credentials of foreign diplomats. The President also has several important functions in government. The President is the only government official with the power to pardon or commute prisoners. The President also appoints the Governor of the Bank of Israel, the State Comptroller upon recommendation of the Knesset House Committee, the President of Magen David Adom, and the members and leaders of several institutions. The President also ceremonially appoints judges to their posts after their selection.

PRESIDENT

Reuven Rivlin since 24 July 2014	
Style	His Excellency
Residence	Beit HaNassi
Appointer	Knesset
Term length	Seven years, single term
Inaugural holder	Chaim Weizmann
Formation	16 February 1949
Website	Israel presidential website

The **President of the State of Israel** literally *President of the State*) is the head of state of Israel. The position is largely a ceremonial figurehead role, with executive power vested in the Government and the Prime Minister. The current president is Reuven Rivlin, who took office on 24 July 2014. Presidents are elected by the Knesset for a seven-year term and are limited to a single term.

The President of Israel is elected by an absolute majority in the Knesset, by secret ballot. If no candidate has received an absolute majority of votes by the first round of voting, a second round, in which only the two most-voted candidates in the first round may participate, is held; the top vote-getter in the second round is the winner. From 1949 to 2000, the president was elected for a five-year term, and was allowed to serve up to two terms in office. Since 2000, the president serves a single seven-year term.

Any Israeli resident citizen is eligible to run for President. The office falls vacant upon completion of a term, death, resignation, or the decision of three-quarters of the Knesset to remove the president on grounds of misconduct or incapacity. Presidential tenure is not keyed to that of the Knesset in order to assure continuity in government and the nonpartisan character of the office. There is no vice president in the Israeli governmental system. If the president is temporarily incapacitated or leaves office, the speaker of the Knesset becomes acting president.

The first presidential election took place on 16 February 1949, and the winner was Chaim Weizmann. The second took place in 1951, as at the time presidential terms were linked to the length of the Knesset term (the first Knesset lasted only two years). Another election took place the following year after Weizmann's death.

Since then, elections have been held in 1957, 1962, 1963 (an early election following Yitzhak Ben-Zvi's death), 1968, 1973, 1978, 1983, 1988, 1993, 1998, 2000, 2007 and 2014. Six elections (1951, 1957, 1962, 1968, 1978 and 1988) have taken place with no opposition candidate, although a vote was still held.

The powers of the President of Israel are generally equivalent to those held by heads of state in other parliamentary democracies and are largely dictated by Basic Law: The Presidency, which was passed in 1964. The Basic Law: The Government also includes sections on the powers of the president with reference to the government. The president signs every law (except those that pertain to the president's powers) and international or bilateral treaties approved by the Knesset. In addition, the president endorses the credentials of ambassadors and receives the credentials of foreign diplomats, appoints the Governor of the Bank of Israel, the State Comptroller upon recommendation of the Knesset House Committee, members of the Council on Higher Education, the National Academy of Science, the Broadcasting Authority, the Authority to Rehabilitate Prisoners, the Chief Rabbinical Council, the Wolf Foundation, the president of Magen David Adom, the president of the Israel Academy of Sciences and Humanities, and ceremonially appoints the Prime Minister. The president also has the power to pardon or commute the sentences of both soldiers and civilians, and ceremonially appoints judges to courts, including the Supreme Court, after appointment by the Judicial Selection Committee.

In addition, paragraph 29a of *The Government* basic law also states that the president must consent to the dissolution of the Knesset at the request of the Prime Minister when the government has lost its majority and can therefore no longer function effectively.

Unlike most presidents in parliamentary republics, the President of Israel is not even the *nominal* chief executive. Basic Law: The Government explicitly vests executive power in the Government (as the Cabinet is officially called). Presidential powers are usually exercised based on the recommendation of appropriate government ministers.

The president's most important role, in practice, is to help lead the process of forming a government. Israel's electoral system and fractured political landscape make it all but impossible for one party to govern alone, let alone win an outright majority of Knesset seats. After each election, the president consults with party leaders to determine who is most likely to command a majority in the Knesset.

PRIME MINISTER

	Prime Minister of Israel
	Incumbent
	Assumed office 31 March 2009
President	Shimon Peres
Preceded by	Ehud Olmert
	In office 18 June 1996 – 6 July 1999
President	Ezer Weizman
Preceded by	Shimon Peres
Succeeded by	Ehud Barak
	Minister of Foreign Affairs
	Incumbent
	Assumed office 18 December 2012
Preceded by	Avigdor Lieberman
	In office 6 November 2002 – 28 February 2003
Prime Minister	Ariel Sharon
Preceded by	Shimon Peres
Succeeded by	Silvan Shalom
	Leader of the Opposition
	In office 28 March 2006 – 31 March 2009
Prime Minister	Ehud Olmert
Preceded by	Amir Peretz
Succeeded by	Tzipi Livni
	Minister of Finance
	In office 28 February 2003 – 9 August 2005
Prime Minister	Ariel Sharon
Preceded by	Silvan Shalom

Succeeded by	Ehud Olmert
	Personal details
Born	21 October 1949 (age 63) Tel Aviv, Israel
Nationality	Israeli
Political party	Likud
Spouse(s)	• Miriam Weizmann (m. 1972–d. 1978) • Fleur Cates (m. 1981–d. 1984) • Sara Ben-Artzi (m. 1991)
Relations	• Benzion Netanyahu (father) • Yonatan Netanyahu (brother) • Iddo Netanyahu (brother)
Children	3
Residence	Jerusalem, Israel
Alma mater	Massachusetts Institute of Technology
Religion	Judaism
Website	netanyahu.org.il
	Military service
Allegiance	Israel
Service/branch	Israel Defense Forces
Years of service	1967–1973
Rank	Captain
Unit	Sayeret Matkal
Battles/wars	War of Attrition, Yom Kippur War

	Benjamin Netanyahu
Knessets	12, 13, 14, 15, 16, 17, 18, 19
	Ministerial roles
1996–1997	Minister of Science and Technology
1996–1999	Minister of Housing and Construction
2002–2003	Minister of Foreign Affairs
2003–2005	Minister of Finance
2009–2013	Minister of Economic Strategy
2009–2013	Minister of Pensioner Affairs
2009–2013	Minister of Health
2012–present	Minister of Foreign Affairs
2013–present	Minister of Public Diplomacy and Diaspora Affairs

Benjamin "Bibi" Netanyahu born 21 October 1949) is an Israeli politician and the current Prime Minister of Israel. He serves also as a member of the Knesset, the Chairman of the Likud party, Foreign Affairs Minister and Minister of Public Diplomacy and Diaspora Affairs. Netanyahu is the first Israeli prime minister born in Israel after the establishment of the state.

Netanyahu joined the Israel Defense Forces during the Six-Day War in 1967, and became a team leader in the Sayeret Matkal special forces unit. He took part in many missions, including Operation Gift (1968) and Operation Isotope (1972), during which he was shot in the shoulder. He fought on the front lines in the War of Attrition and the Yom Kippur War in 1973, taking part in special forces raids along the Suez Canal, and then leading a commando assault deep into Syrian territory. He achieved the rank of captain before being discharged. Netanyahu served as the Israeli ambassador to the United Nations from 1984 to 1988, member of the Likud party, and was Prime Minister from June 1996 to July 1999. He moved from the political arena to the private sector after being defeated in the 1999 election for Prime Minister by Ehud Barak.

Netanyahu returned to politics in 2002 as Foreign Affairs Minister (2002–2003) and Finance Minister (2003–2005) in Ariel Sharon's governments, but he departed the government over disagreements regarding the Gaza disengagement plan. He retook the Likud leadership in December 2005, after Sharon left to form a new party. In the 2006 election, Likud did poorly, winning 12 seats. In December 2006, Netanyahu became the official Leader of the Opposition in the Knesset and Chairman of Likud. In 2007, he retained the Likud leadership by beating Moshe Feiglin in party elections. Following the 2009 parliamentary election, in which Likud placed second and right-wing parties won a majority, Netanyahu formed a coalition government. After the victory in the 2013 elections, he became the second person to be elected to the position of Prime Minister for a third term, after Israel's founder David Ben-Gurion.

Benjamin Netanyahu's older brother, Yonatan Netanyahu, commander of Sayeret Matkal, was killed in 1976 while commanding an Operation Entebbe. The younger brother, Iddo Netanyahu, is a playwright. Their father, Benzion Netanyahu, was a prominent Israeli historian.

In 2005, Benjamin Netanyahu was voted the 18th-greatest Israeli of all time, in a poll by the Israeli news website *Ynet* to determine whom the general public considered the 200 Greatest Israelis. In 2012, he was ranked first on the list of the "Most Influential Jews in the World" by *The Jerusalem Post*. In 2012, Netanyahu was listed 23rd on the *Forbes* magazine's list of "The World's Most Powerful People."

On 31 March 2009 the Knesset approved the appointment of Benjamin Netanyahu as Prime Minister, despite Kadima having won slightly more votes than Netanyahu's Likud. Netanyahu's government took office the following day, 1 April 2009.

POLITICAL POSITIONS

The 2013 election returned Netanyahu's Likud Yisrael Beiteinu coalition with 11 fewer seats than the combined Likud and Yisrael Beitanu parties had going into the vote. Nevertheless, as leader of what remained the largest faction in the Knesset, Israeli president Shimon Peres charged Netanyahu with the task of forming the Thirty-third government of Israel. The new coalition included the Yesh Atid, the Jewish Home and Hatnuah parties and excludes the ultra-Orthodox parties at the insistence of Yesh Atid and the Jewish Home.

Defense and security

Since 2009, an estimated 60,000 illegal immigrants from various African countries have crossed into Israel. Netanyahu said that "This phenomenon is very grave and threatens the social fabric of society, our national security and our national identity." In 2011, Netanyahu arranged for 1000 prisoners to be swapped for Gilad Shalit, including terrorists with "blood on their hands." About 60% of the released terrorists were expected to return to terrorism.

In 2011, Israeli General Staff concluded that the armed forces cannot maintain their battle readiness under Netanyahu's proposed cuts. However Netanyahu decided to cut social programs instead, and promised to increase the defense budget by about six percent. In spite of this, the Israeli military still fell NIS 3.7 million short from its projected budget, which could damage their war capabilities. According to a U.S. State Department representative in November 2011, under the leadership of Netanyahu and Obama, Israel and the United States have enjoyed unprecedented security cooperation

Oslo Accords

From the inception of the Oslo accords, Netanyahu opposed them. During his term as prime minister in the late 1990s, Netanyahu consistently reneged on commitments made by previous Israeli governments as part of the Oslo peace process, leading American peace envoy Dennis Ross to note that "neither President Clinton nor Secretary [of State Madeleine] Albright believed that Bibi had any real interest in pursuing peace."

In a 2001 video, Netanyahu, reportedly unaware he was being recorded, said: "They asked me before the election if I'd honor [the Oslo Accords]," "I said I would, but ... I'm going to interpret the accords in such a way that would allow me to put an end to this galloping forward to the '67 borders. How did we do it? Nobody said what defined military zones were.

Defined military zones are security zones; as far as I'm concerned, the entire Jordan Valley is a defined military zone. Go argue." However, this is clearly consistent with Yitzhak Rabin's October 1995 statement to the Knesset on the ratification of the interim Oslo agreement: "B. The security border of the State of Israel will be located in the Jordan Valley, in the broadest meaning of that term."

LEGISLATIVE BRANCH

Legislative power is vested in the Knesset (Hebrew - "Assembly"), a unicameral parliament, which consists of 120 deputies elected on the basis of universal, direct and equal suffrage by secret ballot on a proportional representation system and party lists for a four-year term. Every citizen of the country who has reached the age of 18 has the right to vote (except for those deprived of this right by the court), and every citizen who has reached 21 years of age has the right to be elected to the Knesset, except for those who are deprived of the right to stand as a candidate categories of civil servants. The whole country in the counting of votes is considered a single constituency. Parties that receive less than 1.5% of the vote cannot be represented in parliament. Each party faction in the Knesset currently consists of at least two deputies. From 1996 to 2001, voters were also granted the right to elect a prime minister.

The main functions of the Knesset are generally the same as those of parliament in other democratic countries. They include the election of the president of the country, approval of activities or the resignation of the government and each member, discussion of the reports of ministers and senior officials, lawmaking, participation in the formulation of the country's political course, consideration of the budget and taxation issues, and control over the activities of administrative bodies. The legislative acts submitted for discussion are put to a vote up to three times (a bill put forward by one of the Knesset deputies must undergo a preliminary reading) and are passed by the participants at the meeting by a simple majority vote.

To elect a president and state controller, to decide on the early dissolution of parliament, as well as to change the system of proportional representation and the main laws, it is necessary to get an absolute majority of votes.

The State Comptroller is appointed by the President on the proposal of the Knesset for a term of five years, but may be re-elected to this post again. The State Comptroller is at the head of the Office of State Control, and is independent of the government in its activities, bearing responsibility only to parliament. Its functions include checking accounts, economic activities and overseeing the activities of ministries, local governments and any other institutions in whose management the government or local governments that are funded directly or indirectly from public funds takes part.

Local government. Israel is divided into six administrative districts (Central, Haifa, Jerusalem, Northern, Southern and Tel Aviv), which are under the jurisdiction of district administrators appointed by the Minister of the Interior and responsible to him, and thirteen subdistricts (nafot).

The local government in Israel is based on municipalities (Mo'atsot iriot) in cities, local councils (Mo'atsot Mekomiot) in urban-type settlements and large villages, and district councils (Mo'atsot Esoriot), which unite groups of small settlements. There are 66 municipalities, 148 local and 53 district councils in Israel. Local authorities are responsible for health, education and culture, social welfare and public utilities (maintenance of water supply and sewage, repair of roads, garbage disposal, etc.), as well as the appointment and collection of local taxes and fees, maintenance of parks and recreation areas, fire service, etc.

Control over the activities of local governments is exercised by the Ministry of the Interior, which approves their budget, the size of municipal taxes and state subsidies, as well as various laws and regulations adopted by local authorities. In addition, the Minister of the Interior is called upon to recommend to local authorities standard formulations of legal provisions relating to these fields of activity of local authorities, which can then be adopted by an appropriate decree of the local government. If the local authority fails to cope with its duties, the Minister of the Interior has the right to dissolve the local administration and temporarily transfer the management to a specially authorized person or commission.

KNESSET - BASIC INFORMATION

The Knesset is the **house of representatives** (parliament) of the State of Israel, in which the full range of current opinions are represented. Nevertheless, parties that reject the existence of the State of Israel as the state of the Jewish People, its democratic nature, or that incite racism may not participate in the elections.

Within the framework of the Israeli democratic system, in which there is a separation of powers amongst the legislature, the executive branch, and the judiciary, the Knesset is the **legislative branch**, with the exclusive authority to enact laws. The Knesset may pass laws on any subject and in any matter, as long as a proposed law does not contradict an existing basic law, and the legislative process is carried out as required by the law. Legislation constitutes an important part of the Knesset's work.

As heir to the authority of the Constituent Assembly, the Knesset has a **constituent-constitutional role**, even though this role was denied by some in the past. According to the Proclamation of Independence, the constitution of the State of Israel should have been prepared by October 1, 1948, but even today Israel does not yet have a complete written constitution. Once all the basic laws are passed, they will together constitute the state's constitution.

The Knesset **supervises the work of the Government** through its committees and the work of the plenum.

The Knesset has several **quasi-judicial** functions, which include the power to lift the immunity of its members, and the power to have the President of the State and State Comptroller removed.

The Knesset also has an **elective function** through which several public officials are elected.

The Knesset is Israel's unicameral legislature and is seated in Jerusalem. Its 120 members are elected to 4-year terms through party-list proportional representation. (*see* electoral system, below), as mandated by the 1958 Basic Law: The Knesset. Knesset seats are allocated among parties using the D'Hondt method of party list proportional representation. Parties select candidates using a closed list. Thus, voters select the party of their choice, rather than any specific candidate. Israel requires a party to meet an election threshold of 2% to be allocated a Knesset seat. All Israeli citizens 18 years of age or older may participate in legislative elections, which are conducted by secret ballot.

As the legislative branch of the Israeli government, the Knesset has the power to enact and repeal all laws. It enjoys *de jure* parliamentary supremacy, and can pass any law by a simple majority, even one that might arguably conflict with a Basic Law, unless it has specific conditions for its modification. The Knesset can adopt and amend Basic Laws acting through its capacity as a Constituent Assembly. The Knesset also supervises government activities through its committees, elects the Prime Minister and approves the cabinet, elects the President of the State, and recommends the State Comptroller. It also has the power to remove the President and State Comptroller from office, revoke the immunity of its members, and to dissolve itself and call new elections.

One of the functions of the Knesset is to supervise the government (ministerial cabinet), most of whose ministers and deputy ministers are elected Knesset members. The Knesset fulfills its supervisory role in various ways: Every law that the government wants to enact must pass the Knesset's approval, including the budget and taxation laws. The Knesset may also demand that the government provide it with information, whether within the framework of its Permanent Committees, sub-committees, and parliamentary inquiry committees, or in the plenum - by means of debates, motions for the agenda, or parliamentary questions.

An additional means of supervision are the reports of the State Comptroller, which are presented to the Knesset by means of the State Control Committee. Following its deliberations on the report, the committee submits its conclusions and proposals to the Knesset plenum, which debates and approves them. Some view the State Comptroller as the Knesset's "arm".

Israel operates under a parliamentary system as a democratic republic with universal suffrage. A member of parliament supported by a parliamentary majority becomes the prime minister—usually this is the chair of the largest party. The prime minister is the head of government and head of the cabinet. Israel is governed by a 120-member parliament, known as the Knesset. Membership of the Knesset is based on proportional representation of political parties, with a 2% electoral threshold, which in practice has resulted in coalition governments.

Parliamentary elections are scheduled every four years, but unstable coalitions or a no-confidence vote by the Knesset can dissolve a government earlier. The Basic Laws of Israel function as an uncodified constitution. In 2003, the Knesset began to draft an official constitution based on these laws. The president of Israel is head of state, with limited and largely ceremonial duties.

POLITICAL PARTIES IN ISRAEL

The Israeli parliament, the Knesset, has 120 elected members. The table below shows a list of the parties and the number of their members in the Knesset. Click the election year to reach the Kneesset web site for the particular election. The parties that are members of the current coalition government are marked by a green background.

Parties	2015	2013	2009	2006	2003	1999
No. of Knesset	20	19	18	17	16	15
Likud	30	31	27	12	38	19
Labor	24	15	13	19	19	26

United Arab List (Raam)	13	4	4	4	2	5
Yesh Atid	11	19				
Kulanu	10					
Habayit HaYehudi	8	12	3		6	5
Shas	7	11	11	12	11	17
Israel Beytenu	6		15	11		4
Torah Judaism	6	7	5	6	5	5
Meretz	5	6	3	5	6	10
Am Ehad					3	2
Center Party						6
Democratic Front for Peace and Equality		4	4	3	3	3
Gil - Gimla'ey Yisrael				7		
Hatnua		6				
Kadima		2	28	29		
National Democratic Alliance (Balad)		3	3	3	3	2
National Union			4		7	4
National Union - Mafdal				9		
Shinui					15	6
Yisrael B'Aliya					2	6
Total number of MKs	120	120	120	120	120	120

ISRAELI KNESSET PARTIES AND THEIR LEADERS

COALITION	
	Likud (Consolidation)—30 seats Israel's historical repository of right-of-center nationalist ideology; skeptical of territorial compromise; has also championed free-market policies. Leader: Binyamin Netanyahu Born in 1949, Netanyahu has served as prime minister since 2009 and also was prime minister from 1996 to 1999. Netanyahu served in an elite special forces unit (Sayeret Matkal), and received his higher education at MIT. Throughout a career in politics and diplomacy, he has been renowned both for his skepticism regarding the exchange of land for peace with the Palestinians and his desire to counter Iran's nuclear program and regional influence. He is generally regarded as both a consummate political dealmaker and a security-minded nationalist. However, he has negotiated with the Palestinians, and many observers discern cautiousness in Netanyahu's decisions regarding the nature and scale of military operations.
	Kulanu (All of Us)—10 seats New pro-secular, center-right party focusing largely on socioeconomic issues. Leader: Moshe Kahlon Born in 1960, Kahlon is Israel's finance minister and a key member of the current coalition government. While serving as communications minister from 2009 to 2013 as a Likud member, Kahlon gained notoriety and popularity for liberalizing the mobile phone market and bringing down costs. He then served as welfare minister before choosing not to run in the 2013 elections and later re-emerging at the head of Kulanu in late 2014.

	Ha'bayit Ha'Yehudi (The Jewish Home)—8 seats Right-of-center nationalist party with base of support among religious Zionists (Ashkenazi Orthodox Jews); includes core constituencies supporting West Bank settlements and annexation. Leader: Naftali Bennett Born in 1972, Bennett is Israel's education minister and served as economy minister in the previous government. He served in various special forces units (including as a reservist during the 2006 Hezbollah conflict in Lebanon). Bennett was a successful software entrepreneur and has lived in America. He served as Netanyahu's chief of staff from 2006 to 2008 while Netanyahu was opposition leader. He led the Yesha Council (the umbrella organization for Israeli West Bank settlers) from 2010 to 2012, and then became leader of Ha'bayit Ha'Yehudi shortly before the 2013 elections.
	Shas (Sephardic Torah Guardians)—7 seats Mizrahi Haredi ("ultra-Orthodox") party; favors welfare and education funds in support of Haredi lifestyle; opposes compromise with Palestinians on control over Jerusalem. Leader: Aryeh Deri Born in 1959, Deri is Israel's interior minister and minister for Negev and Galilee development. He led Shas from 1983 to 1999 before being convicted for bribery, fraud, and breach of trust in 1999 for actions taken while serving as interior minister. He returned as the party's leader in 2013. Deri originally served as the current government's economy minister, but reported differences with Prime Minister Netanyahu over government dealings with private natural gas consortiums led to his resignation from that office.

United Torah Judaism—6 seats Ashkenazi Haredi coalition (Agudat Yisrael and Degel Ha'torah); favors welfare and education funds in support of Haredi lifestyle; opposes territorial compromise with Palestinians and conscription of Haredim; generally seeks greater application of Jewish law.

Leader: Yaakov Litzman Born in 1948, Litzman is Israel's health minister. He was born in Germany and raised in the United States before immigrating to Israel in 1965. Educated in yeshivas (traditional Jewish schools), he later served as principal of a Hasidic girls' school in Jerusalem. He was first elected to the Knesset in 1999 and has previously served as deputy health minister and as a member of the Knesset's finance committee.

Yisrael Beiteinu (Israel Our Home)—5 seats Pro-secular, right-of-center nationalist party with base of support among Russian speakers from the former Soviet Union.

Leader: Avigdor Lieberman Born in 1958, Lieberman is Israel's defense minister, and upon his appointment to this position he resigned his Knesset seat. He served as Israel's foreign minister for most of the period from 2009 to May 2015 and is generally viewed as an ardent nationalist and canny political actor with prime ministerial aspirations. He and Yisrael Beiteinu were in opposition to the current government before joining it in May 2016. Lieberman was born in the Soviet Union (in what is now Moldova) and immigrated to Israel in 1978. He worked under

Netanyahu from 1988 to 1997. Disillusioned by Netanyahu's willingness to consider concessions to the Palestinians, Lieberman founded Yisrael Beiteinu as a platform for former Soviet immigrants. He and other members of his party have faced corruption allegations, but he was acquitted in a 2013 case.

OPPOSITION

המחנה הציוני

Zionist Union—24 seats Joint list of Avoda (Labor) and Ha'tnua (The Movement). Labor is Israel's historical repository of social democratic, left-of-center, pro-secular Zionist ideology; both Labor and Ha'tnua are associated with efforts to end Israel's responsibility for Palestinians in the West Bank and Gaza.

Leader: Avi Gabbay Born in 1967, Gabbay was elected leader of the Labor party in 2017 after having resigned in 2016 as Israel's environment minister (while a member of Kulanu) to protest Yisrael Beiteinu joining the coalition. Gabbay hails from a working class Moroccan Jewish family and became a successful businessman—serving as CEO of Bezeq (Israel's largest telecommunications company) from 2007 to 2013. Observers speculate on the potential for Gabbay's Mizrahi background and centrist positions to broaden the appeal of the Labor party, but the spike in reported popular support for Labor immediately after he was elected leader has not lasted.

القائمة المشتركة

Joint List—13 seats Joint list of four Arab Israeli parties (Hadash, Ra'am, Ta'al, and Balad) that include socialist, Islamist, and Arab nationalist political strains.

Leader: Ayman Odeh Born in 1975, Odeh is the leader of the Joint List and of Hadash, an Arab Israeli socialist party. An attorney, he served on the Haifa city council before becoming Hadash's national leader in 2006. Supports a more democratic, egalitarian, and peace-seeking society, and has sought protection for unrecognized Bedouin villages and advocated for drafting young Arab Israelis for military or civilian national service.

יש עתיד
בראשות יאיר לפיד

Yesh Atid (There Is a Future)—11 seats Pro-secular, centrist party focusing largely on socioeconomic issues.

Leader: Yair Lapid Born in 1963, Lapid served as Israel's finance minister from 2013 until that coalition government collapsed in December 2014. Like his father Tommy, Lapid has parlayed a journalistic career into electoral success. Lapid's popularity fell during his time as finance minister, presumably because the government faced continuing challenges in improving cost-of-living and economic inequality issues while maintaining fiscal discipline. He has since become one of the most popular figures of the center-left opposition.

	Meretz (Vigor)—5 seats Left-of-center, pro-secular Zionist party that supports initiatives for social justice and for peace with the Palestinians Leader: Tamar Zandberg Born in 1976, Zandberg became Meretz's leader in 2018 and was first elected to the Knesset in 2013. Before joining the Knesset, she served on the Tel Aviv city council and was a college instructor. She was a leading figure in 2011 cost-of-living protests.

ELECTORAL SYSTEM

Israel's electoral system operates within the parameters of a Basic Law (*The Knesset*) and of the 1969 *Knesset Elections Law.*

The Knesset's 120 members are elected by secret ballot to 4-year terms, although the Knesset may decide to call for new elections before the end of the 4-year term, and a government can change without a general election; since the 1988 election, no Knesset has finished its 4-year term. In addition a motion of confidence may be called Voting in general elections takes place using the highest averages method of party-list proportional representation, using the d'Hondt formula.

General elections use closed lists: voters vote only for party lists and cannot affect the order of candidates within the lists. Since the 1992 *Parties Law*, only registered parties may stand. There are no separate electoral districts; all voters vote on the same party lists. Suffrage is universal among Israeli citizens aged 18 years or older, but voting is optional. Polling locations are open throughout Israel; absentee ballots are limited to diplomatic staff and the merchant marine. While each party attains one seat for 1 in 120 votes, there is a minimum threshold (recently increased to 2%) for parties to attain their first seat in an election. This requirement aimed to bar smaller parties from parliament but spurred some parties to join together simply to overcome the threshold. The low vote-threshold for entry into parliament, as well as the need for parties with small numbers of seats to form coalition governments, results in a highly fragmented political spectrum, with small parties exercising extensive power (relative to their electoral support) within coalitions.

The president selects the prime minister as the party leader most able to form a government, based on the number of parliament seats his or her coalition has won. After the president's selection, the prime minister has forty-five days to form a government. The Knesset collectively must approve the members of the cabinet. This electoral system, inherited from the Yishuv (Jewish settlement organization during the British Mandate), makes it very difficult for any party to gain a working majority in the Knesset and thus governments generally form on the basis of coalitions. Due to the difficulties in holding coalitions together, elections often occur earlier than scheduled. The average life-span of an Israeli government is 25 months. Over the years, the peace process, the role of religion in the state, and political scandals have caused coalitions to break apart or have produced early elections

ORGANISATION OF THE KNESSET

SPEAKER AND THE DEPUTY SPEAKERS

Election of the Speaker and his Deputies (amendment No. 105)

(a) The Knesset shall elect the Speaker of the Knesset and the Deputies of the Speaker of the Knesset, by means of open elections, in accordance with the provisions of article 20 of Basic Law: the Knesset, and article 10 of the Knesset Law. The Deputies shall be elected upon the recommendation of the Organizing Committee, taking into account the Parliamentary Group make-up of the Knesset and the size of the Parliamentary Groups. The election of several Deputies on the same occasion shall take place by means of a single vote.

(b) The Speaker shall be elected no later than the date on which the Knesset convened for the purpose of establishing the Government, as stated in article13 of Basic Law: the Government. Should the elections of the Knesset Speaker be scheduled for the same date set for the sitting for the purpose of establishing the Government, the Speaker shall be elected first.

(c) The Speaker of the Knesset and the Deputies shall be elected for the whole Knesset term. However, the Knesset is entitled to elect Deputies to the Speaker of the Knesset, on the basis of a recommendation as stated in clause (a), for shorter terms of office, and determine their commencement and termination.

(d) A Minister or a Deputy Minister shall not be Speaker of the Knesset Speaker or a Deputy to the Speaker of the Knesset.

(e)

(1) Should the position of Knesset Speaker be vacated, the Knesset shall elect a new Speaker within 21 days, in the manner laid down in clause (a); should the position of a Deputy to the Speaker of the Knesset be vacated, the Knesset is entitled to elect another Knesset Member in his place, in the said manner.

(2) Should a Deputy to the Speaker of the Knesset be suspended from his position, the Knesset is entitled to elect another Knesset Member in his place in the said manner, and despite what is said in the beginning of clause (c), he shall serve as a Deputy to the Speaker for the period of the suspension only.

Restrictions to the election of the Speaker of the Knesset or a Deputy to the Speaker of the Knesset

3.

(a) The House Committee, and before it is selected – the Arranging Committee, is entitled to decide, on the basis of a recommendation by the Ethics Committee, if it has been appointed, that a Member of the Knesset shall not be a candidate for the position of Speaker of the Knesset Speaker or Deputy to the Speaker of the Knesset, should one of the following apply: (Amendments Nos. 105,

(1) The Attorney General has submitted a copy of a bill of indictment against him, as stated in article 4(a) of the 107, 115 & 120)

Immunity Law, or criminal proceedings, as defined in article 7(a) of the Knesset Law (henceforth – criminal proceedings) are being carried out against him, and this whether or not it has decided that he should have immunity from criminal proceedings. Should the House Committee decide that the Knesset Member shall not be a candidate as stated in this clause, its decision shall remain in force as long as the criminal proceedings in his case have not terminated, and should it be decided that he shall have immunity from criminal proceedings - for the whole period of his membership in that Knesset, or for a shorter period determined by the Committee.

(2) The Knesset Member was convicted in a final verdict on a criminal offence, whether while he was a Member of the Knesset or beforehand, and ten year have not yet elapsed from the day on which the sentence became final, or from the day on which he completed serving his sentence, whichever is later.

(b) The House Committee shall not take a decision, in accordance with clause (a), until after it has given the Knesset Member an opportunity to present his case.

(c) The deliberation proceedings in the House Committee, and in the Ethics committee shall come to an end, in each of them, within a week.

(d) (1) Should the House Committee decide that the Knesset Member shall not be a candidate as stated, the Member is entitled to appeal the decision to the Knesset, within 48 hours.

(2) The debate in the Knesset shall take place within 48 hours of the appeal being submitted, or the following day on which a Knesset sitting may be held in accordance with the provisions of article 19(a), at the latest. The appellant is entitled to explain his appeal, and is entitled to lay on the Knesset table documents connected with the appeal. The Chairpman of the House Committee is entitled to reply to the appeal, each one of them for a time limited of no more than15 minutes, and the Knesset shall decide without a debate.

(e) The voting in the House Committee and the Knesset shall be open.

Suspension from office in accordance with article 7 of the Knesset Law (Amendment Nos. 105, 115 & 120)

4.

(a) Should the Knesset Speaker or a Deputy to the Knesset Speaker be suspended, or should limitations be placed on his office on the basis of the provisions of article 7 of the Knesset Law, the suspension shall be terminated, or the limitations cancelled upon the delivery of a final verdict that finds him innocent, or does not state that the offence involves disgrace, and should it be decided that he shall be immune from criminal proceedings – upon the end of term of that Knesset, and all this as long as the Knesset has not decided, on the basis of a recommendation by the House Committee, on a shorter period for the suspension or limitations.

(b) Should the House Committee propose to the Knesset to suspend the Speaker of the Knesset, or a Deputy Speaker of the Knesset from his office, or lay down limitations to his office, the Chairman of the House Committee, shall present the proposal of the House Committee to the Knesset, and the Knesset Member to whom the proposal relates is entitled to answer, each within a time limit that shall not exceed 15 minutes, and the Knesset shall decide without a debate.

Resignation of the Knesset Speaker or a Deputy to the Knesset Speaker

5.

(a) (1) The Knesset Speaker is entitled to resign from his position by laying a letter of resignation on the Knesset table. Should the Speaker choose to resign during the Knesset recess, and no special session is to take place, he shall hand the resignation letter over to the Secretary General of the Knesset, who shall bring it immediately to the attention of the Knesset Members.

(2) The term of office of the Knesset Speaker, who has resigned, shall end 48 hours after the letter of resignation was laid on the Knesset table, or handed over to the Secretary General of the Knesset, as the case may be, unless he withdrew his resignation beforehand.

(3) The Speaker of the Knesset who submitted or handed over a resignation letter, is entitled to inform the Knesset of the reasons for his resignation.

(b) (1) A Deputy to the Speaker of the Knesset is entitled to resign from his position by handing over a letter of resignation to the Speaker of the Knesset.

(2) The term of office of a Deputy to the Speaker of the Knesset, who has resigned, shall end 48 hours after the letter of resignation was handed over to the Speaker of the Knesset, unless he withdrew his resignation beforehand.

(3) The Speaker of the Knesset shall inform the Knesset of the resignation of a Deputy to the Speaker of the Knesset.

Duties of the Knesset Speaker and a Deputy to the Knesset Speaker

6. (a) The Speaker shall run the affairs of the Knesset, represent it externally, uphold its dignity, maintain order during its sittings, and oversee the observance of its Rules of Procedure. He shall preside over the sittings of the Knesset, and run them, determine the results of votes, and in addition fulfill any task assigned to him by law.

(b) The Speaker is responsible for the preparation of the preparation and implementation of the Knesset budget. Once the annual budget proposal has been approved in First Reading within the framework of the annual Budget Bill, it shall be referred for deliberation in the Joint Committee of the House Committee and the Finance Committee stated in article 11(b) of the Budget Foundations Law. Theshall be brought for Second Reading and Third Reading within the framework of the annual Budget Bill.

(c) The Speaker of the Knesset is responsible for the administration of the Knesset and the Knesset Secretariat.

(d) While serving as acting President of the State, as stated in article 23(a) of Basic Law: the President of the State, the Speaker of the Knesset shall not run the sittings of the Knesset, unless the House

Committee has decided otherwise.

(e) The Speaker of the Knesset shall not be a member of any of the Knesset Committees, except for the Interpretations Committee, but he is entitled to participate in the deliberations of each of the Knesset Committees, including joint committees, and subcommittees, even if their minutes are confidential.

(f) The Speaker of the Knesset is entitled, from time to time, to hand over to one of the Deputies, the running of the Knesset sitting, or any of his tasks as determined in these Rules of Procedure, except for his duties in accordance with clauses (b) and (c).

(g) The Deputy Speaker of the Knesset, who is replacing the Speaker of the Knesset as stated in article 29 of the Knesset Premises Law, or to whom the Speaker of the Knesset has delegated some of his powers as stated in article 30(a) of the said law, or who is running the sitting of the Knesset, or fulfilling one of the tasks of the Speaker of the Knesset, shall have, on that occasion, all the duties and powers that are vested in the Speaker of the Knesset.

(h) A Deputy to the Speaker of the Knesset shall not be a chairman of the House Committee, or his substitute.

Publication in the Official Gazette of matters regarding the Knesset Speaker and his Deputies (Amendment

7. Regarding the Speaker of the Knesset and his Deputies, a notice shall be published in the Official Gazette on behalf of the Knesset on the following matters:

(1) The elections, suspension or termination of the service of the Speaker of the Knesset' or of a Deputy to the Speaker of the Knesset;

(2) The service of a Deputy to the Speaker of the Knesset as Acting Speaker of the Knesset according to article 20a of Basic Law: the Knesset.

ELECTION AND APPOINTMENT OF POSITION HOLDERS

ELECTION OF REPRESENTATIVES TO APPOINTMENTS COMMITTEES BY THE KNESSET

Representatives to appointments committees for holders of judicial office (Amendments Nos. 115 & 117)

62.

(a) Within four months from the beginning of its term, and within 60 days from the day on which the place of a representative in the course of the term of the Knesset has been vacated, the Knesset shall elect its representatives to each of the Appointments and Selection Committees enumerated below (in this chapter – appointments committees):

(1) The Committee for the election of *Dayanim,* on the basis of article 6 of the *Dayanim* [Jewish religious judges] Law, 5715-1955;

(2) The Committee for the election of Kadim, in accordance with article 4 of the *Kadim* [Muslim religious judges] Law, 5721-1961;

(3) The Appointments Committee on the basis of article 11 of the Druze Religious Courts Law, 5723-1962 (in this article – the Appointments Committee for *Kadim Madhab* [Druze religious judges]);

(4) The Committee for the Selection of Judges on the basis of article 4 of Basic Law: Adjudication, and article 6 of the Courts Law.

(b)

(1) The Secretary General of the Knesset shall inform all the Knesset Members of the time of the election for each of the Appointments Committees, as laid down by the Speaker of the Knesset, no later than two weeks before that date;

(2) The proposal of candidature shall be submitted to the Speaker of the Knesset in writing by the adjournment of the Knesset sitting on the last day of the week before the day of election, and if that week falls on a recess – no later than a week before the date of the elections;

(3) Each of the Knesset Members, who is not a minister or a deputy minister, is entitled to offer his candidature to an appointments committee, except for the Appointments Committee for *Kadim Madhab*. However, with regards to the Committee for the Election of Kadim, only someone, who is a member of a party other than the party in which a representative of the Government, or the Knesset representative in the Committee, is entitled to offer his candidacy;

(4) Every Druze Member of the Knesset, who is not a minister or a deputy minister, may offer his own candidature to the Committee for the Appointment of *Kadim Madhab*, and any ten Members of the Knesset are entitled to propose the candidature of a Druze, who is not a Member of the Knesset, to the said Committee. The consent of the candidate, and his declaration regarding his fulfillment of the conditions for election on the basis of this chapter, shall be attached to this proposal;

(c) The Secretary General of the Knesset shall inform all the Knesset Members of the candidates' names at least 48 hours before the opening of the Knesset sitting at which the election to the Appointments Committee shall take place.

(d) The election of the Knesset representatives to an appointments committee shall be by secret ballot, as elaborated below:

(1) Before the beginning of the voting, the Speaker of the Knesset shall announce to the Knesset the make-up of the Ballot Committee, which he appointed for this purpose, which shall include four Members of the Knesset, who are not candidates in those elections – two from the Coalition Parliamentary Groups, and two from the Opposition Parliamentary Groups;

(2) The Secretary General of the Knesset shall call the names of the Knesset Members by the alphabetical order of their surnames, and each of the Knesset Members in turn shall walk over to vote in the locations designated for this purpose in the Plenary Hall, and hidden from the sight of others. The provisions of article 36(b) shall apply to this matter, with the required changes;

(3) The Knesset Member shall receive a form that lists the names of the candidates, with the indication of the number of Knesset representatives in the Appointments Committee that are to be elected. Should the number of candidates be equal to the number of the Knesset representatives that are to be elect6ed, the indication of opposition to the election of any of them shall be enabled;

(4) The election shall take place by marking the names of the candidates on the form, up to the number of the Knesset representatives in the Appointments Committee that are to be elected, or by indicating opposition to their election, as stated in paragraph (3). A form on which a larger number of candidates from the said number has been marked – is invalid, and if the form included candidates for several Appointments Committees – it shall be invalid with regards to the Committee to which more candidates were marked, as stated;

(5) The Knesset Member shall place the form in the ballot box;

(6) Once the voting has ended, the ballot box shall be handed over to the Ballot Committee that will count the votes immediately;

(7) The results of the vote shall be determined on the basis of the following provisions:

(a) Should the number of candidates be larger than the number of Knesset representatives, who are to be elected, the candidates who received the largest number of votes shall be elected. Should a number of candidates receive an equal number of votes, as a result of which it is not possible to determine who all, or part of the Knesset representatives are, as stated, the voting among them shall be repeated immediately, until a decision is obtained;

(b) Should the number of candidates be the same as the number of Knesset representatives, who are to be elected –

(1) They shall be elected if the number of votes in their favour is greater than the number of votes against them;

(2) Should the number of votes in their favour fail to be larger than the number of votes against them, new elections shall take place for the election of the remaining representatives, within 30 days, and the provisions of this article shall apply to them;

(c) Despite what is said in subparagraph (a), if a female Knesset Member was not elected to the Committee for the election of *Dayanim*, or the Committee for the election of judges, as stated in article 6(a1) of the *Dayanim* Law, 5715-1955, or as stated in article 6(3a) to the Courts Law, as the case may be, a second vote shall take place immediately. In the second vote only the two female Knesset Members, who were candidates in the first vote, shall stand for election, and the female Knesset Member, who received the largest number of votes shall be considered to be the one elected instead of the male Knesset Member who received the second largest number of votes;

(d) Despite what is said in subparagraph (a), if two Muslim Knesset Members were not elected to serve on the Committee for the Election of Kadis as stated in article 4(a), the Muslim candidate, who was not elected, and received the largest number of votes, as having been elected instead of a Knesset Member, who is not Muslim, who received the second or third largest number of votes, as the case may be;

(e) Despite what is said in subparagraph (a), if more than one Knesset Member from the same party were elected to the Committee for the election of Kadis, contrary to article 4(a1) of the Kadis Law, only the Knesset member from this party, who received the largest number of votes shall be considered to have been elected, and instead of the additional member from his party elected as stated, shall come a candidate from another party, who received the number of votes next in size.

(8) The Ballot Committee shall inform the Speaker of the Knesset of the results of the vote. The Speaker of the Knesset shall inform the Knesset of the results of the elections at the same sitting in which they took place.

(e) Should a representative of the Knesset to an appointments committee be appointed as a minister or a deputy minister, he shall cease to serve as a representative, as stated, upon his appointment, and elections shall be held for a representative to replace him, in accordance with the provisions of this article.

Limitations to service, suspensions, and removal from service on the basis of article 6 of the Knesset Law (Amendments Nos. 115 and 119)

63.

(a) The House Committee, and as long as it has not yet been selected – the Arrangements Committee, is entitled to decide that a Member of the Knesset shall not be a candidate for service as a representative of the Knesset in an appointments committee, should what is stated in the introductory section of paragraph (1) or (2) of article 3(a) apply to him. The provisions of clauses (a)(1) and of (b) to (e) in article 3 shall apply to this matter, with the required changes.

(b) The Knesset is entitled, on the basis of a proposal by the House Committee to suspend the membership of a Knesset Member in an appointments committee should what is stated in the introductory section of paragraph (1) , and in article 3(a) apply to him. The provisions of article 3(b), (c) and (e) shall apply to this matter, with the required changes. Should the Knesset's representative in an appointments committee be suspended, the Knesset shall elect another representative in his place, for the period of the suspension, in the manner described in article 62.

(c) Should a Member of the Knesset be convicted in a final verdict on a criminal offence in the course of the term of that Knesset, he shall cease to serve as the representative of the Knesset in the Appointments Committee.

(d) Regarding a Druze, who is not a Member of the Knesset, as a representative of the Knesset in an appointments committee for *Kadim-Madhab* the following provisions shall apply:

(1) Anyone, against whom criminal proceedings are being held, or has been convicted in a final verdict of a criminal offence, and ten years have not gone by since the verdict became final, or from the day on which he finished serving his sentence, whichever is later, shall not be a candidate as a representative of the Knesset in a committee;

(2) Should criminal proceedings be held against him after his election – he shall be suspended from his service as a representative of the Knesset in the Committee, until a final verdict is given, and the Knesset shall elect another representative in his place for the period of the suspension, in the manner described in article 62;

(3) Should he be convicted in a final verdict of a criminal offence, he shall cease to serve as a representative of the Knesset in the Committee.

Representatives on the basis of the Chief Rabbinate of Israel Law (Amendment No. X)

64.

(a) The election of the Knesset representatives to the Electing Assembly on the basis of article 8(7) of the Chief Rabbinate of Israel Law 5740-1980, shall take place no later than thirty days before the date set for the convening of the Electing Assembly for the purpose of holding elections, as stated in article 12 of the said law. Should a date not have been set as stated, the election shall take place no later than thirty days before the last date for electing the Chief Rabbis of Israel, or the members of the Council on the basis of article 16(c) of the said law, as the case may be.

(b) The proposal to authorize one of the Knesset Committees to elect the Knesset representatives as stated in clause (a), shall be brought to the Knesset by the Knesset Speaker.

(c) The following provisions shall apply to the election of the Knesset representatives as stated in clause (a), with the required changes:

(1) Should the election take place in the Knesset plenum, the provisions of articles 62(b) to (e) and 63(a) to (c) shall apply;

(2) Should the election take place in the Committee authorized for this purpose by the Knesset, the provisions of articles 62(e), 63(a) to (c), the final section of article 65(a), articles 63(b) and (c), and 66(c) shall apply.

(d) The Knesset representatives elected on the basis of this article shall serve as long as they are Members of the Knesset, and should the term of the Knesset end – until the new Knesset shall elect other Members in their place.

ELECTION OF REPRESENTATIVES BY A COMMITTEE OF THE KNEESSET

A representative to the Committee that proposes candidates for the position of Attorney General (Amendment No. 115)

65.

(a) Within four months from the beginning of its service, as well as within 60 days from the day on which the place of a representative has been vacated in the course of the Knesset's term, the Constitution, Law and Justice Committee shall elect the Knesset representative to the Committee that proposes candidates for the position of Attorney General. The Chairman of the Constitution, Law and Justice Committee shall inform all the Knesset Members of the time of the election, no later than two weeks before that date.

(b) Each of the Knesset Members, who is not a Minister or Deputy Minister, is entitled to offer his candidature in writing to the Chairman of the Constitution, Law and Justice Committee, until the adjournment of the Knesset sitting on the last day of the week before the election day, and should that week occur during a recess – no later than one week before the date of the election.

(c) The Chairman of the Constitution, Law and Justice Committee shall inform all the Knesset Members of the candidates' names at least 48 hours before the time of the opening of the Committee's meeting at which the elections shall take place.

(d) The election of the Knesset representative shall take place in an open vote, as elaborated below:

(1) Should there be more than a single candidate, each of the Committee members participating in the voting shall announce the name of the candidate who he supports, and the candidate who received the largest number of participants' votes – shall be elected. Should several candidates receive an equal number of votes, so that it is not possible to determine who was elected, the voting among them shall be repeated immediately, until there is a decision;

(2) Should there be a single candidate, each of the Committee members participating in the vote shall state if he supports him or objects to his election, and the following provisions shall apply -

(a) He shall be elected if the number of votes in his favour is larger than the number of votes against him;

(b) Should the number of votes in his favour be no greater that the number of votes against him, new elections shall take place within 30 days, and the provisions of this article shall apply to them.

(e) The provisions of articles 62(e) and 63(a) to (c), shall apply to the matter of the Knesset representative on the basis of this article, with the required changes.

66.

(a) The Education, Culture and Sports Committee shall elect the three Knesset representatives to the Council of *Yad Ben-Zvi* on the basis of article 4 of the *Yad Yitzhak Ben-Zvi* Law, 5729-1969.

(b) The provisions of articles 62(e) and 65(a) to (c) shall apply to the elections of the representatives with the required changes, and with the following difference: instead of the Constitution, Law and Justice Committee shall come the Education, Culture and Sports Committee.

(c) The election of the Knesset representatives shall take place by an open vote, as elaborated below:

(1) Should the number of candidates be larger than the number of Knesset representatives who are to be elected, each of the Committee members participating in the vote shall state the name of the candidate or candidates who he supports, up to the number of Knesset representatives that is to be elected, and the candidates, who received the largest number of votes from the participants - shall be elected. Should several candidates receive an equal number of votes, and consequently it is not possible to determine who the Knesset representatives - all or part of them – are, the voting among them shall be repeated immediately until there is a decision;

(2) Should the number of candidates be the same as the number of Knesset representatives, who are to be elected, each of the Committee members participating in the vote shall announce whether he supports each of them, or objects to their elections, and the following provisions shall apply –

(a) Candidates who received a larger number of votes in their favour than votes against them, shall be elected;

(b) Should the number of candidates elected be smaller than the number of Knesset representatives as stated, new elections shall be held for the remaining representatives who are to be elected, within 30 days, and the provisions of this article shall apply to them.

DETERMINING THE NUMBER OF SUPREME COURT JUSTICES

Determining the number of Supreme Court Justices on the basis of article 25 of the Courts Law

67.

(a) A decision of the Knesset regarding the number of justices in the Supreme Court on the basis of article 25 of the Court Law (combined version), 5744-1984, shall not be adopted except on the basis of a proposal by the Constitution, Law and Justice Committee.

(b) Any ten Member of the Knesset, as well as the Government, are entitled to submit to the Chairman of the Constitution, Law and Justice Committee a proposal that the Knesset should change the number of justices in the Supreme Court, and shall indicate in it the number of proposed justices.

(c)1 The Constitution, Law and Justice Committee shall deliberate and shall decide on the proposal as stated in clause (b) within 120 days from the day that it was submitted, and recess days shall not be counted.

(d) The decision of the Constitution, Law and Justice Committee regarding the proposal as stated in clause (b), shall be laid on the Knesset table, together with reservations submitted and explained by Members of the Knesset at the deliberation in the Committee, even if they are not members of the Committee. A Member of the Knesset shall not submit more than one reservation.

(e) The Speaker of the Knesset shall bring the decision of the Constitution, Law and Justice Committee for a debate in the Knesset within 30 days from its being laid down, and recess days shall not be taken into account. The Chairman of the Committee shall present the Committee's proposal to the Knesset, and he is entitled to sum up the debate, as stated in article 29(2) and (3). Anyone who has reservations is entitled to explain his reservation within a time limit that shall not exceed five minutes. After the explanation of the reservations a personal debate shall take place.

(f) At the end of the debate the Knesset shall vote on the proposal of the Constitution, Law and Justice Committee, and on the reservations as elaborated below:

(1) Should the proposal of the Committee be adopted – it shall be the resolution of the Knesset, and there is no vote on the reservations;

(2) Should the proposal of the Committee fail to be adopted and all the reservations were voted upon

1 Article 67(c) shall come into force upon the inception of the 19th Knesset.

(a) Should one reservation be adopted – it shall be the resolution of the Knesset;

(b) Should several reservations be adopted – the Knesset shall decide among them.

(g) The Constitution Law and Justice Committee shall not deliberate a proposal as stated in clause (b), unless a year has gone by since the Knesset resolution on the basis of clause (f).

KNESSET ORGANIZATION AND ADMINISTRATIVE PROCEDURES

SITTINGS

The dates of the sessions

18. The Speaker of the Knesset, after consulting his Deputies, and with the approval of the House Committee, shall set the dates on which the Knesset Sessions shall open and close, subject to what is said in article 9 of the Knesset Law.

The Knesset sittings

19.

(a) (1) The Knesset shall hold sittings on Mondays and Tuesdays from 16:00, and on Wednesdays as of 11:00. The Speaker of the Knesset, with the approval of the House Committee, is entitled to change the time of a sitting, to cancel a sitting, and to set an additional sitting and its time – whether on one of the said days, or on another day that is not one of the Jewish holidays that are listed in article 18a(a) of the Government and Justice Arrangements Ordinance.

(2) The Speaker of the Knesset is entitled to declare a break in the course of a sitting of the Knesset.

(b) Should the Speaker take note of the fact that an event of exceptional importance has taken place, which requires the convening of the Knesset for an urgent sitting that diverges from the weekly agenda, he is entitled, after consulting with the Chairman of the House Committee, to convene the Knesset for a debate on the said event, and he shall determine the debate procedures in the sitting.

(c) The Speaker of the Knesset is entitled to declare a sitting to mark an event, and he shall determine the debate procedures in it.

(d) At every sitting of the Knesset, and in the course of the whole sitting, at least one of the Government Ministers shall be present.

The opening of the Knesset Session

20.

(a) The President of the state is entitled to open the first Knesset sitting in every Knesset Session, and shall speak immediately after the Speaker of the Knesset.

(b) Immediately after the President of the State has opened the Knesset sitting as stated in clause (a), the Prime Minister shall deliver a statement regarding the activity of the Government in the period following the previous Session, and regarding the Government's plans for the coming Session. If the President of the State has not opened the Knesset sitting, the Prime Minister shall open the sitting with a statement as mentioned. A parliamentary group debate shall take place on the statement, and the Knesset shall vote on it.

(c) Should the Knesset debate a motion to express no-confidence in the Government on the opening day of the Knesset Session, the Motion shall be explained after the Prime Minister's statement, a combined parliamentary group debate shall take place on both topics, and at its end the Knesset shall vote on the Prime

Minister's statement, and after that on the proposal to express no-confidence in the Government

Convening the Knesset during recess

21.

(a) Twenty Five Members of the Knesset, who request that the Knesset convene during the recess, in accordance with article 9(b) of the Knesset Law, are entitled to specify in their demand one or two topics. The Speaker of the Knesset shall place the topics on the agenda of the sitting as Motions for the Agenda. Nothing of what was said prevents the Speaker of the Knesset from placing on the agenda of the sitting one or two additional topics, on the basis of the request of 25 other Members of the Knesset.

(b) Should 25 Members of the Knesset request that the Knesset should be convened, as stated in clause (a), they cannot request to add topics to that sitting of the Knesset, but the Speaker of the Knesset is entitled, at their request, to change a topic that they listed in their demand, as long as they made the request at least 36 hours before the opening of the sitting. The Knesset shall not debate a topic that was not listed in the request of the 25 Knesset members.

(c) In a Knesset sitting, on the basis of this article, two Members of the Knesset only are allowed to explain every Motion for the Agenda, within a time limit that shall not exceed 10 minutes for each of them.

(d) Canceled

(e) The request of the Government to convene the Knesset during the recess, in accordance with article 9(b) of the Knesset Law, shall be submitted in a written notice by the Government Secretary to the Knesset Secretary General.

Speeches in the plenum

22.

The following are entitled to speak in the Knesset Plenum:

Members of the Knesset, Ministers and Deputy Ministerss, who are not Members of the Knesset, as well as the President of the State in accordance with the provisions of any law, or upon the invitation of the Knesset Speaker, and with the approval of the House Committee. The Speaker of the Knesset, with the approval of the House Committee, is also entitled to invite a Head of state, a prime Minister or the head of a foreign parliament to speak, as well as the head of an international organization in which Israel is a member, and they shall be entitled to speak in their own language.1

Maiden speech and farewell speech

23.

(a) A Member of the Knesset, who has started to serve in the Knesset, and did not serve previously as a Member of the Knesset, or as a minister, is entitled to deliver a maiden speech at one of the sittings after he has declared his allegiance.

(b) The Speaker of the Knesset is entitled to enable a Member of the Knesset, who has resigned from his position, to deliver a farewell speech, after he has presented his resignation letter, and before his resignation has entered into force, as long as a sitting of the Knesset is scheduled to be held.

(c) A minister or deputy minister, with regards to whose termination of service a notice has been submitted to the Knesset, as mentioned in article 9(a)(6) or (8), is entitled to deliver a speech concerning the termination of his service at the sitting at which the notice was given, as long as he serves as a Member of the Knesset at the time of the sitting.

1 On 15.6.2011 the President of the European Parliament spoke in the Plenum (decision of the House Committee on 14.6.2011); on 15.2.2012 the President of Croatia spoke in the Plenum (decision of the House Committee on 13.2.2012).

(d) The Speaker of the Knesset shall set a date for the delivery of speeches in accordance with the provisions of this article, and the time limit for each speech.

Commemoration of those who have passed away

24.

(a) Should a former Member of the Knesset pass away, the Knesset shall pay respect to his memory by rising at one of the sittings close to his passing away. The Speaker of the Knesset shall speak in memory of the deceased, and he is entitled to enable additional Members of the Knesset to speak, in numbers and a time limit to be decided.

(b) Should the President of the State, a Member of the Knesset, a minister or a deputy minister pass away while he is still in office, or should a former President of the State, a former Speaker of the Knesset, or a former Prime Minister pass away, the Knesset shall hold a sitting in his memory, and shall pay its respects to his memory by rising. The Speaker of the Knesset shall open the sitting with a speech in memory of the deceased, and shall enable additional Members of the Knesset to speak, in numbers and a time limit to be decided.

AGENDA

Weekly agenda (Amendments Nos. 108 and 112)

25.

(a) The Secretary General of the Knesset shall publish, no later than the last sitting day of the week, the list of topics on the Knesset agenda.

(b) The Speaker of the Knesset shall set the detailed weekly agenda of the Knesset at the beginning of each week, in accordance with the provisions of this article, and shall present it at the weekly meeting of the Knesset Presidium. The Secretary General of the Knesset shall publish the agenda that was set, after the meeting of the Presidium.

(c) The agenda of the Knesset sittings shall begin with the following: on Monday – motions to express no-confidence in the Government, should they have been tabled; on Tuesday – one minute speeches; and on Wednesday - replies to urgent questions.

(d) (1) The Speaker of the Knesset shall set the agenda of the Knesset so that the sittings of the Knesset on Mondays and Tuesdays shall be devoted to debates on Government motions and debates on private members' bills of Knesset Members on first reading, on second reading, and on third reading, and the sitting of the Knesset on Wednesday shall be devoted to debating private members bills brought for preliminary reading and motions for the agenda. Replies to questions may be given at any one of the Knesset sittings.

(2) Despite what is said in paragraph (1), the Speaker of the Knesset is entitled to place on the agenda of the Knesset a debate on private members' bills as stated in that paragraph, on Monday and Tuesday, and a debate at the request of the Government on Wednesday, as long as the topic that was placed as stated on the agenda shall be debated after the topics that were set for debate on the basis of paragraph (1), and a notice in this sense shall be submitted to the Knesset Members before the beginning of the debate on it.

(e) The Speaker of the Knesset is entitled to set an agenda that diverges from the provisions of clauses (c) and (d), when this is what the circumstances require, including in weeks in which three regular sitting of the Knesset do not take place, in a week in which the Knesset debates the annual Budget Bill or the accompanying Bills, and in the last week of the Knesset sessions.

Notice on the laying of documents on the Knesset table (Amendment No. 108)

26. The Secretary General of the Knesset or a deputy to the Secretary General shall submit to the Knesset, in the course of its sitting, a notice regarding the documents that have been laid on the Knesset tabled.

DEBATE PROCEDURES

Form of debate (Amendment No. 108 & 113)

27.

(a) The debates in the Knesset are based on parliamentary groups, or are personal.

(b) The debate on the following shall be parliamentary group based:

(1) The establishment of the Government or its resignation;

(2) An announcement by the Government on the basis of article 32;

(3) The expression of no-confidence in the Government;

(4) A debate with the participation of the Prime Minister on the basis of article 42(b) of Basic Law: the Government.

The procedure in a parliamentary group debate and a personal debate

28.

(a) In a Parliamentary Group debate -

(1) The House Committee shall set the time frame devoted to the debate;

(2) Every Parliamentary Group shall determine the names of its members, who shall participate in the debate, and the order of their appearance, as long as the time frame for each speaker shall be no less than three minutes;

(3) The Secretary general of the Knesset shall set the order of the speakers among the Parliamentary Groups on the basis of their size, but a Knesset member from the Parliamentary Group of the Leader of the Opposition shall be called upon to speak first, and a Knesset Member from the Prime Minister's Parliamentary Group shall be called upon to speak last;

(4) A Member of the Knesset who is absent from the sitting when his turn to speak arrives, without notifying on the fact in advance, shall not be entitled to speak in the debate, but his Parliamentary Group is entitled to transfer the time frame that was allotted to him to another member of the Parliamentary Group.

(b) In a personal debate –

(1) The time frame for every speaker shall be three minutes, unless the Speaker of the Knesset has decided on a longer time frame;

(2) Every Knesset Member is entitled to inform the Secretary General of the Knesset of his wish to participate in a debate, and his name shall be placed on the list of speakers. A notice, as aforesaid, shall be given before the beginning of the debate, but a Knesset Member is entitled to make a statement after the debate has begun, as long as the Speaker of the Knesset has not announced that the list is closed;

(3) A Member of the Knesset is entitled to ask that his place in the list of speakers be changed. A Member of the Knesset who is absent from the sitting when his turn has come to speak, without having notified on the fact in advance, shall not be entitled to speak in the debate.

Opening the debate and closing it (Amendments Nos. 108 & 120)

29. On an item on the agenda of the Knesset, based on the recommendation of the Government, or of one of the Knesset Committees, except for a debate on Bills, the debate shall open and shall be closed in accordance with the following provisions:

(1) On a topic raised by the Government, a Minister, or Deputy Minister, shall open the debate, and he is entitled to sum up the debate;

(2) On a topic raised by a committee, the Chairman of the Committee is entitled to sum up the debate;

(3) The opening speech shall be within a time frame that shall not exceed ten minutes. The summing up shall be within a time frame that shall not exceed five minutes.

A proposal regarding the procedures for running the sitting or a vote (Amendment No. 108)

30.

(a) Should a Member of the Knesset ask the Chairman of the sitting for permission to make a proposal regarding the procedures for running the sitting, or for the voting, the Chairman shall decide whether to give the Knesset Member the floor in order to raise his proposal. The time frame for explaining t he said proposal shall be no more than one minute.

(b) In the course of the vote or series of votes, the floor shall not be given, except for a motion regarding the order of the voting.

(c) The Chairman of the sitting shall decide on the proposals on the basis of this article.

The right of a Minister or Deputy Minister to speak (Amendments Nos. 108 & 117)

31.

(a) One Minister, who speaks on behalf of the Government, is entitled to receive the right to speak at any stage of the debate, and before the voting begins. Should an additional Minister ask to speak behalf of the Government, the Chairman of the sitting is entitled to give him the floor, within a time frame that does not exceed five minutes.

(b) (Cancelled)

(c) What is stated in this article with regards to a Minister shall also apply to a Deputy Minister, who asks to speak on behalf of the Government on the affairs of the Ministry in which he serves.

Government statements and expressions of no-confidence in the Government (Amendments Nos. 108' 110' 113 & 119)

32.

(a) The Government is entitled at any time to make a statement in the Knesset, without its being included in advance in the agenda, and on the basis of the demand of 25 Members of the Knesset in writing within a week of the statement being made, a debate and a vote shall be held about it in the first regular sitting of the Knesset during the Knesset's Session after the demand was submitted, but on the basis of a request of the Government, the debate and the vote shall be put off to the following regular Knesset sitting during the Knesset's Session.

(b)

(1) The Prime Minister is entitled to give notice to the Chairman of the sitting that he shall consider the vote of the Knesset on an item that is on the agenda as a matter of expressing confidence in the Government, and shall announce the position of the Government with regards to it. Should he give notice as aforesaid, a single vote only shall take place, both on the item on the agenda, and on the announcement of the Prime Minister. The provisions of this clause shall not apply in a vote on a bill in preliminary debate, and a motion for the agenda.

(2) Should the Prime Minister announce that the Government supports an item on the agenda, or objects to it, and should the position of the Government receive the support of a majority of the participants, the Government shall be considered to have received the confidence of the Knesset. Should the position of the Government fail to receive the support of a majority as aforesaid – it shall be considered to have failed to receive the confidence of the Knesset.

A statement by a parliamentary group on a matter that is not a bill (amendment No. 108)

33. In a debate on a topic that is not a bill, ev3ery parliamentary group, that did not participate both in the debate and the voting, is entitled at the end of the voting to make a statement within a time frame that does not exceed five minutes.

Personal announcement (amendment No. 108)

34.

(a) The Chairman of the sitting is entitled to enable a Member of the Knesset to make a personal statement, if he has asked to do so for the purpose of correcting a misunderstanding regarding what he said in the Knesset, or in connection with an accusation made against him in the Knesset. Should the accusation have been made against a parliamentary group, the Chairman is entitled to enable one of its members to make a statement, as aforesaid.

(b) The Knesset Member shall submit a summary of his statement in advance , and in writing to the Chairman of the sitting.

(c) The statement of the Knesset Member shall be given at the end of the debate on the item in which the words, as a result of which the statement was requested were said, and if the debate ended with a vote – upon the termination of the voting, within a time frame that shall not exceed five minutes.

VOTING IN THE KNESSET PLENUM

Procedure for voting (Amendment No. 109)

35.

(a) Upon the termination of the debate in the Knesset Plenum on a topic on the agenda, a vote shall take place, unless the Chairman of the sitting has decided, under special circumstances, to put off the voting, and a notice to this effect has been conveyed to the Knesset Members. At the request of the Knesset Member, who initiated or proposed the topic on the agenda, or with his consent and the consent of the Government, the Chairman of the sitting is entitled to decide that the voting shall be put off , even if there are no special circumstances as stated, and the notice on this shall be conveyed to the Knesset Members before the beginning of the debate on the topic, or in its course.

(b) The chairman of the sitting shall determine the procedure of voting.

(c) Before every vote or set of votes, the Secretary General of the Knesset shall announce the voting by sounding the bell.

Manner of voting (Amendments Nos. 109 113 & 120)

36.

(a) (1) The Knesset Member shall vote by means of the electronic voting system, from his permanent seat only.

(2) The Chairman of the sitting is entitled to decide that a vote that is taking place as part of a series of votes, shall be held by means of the raising of hands, unless there has been an objection to this from one of the Parliamentary Groups.

(b) By demand in writing of at least twenty Knesset Members, or by demand of the Government, a roll call shall take as described below:

(1) The Secretary General of the Knesset shall call the names of all the Knesset Members according to the alphabetical order of their surnames, and each of the Knesset Members, in turn, shall declare his vote out loud, and he is entitled to state that he is not participating in the vote;

(2) After the names have been called, the Secretary General of the Knesset shall once again call the names of the Knesset Members who did not vote, or did not say that they are not participating in the vote, so that they may state their votes;

(3) The Chairman of the sitting shall ask if there is in the Chamber a Knesset Member whose vote was not registered, and shall enable him to vote, and immediately after that he shall announce that the voting has terminated;

(4) The Secretary general shall register the results of the vote, and shall hand them over to the Chairman of the sitting, so that he shall announce them to the Knesset;

(5) A Member of the Knesset who has stated his vote, or who stated that he is not participating in the vote, is not entitled to change his statement after the next Knesset Member has been called upon to vote.

Results of the vote

37.

(a) At the end of the voting the Chairman of the sitting shall announce its results.

(b) A Member of the Knesset who has participated in an electronic vote, and claimed that his vote was not recorded, or he has requested that his vote be changed due to a mistake, shall announce the fact immediately after the voting. The Chairman of the sitting shall consider the request, and shall immediately announce the request and his decision whether to change the results of the vote.

(c) In a vote by the raising of hands –

(1) Should the Chairman of the sitting see that the motion that was put to the vote was supported by a majority, or was rejected by a majority, the votes need not be counted, unless there is in the law a requirement for a certain majority of votes. However, the Chairman of the sitting in entitled to announce, before any vote, that the votes shall be counted;

(2) Should the Chairman of the sitting decide that the results of the vote were not clear, he shall immediately instruct to hold an additional vote, by the raising of hands, or electronic.

(d) Should the results of the vote be a tie, the motion is not adopted, and the vote is not repeated.

COMMITTEE CHAIRS

Committee	Chairman	Party
Economic Affairs Committee	Eitan Cabel	Zionist Union
Education, Culture, and Sports Committee	Ya'akov Margi	Shas
Ethics Committee	Yitzhak Vaknin	Shas
Finance Committee	Moshe Gafni	United Torah

		Judaism
Foreign Affairs and Defense Committee	Avi Dichter	Likud
House Committee	David Bitan	Likud
Committee for Immigration, Absorption and Diaspora Affairs	Avraham Neguise	Likud
Internal Affairs and Environment Committee	Dudu Amsalem	Likud
Labor, Welfare and Health Committee	Eli Alaluf	Kulanu
Constitution, Law and Justice Committee	Nissan Slomiansky	The Jewish Home
Science and Technology Committee	Uri Maklev	United Torah Judaism
State Control Committee	Karin Elharar	Yesh Atid
Committee on the Status of Women and Gender Equality	Aida Touma-Suleiman	Joint List
Special Committee for Discussion of the Public Broadcast Bill 2015	Stav Shaffir	Zionist Union
Special Committee for Public Petitions	Yisrael Eichler	United Torah Judaism
Special Committee for the Rights of the Child	Yifat Shasha-Biton	Kulanu
Special Committee for the Transparency and Accessibility of Government Information	Stav Shaffir	Zionist Union
Special Committee on Drug and Alcohol Abuse	Tamar Zandberg	Meretz
Special Committee to Discuss the National Authority for Urban Renewal Bill	Eli Cohen	Kulanu

EXECUTIVE BRANCH - CABINET OF MINISTERS

The **Government of Israel** exercises executive authority in the State of Israel. It consists of ministers who are chosen and led by the prime minister. The composition of the government must be approved by a vote of confidence in the Knesset (the Israeli parliament). Under Israeli law, the prime minister may dismiss members of the government, but must do so in writing, and new appointees must be approved by the Knesset. Most ministers lead ministries, though some are ministers without portfolio. Most ministers are members of the Knesset, though only the Prime Minister and the "designated acting prime minister" are required to be Knesset members. Some ministers are also called deputy and vice prime ministers. Unlike the designated acting prime minister, these roles have no statutory meanings. The government operates in accordance with the Basic Law. It meets on Sundays weekly in Jerusalem. There may be additional meetings if circumstances require it. The prime minister convenes these meetings.

The first government was the provisional government of Israel (*HaMemshala HaZmanit*) which governed from shortly before independence until the formation of the first formal government in March 1949 following the first Knesset elections in January that year. It was formed as the People's Administration (*Minhelet HaAm*) on 12 April 1948, in preparation for independence just over a month later. All its thirteen members were taken from Moetzet HaAm, the temporary legislative body set up at the same time.

THIRTY-FOURTH GOVERNMENT OF ISRAE

Date formed	14 May 2015
People and organisations	
Head of state	Reuven Rivlin
Head of government	Benjamin Netanyahu
No. of ministers	21
Member parties	Likud The Jewish Home Kulanu Shas United Torah Judaism Yisrael Beiteinu
Status in legislature	Coalition government
Opposition party	Zionist Union
Opposition leader	Isaac Herzog
History	

Election(s)	2015 Knesset election
Legislature term(s)	20th Knesset
Predecessor	33rd Cabinet
Successor	35th Cabinet

The **thirty-fourth government of Israel**, also known as the *Fourth Netanyahu Government*, is the current government of Israel, headed by Prime Minister Benjamin Netanyahu. It was formed after the March 2015 Knesset elections. The coalition that makes up the government, consisting of the parties Likud, United Torah Judaism, Shas, Kulanu and the Jewish Home, was submitted to the President of Israel just before the deadline on 6 May 2015. The government ministers were introduced, approved by the Knesset and sworn in on 14 May. The government deputy ministers were sworn in on 19 May.

Between them, the parties hold 61 of the 120 seats in the Knesset. The elections that led to the formation of the government were a result of events on 2 December 2014, when Netanyahu dismissed two of his ministers whose parties' members subsequently resigned from the 33rd government of Israel, dissolving the government ahead of schedule.

During the 34th government, several corruption cases arose in regards to Netanyahu. Justice Minister Ayelet Shaked stated that even if indicted, Netanyahu will still be able to continue as Prime Minister.

POLICY GUIDELINES

The policy guidelines for the 34th government include but are not limited to:

- Strengthening the rule of law
- Reducing the cost of living
- Increasing competition, especially in the financial sector, and granting easier access to credit for small and medium businesses
- Integrating disabled persons into society, in providing education and employment aid
- Advancing the peace process with the Palestinians and other neighbors while keeping Israel's national interests

CABINET MEMBERS

Portfolio	Minister	Party
Prime Minister Minister of Foreign Affairs	Benjamin Netanyahu	Likud
Minister of Agriculture and Rural Development	Uri Ariel	The Jewish Home
Minister of Aliyah and Integration	Sofa Landver	Yisrael Beiteinu
Minister of Construction	Yoav Galant	Kulanu
Minister of Culture and Sport	Miri Regev	Likud
Minister of Defense	Avigdor Lieberman	Yisrael Beiteinu
Minister of the Interior Minister of the Development of the Negev and Galilee	Aryeh Deri	Shas

Minister of the Economy	Eli Cohen	Kulanu
Minister of Education Minister of Diaspora Affairs	Naftali Bennett	The Jewish Home
Minister of Finance	Moshe Kahlon	Kulanu
Minister of Health	Yaakov Litzman	United Torah Judaism
Minister of Intelligence and Atomic Energy Minister of Transportation	Yisrael Katz	Likud
Minister of Jerusalem Minister of Environmental Protection	Ze'ev Elkin	Likud
Minister of Internal Security Minister of Strategic Affairs Minister of Information	Gilad Erdan	Likud
Minister of Tourism	Yariv Levin	Likud
Minister of Justice	Ayelet Shaked	The Jewish Home
Minister of National Infrastructure, Energy, and Water	Yuval Steinitz	Likud
Minister of Regional Cooperation Minister of Communications	Tzachi Hanegbi	Likud
Minister of Religious Affairs	vacant	Shas
Minister of Science, Technology and Space	Ofir Akunis	Likud
Minister for Senior Citizens	Gila Gamliel	Likud
Minister of Welfare and Social Services	Haim Katz	Likud
Minister in the Prime Minister's Office	Ayoob Kara	Likud

SECURITY CABINET

The State Security Cabinet (SSC) or **Ministerial Committee on National Security Affairs (NSAC- National Security Affairs Committe)** (Hebrew: ועדת השרים לענייני ביטחון, *Va'adat HaSarim Le'Inyanei Bitahon*) is a narrow forum of "Inner Cabinet" within the Israeli Cabinet, headed by the Prime Minister of Israel, with the purpose of outlining a foreign and defense policy and implementing it. This smaller forum of the cabinet members, is designated to coordinate the diplomatic negotiations, and in times of crisis, especially war, it is designed to make quick and effective decisions.

Minister	Party
Benjamin Netanyahu (Chairman)	Likud
Naftali Bennett	The Jewish Home
Aryeh Deri	Shas
Gilad Erdan	Likud
Yoav Galant	Kulanu

Moshe Kahlon	Kulanu
Yisrael Katz	Likud
Sofa Landver	Yisrael Beiteinu
Avigdor Lieberman	Yisrael Beiteinu
Ayelet Shaked	The Jewish Home

GOVERNMENT AGENCIES AND SPECIAL COMMITTEES

Agency / Committee	Chairman	Party
Israel Land Administration	Yoav Galant	Kulanu
World Zionist Organization's Settlement Division	Uri Ariel	The Jewish Home
Israel Atomic Energy Commission	Yuval Steinitz	Likud

GOVERNMENT MINISTRIES

THE OFFICE OF THE PRESIDENT

Hanassi St.
Jerusalem 92188
Tel: 972-2-6707211
Fax: 972-2-5610037
Website: http://www.president.gov.il

THE KNESSET

Kiryat Ben-Gurion
Jerusalem 91950
Tel: 972-2-6753333
Fax: 972-2-6521599
E-mail Knesset Members
Website: http://www.knesset.gov.il

PRIME MINISTER'S OFFICE

3 Kaplan St.
P.O.B. 187
Kiryat Ben-Gurion
Jerusalem 91919
Tel: 972-2-6705555
Fax: 972-2-5664838
Website: http://www.pmo.gov.il
E-mail: pm_eng@pmo.gov.il

Central Bureau of Statistics
3 Kaplan St.
P.O.B. 187
Kiryat Ben-Gurion

Jerusalem 91919
Tel: 972-2-6553553
Fax: 972-2-6553325
Website: http://www.cbs.gov.il

MINISTRY OF AGRICULTURE

Agricultural Center
POB 50200
Bet-Dagan
Tel: 972-3-9485555
Fax: 972-3-9485858
Email: http://www.moag.gov.il/Pages/ContactUs.aspx
Website: http://www.moag.gov.il

MINISTRY OF COMMUNICATION

23 Yaffo St.
Jerusalem 91999
Tel: 972-2-6706320
Fax: 972-2-6706372
Website: http://www.moc.gov.il

Postal Authority
237 Yaffo St.
Jerusalem 91999
Tel: 972-2-6290808
Fax: 972-2-6290921
Website: http://www.postil.com

MINISTRY OF CONSTRUCTION AND HOUSING

Kiryat Hamemshala
P.O.B. 18110
Jerusalem 91180
Tel: 972-2-5847211
Fax: 972-2-5811904
Website: http://www.moch.gov.il

MINISTRY OF DEFENSE

Kaplan St.
Hakirya
Tel-Aviv 61909
Tel: 972-3-5692010
Fax: 972-3-6916940
Website: http://www.mod.gov.il

MINISTRY FOR THE DEVELOPMENT OF THE NEGEV AND THE GALILEE

Shaul Hamelech 8
Tel Aviv 64733

Tel: 972-3-6060700
Fax: 972-3-6958414
Website: http://www.vpmo.gov.il

MINISTRY OF EDUCATION, CULTURE AND SPORTS

34 Shivtei Israel St.
P.O.B. 292
Jerusalem 91911
Tel: 972-2-5602222
Fax: 972-2-5602223
Website: http://www.education.gov.il

The Israel Academy of Sciences and Humanities
Albert Einstein Square, Talbieh
P.O.B. 4040
Jerusalem 91040
Tel: 972-2-5636211
Website: http://www.academy.ac.il

MINISTRY OF ENERGY AND WATER RESOURCES

Jaffa Road 216
Jerusalem
P.O.B. 36148
Jerusalem 91360
Tel: 972-2-5006777
Fax: 972-2-5006888
Website: http://www.mni.gov.il

MINISTRY OF ENVIRONMENTAL PROTECTION

5 Kanfei Nesharim St., Givat Shaul
P.O.B. 34033
Jerusalem 95464
Tel: 972-2-6553777
Fax: 972-2-6535934
Website: http://www.sviva.gov.il

MINISTRY OF FINANCE

1 Kaplan St.
Kiryat Ben-Gurion
P.O.B. 13195
Jerusalem 13195
Tel: 972-2-5317111
Fax: 972-2-5637891
Website: http://www.mof.gov.il

MINISTRY OF FOREIGN AFFAIRS

9 Yitzhak Rabin Blvd.
Kiryat Ben-Gurion
Jerusalem 91035
Tel: 972-2-5303111
Fax: 972-2-5303367
Website: http://www.mfa.gov.il
Contact information

MINISTRY OF HEALTH

2 Ben-Tabai St.
P.O.B. 1176
Jerusalem 91010
Tel: 972-2-6705705
Fax: 972-2-6233026
Website: http://www.health.gov.il

MINISTRY OF IMMIGRANT ABSORPTION

1 Kaplan St.
Kiryat Gen-Gurion
P.O.B. 13061
Jerusalem 91130
Tel: 972-2-6752696/7
Fax: 972-2-5618138
Website: http://www.moia.gov.il

MINISTRY OF INDUSTRY AND TRADE

5, Bank of Israel Street
Kiryat Ben-Gurion
Jerusalem 91009
Tel: 972-2-6662299
Fax: 972-2-6662947
Website: http://www.moit.gov.il

Israel Land Adminstration
6 Shamai St.
P.O.B. 2600
Jerusalem 94631
Tel: 972-2-6208322/422
Fax: 972-2-6241286
Website: http://www.mmi.gov.il

MINISTRY OF THE INTERIOR

2 Kaplan St.
P.O.B. 6158
Kiryat Ben-Gurion
Jerusalem 91061
Tel: 972-2-6701411

Fax: 972-2-6701628
Website: http://www.moin.gov.il/

MINISTRY OF JUSTICE

29 Salah A-din St.
Jerusalem 91010
Tel: 972-2-6708511
Fax: 972-2-6288618
Website: http://www.justice.gov.il

MINISTRY OF LABOR AND SOCIAL WELFARE

2 Kaplan St.
Kiryat Ben-Gurion
P.O.B. 915
Jerusalem 91008
Tel: 972-2-6752311
Fax: 972-2-6752803
Website: http://www.molsa.gov.il/

National Insurance Institute
13 Weizmann Blvd.
Jerusalem 91909
Tel: 972-2-6709211
Fax: 972-2-6709792
Website: http://www.btl.gov.il

MINISTRY OF PUBLIC SECURITY

Kiryat Hamemshala
P.O.B. 18182
Jerusalem 91181
Tel: 972-2-5309999
Fax: 972-2-5847872
Website: http://www.mops.gov.il/

Israel Police
Website: http://www.police.gov.il

Israel Prison Service
Hahistadrut 5
Jerusalem
Tel: 972-2-6225222
Website: http://www.ips.gov.il

MINISTRY OF SCIENCE AND TECHNOLOGY

Kiryat Hamemshala Hamizrahit
Building No. 3
Jerusalem 91181

Tel: 972-2-5411111
Website: http://www.most.gov.il

MINISTRY OF TOURISM

5, Bank of Israel Street
Kiryat Ben-Gurion
Jerusalem 91009
Tel: 972-2-6754811
Fax: 972-2-6733592
Websites: http://www.tourism.gov.il/

Ministry of Transport
5, Bank of Israel Street
Kiryat Ben-Gurion
Jerusalem 91009
[P.O.B. 867, Jerusalem 91008]
Tel: 972-2-6663333
Contact information
Website: http://www.mot.gov.il

Ports and Railways Authority
Public Relations
74 Derech Petah-Tikva
P.O.B. 2021
Tel-Aviv 61201
Tel: 972-3-5657000
Fax: 972-3-5617142
Website: http://www.israports.org.il

Israel Airports Authority
Ben-Gurion Airport
Tel: 972-3-9712804
Fax: 972-3-9712436
For information on taxes and tarrifs:
Tel: 972-3-9715596
Website: http://www.iaa.gov.il

BANK OF ISRAEL

P.O.B. 780
Kiryat Ben-Gurion
Jerusalem 91007
Tel: 972-2-6552211
Fax: 972-2-6528805
Website: http://www.bankisrael.gov.il

NATIONAL AUTHORITY OF RELIGIOUS SERVICES

7 Kanfei Nesharim
Jerusalem
Tel: 972-2-5311385
Fax: 972-2-5311310
Website: http://www.religions.gov.il

CHIEF RABBINATE OF ISRAEL

80 Yirmiyahu Street
Jerusalem
- Chief Ashkenazi Rabbi
  Tel: 972-2-5313191
  Fax: 972-2-5377872
  E-mail: rabbiae@rabbinate.gov.il
- Chief Sephardi Rabbi
  Tel: 972-2-5313190
  Fax: 972-2-5371305
  E-mail: rabbis@rabbinate.gov.il

STATE COMPTROLLER AND OMBUDSMAN

12 Beit Hadfus St.
Givat Shaul, Jerusalem
POB 1081,
Jerusalem 91010
Tel: 972-2-6665000
Fax: 972-2-6665204
Website: http://www.mevaker.gov.il

MINISTERSS - NAMES AND CONTACTS

Ministry	Minister	Phone
Agriculture and Rural Development	Uri Ariel	02.6553701
Communications	Eyub Kara	02.6706301
Construction and Housing	Yoav Galant	02.5847211
Culture and Sport	Miri Regev	
Defense	Avigdor Lieberman	03.6955476
Economy	Eli Cohen	02.6220383
Education	Naftali Bennett	02.5602330
Energy and Water Resources	Yuval Steinitz	02.5316100
Environment	Zeev Elkin	02.6553777
Finance	Moshe Kahlon	02.5317200
Foreign Affairs	Benjamin Netanyahu	02.6535015
Health	Yakov Litzman	02.6787626
Immigrant Absorption	Ze'ev Elkin	02.5618163
Justice	Ayelet Shaked	02.6708527
Labor, Welfare and Social Services	Haim Katz	02.6752523
Prime Minister	Benjamin Netanyahu	02.6705555
Public Security	Gilad Erdan	02.5821191

Ministry	Minister	Phone
Religious Services	David Azoulay	
Science	Ophir Akunis	02.3847400
Senior Citizens	Gila Gamliel	02.6547002
The Interior	Arie Deri	02.5660166
Tourism	Yariv Levin	02.6754852
Transport	Yisrael Katz	02.6228200

Note: * Ministry of Energy was called Ministry of National Infrastructures prior to 2012.

ISRAELI SECURITY FORCES

Security forces in **Israel** (also known as **Israel security establishment**, include a variety of organizations, including law enforcement, military, paramilitary, governmental, and intelligence agencies.

MILITARY

- **Israel Defense Forces**: Israel's Defense forces, comprising the Army, Air Force and Navy.

POLICE

- **Israel Police**: a civilian force. As with most other police forces in the world, its duties include crime fighting, traffic control and maintaining public safety.

- **Civil Guard** (*Mishmar Ezrahi*): A volunteer organization of Israeli citizens which assists in daily police work. It is a subdivision of the Israel Police.
- **Border Police** (*Magav*): the military branch (gendarmerie) of the Israeli Police.

INTELLIGENCE

- **Shabak (Israel Security Agency)** *Sherut HaBitahon HaKlali* (Hebrew: שירות הבטחון הכללי, "General Security Agency"): the organization responsible for internal security, including in the Israeli-occupied territories.
- **Mossad (The Institute)** *HaMosad LeModi'in VLeTafkidim Meyuhadim* (Hebrew: המוסד למודיעין ולתפקידים מיוחדים, "The Institute for Intelligence and for Special Tasks"): the agency responsible for foreign intelligence.
- **Aman (Directorate of Military Intelligence)** *Agaf HaModi'in*: Military intelligence, or Aman, produces comprehensive national intelligence estimates for the prime minister and cabinet, daily intelligence reports, risk of war estimates, target studies on nearby countries, and communications intercepts. Aman also conducts across-border agent operations. Aman is an independent service, co-equal with the army, navy and air force. Aman has an estimated staff of 7,000.

EMERGENCY SERVICES

- **Magen David Adom (Red Shield of David)**: Magen David Adom (MDA) is made up of volunteer and professional medical responders and provides the Israel's pre-hospital emergency medical needs, including disaster, ambulance, and blood services.
- **Israel Fire and Rescue Services**: They are responsible for extinguishing fires and extracting people trapped in structures (ranging from stuck elevators to collapsed buildings).
- **Home Front Command**: part of the IDF. A military rescue team which handles large-scale civilian disasters such as earthquakes, collapsed buildings and missile attacks on cities.
- **Unit 669**: the Israeli Air Force airborne medevac extraction unit.
- 11 Local Rescue teams in the Golan Heights, Galilee-Carmel, Jezreel Valley, Samaria, Ein Gedi, Megilot, Gush Etzion, Arad, Negev, Arava, and Eilat-Eilot.

OTHER ORGANIZATIONS

- **Israel Prison Service**: *Sherut Batei ha-Sohar*. The Israel Prison Service (IPS), sometimes called by its acronym SHABAS, is a security organization which is an integral part of Israel's system of law enforcement. Its chief roles include the holding of prisoners and detainees under secure and suitable conditions, while preserving their dignity, and meeting their basic needs. The IPS coordinates with relevant national, regional and municipal authorities and organizations.
- **Knesset Guard**: The Knesset has its own guard and usher unit, headed by the Sergeant-at-Arms. The Knesset Guard is in charge of security in the Knesset compound and building. The Serjeant-at-Arms ("Katzin ha-Knesset") is the commander of the Knesset Guard

LOCAL GOV ERNMENT

BASIC INFORMATION

The **local governments of Israel** also known as local authorities), are the set of bodies charged with providing services such as urban planning, zoning, and the provision of drinking water and emergency services, as well as education and culture, as per guidelines of the Interior Ministry for communities of all sizes in the country. Almost all local governments take one of three forms: city councils, which governs a large municipality, local councils, which governs a small municipality, and regional councils, which governs a group of communities, often but not necessarily of a rural nature.

The basis of local government in Israel are municipalities (Moats iriot) in the cities, local councils (Moatsot mecomiot) in townships of urban or rural type and district councils (Moatsot esoriot), which unite groups of small settlements. There are 66 municipalities, 148 local and 53 district councils in Israel. Local authorities are responsible for health, education and culture, social welfare and public utilities (maintenance of water supply and sewage, repair of roads, garbage collection, etc.), as well as the appointment and collection of local taxes and fees, maintenance of parks and areas recreation, fire service and the like. Control over the activities of local governments is entrusted to the Ministry of Internal Affairs, which approves their budget, the size of municipal taxes and state subsidies,

The law defines three types of local authorities: municipalities, local councils and regional councils. Municipalities administer urban towns, generally with a population of over 20,000. In 1995, the number of such municipalities totaled 51. The three largest cities are Jerusalem, the capital (population 670,000), Tel Aviv (population 359,000) and Haifa (population 272,000). There are nine medium-sized municipalities of 110,000 to 160,000 residents, while most municipalities have a population of about 20,000 to 80,000.

Smaller urban towns and large rural settlements are governed by local councils, with powers similar to those of a municipality. More than 70 out of 150 local councils serve a population of more than 5,000.

The regional councils are in fact two-tier local authorities. The lower tier is the settlements, which are mostly agricultural; they are authorized to elect a local committee for providing municipal services. The upper tier is the regional council, which includes candidates from each settlement in the council's jurisdiction. It possesses the powers of a local council.

Municipal federations of adjacent local authorities are a single-purpose local authority, providing certain services such as fire-fighting, working together mainly because of economies of scale. The federation has a separate budgetary framework and may sign contracts, legislate by-laws, levy taxes and so forth.

Functions

The local authority provides its residents, commercial firms, and other institutions within its area of jurisdiction with a wide range of services. It develops its physical infrastructure, road system, water supply, refuse collection and disposal system, sewage system, and parks. It is responsible for environmental protection (public health, nuisances, cleanliness, etc.) and, with the Ministry of Education, Culture and Sport, the education system. The local authority builds schools and provides for their equipment and maintenance. Pre-kindergartens and secondary education institutions are established and administered by the local authority, but some of these facilities may be owned by non-profit organizations with aid given by the local authority. Local authorities also promote and financially assist cultural and sports activities (libraries, museums, youth clubs, etc.) and some maintain orchestras, choirs, theaters and similar enterprises.

The local authority provides social welfare services, with its social workers taking care of families in need, as well as special groups such as the elderly, retarded children, drug addicts and the like.

The local council has an important role in town planning. The Planning and Building Law, 5725-1965, sets forth the principles according to which town planning is undertaken, as well as planning institutions that must act at the local, district, and countrywide geographic and administrative levels. The law grants the local planning commission considerable independence, while also expanding the regional and countrywide dimensions in planning. The local planning commission is comprised of members of the local council. The law gives the local planning commission responsibility for day-to-day management and on-site compliance with regulations.

The district planning commission is a joint state-local authority comprised of representatives of those government ministries whose field of action is relevant to the issues of planning, and of representatives of the local authorities in the region. The district commission approves detailed local plans and also acts as a forum for handling appeals of decisions made by local commissions. The local council is authorized to issue by-laws in every area in which it has jurisdiction. It has the power to enforce those by-laws as well as the laws and regulations applicable to its functions.

The local authorities are empowered to levy local taxes and imposts and collect various payments for services and concessions. In general, they have the powers and means to manage their finances. The prepare their own budgets, which then must be approved by the Ministry of the Interior. Each municipality must employ an auditor to check its activities.

The Union of Local Authorities is a voluntary organization of municipalities and local councils. The regional councils are organized separately in the Organization of Regional Councils, since they have special problems which differ from other local authorities. Both organizations have a central goal, to further the mutual interests of the local authorities in their relations with government ministries and the Knesset (parliament). The Union represents the local authorities in negotiations for collective wage agreements and it signs such agreements together with the Histadrut (New General Federation of Labor) and the government. It also hosts various associations of key local officials such as the Association of Town Clerks and the Association of Local Treasurers.

All Israeli local governments are operated under a strong Mayor–council system. They appoint a head, or mayor, who is selected through a process of democratic elections along with his fellow council members. If a council's operation is impeded by a severe financial crisis, the Interior Minister may dissolve it, fire the council head, and appoint a special commission to operate the council until normalisation. Councils may enact bylaws for improvement of the residents' quality of life, and in addition to the levy of direct taxes, are allocated funds from the national government via the Interior Ministry. City and local councils are united in the framework of the "Centre for Local Government in Israel", founded in 1938, while regional councils are organised in a separate body.

Local authorities are responsible for providing citizens, firms, and institutions within its jurisdiction with a number of services:

- Physical infrastructure
    - Road system

    - Water supply
    - Refuse collection and disposal
    - Sewage systems
    - Parks
- Environmental protection
    - Public health
    - Nuisances
    - Cleanliness
- Education (joint responsibility with Ministry of Education)
    - Education
        - Construction of schools
        - Provision of equipment
        - Maintenance
- Culture & Sports (financial support and promotion)
    - Libraries
    - Museums
    - Youth clubs
    - Orchestras
    - Theaters
    - Sport facilities
- Social welfare
    - Families in need,
    - Special groups such as the elderly, disabled children, drug addicts

The income in the ordinary budget of local authorities comes from three sources: locally-generated income, government participation and loans for balancing the ordinary budget. From the early 1970s to the mid-1980s, locally-generated income was low and government participation was high; from then on the proportions were reversed.

Government financial participation includes two categories: the general grant and earmarked participation. The general grant is provided to the local authorities without being tied to any specific expenditure, since it is meant to be a supplement to local taxes for those authorities with a low collection potential.

Most of the earmarked income originates in the Ministry of Education, Culture and Sport and the Ministry of Labor and Social Welfare. The former covers the salaries of some educational personnel, as well as full or partial coverage of other projects operated by the local authority. The Ministry of Labor and Social Welfare finances 75 percent or more of local authority welfare activities according to standards set by the Ministry. As most local authorities exceed these standards, actual government participation amounts to 60-66 percent of local welfare expenditures.

Government ministries provide grants and loans to finance development projects such as educational and cultural facilities, roads, water and sewage systems, as well as general development grants for projects selected by local preference. Occasionally loans have been granted to balance the authorities' regular budgets and reduce deficits.

The State Commission on Local Government, which was appointed by a decision of the central government, presented its final report in 1981. Its main recommendations related to new financial relations with the central government and to the minimizing of central supervision over local authorities. Thus, in the 1980s and 1990s, some additional functions and responsibilities were given to local government in physical, social and educational arenas. Studies show that local authorities generally succeed in fulfilling their duties and in completing projects which they initiate, even though many approvals are involved in the process. The influence of the local authority is relatively wide in many areas, even when the central government controls the purse strings or other factors.

POLITICS AND DEVELOPMENTS

The **politics of Israel** is dominated by Zionist parties. They traditionally fall into three camps, the first two being the largest: Labor Zionism (social democrat), Revisionist Zionism (conservative) and Religious Zionism. There are also several non-Zionist Orthodox religious parties, non-Zionist left-wing groups, as well as non-Zionist and anti-Zionist Israeli Arab parties.

POLITICAL CONDITIONS

Golda Meir, Prime Minister of Israel from 1969 to 1974, once joked that "in Israel, there are 3 million prime ministers". The particular version of proportional representation used, in which the whole country is a single constituency, encourages the formation of a large number of political parties, many with very specialized platforms, and often advocating the tenets of particular interest-groups.

The prevalent balance between the largest parties means that the smaller parties can have strong influence disproportionate to their size. Due to their ability to act as tie breakers, they often use this status to block legislation or promote their own agenda, even contrary to the manifesto of the larger party in office.

From the founding of Israel in 1948 until the election of May 1977, Israel was ruled by successive coalition governments led by the Labor Alignment (or Mapai prior to 1967). From 1967 to 1970, a national unity government included all of Israel's parties except for the two factions of the Communist Party of Israel. After the 1977 election, the Revisionist Zionist Likud bloc (then composed of Herut, the Liberals, and the smaller La'am Party) came to power, forming a coalition with the National Religious Party, Agudat Israel, and with others.

The 2013 Freedom in the World annual survey and report by U.S.-based Freedom House, which attempts to measure the degree of democracy and political freedom in every nation, ranked Israel as the Middle East and North Africa's only free country

POLITICAL ISSUES

Major issues in Israeli political life include:

- The Israeli-Palestinian conflict and Arab-Israeli conflict
- The relationships between Jewish religious movements
- The nature of the state of Israel; (e.g. in what ways should it represent Judaism and in what ways should it represent secular democracy?) (see Jewish State and Religion in Israel)
- The Economy, and social issues.

JUDICIAL SYSTEM

The **Israeli judicial system** consists of secular courts and religious courts. The law courts constitute a separate and independent unit of Israel's Ministry of Justice. The system is headed by the President of the Supreme Court and the Minister of Justice

Israel has a three-tier court system. At the lowest level are magistrate courts, situated in most cities across the country. Above them are district courts, serving both as appellate courts and courts of first instance; they are situated in five of Israel's six districts. The third and highest tier is the Supreme Court, located in Jerusalem; it serves a dual role as the highest court of appeals and the High Court of Justice. In the latter role, the Supreme Court rules as a court of first instance, allowing individuals, both citizens and non-citizens, to petition against the decisions of state authorities. Although Israel supports the goals of the International Criminal Court, it has not ratified the Rome Statute, citing concerns about the ability of the court to remain free from political impartiality.

Israel's legal system combines three legal traditions: English common law, civil law, and Jewish law. It is based on the principle of *stare decisis* (precedent) and is an adversarial system, where the parties in the suit bring evidence before the court. Court cases are decided by professional judges rather than juries. Marriage and divorce are under the jurisdiction of the religious courts: Jewish, Muslim, Druze, and Christian. A committee of Knesset members, Supreme Court justices, and Israeli Bar members carries out the election of judges. Administration of Israel's courts (both the "General" courts and the Labor Courts) is carried by the Administration of Courts, situated in Jerusalem. Both General and Labor courts are paperless courts: the storage of court files, as well as court decisions, are conducted electronically. Israel's Basic Law: Human Dignity and Liberty seeks to defend human rights and liberties in Israel.

SECULAR COURTS

SUPREME COURT

Located in Jerusalem, the Supreme Court acts as a further appellate court, hearing both criminal and civil cases. The Supreme Court re-evaluates decisions by the lower, district courts. Sitting as the **High Court of Justice**, it acts as a court of first instance, often in matters concerning the legality of decisions regarding state authorities.

DISTRICT COURTS

The District Courts constitute the middle level courts of the judicial system, and have jurisdiction in any matter not within the sole jurisdiction of another court. In criminal matters, the courts have jurisdiction over cases where the accused faces a penalty of at least seven years imprisonment. In civil cases, they have jurisdiction over cases in which more than two and a half million shekels are in dispute. District courts also hear appeals of judgments of the magistrate courts, as well as cases involving companies and partnership, abritration, prisoners petitions, and appeals on tax matters. Sitting as courts for administrative matters, they can hear petitions against arms of the government. One also sits as the court of admiralty, hearing all cases involving shipping commerce, accidents on the sea and the like.

Most cases are heard by a single judge, though the court president can choose to appoint a three-judge panel. Cases where the accused is charged with an offense punishable by at least ten years in prison and appeals from magistrate courts are heard by three-judge panels. There are six such courts, one in each district of Israel.

MAGISTRATE COURTS

The Magistrate courts serve as basic trial courts. In criminal matters, they hear cases where the accused faces up to seven years imprisonment, and in civil cases, have jurisdiction over matters up to two and a half million shekels. They also have jurisdiction over the use and possession of real property. The courts also act as traffic courts, municipal courts and family courts. Sitting as small-claims courts, they have jurisdiction over cases involving claims up to 30,000 shekels. Rather than following standard evidentiary rules, they require extensive pleadings and documentation upon filing of a formally written complaint. Verdicts are expected seven days from trial. Cases are heard by a single judge unless the court president decides to appoint a three-judge panel. There are 30 magistrate courts.

LABOR COURTS

There are five Regional Labor Courts in Israel as a tribunal of first instance, and one National labor court in Jerusalem hearing appeals and few cases of national importance, as first tier. They are vested with exclusive jurisdiction over cases involving employer-employee relationship, pre-employment, post-employment strikes and labor union disputes, as well as labor related complaints against the National Insurance Institute, and claims under the *National Health Insurance Law.*

The Labor Courts Law sets forth those matters within the jurisdiction of the Labor Court. Substantially all causes of action arising from the employer-employee relationship are within the court's jurisdiction.

In civil matters, the Labor Courts are not bound by the rules of evidence. Most cases are heard by a panel of three, including a Judge, a representative on behalf of employees and a representative on behalf of employers.

MILITARY COURTS

The Military Court of Appeals is the highest judicial body in the Israel Defense Forces (IDF). The land, air and naval branches of the IDF, each of its military districts, the General Staff and the Home Front Command maintain their own special military courts. Military courts are used to try soldiers charged with military offenses, and deal with most criminal and security cases in the Israeli-occupied territories.

CRIMINAL PROCEDURE

Israel is unique among Western nations due to the absence of juries in its legal system. Rather, all trials are conducted before either one judge or a three-judge panel.

A suspect arrested in Israel is typically interrogated by police. Though police are allowed to lie to a suspect during interrogation, anyone facing police interrogation has the right to consult a lawyer beforehand, and an interrogating officer must warn a suspect that he or she does not have to say anything self-incriminating, and that anything said might be used against them in court.

Everyone accused of a criminal offense has the right to be represented by an attorney, and if the accused cannot afford a private attorney, one is assigned to them from the Public Defender's Office. Prosecutions are handled by the State Attorney's Office, which consists of a central bureau and eight regional offices.

Following a verdict, the defense or prosecution has the right to appeal to a higher court. Israeli law also provides for the possibility to ask the Supreme Court for a new trial, though it is very rare to be granted a retrial. Between 1948 and 2012, only 21 cases were granted a retrial, about half of which ended in reconfirmation of a defendant's guilt.

Administrative detention and closed trials are allowed in cases involving security and illegal immigration. Anyone subjected to administrative detention and a possible closed trial has the right to be represented by an attorney, and may appeal their detention to the Supreme Court. The burden of proof rests on the prosecution to prove that closed proceedings are necessary.

The vast majority of criminal cases investigated by police and considered for indictment are closed due to lack of evidence or lack of public interest. Of those cases that do go to court, over 85% end with a plea bargain. Though accepting a plea bargain is considered a *de facto* guilty plea, it also leads to a lighter sentence. Of the cases that do go to trial, 71.5% end with a conviction on some of the charges and acquittal on others, 21.6% with a conviction on all charges, and 0.3% with a full acquittal. Another 2.1% of cases are dismissed after the defendant is found incompetent to stand trial, 1.2% are dismissed over technicalities, and in 0.9% pf cases the charges are dropped.

JUDICIAL SELECTION

Judges who serve on the Supreme Court, as well as the district and magistrate courts, are appointed by the Judicial Selection Committee, which consists of nine members: the Minister of Justice and another cabinet member, two Knesset members, two members of the Israel Bar Association, and the President of the Supreme Court and two other Supreme Court justices. The committee is chaired by the Minister of Justice.

RELIGIOUS COURTS

JEWISH RELIGIOUS COURTS

The Jewish religious courts, known as Rabbinic Courts, whose *dayanim* ("judges") are selected by a committee headed by the Minister of Justice, have jurisdiction regarding marital issues of Jews (especially divorce). Divorce of a Jewish couple can only be obtained at the Rabbinical Batei Din. However, if a petition for ancillary matrimonial reliefs, such as custody, support or equitable distribution of property is filed with the Civil Courts before a case for divorce is opened at the Batei Din, then all other marital issues may also be taken by Magistrate Courts sitting as Family Courts. Otherwise, if one spouse opens some sort of an action with the Batei Din, (including asking the couple for reconciliation), the Batei Din assume that all ancillary relief is aggregated into the main complaint, and the spouses may find themselves facing judicial deermination pursuant to Halakha (Jewish religious law), and not pursuant to the secular law. Thus, spouses may lose the equal protection and anti gender discrimination protections of the secular civil law.

The Supreme Rabbinic Court acts as the court of last resort for cases brought before the rabbinic courts.

NON-JEWISH RELIGIOUS COURTS

The Muslim, Christian and Druze have their own religious courts which have similar jurisdiction over their followers, although Muslim religious courts have more control over family affairs. They are supervised by their own official religious establishments (although the Muslim and Druze *kaddis* judges are also elected by the Knesset). This is the maintenance of an agreement reached with the British Mandatory Authorities before the State of Israel's establishment in 1948.

LEGAL PRACTICE

As of 2012, there are 52,142 active lawyers in Israel, making it the country with the highest number of active lawyers per capital in the world. Law schools produce new graduates at the rate of 2,000 new lawyers a year. This creates a tight and highly competitive market

LOCAL GOVERNMENT IN ISRAEL

The **local governments of Israel** (Hebrew: רשות מקומית; also known as local authorities), are the set of bodies charged with providing services such as urban planning, zoning, and the provision of drinking water and emergency services, as well as education and culture, as per guidelines of the Interior Ministry for communities of all sizes in the country. Almost all local governments take one of three forms: city councils, which governs a large municipality, local councils, which governs a small municipality, and regional councils, which governs a group of communities, often but not necessarily of a rural nature.

All Israeli local governments are operated under a strong Mayor–council system. They appoint a head, or mayor, who is selected through a process of democratic elections along with his fellow council members. If a council's operation is impeded by a severe financial crisis, the Interior Minister may dissolve it, fire the council head, and appoint a special commission to operate the council until normalisation. Councils may enact bylaws for improvement of the residents' quality of life, and in addition to the levy of direct taxes, are allocated funds from the national government via the Interior Ministry. City and local councils are united in the framework of the "Centre for Local Government in Israel", founded in 1938, while regional councils are organised in a separate body.

ROLES

Local authorities are responsible for providing citizens, firms, and institutions within its jurisdiction with a number of services:

- Physical infrastructure
    - Road system
    - Water supply
    - Refuse collection and disposal
    - Sewage systems
    - Parks
- Environmental protection
    - Public health
    - Nuisances
    - Cleanliness
- Education (joint responsibility with Ministry of Education)
    - Education
        - Construction of schools
        - Provision of equipment
        - Maintenance
- Culture & Sports (financial support and promotion)
    - Libraries
    - Museums

    - Youth clubs
    - Orchestras
    - Theaters
    - Sport facilities
- Social welfare
    - Families in need,
    - Special groups such as the elderly, retarded children, drug addicts

OTHER ABILITIES AND RESPONSIBILITIES

Local councils in particular have an important role in ensuring the principles put forward in the Planning and Building Law, 5725-1965, are adhered to. The district planning commission is a joint state-local authority which approves detailed local plans and acts as a forum for handling appeals of decisions. The local council is also authorized to issue by-laws in every area in which it has jurisdiction and has the power to enforce these laws as well as the laws and regulations applicable to its functions. Furthermore local authorities are allowed to levy local taxes and collect various payments for services and concessions. They prepare their own budgets, although these then must be approved by the Ministry of the Interior.

GOVERNMENT, ELECTIONS AND POLITICAL DEVELOPMENTS

ISRAELI GOVERNMENTAL AND POLITICAL structures stem from certain premises and institutional arrangements generally associated with West European parliamentary democracies, East European and Central European institutions and traditions, and even some Middle Eastern sociopolitical patterns. These influences were transmitted though the unique history, political culture, and political institutions of Israel's formative prestate period and the Middle Eastern environment in which it is situated. The legitimacy of Israeli society and the identification by the majority Jewish population with the state and its institutions rest on several foundations: Zionist Jewish nationalism, the existence of an outside threat to Israeli security, Judaism, collectivism, and democracy. These bases are affected by the Arab/Palestinian-Israeli conflict (hereafter the Arab-Israeli conflict) and by the pluralist nature of Israeli society, in which a substantial Arab minority participates in the country's political system, but has an ambivalent role within the majority Jewish society

The Israeli political system is characterized by certain West European democratic arrangements: elected government, multiparty competition, a high level of voter participation in local and national elections, an independent judiciary that is the country's foremost guardian of civil liberties, a vigorous and free press, and the supremacy of civilian rule. Other features, such as collectivism and a lack of expension of the liberal component in Israeli politics, are distinctly East European and Central European in origin. These features are expressed by the absence of a written constitution limiting the powers of government and imposing restraints on the majority to safeguard the rights of individuals, particularly in matters of civil rights and relations between state and religious interests. In the late 1980s, increasing disagreement over some fundamental questions, for instance, the state's territorial boundaries and the role of religion in the state, led to a breakdown in the pre-1967 national consensus over such issues. Such disagreement has resulted in intense ideological polarization as reflected in electoral and parliamentary stalemates between the two major political parties--Likud (Union) and the Israel Labor Party (generally referred to as the Labor Party or simply Labor)-- and their allies.

In July 1984, the political system faced a challenge of unprecedented magnitude. For the first time in the country's thirty-six-year postindependence history, neither major party was able to form a coalition government without the other's equal participation. The result, the National Unity Government formed in September 1984, represented a milestone in the country's political development. That development had already undergone an unprecedented shock in May 1977, when the left-of-center Labor Party was voted out of office for the first time after nearly half a century of unbroken political dominance in pre- and post-state Israel. In 1977 a newly mandated regime was ushered in under Prime Minister Menachem Begin, who led the right-of-center Likud Bloc and who differed sharply with the Labor Party over political philosophy and both domestic and foreign policy. Likud was reconfirmed in power by the 1981 elections, but it suffered an almost irreparable blow with Begin's resignation in September 1983, which followed a series of failed policies concerning the 1982 invasion of Lebanon and the domestic economy.

The less charismatic and more cautious Yitzhak Shamir succeeded Begin. Under the terms of the National Unity Government, established in September 1984, the leader of the Labor Party, Shimon Peres, was entrusted with the formation of a government with himself as prime minister, on the written understanding that he would relinquish the prime ministership in two years' time--halfway through the parliamentary term--to his designated "vice prime minister" (or vice premier) Shamir. The next elections to the Knesset (parliament--see Glossary) were held in November 1988; by reproducing the same inconclusive electoral results as in 1984, they led to the formation of a second Likud-and-Labor-led National Unity Government, except that this time Labor joined as a junior partner. Following a period of protracted coalition bargaining, Shamir was reinstated as prime minister, with Peres moving from the Ministry of Foreign Affairs to the Ministry of Finance. Moshe Arens, a former Likud minister of defense and a Shamir ally, was appointed minister of foreign affairs, and Labor's Yitzhak Rabin became minister of defense.

From 1984 to 1988, the National Unity Government acted as a joint executive committee of Labor and Likud. Under its direction, the Israel Defense Forces (IDF) withdrew to an Israeli-dominated security zone in southern Lebanon; Israel's runaway inflation, which had plagued the economy under previous Likud rule, was curbed; and divisive political debates on major national issues were, to some extent, subdued. Nevertheless, on major issues such as participation in United States-sponsored peace initiatives to resolve the Arab-Israeli conflict, the exchange of "land for peace," and the political future of the West Bank (see Glossary) and Gaza Strip territories, unity between Labor and Likud was lacking. The unity cabinet became deadlocked as each partner continuously strove to advance its own foreign policy agenda. In the latter half of the unity government's term, from 1986 to 1988, consensus on domestic issues disintegrated as the parties prepared for the 1988 Knesset elections. For the most part, this breakdown in consensus continued following the elections; although the United States began a dialogue with the Palestine Liberation Organization (PLO), the government continued to preserve the status quo on security issues.

In the State of Israel, which was founded on May 14, 1948, as in other democratic states, the democratic rule is rooted in the following principles and institutions: basic laws which lay down the order of government and of the citizens' rights; the holding of elections to the house of representatives and to municipal councils every few years, following which, a central government and local authorities are set up, based on the principle of the rule of the majority, with the rights of the minority guaranteed by law; the principle of the separation between the legislative branch, the executive branch, and the judiciary, to which the institution of state control has been added; freedom of the press.

THE ELECTORAL SYSTEM

The elections in Israel are general, equal and secret. On the national level they are held at least once every four years, and on the municipal level at least once every five years. Israel has a system of proportional representation, and the whole state is considered a single constituency. Every party running for election presents a list of candidates, and the number of candidates entering the house of representatives is proportional to the percentage of support the list receives. Every citizen over the age of 18, whose name appears in the list of voters, may vote.

POLITICAL FRAMEWORK: ELITE, VALUES, AND ORIENTATIONS

When Israel became independent, its founding political elite, associated mainly with Mapai, had almost three decades of experience in operating self-governing institutions under the British Mandate. The top Mapai/Labor Party leaders continued to dominate Israeli politics for another three decades. Their paramount influence for over half a century as founders, architects, and prime movers of a Jewish national homeland has had an enduring effect on their successor generation and the political scene in Israel. The elite, political culture, social structure, and social makeup of any nation entwine in complex ways and in the process shape the character and direction of a given political system. This process holds true especially in Israel, where ideological imperatives and their institutionalization have constituted an important part of the country's evolution.

The first generation of Israeli leaders came to Palestine (which they called Eretz Yisrael, or Land of Israel) mainly during the Second Aliyah (see Glossary) between 1900 and 1920. The Ashkenazim (Jews of European origin), who constituted the majority among the Yishuv's mostly Labor Zionist political and socioeconomic elites, were impelled by Zionist ideals. The majority held to Labor Zionism, while others adhered to moderate General Zionism (sometimes called Political Zionism) or right-wing Revisionist Zionism.

To the early immigrants, the themes promoted by the different Zionist movements provided powerful impulses for sociopolitical action. These pioneers were essentially Labor Zionists with an abiding faith in the rectitude of values that stressed, among other things, the establishment of a modern Jewish nation promoting mutual assistance under the principle of "from each according to his ability, to each according to his needs," abolition of private ownership of the means of production, and the idea that human consciousness and character were conditioned by the social environment.

They also held that Jewish land should be developed in a collectivist agricultural framework, that well-to-do Jews in the Diaspora should materially aid the cause of the Jewish homeland, and that the Jews of the Diaspora should seek the fullest measure of redemption by immigrating to the new Yishuv. In addition, collectivist values of East European and Central European origin, in which the founding generation had been socialized, affected the political orientation of Israel both before and after independence.

The value system of the first generation came to be exemplified first and foremost in the communal and egalitarian kibbutz and to a lesser extent in the moshav. Together these institutions accounted for less than 3 percent of the Jewish population at any given time, but they have held a special place in Israeli society as the citadel of pioneer ideology. They also gave Israel a distinctive self-image as a robust, dedicated, egalitarian, "farmer- or citizen-soldier" society. The kibbutzim also produced numbers of national leaders out of proportion to their small population; they also provided the country with some of its best soldiers and officers.

The founding generation of Israeli leaders, including David Ben-Gurion, Yitzhak Ben-Zvi, Berl Katznelson, Moshe Sharett, and later, Levi Eshkol and Golda Meir, in effect shaped the country's socioeconomic structures and political patterns. These people were instrumental in establishing the original Labor Zionist parties beginning in 1905, in merging them to establish Mapai in 1930, and in organizing the Histadrut and Jewish self-defense institutions, such as the Haganah (see Glossary), which later became the Israel Defense Forces (IDF) in 1920. These formative, nation-building organizations, along with the quasi-governmental Elected Assembly (Asefat Hanivharim--see Glossary), the National Council (Vaad Leumi), the WZO, and the Jewish Agency, served as the Yishuv's national institutions, shaping the character of postindependence Israel.

From its earliest days, Mapai, which had an interlocking leadership with the Histadrut, dominated Israeli public life, including the top echelons of the IDF, the WZO, and the Jewish Agency. Its legitimacy as a ruling party was seldom questioned because it was identified with the mystique of the Zionist struggle for independence, patriotism, and the successful consolidation of statehood. The essentially secular political values espoused by Mapai leaders were endorsed by most of the Jewish population. The absence of effective alternative governing elites or countervalues within the country's multiparty coalition-type government system made it difficult to challenge the Mapai-controlled political mainstream. Moreover, political patterns from the 1920s until the June 1967 War generally discouraged the rise of radical right-wing or left-wing destabilizing tendencies. This trend was rooted in the overall political dominance of Israel's Labor Party and its predecessors and the strength of the mutual restraints inherent in Israel's political subcultures.

Mainstream Israeli society is composed of persons who represent pluralistic cultural and political backgrounds. Politically, some Israeli Jews have liberal West European orientations; others were reared in more collectivist Central European and East European environments, or in authoritarian Middle Eastern political cultures. Some are religiously more traditional than others, but even among Orthodox Jews, shades of conviction vary substantially over the role of Jewish customary laws and the relationship between the state and religion. Thus, the founding generation had to develop a political system that reconciled and accommodated the varied needs of a wide range of groups.

The political system within Israel proper, excluding the West Bank and the Gaza Strip, is geared to the broadest possible level of public participation. Political activities are relatively free, although authoritarian and antidemocratic tendencies were evident among some of the leaders and supporters of right-wing ultranationalist parties and factions. In the late 1980s, the impetus to "agree to disagree" within the democratic framework of conciliation began to show some weakening as a result of intense polarizing controversies over the future of the occupied territories and various disputes over issues concerning the state and religion.

By the early 1970s, Jews of Sephardic origin (popularly referred to in Israel as Oriental Jews) outnumbered their Ashkenazic counterparts as a demographic group. The older Sephardim were, in general, from politically authoritarian and religiously traditional North African and Middle Eastern societies that regarded the Central European and West European secular and social democratic political value spectrum as too modern and far-reaching as compared to their own. They were accustomed to strong authoritarian leaders rather than ideals emphasizing social democratic collectivism and popular sovereignty. Nonetheless, a sizable proportion of Sephardim joined Labor's ranks both as leaders and rank-and-file party members.

Oriental Jews came to be referred to in the 1960s as "the Second Israel"--the numerically larger but socially, culturally, economically, and politically disadvantaged half of the nation. Not all Orientals were economically deprived, but nearly all of those who were relatively poor belonged to Sephardic communities. The communal gap and attendant tensions between Ashkenazic and Sephardic Jews have naturally engaged the remedial efforts of successive governments, but results have fallen far short of Oriental expectations. The problem was partly rooted in the country's political institutions and processes. Ashkenazic dominance of sociopolitical and economic life had been firmly institutionalized before independence. Over the years, however, Sephardic representation substantially increased in the country's major political parties, and as of the 1980s, Sephardic Jews occupied leadership positions in many municipalities.

Not surprisingly, beginning in the 1950s, most Sephardim tended to vote against Mapai and its successor, Labor. Both were perceived as representing the Ashkenazic establishment, even though Sephardim were always represented among the ranks of party leaders. In the 1950s and early 1960s, while many Sephardim were impressed with Ben-Gurion's charismatic and authoritative leadership, they nevertheless tended to support Herut, the major opposition party led by Menachem Begin, whose right-wing populism and ultranationalist, anti-Arab national security posture appealed to them. Paradoxically, the socialist-inspired social welfare system, a system built by Mapai and sustained by Labor and the Labor-dominated Histadrut, benefited the Sephardim particularly. In general, the Sephardim tended to support the right-wing Gahal/Likud blocs that for years had advocated a substantial modification of the welfare system so as to decrease its socialist emphasis. In terms of long-range electoral trends, the Sephardic position did not augur well for the Labor Zionist elite of the Labor Party.

Pressure for greater political representation and power has come from the younger, Israeli-born generation of both Ashkenazic and Sephardic origins. As a group, they were less obsessed with the past than their elders. The youth have been moving toward a strong, industrialized, capitalist, Western-style, middle-class society as the national norm. Although some younger right-wing ultranationalists and right-wing religious advocates continued to be imbued with the extremist nationalism and religious messianism of their elders--as shown, for example, by their support of parties favoring annexation of the occupied territories--most of the younger generation were more secular, pragmatic, and moderate on such issues.

The concerns of secular young people went beyond the question of "Who is a Jew"--which they continuously had to confront because of right-wing religious pressures--to such critical issues as the quality of education, social status, economic conditions, and the comforts of modern life. Their primary interests have been how to make Israel more secure from external threat and how to improve the quality of life for all. Nevertheless, for many Israelis, the founding ideologies remained a ritualized part of national politics.

Urbanization and industrialization were equally potent forces of change; their adulterating effect on Israel's founding ideology has been particularly significant. They have led to new demands, new opportunities, and new stresses in social and economic life affecting all social and political strata. The older commitment to agriculture, pioneering, and collectivism has crumbled before the relentless pressure of industrialization and the bridging of the gap between urban and rural life. Collective and communal settlements have become increasingly industrialized; factories and high-technology industries have been set up; the mass media have faciliated an influx of new information and ideas; and additional layers of bureaucratic and institutional arrangements have emerged. Kibbutz idealism, the pride of Israel, has declined, especially among increasingly individualistic and consumer-oriented young people. To stem this tide and to retain young members, kibbutz federations and individual kibbutzim have established many educational and vocational programs and activities.

As the 1970s began, the social base of Israeli politics had become highly complex, and political fluidity resulted. A major catalyst in creating a new mood was the October 1973 War, known in Israel as the Yom Kippur War, which dealt a crushing blow to popular belief in Israel's strength and preparedness in the face of its Arab adversaries. The result was a loss of confidence in the political and national security elite, headed at the time by Prime Minister Golda Meir, Minister of Defense Moshe Dayan, and Minister-without-Portfolio Israel Galilee. After the war, in which Egyptian and Syrian forces scored military gains, many charges and countercharges concerned inadequate military preparedness. Nevertheless, Meir's government returned to power in the country's parliamentary elections held on December 31, 1973. Apparently, despite widespread misgivings, many Israelis believed that continuity was preferable to change and uncertainty under Begin's newly formed and untried center-right Likud Bloc.

Meir's resignation from the prime ministership in April 1974 resulted in a succession crisis and the departure of the last of Labor's old guard party leaders, mostly in their late sixties and seventies, such as Meir, Pinchas Sapir, and Israel Galilee. Meir's departure triggered political infighting among the Labor elite, specifically between the former Mapai and Rafi (Israel Labor List--see Appendix B) factions; a new generation centered around the triumvirate of Yitzhak Rabin, Shimon Peres, and Yigal Allon, succeeded Meir.

The second most striking political development in the 1970s was the ascendance of a new right-wing counterelite in May 1977. An upset victory in the ninth parliamentary elections, called an "earthquake" by some, brought Begin's center-right Likud to power, ending Labor's half a century of political dominance. The new political elite won primarily because of the defection of former Labor leaders and previous Labor voters to the Democratic Movement for Change (DMC), which had been founded in 1976 by Yigal Yadin and several other groups. Despite the subsequent collapse of the DMC and the defection of moderates from the Likud-led cabinet--for example, former Minister of Defense Ezer Weizman formed his own list Yahad (Together--see Appendix B) in 1981 and Minister of Foreign Affairs Moshe Dayan created Telem--Likud's success in the tenth parliamentary elections of 1981 resulted from its continued ability to present itself as a viable governing group and a party dedicated to ultranationalism and territorial expansionism.

The top echelons of the Israeli political elite as of the late 1980s were still predominantly of European background; many of them had either immigrated to Palestine during the 1930s and the 1940s or had been born in the Yishuv to parents of East European or Central European origin. A growing number of Oriental politicians, however, were making their mark in the top ranks of all the major parties and at the ministerial and subministerial levels. A majority of the elite had a secular university education, while a minority had a more traditional religious education. The political elite was overwhelmingly urban--most resided in Tel Aviv, Jerusalem, or Haifa. A minority, particularly the Sephardim, came from the newer development towns. Among the elite who resided in rural areas most, especially members of Labor and its satellites, represented communal kibbutzim and, to a lesser extent, moshavim.

By occupational category, professional party politicians constituted by far the largest single group, followed, in numerical order, by lawyers, kibbutz officials, educators, Histadrut or private sector corporate managers, journalists, ex-military officers, and, to a lesser degree, functionaries of religious institutions. Many of the elite were in the forty-to-mid-sixty age bracket. In 1988 the political elite numbered more than 200 individuals, excluding the broader social elite encompassing business, military, religious, educational, cultural, and agricultural figures. The number would be greater if senior officials in such key offices as the Office of the Prime Minister and the ministries of defense, foreign affairs, finance, and commerce, as well as the Histadrut and its industrial and financial enterprises and trade unions, were included.

The power of individual members of the elite varied depending on their personal reputation and their offices. The most influential were found in the cabinet. Members of the Knesset came next. Elected mayors of large municipalities such as Tel Aviv, Jerusalem, and Haifa had considerable importance because of the influence of local politics on national-level politics. In addition, the president, Supreme Court justices, and the head of the Office of the State Comptroller had the prestige of cabinet members although they lacked decision-making responsibility.

During the late 1980s, the criteria for entrance into the top elite were more open and competitive than previously. Political parties, and, to some extent, the civil service, continued to be the principal vehicles for upward mobility. Under the country's electoral system of proportional representation, participation in party politics remained essential for gaining top positions, except in limited cases of co-optation from nonparty circles, principally the military. In earlier periods, party nominating committees primarily determined a politician's entry into a parliamentary delegation; in the 1980s, internal party elections increasingly governed this decision. This system placed a high premium on partisan loyalty, membership in a party faction, and individual competence.

The political establishment, whether in office or in opposition, secularist or Orthodox, left-wing or right-wing, has remained basically loyal to the state. Establishment interpretations of classical Zionist ideologies have varied according to the adherents' diverse backgrounds and political and religious orientations, but internal political cleavages have not undermined the essential unity of Israeli society and political institutions. Except for certain segments among a minority of extremist right-wing religious or secular ultranationalists, most Israeli citizens have sought to maintain democratic values and procedures; their differences have centered mainly on tactics rather than on the goal of realizing a modern, democratic, prosperous social welfare state.

MULTIPARTY SYSTEM

Political power in Israel has been contested within the framework of multiparty competition. Parliamentary elections are held every four years, and, unlike many parliamentary systems, the electorate votes as a single national constituency. Power has revolved around the system of government by coalition led by one of the two major parties, or in partnership among them. From the establishment of Mapai in 1930 until the 1977 Knesset elections, Labor (and its predecessor, Mapai) was the dominant party. Labor's defeat in the 1977 Knesset election, however, transformed the dominant party system into a multiparty system dominated by two major parties, Labor and Likud, in which neither was capable of governing except in alliance with smaller parties or, as in 1984 and 1988, in alliance with each other.

Since 1920, when the first Elected Assembly was held, no party has been able to command a simple majority in any parliamentary election. Israel has always had a pluralistic political culture featuring at least three major polarizing social and political tendencies: secular left-of-center, secular right-of-center, and religious right-of-center. No single tendency was dominant in the 1980s. Political fragmentation, as marked by the proliferation of parties, is a long-standing feature of Israeli society.

For example, in the prestate period, between 1920 and 1944, from twelve to twenty-six party lists were represented in the Elected Assembly. In the first Knesset election in 1949, twenty-four political parties and groups competed. Since then the number has fluctuated as a result of occasional splits, realignments, and mergers. However, dominance by two major parties and a multiplicity of smaller parties remained deeply embedded in Israeli political culture (for details of individual political parties, see Appendix B).

In addition to political operations, party functions during the prestate period included "democratic integration," that is, the provision of social, economic, military, and cultural services for party members and supporters. During the postindependence period, party politics, in particular regarding competition between Labor and Likud and their respective allies, continued to be vigorous. Many analysts saw signs of a political crisis looming with the emergence of extremist minor parties and extraparliamentary protest movements (e.g., Kach and Gush Emunim). These groups challenged the traditional parties on such issues as the roles of the state and religion and the future territorial boundaries of the Jewish state.

Israel's major parties originated from the East European and Central European branches of the WZO, founded by Theodor Herzl in 1897, and from political and religious groups in the Mandate period. For example, a faction called the Democratic Zionists, including among its members Chaim Weizmann, Israel's first president, was active in 1900; Mizrahi (Spiritual Center), an Orthodox religious movement, was founded in 1902; and the non-Marxist Labor Zionist HaPoel HaTzair (The Young Worker), was established in 1905. Aaron David Gordon, the latter group's spiritual leader, was instrumental in founding the first kibbutz and moshav soon after the party's establishment (see Political Zionism , ch. 1). Moreover, in 1906 the Marxist Poalei Tziyyon (Workers of Zion--see Appendix B) was created to initiate a socialist-inspired class struggle in Palestine. Ber Borochov was its ideological mentor, and Ben-Gurion and Ben-Zvi were among its founding leaders. Vladimir Jabotinsky founded the right-wing Revisionist Party in 1925 to oppose what he considered the WZO executive's conciliatory policy toward the British mandatory government and toward the pace of overall Zionist settlement activity in Palestine.

These early, formative experiences in political activity produced three major alignments. All were Zionist, but they had varying shades of secularism and religious orthodoxy. Two of the alignments were secular but ideologically opposed. The first consisted of leftist or socialist labor parties of which Mapai, founded in 1930, was the dominant party. The second consisted of centrist-rightist parties; Herut (Freedom Movement--see Appendix B), founded in 1949, the Revisionist Party's successor and the present Likud's mainstay, dominated that alignment. Herut, which had become part of Likud, eventually won a mandate to govern in 1977 under Begin. The third major political alignment consisted of Orthodox religious Zionists. A fourth category of minor Zionist parties also emerged, traditionally allied with one of the two major alignments; non-Zionist communist Arab or nationalist Arab parties constituted the fifth grouping.

In the late 1980s, the stated values of Israeli political parties, including religious, communist, Arab nationalist, and mainstream parties, could not properly be placed on the left-right or liberal-conservative spectrum except, perhaps, on the issue of the future of the occupied territories. The positions advocated by Labor, Likud, Orthodox religious parties, and the constellation of smaller parties allied to them have varied greatly. On the extreme left, the most anti-Western element in Israeli politics was Rakah (New Communist List--see Appendix B), a Moscow-oriented group with a contingent of former Sephardic Black Panther activists that appealed to Palestinian Arab nationalist sentiment. Of the long-established minor parties, the moderate left-of-center Mapam (formally Mifleget Poalin Meuchedet, United Workers' Party--see Appendix B), which from 1969 to 1984 constituted a faction in the electoral alignment with Labor, the Citizens' Rights Movement and Shinui, were Labor's traditional satellites. Labor, in alignment with Mapam from 1969 until 1984, favored a negotiated settlement concerning the occupied territories involving the exchange of land for peace.

On the center-right of the political spectrum were Likud and its satellite parties, Tehiya, Tsomet, and Moledet. On the fringe right was Kach, which the Knesset outlawed in 1988 because of its racist platform that wished to expel all Arabs from the occupied territories. Likud, especially its Herut component, favored retaining much of the occupied territories to regain what it considered to be the ancient boundaries of Eretz Yisrael. The positions of the religious parties--the National Religious Party (NRP--see Appendix B), Agudat Israel, Shas (Sephardic Torah Guardians--see Appendix B), and Degel HaTorah (Torah Flag--see Appendix B)--generally coincided with the right-of-center parties, although the NRP trade-union component has continued its alliance with Labor in the Histadrut.

Israeli parties have engaged in many activities even in nonelection years. Indoctrination of young people has been important, although in the case of the Labor Party it had markedly lessened in the 1980s in comparison to the prestate period. Political parties retained much of their early character as mutual aid societies. Consequently, voters have tended to support the country's political parties as a civic duty. Membership in a registered party has not been a requirement for voting, but formal party membership was high and party members have accounted for 25 to 50 percent of the vote.

Except for small Arab and communist groups, Israeli political parties have been basically Zionist in their orientation. Given the shades of interpretation inherent in Zionism, parties drew their support from adherents who might be secular, religious, or antireligious, adherents of social welfare policies or free enterprise (the distinction was not always clear because Mapai/Labor in fact created Israel's capitalist economy), advocates of territorial compromise or territorial expansion. In general, attempts to organize parties on the basis of ethnic origin--for example, in the cases of Yemeni, Iraqi, or Moroccan Jews--had been unsuccessful until the early 1980s, when the Sephardi-based Tami (Traditional Movement of Israel--see Appendix B) and Shas were formed.

With the exception of religious parties, Israeli parties possessed national constituencies but also engaged in politics based on territorial subdivisions and local interests. Increasingly during the late 1980s, local party branches enjoyed greater independence in selecting local personalities in internal party nominations for mayoral, municipal council, Histadrut, and Knesset elections, as well as their own parties' central committees and conventions. This independence resulted in part from the growing tendency to vote on the basis of individual merit--mayoral elections, for example, reflected an emerging pattern of split-ticket voting--rather than traditional party loyalty. This trend, if sustained, is likely to lead to the decentralization of party control, if only to ensure that voters will support the same party in national as well as local elections.

CIVIL-MILITARY RELATIONS

The supremacy of civilian authorities over the military has rarely been challenged in Israel's history. The Lavon affair of 1954 remains the major exception. Factors weighing against military interference have included the prohibition on active officers engaging in politics and the population's broad support for the nonpartisan behavior of the armed forces. Given the ever-present external threat to Israeli security, however, the military looms large in everyday life. This has led some foreign observers to call Israel a "garrison democracy." The military has also served as a channel into politics, with political activity providing a "second career" for retired or reservist officers after they complete their military careers, usually between the ages of forty and fifty. This phenomenon has left its mark on Israeli politics as high-ranking retired or reservist IDF figures have often "parachuted" into the leadership ranks of political parties and public institutions.

The most frequent instances of this tendency have occurred during the demobilization of officers in postwar periods, for example, following the 1948, 1967, and 1973 wars.

Until the June 1967 War, the great majority of reservist or retired officers joined Labor's ranks. In the 1950s, the first generation of such officers included Moshe Dayan, Yigal Allon, Yigal Yadin, Israel Galilee, and Chaim Herzog. After 1967, the number of such officers co-opted into the political elite rose sharply, with many for the first time joining center-right parties. Among those joining the Labor Party were Yitzhak Rabin, Haim Bar-Lev (*bar*, son of-- see Glossary), Aharon Yariv, and Meir Amit. Ezer Weizman, Ariel (Arik) Sharon, Mordechai Zipori, and Shlomo Lahat joined Likud. Despite their widespread participation in politics, these exmilitary officers have not formed a distinct pressure group. The armed forces have generally remained shielded from partisan politics. The only possible exception was the IDF's military action in Lebanon in June 1982, which disregarded the cabinet's decision on the limits of the advance. The invasion occurred while Ariel Sharon was minister of defense (1981-83) and Rafael Eitan was chief of staff (1979-83); both individuals had stressed the independent policy role of the IDF

VOTING METHOD

Israel's voting method is simplified by the fact that voters vote for a political party and not specific candidates in a closed list system.

On election day, and upon entry to a polling station, the voter is given an official envelope, and shown to a voting booth.

Inside the booth is a tray of slips, one for each party. The slips are printed with the "ballot letters" of the party (between one and three Hebrew or Arabic letters), the full official name of the party, and sometimes a slogan in small print. Each party publicizes their letter prior to election day, with most election posters featuring them. As many political parties in Israel are known by their acronyms, several parties can spell out their name in two or three letters, and thus use their name as their ballot letters (e.g. Meretz and Hetz).

The voter chooses the relevant slip for their party, puts it in the envelope, seals it, and then places the envelope into the ballot box.

Parties use the equivalent letters in both official languages, Arabic and Hebrew; for instance Kadima use כן (Kaph-Nun) in Hebrew and كن (also Kaph-Nun) in Arabic. Because the Arabic alphabet shares a common source with the Hebrew (the Aramaic alphabet), each Hebrew letter has a perfectly corresponding Arabic one, facilitating this system.

The system has the advantage of being simple to use for those with limited literacy. This is especially important in Israel where many new immigrants struggle with the language, especially reading and writing, as Hebrew uses a unique alphabet.

Each party must register its chosen letters with the Israeli Central Elections Committee, and certain letters are reserved. If a new party wishes to use letters from an older party, it must receive permission from that party. Example of reserved letters are Mem, Het and Lamedh for Likud and Shin and Samekh for Shas.

ISRAELI LEGISLATIVE ELECTION, 2015

FOREIGN POLICY AND NATIONAL SECURITY

Israel maintains diplomatic relations with 157 countries and has 100 diplomatic missions around the world.

Only three members of the Arab League have normalized relations with Israel: Egypt and Jordan signed peace treaties in 1979 and 1994, respectively, and Mauritania opted for full diplomatic relations with Israel in 1999. Despite the peace treaty between Israel and Egypt, Israel is still widely considered an enemy country among Egyptians. Under Israeli law, Lebanon, Syria, Saudi Arabia, Iraq, Iran, Sudan, and Yemen are enemy countries and Israeli citizens may not visit them without permission from the Ministry of the Interior.

The Soviet Union and the United States were the first two countries to recognize the State of Israel, having declared recognition roughly simultaneously, although to be strictly correct the initial recognition by the United States on 14 May 1948 was only to recognise *the provisional government as the de facto authority of the new State of Israel.*

The United States may regard Israel as its primary ally in the Middle East, based on "common democratic values, religious affinities, and security interests".The United States has provided $68 billion in military assistance and $32 billion in grants to Israel since 1967, under the Foreign Assistance Act (period beginning 1962), more than any other country for that period until 2003. Their bilateral relations are multidimensional and the United States is the principal proponent of the Arab-Israeli peace process. The United States and Israeli views differ on some issues, such as the Golan Heights, Jerusalem, and settlements.

India established full diplomatic ties with Israel in 1992 and has fostered a strong military, technological and cultural partnership with the country since then. According to an international opinion survey conducted in 2009 on behalf of the Israeli Foreign Ministry, India is the most pro-Israel country in the world. India is the largest customer of Israeli military equipment and Israel is the second-largest military partner of India after the Russian Federation. India is also the third-largest Asian economic partner of Israel and the two countries enjoy extensive space technology ties. India became the top source market for Israel from Asia in 2010 with 41,000 tourist arrivals in that year.

Germany's strong ties with Israel include cooperation on scientific and educational endeavors and the two states remain strong economic and military partners. Under the reparations agreement, as of 2007 Germany had paid 25 billion euros in reparations to the Israeli state and individual Israeli holocaust survivors. The UK has kept full diplomatic relations with Israel since its formation having had two visits from heads of state in 2007. Relations between the two countries were also made stronger by former prime minister Tony Blair's efforts for a two state resolution. The UK is seen as having a "natural" relationship with Israel on account of the British Mandate for Palestine. Iran had diplomatic relations with Israel under the Pahlavi dynasty but withdrew its recognition of Israel during the Islamic Revolution.

Although Turkey and Israel did not establish full diplomatic relations until 1991, Turkey has cooperated with the State since its recognition of Israel in 1949. Turkey's ties to the other Muslim-majority nations in the region have at times resulted in pressure from Arab and Muslim states to temper its relationship with Israel. Relations between Turkey and Israel took a downturn after the Gaza War and Israel's raid of the Gaza flotilla. IHH, which organized the flotilla, is a Turkish charity that some believe has ties to Hamas and Al-Qaeda.

Relation between Israel and Greece have improved since 1995 due to the decline of Israeli-Turkish relations. The two countries have a defense cooperation agreement and in 2010, the Israeli Air Force hosted Greece's Hellenic Air Force in a joint exercise at the Uvda base. The joint Cyprus-Israel oil and gas explorations centered on the Leviathan gas field are also an important factor for Greece, given its strong links with Cyprus. Israel is the second largest importer of Greek products in the Middle East. In 2010, the Greek Prime minister George Papandreou made an official visit to Israel after many years, in order to improve bilateral relations between the two countries.

Israel and Cyprus have a number of bilateral agreements and many official visits have taken place between the two countries. The countries have ties on energy, agricultural, military and tourism matters. The prospects of joint exploitation of oil and gas fields off Cyprus, as well as cooperation in the world's longest sub-sea electric power cable has strengthened relations between the countries.

Azerbaijan is one of the few majority Muslim countries to develop bilateral strategic and economic relations with Israel. The relationship includes cooperation in trade and security matters and cultural and educational exchanges. Azerbaijan supplies Israel with a substantial amount of its oil needs, and Israel has helped modernize the Armed Forces of Azerbaijan. In the spring of 2012, the two countries reportedly concluded an arms deal worth $1.6 billion. In 2005, Azerbaijan was Israel's fifth largest trading partner.

In Africa, Ethiopia is Israel's main and closest ally in the continent due to common political, religious and security interests. Israel provides expertise to Ethiopia on irrigation projects and thousands of Ethiopian Jews (Beta Israel) live in Israel.

As a result of the 2009 Gaza War, Mauritania, Qatar, Bolivia, and Venezuela suspended political and economic ties with Israel

The cabinet, and particularly the inner cabinet, consisting of the prime minister, minister of foreign affairs, minister of defense, and other selected ministers, are responsible for formulating Israel's major foreign policy decisions. Within the inner cabinet, the prime minister customarily plays the major role in foreign policy decision making, with policies implemented by the minister of foreign affairs. Other officials at the Ministry of Foreign Affairs include, in order of their rank, the director general, assistant directors general, legal and political advisers, heads of departments, and heads of missions or ambassadors. While the director general may initiate and decide an issue, commit the ministry by making public statements, and respond directly to queries from ambassadors, assistant directors general supervise the implementation of policy. Legal and political advisers have consultative, not operational, roles. Heads of departments serve as aides to assistant directors general, administer the ministry's departments, and maintain routine contact with envoys. The influence of ambassadors depends on their status within the diplomatic service and the importance to the ministry's policy makers of the nation to which they are accredited.

In the Knesset, the Foreign Affairs and Security Committee, with twenty-six members, although prestigious, is not as independent as the foreign affairs committees of the United States Congress. Its role, according to Samuel Sager, an Israeli Knesset official, is not to initiate new policies, but to "legitimize Government policy choices on controversial issues." Members of the committee frequently complain that they do not receive detailed information during briefings by government officials; government spokesmen reply that committee members tend to leak briefing reports to the media.

Israeli foreign policy is chiefly influenced by Israel's strategic situation, the Arab-Israeli conflict, and the rejection of Israel by most of the Arab states. The goals of Israeli policy are therefore to overcome diplomatic isolation and to achieve recognition and friendly relations with as many nations as possible, both in the Middle East and beyond. Like many other states, throughout its history Israel has simultaneously practiced open and secret diplomacy to further its main national goals. For example, it has engaged in military procurement, the export of arms and military assistance, intelligence cooperation with its allies, commercial trade, the importation of strategic raw materials, and prisoner-of-war exchanges and other arrangements for hostage releases. It has also sought to foster increased Jewish immigration to Israel and to protect vulnerable Jewish communities in the Diaspora.

MINISTRY OF FOREIGN AFFAIRS (ISRAEL)

The **Israeli Ministry of Foreign Affairs** is one of the most important ministries in the Israeli government. The ministry's role is to implement Israel's foreign policy, and promote economic, cultural, and scientific relations with other countries. The Ministry of Foreign Affairs is located in the government complex in Givat Ram, Jerusalem.The current Foreign Affairs Minister is Avigdor Lieberman.

In the early months of 1948, when the government of the future State of Israel was being formed, the Ministry of Foreign Affairs was housed in a building in the abandoned Templer village of Sarona, on the outskirts of Tel Aviv. Moshe Sharett, formerly head of the Political Department of the Jewish Agency, was placed in charge of foreign relations.

Israel maintains diplomatic relations with 160 countries. It operates 70 embassies, 18 consulates-general and 5 special missions: a mission to the United Nations (New York), a mission to the United Nations institutions in Geneva), a mission to the United Nations institutions in Paris, a mission to the United Nations institutions in Vienna and an ambassdor to the European Union (Brussels).

In October 2000, Morocco, Tunisia and the Sultanate of Oman closed the Israeli offices in their countries and suspended relations with Israel. Niger, which renewed relations with Israel in November 1996, severed them in April 2002. Venezuela and Bolivia severed diplomatic ties with Israel in January 2009, in the wake of the IDF operation against Hamas in Gaza.

The new building of the Israeli Ministry of Foreign Affairs in Kiryat Ben-Gurion, the government complex near the Knesset, was designed by Jerusalem architects Kolker, Kolker and Epstein in association with Diamond, Donald, Schmidt & Co. of Toronto. The building consists of three wings: One houses the offices of the Foreign Minister and director-general, another houses the diplomatic corps and the library, and the third is used for receptions. The outside walls of the reception hall incorporate onyx plates that diffuse an amber light. In June 2001, the design won the prize for excellence from the Royal Institute of Architects of Canada. The building is described as a "sophisticated essay in the play between solid and void, mass and volume, and light and shadow

MINISTER

Avigdor Liberman, MK
Deputy Prime Minister and Minister of Foreign Affairs
(Yisrael Beitenu)

Avigdor Liberman

Avigdor Liberman was born in 1958 in Moldova and immigrated to Israel in 1978.
He served in the IDF, and has a B.A. in International Relations and Political Science from the Hebrew University of Jerusalem.

One of the founders of the Zionist Forum for Soviet Jewry, Avigdor Liberman was a member of the Board of the Jerusalem Economic Corporation and the Secretary of the Jerusalem branch of the Histadrut Ovdim Le'umit and was the editor of a newspaper (Yoman Yisraeli). Liberman served as Director-General of the Likud Movement from 1993-1996, and then as Director-General of the Prime Minister's Office (1996-1997). In 1999, he founded and became Head of the Yisrael Beiteinu Party.

First elected to the Knesset in 1999, he has served as a member of the Foreign Affairs & Defense Committee and State Control Committees, and as Chairman of the Israel-Moldova Parliamentary Friendship League.

In March 2001, Liberman was appointed Minister of National Infrastructures. He resigned his post in March 2002. He served as Minister of Transportation from February 2003 until June 2004. He served as Deputy Prime Minister and Minister of Strategic Affairs from October 2006 until his resignation in January 2008.

In March 2009, Avigdor Liberman was appointed Deputy Prime Minister and Minister of Foreign Affairs.

He is married, with three children.

THE IRANIAN THREAT: OVERVIEW

Iran, under the leadership of President Mahmud Ahmadinejad, is a rapidly growing threat to its own people, the peoples of the Middle East region, and the Western world.

Iran has long been involved in the sponsoring and support of worldwide terror groups and has been officially implicated for its involvement in terrorist activities in several Western states. It provides aid in the form of weapons, training, and funding to Hamas and other Palestinian terrorist groups, Hizbullah in Lebanon, Iraq-based militants, and Taliban fighters in Afghanistan.

Iran's behavior over the past several years suggests that it is actively pursuing a nuclear weapons program. While denying these allegations, Iran's behavior has led to its being sanctioned by various international bodies, including the IAEA and the U.N Security Council.

In the past decade, Iran has pursued all stages of developing nuclear weapons, including mining uranium, converting uranium to uranium hexafluoride, enriching uranium hexafluoride to obtain high-grade fissile material necessary for military use, and developing an implosion system needed for the detonation of nuclear devices. All this despite Iran's commitment to and ratification of the Treaty on the Non-Proliferation of Nuclear Weapons. In addition, Iran has developed weapons systems - primarily medium- and long-range ballistic missiles capable of delivering nuclear payloads to countries in the Middle East, Europe and soon North America.

In addition, Iran continues to violate and disregard the human rights of its own citizens, and represses freedom of the press, freedom of association, freedom of religion, equality, and children's rights.

Iran publically denies the Holocaust, and is the only country that openly calls for the annihilation of another state - the State of Israel.

President Ahmadinejad actively endorses chaos, so as to hasten the re-emergence of the Hidden Imam and spread true Islamic rule worldwide. He believes that the Hidden Imam will return only following an apocalyptic war against Israel and the West.

Prime Minister Benjamin Netanyahu (17 Feb 2010):

"We are threatened by an extremist form of Islam, headed by Tehran, which sends out its tentacles in the form of Hamas and Hizbullah and other terrorist organizations, which undermine the very existence of the State of Israel and speak openly about their desire to destroy it. This is not just a threat against Israel, but against the entire world...

There are tens of millions of people in Iran, the vast majority, aspiring to one thing - freedom from this brutal tyranny.

The character of this regime was exposed and their secret nuclear program was exposed. Now the question is what the international community will do in the face of this challenge. If sanctions include preventing the export of gasoline and, equally important, the importation of petroleum products, Iran's economy will be stopped. I hope the international community will rise to the occasion. I hope they understand the magnitude of this moment, this historic moment in time when the responsible countries of the world, which already understand the magnitude of the threat and the short period of time we have left, will do what is necessary."

ELECTORAL SYSTEM AND POLITICAL DEVELOPMENTS

BASIC INFORMATION

Elections in Israel are based on nationwide proportional representation. The electoral threshold is currently set at 3.25%, with the number of seats a party receives in the Knesset being proportional to the number of votes it receives. The Knesset is elected for a four-year term, although most governments have not served a full term and early elections are a frequent occurrence. Israel has a multi-party system based on coalition governments as no party has ever won a majority of seats in a national election, although the Alignment briefly held a majority following its formation by an alliance of several different parties prior to the 1969 elections. The legal voting age for Israeli citizens is 18. Elections are overseen by the Central Elections Committee and are held according to the Knesset Elections Law.

ELECTORAL PROCEDURE

Under normal circumstances, Israel's basic law requires national elections for the Knesset to take place on a Tuesday in the Jewish month of Cheshvan (late September through early November) four years following the previous elections. However, it is possible, and it often happens, that early elections can take place prior to the date set in the basic law. Early elections can be called by a vote of the majority of Knesset members, or by an edict of the President, and normally occur on occasions of political stalemate and of the inability of the government to get the parliament's support for its policies. Failure to get the annual budget bill approved by the Knesset by March 31 (3 months after the start of the fiscal year) also leads automatically to early elections. It is also possible to postpone the date of the election by a special majority of the Knesset members.

Israel uses the closed-list method of party-list proportional representation; thus citizens vote for their preferred party and not for any individual candidates. The 120 seats in the Knesset are then assigned (using the D'Hondt method) proportionally to each party that received votes, provided that the party gained votes which met or exceeded the electoral threshold. Parties are permitted to form electoral alliances so as to gain enough collective votes to meet the threshold (if so, the alliance ***as a whole*** must meet the threshold, not the individual parties) and thus be allocated seats. The low threshold makes the Israeli electoral system more favourable to minor parties than systems used in most other countries. Two parties can make an agreement so that both parties' sum of surplus votes are combined, and if the combined surplus votes amount to an extra seat, the extra seat goes to the party with the greater number of surplus votes.

Any Israeli citizen over 21 may be elected to the Knesset, except holders of several high positions in the civil service and officers or career soldiers (those should resign from their post before the elections), soldiers in compulsory service, and felons who were convicted and sentenced to prison terms exceeding three months (until seven years after their prison term expired).

The following people may not serve as a Member of Knesset (MK) due to their conflicting functions:

1. The President of the State of Israel
2. The two Chief Rabbis of the State of Israel
3. Any judge in the judicial system, so long as they still hold office
4. Any *dayan*, or judge in the Rabbinical Court system, so long as they still hold office
5. The State Comptroller
6. Rabbis or Ministers of religions, while receiving salaries for such a position

7. Senior state employees and senior army officers of such grades or ranks and in such functions as shall be determined by law

The following prevents a party from running a list in Knesset elections:

1. Negating the State of Israel as the state of the Jewish people
2. Negating the democratic nature of the State
3. Incitement to racism
4. Support of armed struggle against the State of Israel

After an election, the President, following consultations with the elected party leaders, chooses the Knesset member most likely to have the ability to form a viable (coalition) government. While this typically is the leader of the party receiving the most seats, it is not required to be so. In the event a party wins 61 or more seats in an election, it can form a viable government without having to form a coalition. However, no party has ever won more than 56 seats in an election; thus, a coalition has always been required. That member has up to 42 days to negotiate with the different parties, and then present his or her government to the Knesset for a vote of confidence. If the Knesset approves the proposed government (by a vote of at least 61 members), he or she becomes Prime Minister.

As the coalitions often prove highly unstable - given the number and diverse views of the political parties involved - parties (or portions thereof) quite commonly leave them. However, so long as the coalition has at least 61 members (and it is free to recruit from parties not originally in the coalition) it is entitled to remain in power. Such a case occurred with the 19th Knesset: Ehud Barak and four other members left the Labor in 2011 to form the Independence Party and continued their alignment with Likud, while the remaining eight Labor members remained with the party but left the coalition; after all the changes the Likud coalition retained the support of the minimum 61 members and so it remained in power. Once a coalition fails a motion of confidence it ceases to be in power, but has a prescribed time to form a new coalition, after which other parties can attempt to form one, before early elections must be called.

ISRAEL FOREIGN POLICY STRATEGY AND DEVELOPMENTS

The **foreign relations of Israel** refers to diplomatic relations and international agreements between the State of Israel and other countries around the world. Israel joined the United Nations on May 11, 1949. Today, Israel has diplomatic ties with 157 foreign states. Since 1967, diplomatic relations have been established with several Arab and Muslim countries. After signing peace treaties, Israel maintains full diplomatic relations and open borders with Egypt and Jordan.

After the establishment of the State of Israel in 1948, the Jewish state experienced diplomatic isolation and Arab League boycotts. Currently, of the 203 sovereign states today, Israel has diplomatic relations with 157 states. Some states recognize Israel as a state, but have no diplomatic relations. Others explicitly do not recognize Israel as a state. Several states below had once had diplomatic relations with Israel, but have since broken or suspended such relations (Bolivia, Venezuela, Nicaragua, Cuba in Latin America; Bahrain, Qatar, Mauritania, Morocco, Tunisia, Oman in Arab League; and Iran before the Islamic revolution).

NO RECOGNITION OR DIPLOMATIC RELATIONS

Israel has no diplomatic relations with 36 UN member states, 20 of them members of the 22-member Arab League, while majority of the remaining states are Muslim majority countries. Some of the countries, with which Israel has no diplomatic relations, accept Israeli passports and acknowledge other Israeli marks of sovereignty. Period of former relations marked in brackets. Israel has no diplomatic relations with the following 36 states;

- *Africa*: Algeria, Chad, Comoros, Djibouti, Guinea, Libya, Mali, Morocco (1994–2000), Mauritania (1999–2009), Niger, Somalia, Sudan, Tunisia.
- *Americas*: Bolivia (1950–2009), Cuba (1950–1973), Nicaragua (1992–2010), Venezuela (1950–2009).
- *East Asia*: North Korea.
- *Middle East*: Bahrain (1996–2000), Iran (1948–1951, 1953–1979), Iraq, Lebanon, Kuwait, Oman (1996–2000), Qatar (1996–2009), Saudi Arabia, Syria, Yemen, United Arab Emirates.
- *South, Central Asia*: Afghanistan, Bangladesh, Bhutan Pakistan.
- *Southeast Asia*: Brunei, Malaysia, Indonesia.

On January 14, 2009, Bolivia and Venezuela suspended diplomatic ties with Israel, and on January 16, 2009, Qatar and Mauritania suspended political and economic ties after Bashar al-Assad and Khaled Meshaal called on all Arab states to break ties with the Jewish state in the wake of the 2008–2009 Israel–Gaza conflict. On March 6, 2009, the Israeli diplomatic delegation to Mauritania left after nine years of diplomatic ties, following a demand from the Mauritanian authorities to close the Israeli embassy in Nouakchott within 48 hours. The Mauritanian delegation to Israel left earlier without sending official notice to the Israeli Ministry of Foreign Affairs.

The following 19 UN member states do not recognize Israel as a state: Afghanistan Algeria Bahrain Bangladesh, Chad, Cuba, Indonesia, Iran Iraq, Kuwait, Lebanon, Libya North Korea, Pakistan, Saudi Arabia, Sudan, Syria, United Arab Emirates and Yemen.

Non UN-member states: The Republic of China (Taiwan) recognizes Israel, but does not officially conduct relations (though there are "unofficial relations") due to Israel's recognition of the People's Republic of China. The Sahrawi Republic explicitly does not recognise Israel. Apart from the Holy See, which is a UN observer and recognises Israel, Israel recognises no non-UN member states. No other non-UN member states recognize Israel.

PARTIAL RECOGNITION OR TRADE AGREEMENTS

Comoros has no official diplomatic ties with Israel but the countries engage in mutual trade. In October 2000, Israeli diplomatic missions in Bahrain, Morocco, and Oman were closed, although trade and economic ties continue. Israeli tourism to Morocco is warmly welcomed. Israeli citizens are admitted into North Korea with Israeli passports, but like other foreign visitors they are asked to deposit their passport with the local authorities and use specially issued local documents for tourists. Since 2004, Israel has exported apples to Syria through the Quneitra crossing. In 2010, some 10,000 tons of apples grown by Druze farmers in the Golan Heights have been sent to Syria.

RELATIONS WITH MIDDLE EASTERN STATES

Despite the Arab-Israeli conflict, Israel has established formal diplomatic relations with Egypt and maintained a de facto peaceful relationship with Jordan. Israeli leaders have traveled to Morocco to discuss Israeli-Arab issues, and Morocco has often served as an intermediary between Israel and the other Arab states. In 1983 Israel signed a peace treaty with Lebanon, although it was quickly abrogated by the Lebanese as a result of Syrian pressure. Some secret diplomatic contacts may also have occurred between Israel and Tunisia.

EGYPT

In late 1988, about ten years after the signing of the Camp David Accords and the Treaty of Peace Between Egypt and Israel, a "cool" peace characterized Egyptian-Israeli relations. These relations had originally been envisioned as leading to a reconciliation between Israel and the Arab states, but this development has not occurred. EgyptianIsraeli relations have been restrained by a number of developments, including the June 1981 Israeli bombing of an Iraqi nuclear reactor, the Israeli invasion of Lebanon directed against Palestinian forces a year later, the establishment of an increasing number of Jewish settlements in the West Bank and the Gaza Strip, and the "watering down" of proposals for the autonomy of the Palestinian inhabitants of these territories as envisaged by the Camp David Accords and the Egyptian-Israeli peace treaty.

Relations between the two countries warmed somewhat during Peres's tenure as prime minister and minister of foreign affairs in the National Unity Government. They again cooled, however, following the establishment of the Likud-led cabinet in December 1988, and prime minister Shamir's rejection of Israeli participation in an international peace conference with the PLO. Nevertheless, the two countries continued to maintain full diplomatic relations, and in 1985 about 60,000 Israeli tourists visited Egypt, although Egyptian tourism to Israel was much smaller. Cooperation occurred in the academic and scientific areas as well as in a number of joint projects in agriculture, marine science, and disease control.

Another issue that had impeded normal relations between Egypt and Israel concerned the disposition of Taba, an approximately 100- hectare border enclave and tourist area on the Gulf of Aqaba in the Sinai Peninsula claimed by the two countries, but occupied by Israel. Following a September 1988 ruling in Egypt's favor by an international arbitration panel, official delegations from Israel and Egypt met to implement the arbitral award.

JORDAN

Secret or "discreet" contacts between the leaders of the Yishuv and later of Israel and the Hashemite Kingdom of Transjordan or Jordan began in the early days of the British Mandate and continued into the late 1980s. These covert contacts were initiated with King Abdullah, the grandfather of King Hussein, Jordan's present ruler. Some observers have speculated that, together with Jordan's annexation of the West Bank in 1950, these contacts may have been responsible for Abdullah's assassination by a Palestinian gunman in East Jerusalem in July 1951. According to Israeli journalists Yossi Melman and Dan Raviv, Hussein renewed Jordan's ties with Israel in 1963. Following Jordan's ill-fated participation in the June 1967 War, secret meetings took place between Hussein and Israeli leaders in 1968, and they lasted until Begin's accession to power in 1977. This "secret" relationship was revived in 1984, following Labor's participation in the National Unity Government, and intensified in 1986-87. The participants reached agreements on Israeli-Jordanian cooperation on such issues as the role of pro-Jordanian Palestinian moderates in the peace process, setting up branches of Jordan's Cairo-Amman Bank in the West Bank, and generally increasing Amman's influence and involvement in the West Bank's financial, agricultural, education, and health affairs, thus blocking the PLO. The last reported meeting between Minister of Foreign Affairs Peres and King Hussein took place in London in November 1987, when the two leaders signed a "memorandum of understanding" on a peace plan. Upon his return to Israel, however, Peres was unable to win support for the agreement in the Israeli cabinet.

MOROCCO

Morocco has been noted for its generally good relations with its own Jewish community, which in 1988 numbered approximately 18,000; in 1948 there had been about 250,000 Jews in Morocco. Over the years discreet meetings have occurred between Moroccan and Israeli leaders. Beginning in 1976, King Hassan II began to mediate between Arab and Israeli leaders. Then Prime Minister Yitzhak Rabin reportedly made a secret visit to Morocco in 1976, leading to a September 1977 secret meeting between King Hassan and Foreign Minister Moshe Dayan. King Hassan also played a role in the Egyptian-Israeli contacts that led to the 1978 Camp David Accords. In July 1978, and again in March 1981, Peres, as opposition leader, made secret trips to Morocco. In May 1984, thirty-five prominent Israelis of Moroccan origin attended a conference in Rabat. This meeting was followed by an official visit in May 1985 by Avraham Katz-Oz, Israel's deputy minister of agriculture, to discuss possible agricultural cooperation between the two countries. In August 1986, Moroccan agricultural specialists and journalists reportedly visited Israel, and Haim Corfu, Israel's minister of transport, attended a transportation conference in Morocco. On July 22 and 23, 1986, Prime Minister Peres met King Hassan at the king's palace in Ifrane. This was the first instance of a public meeting between an Arab leader and an Israeli prime minister since the Egyptian-Israeli meetings of the late 1970s. Hassan and Peres, however, were unable to agree on ways to resolve the Palestinian dimension of the Arab-Israeli conflict.

IRAN

Until the overthrow of the shah's regime in 1979, Israel and Iran had established government missions in both countries although this relationship was never formalized by an exchange of ambassadors. Under the shah, from 1953 to 1979, Iran was one of Israel's primary suppliers of oil and a major commercial partner. In addition, the intelligence services of the two countries cooperated closely, and Israel exported military hardware and provided training and other assistance to Iranian military forces. These close, but discreet, relations were abruptly terminated in 1979, upon the coming to power of the regime of Ayatollah Sayyid Ruhollah Musavi Khomeini and Iran's joining of the anti-Israel camp. Shortly thereafter, Iran called for the "eradication" of the State of Israel through armed struggle and its replacement by a Palestinian state. As a symbolic gesture, the PLO was given the building of the former Israeli mission in Tehran.

In the 1980s, however, Israeli concern about the fate of the approximately 30,000 Jews remaining in Iran, interest in assisting Iran in its war with Iraq, and cooperation with the United States in its efforts to free American hostages held by Iranian-backed Shia (see Glossary) extremists in Lebanon, led to a renewal of contacts between Israeli and Iranian leaders and shipments of Israeli arms to Tehran. Israel reportedly sent arms to Iran in exchange for Iran's allowing thousands of Jews to leave the country.

RELATIONS WITH THE UNITED STATES

For strategic security and diplomatic support, Israel has depended almost totally upon the United States. Since the establishment of the state in 1948, the United States has expressed its commitment to Israel's security and well-being and has devoted a considerable share of its world-wide economic and security assistance to Israel. Large-scale American military and economic assistance began during the October 1973 War, with a massive American airlift of vital military matériel to Israel at the height of the war. From 1948 through 1985, the United States provided Israel with US$10 billion in economic assistance and US$21 billion in military assistance, 60 percent of which was in the form of grants. From 1986 through 1988, total United States economic and military assistance to Israel averaged more than US$3 billion a year, making Israel the largest recipient of United States aid. Of the annual total, about US$1.8 billion was in Foreign Military Sales credits, and about US$1.2 billion was in economic assistance.

During the administration of President Ronald Reagan, the United States-Israeli relationship was significantly upgraded, with Israel becoming a strategic partner and de facto ally. A number of bilateral arrangements solidified this special relationship. In November 1983, the United States and Israel established a Joint Political-Military Group to coordinate military exercises and security planning between the two countries, as well as to position United States military equipment in Israel for use by American forces in the event of a crisis. In 1984 Israel and the United States concluded the United States-Israel Free Trade Area Agreement to provide tariff-free access to American and Israeli goods. In 1985 the two countries established a Joint Economic Development Group to help Israel solve its economic problems; in 1986 they created a Joint Security Assistance Group to discuss aid issues.

Also in 1986, Israel began participating in research and development programs relating to the United States Strategic Defense Initiative. In January 1987, the United States designated Israel a major non-NATO ally, with status similar to that of Australia and Japan. Two months later, Israel agreed to the construction of a Voice of America relay transmitter on its soil to broadcast programs to the Soviet Union. In December 1987, Israel signed a memorandum of understanding allowing it to bid on United States defense contracts on the same basis as NATO countries. Finally, the two countries signed a memorandum of agreement in April 1988 formalizing existing arrangements for mutually beneficial United States-Israel technology transfers.

Israel has also cooperated with the United States on a number of clandestine operations. It acted as a secret channel for United States arms sales to Iran in 1985 and 1986, and during the same period it cooperated with the United States in Central America.

The United States-Israeli relationship, however, has not been free of friction. The United States expressed indignation with Israel over an espionage operation involving Jonathan Jay Pollard, a United States Navy employee who was sentenced to life imprisonment for selling hundreds of vital intelligence documents to Israel. During the affair, Israeli government and diplomatic personnel in Washington served as Pollard's control officers. Nevertheless, United States government agencies continued to maintain a close relationship with Israel in sensitive areas such as military cooperation, intelligence sharing, and joint weapons research.

The main area of friction between the United States and Israel has concerned Washington's efforts to balance its special ties to Jerusalem with its overall Middle Eastern interests and the need to negotiate an end to the Arab-Israeli conflict, in which the United States has played a major mediating role. In 1948 the United States hoped that peace could be achieved between Israel and the Arab states, but this expectation was quickly dashed when Arab nations refused to recognize Israel's independence. American hopes were dashed again when in 1951 Jordan's King Abdullah, with whom some form of settlement seemed possible, was assassinated and in 1953 when the Johnston Plan, a proposal for neighboring states to share the water of the Jordan River, was rejected.

The June 1967 War provided a major opportunity for the United States to serve as a mediator in the conflict; working with Israel and the Arab states the United States persuaded the United Nations (UN) Security Council to pass Resolution 242 of November 22, 1967. The resolution was designed to serve as the basis for a peace settlement involving an Israeli withdrawal from territories occupied in the June 1967 War in exchange for peace and Arab recognition of Israel's right to exist. Many disputes over the correct interpretation of a clause concerning an Israeli withdrawal followed the passage of the UN resolution, which was accepted by Israel. The resolution lacked any explicit provision for direct negotiations between the parties. Although the Arab states and the Palestinians did not accept the resolution, it has remained the basis of United States policy regarding the Arab-Israeli conflict.

In December 1969, the Rogers Plan, named after United States Secretary of State William P. Rogers, although unsuccessful in producing peace negotiations, succeeded in ending the War of Attrition between Israel and Egypt that followed the June 1967 War and established a cease-fire along the Suez Canal. In 1971 United States Assistant Secretary of State Joseph P. Sisco proposed an "interim Suez Canal agreement" to bring about a limited Israeli withdrawal from the canal, hoping that such an action would lead to a peace settlement. The proposal failed when neither Israel nor Egypt would agree to the other's conditions.

In October 1973, at the height of the Arab-Israeli war, United States-Soviet negotiations paved the way for UN Security Council Resolution 338. In addition to calling for an immediate cease-fire and opening negotiations aimed at implementing Resolution 242, this resolution inserted a requirement that future talk be conducted "between the parties concerned," that is, between the Arab and the Israelis themselves.

In September 1975, United States secretary of state Henry Kissinger's "shuttle diplomacy" achieved the Second Sinai Disengagement Agreement between Israel and Egypt, laying the groundwork for later negotiations between the two nations. The United States also pledged, as part of a memorandum of understanding with Israel, not to negotiate with the PLO until it was prepared to recognize Israel's right to exist and to renounce terrorism.

Another major United States initiative came in 1977 when President Jimmy Carter stressed the need to solve the Arab-Israeli conflict by convening an international peace conference in Geneva, cochaired by the United States and the Soviet Union. Although Egyptian President Anwar as Sadat conducted his initiative in opening direct Egyptian-Israeli peace talks without United States assistance, the United States played an indispensable role in the complex and difficult negotiation process. Negotiations ultimately led to the signing, under United States auspices, of the September 17, 1978, Camp David Accords, as well as the March 1979 Treaty of Peace Between Egypt and Israel. The accords included provisions that called for granting autonomy to Palestinians in the West Bank and the Gaza Strip through a freely elected self-governing authority during a five-year transitional period; at the end of the period the final status of the occupied territories was to be decided. Carter had hoped that this process would enable the Palestinians to fulfill their legitimate national aspirations while at the same time safeguarding

Israeli security concerns. While criticizing the Begin government's settlement policy in the occupied territories, the Carter administration could not prevent the intensified pace of construction of new settlements.

Following Israel's invasion of Lebanon in early June 1982, on September 1, 1982, President Reagan outlined what came to be called the Reagan Plan. This plan upheld the goals of the Camp David Accords regarding autonomy for the Palestinians of the West Bank and the Gaza Strip and disapproved of Israel's establishment of any new settlements in these areas. It further proposed that at the end of a transitional period, the best form of government for the West Bank and the Gaza Strip would be self-government by the resident Palestinian population in association with Jordan. Under the plan, Israel would be obliged to withdraw from the occupied territories in exchange for peace, and the city of Jerusalem would remain undivided; its final status would be decided through negotiations. The plan rejected the creation of an independent Palestinian state. Although Labor leader Peres expressed support for the plan, Prime Minister Menachem Begin and the Likud opposed it, as did the PLO and the Arab states. The plan was subsequently shelved.

The United States nevertheless continued its efforts to facilitate Arab-Israeli peace. In March 1987, the United States undertook intensive diplomatic negotiations with Jordan and Israel to achieve agreement on holding an international peace conference, but differences over Palestinian representation created obstacles. In Israel, Likud prime minister Shamir and Labor minister of foreign affairs Peres were at odds, with Shamir rejecting an international conference and Peres accepting it. Peres and Labor Party minister of defense Rabin reportedly held talks with Jordan's King Hussein, who wanted the conference to include the five permanent members of the UN Security Council, as well as Israel, the Arab states, and the PLO. The Reagan administration, on the other hand, was reluctant to invite the Soviet Union to participate in the diplomatic process. The administration insisted that any prospective conference adjourn speedily and then take the form of direct talks between Israel and Jordan. The administration also insisted that the conference have no power to veto any agreement between Israel and Jordan.

A major difficulty involved the nature of Palestinian representation at a conference. A Soviet-Syrian communiqué repeated the demand for PLO participation, which Israel flatly rejected. The United States asserted that, as the basis for any PLO participation, the PLO must accept UN Resolutions 242 and 338 with their implied recognition of Israel's right to exist. Both the PLO mainstream and its radical wings were unwilling to agree to this demand. The Palestinian uprising (*intifadah*) in the West Bank and the Gaza Strip began in December 1987. In February 1988, Secretary of State George Shultz visited Israel, Egypt, Jordan, and Syria; in a statement issued in Jerusalem he called for Palestinian participation, as part of a Jordanian/Palestinian delegation, in an international peace conference. The PLO rejected this initiative. The United States proposal called for a comprehensive peace providing for the security of all states in the region and for fulfillment of the legitimate rights of the Palestinian people.

The proposal consisted of an "integrated whole" and included the following negotiating framework: "early negotiations between Israel and each of its neighbors willing to do so," with the door "specifically open for Syrian participation"; "bilateral negotiations . . . based on United Nations Security Council Resolutions 242 and 338 in all their parts"; "the parties to each bilateral negotiation" to determine "the procedure and agenda of the negotiation"; "negotiations between an Israeli and a Jordanian/Palestinian delegation on arrangements for a transitional period for the West Bank and Gaza," with the objective of completing "these talks within six months"; and "final status negotiations" beginning "on a date certain seven months after the start of transitional talks," with the objective of completing the talks "within a year."

On March 26, 1988, Shultz met with two members of the Palestine National Council (PNC), which represents Palestinians outside Israel various political and guerrilla groups with the PLO, and associated youth, student, women's and professional bodies. According to a PLO spokesman, the PNC members, Professors Ibrahim Abu Lughod and Edward Said, both Arab Americans, were authorized by Yasir Arafat to speak to Shultz, and they later reported directly to the PLO leader about their talks. Little resulted from this meeting, however, and Shultz found no authoritative party willing to come to the conference table.

The United States once again involved itself in the peace process to break the stalemate among the Arab states, the Palestinians, and Israel following King Hussein's declaration on July 31, 1988, that he was severing most of Jordan's administrative and legal ties with the West Bank, thus throwing the future of the West Bank onto the PLO's shoulders. PLO chairman Yasir Arafat thereby gained new international status, but Shultz barred him from entering the United States to address the UN General Assembly in early December because of Arafat's and the PLO's involvement in terrorist activities. When Arafat, following his December 14 address to a special session of the UN General Assembly in Geneva, met American conditions by recognizing Israel's right to exist in "peace and security," accepted UN Resolutions 242 and 338, and renounced "all forms of terrorism, including individual, group and state terrorism," the United States reversed its thirteen-year policy of not officially speaking to the PLO.

The Israeli National Unity Government, installed in late December, denounced the PLO as an unsuitable negotiating partner. It did not accept the PLO's recognition of Israel and renunciation of terrorism as genuine.

Whether the United States-PLO talks would yield concrete results in terms of Arab-Israeli peace making remained to be seen as of the end of 1988. Notwithstanding the possibility of future progress, the new willingness of the United States to talk to the PLO demonstrated that, despite the special relationship between the United States and Israel and the many areas of mutual agreement and shared geopolitical strategic interests, substantial differences continued to exist between the United States and certain segments of the Israeli government. This was especially true with regard to the Likud and its right-wing allies.

RELATIONS WITH AFRICAN STATES

Until the early 1970s, Israel sent hundreds of agricultural experts and technicians to aid in developing newly independent sub-Saharan African states, seeking diplomatic relations in return. The Arab countries, however, exerted pressure on such states to break ties with Israel. Most African states eventually complied with this pressure because of their need for Arab oil at concessionary prices and because of Arab promises of financial aid. Furthermore, Israel received heavy criticism from African nations because of its relations with South Africa. Moreover, Israeli support for the Biafran secessionist movement in Nigeria alarmed the members of the Organization of African Unity, many of whom faced threatening national liberation movements in their own countries. The June 1967 Israeli occupation of the West Bank, the Gaza Strip, and the Sinai Peninsula stirred a sense of unease among the African states; after the October 1973 War twenty-nine African states severed diplomatic relations with Israel. Malawi, Lesotho, and Swaziland were the only sub-Saharan countries to maintain diplomatic relations with Israel.

The African "embargo" of Israel began to collapse after the 1978 Camp David Accords and the establishment of diplomatic relations between Egypt and Israel. Following Zaire's lead in 1982, Liberia (1983), the Côte d'Ivoire (1986), Cameroon (1986), and Togo (1987) renewed diplomatic ties with Israel. Kenya, Gabon, Senegal, and Equatorial Guinea have also shown interest in renewing diplomatic relations. Several other African countries, although maintaining their diplomatic distance, nevertheless had unofficial ties with Israel, as expressed by the presence of

Israeli advisers and technicians. Ghana had an Israeli "interests office," and Nigeria, Sierra Leone, and the Central African Republic all maintained unofficial ties with Israel.

Israeli military expertise and technical skills, particularly in desert reclamation, have often facilitated ties with the sub-Saharan nations. In Cameroon, Israel built a training center to assist in halting the advance of the Sahara Desert, and in Côte d'Ivoire, Israeli contractors undertook several major building projects. Israel also trained the elite armed units protecting the presidents of Cameroon, Liberia, Togo, and Zaire.

Israel has long had a special interest in Ethiopia, a partially Christian country, because of the presence of Falashas (Ethiopian Jews) in that country. Ethiopian-Israeli relations had been close until the overthrow of Emperor Haile Selassie and the imposition of a Marxist, pro-Soviet military regime in 1974. In 1978 Ethiopia received military aid from Israel as well as from the Soviet Union, Cuba, and Libya in its border war with Somalia. In 1984 and 1985, it was reported that, in exchange for Israeli military aid to Ethiopia in its battle against Muslim Eritrean secessionists supported by Arab states, Israel organized an airlift of more than 10,000 Falashas from ethopia to Israel. In 1988 it was estimated that between 10,000 and 15,000 Falashas still remained in Ethiopia.

Israel has also had a longstanding interest in South Africa because of its approximately 110,000 Jews and 15,000 Israelis. Israeli leaders justified trade with South Africa on the ground that it offered protection for the South African Jewish community and developed export markets for Israel's defense and commercial industries. Excluding the arms trade, in 1986 Israel imported approximately US$181.1 million worth of South African goods, consisting primarily of coal; it exported products worth about US$58.8 million.

Israel has traditionally opposed international trade embargoes as a result of its own vulnerability at the hands of the UN and Third World-dominated bodies. In 1987, however, Israel took steps to reduce its military ties with South Africa so as to bring its policies in line with those of the United States and Western Europe, which had imposed limited trade, diplomatic, and travel sanctions on South Africa. In a speech to the Knesset on March 19, then Minister of Foreign Affairs Peres formally presented the Israeli cabinet's four-point plan to ban military sales contracts with South Africa (Israel's arms trade with South Africa was reportedly between US$400 and US$800 million a year); to condemn apartheid, which Peres characterized as "a policy totally rejected by all human beings;" to reduce cultural and tourist ties to a minimum; and to appoint an official committee to draft a detailed list of economic sanctions in line with those of the United States and other Western nations. The cabinet also announced its decision to establish an educational foundation for South African blacks and people of mixed race in Israel.

RELATIONS WITH LATIN AMERICA

The traditional pro-Western stance of most Latin American states has proven to be politically and economically advantageous to Israel, as they have tended to be more sympathetic to Israel in the UN than African or Asian countries. They have also been more willing to maintain economic and military relations with Israel. Although Latin American states are primarily Roman Catholic and follow the Vatican's position favoring the internationalization of Jerusalem, Israel has obtained crude oil from Mexico, it maintains a lucrative arms trade with Argentina and other countries, and it has assisted Latin American regimes in their counterinsurgency efforts against Cuban and Nicaraguan-supported guerrillas.

RELATIONS WITH WESTERN EUROPE

Israeli relations with the states of Western Europe have been conditioned by European desires to further their own commercial interests and ties with the Arab world and their heavy dependence on Middle Eastern oil. Europeans have provided political support for Arab states and the Palestinian cause, even though Europe has served as the battleground for Arab and Palestinian terrorist groups. For example, beginning in the early 1970s, the ministers of foreign affairs of the European Community called for Israel to withdraw from territories occupied during the June 1967 War, expressed "reservations" over the 1978 Camp David Accords, and accepted the "association" of the PLO in solving the Palestinian problem.

Despite such official declarations, West European states have been important trading partners for Israel; about 40 percent of Israel's foreign trade occurred with European countries. Furthermore, there has been strong European-Israeli cooperation-- except with Greece--in the area of counterterrorism. Britain was Israel's most important European trading partner although relations between the two countries were never free of tensions. In 1979, for example, Britain disallowed Israel's purchase of British crude oil after Israel lost oil deliveries from Iran and Sinai. Moreover, Britain imposed an arms embargo on Israel following its June 1982 invasion of Lebanon.

In the early 1950s, France and Israel maintained close political and military relations, and France was Israel's main weapons supplier until the June 1967 War. At that time, during Charles de Gaulle's presidency, France became highly critical of Israeli policies and imposed an arms embargo on Israel. In the early 1980s, French-Israeli relations markedly improved under the presidency of François Mitterrand, who pursued a more even-handed approach than his predecessors on Arab-Israeli issues. Mitterand was the first French president to visit Israel while in office.

Relations between Israel and the Federal Republic of Germany (West Germany) were "second in importance only to [Israel's] partnership with the United States," according to Michael Wolffsohn, a leading authority on the subject. In Wolffsohn's view, the dominant issues in West German-Israeli relations were: the question of reparations (up to 1953); the establishment of diplomatic relations (up to 1965); the solidification of normal relations (through 1969); the erosion in the West German-Israeli relationship as Chancellor Willi Brandt--the first West German chancellor to visit Israel--began to stress Israel's need to withdraw from all territories occupied in the June 1967 War and to recognize the right of the Palestinian people to self-determination; and, finally, during the 1980s, under the Christian Democrats, West Germany's closer adherence to United States policies on Arab-Israeli issues.

In January 1986, Spain established full diplomatic relations with Israel despite pressures from Arab states and policy differences between Madrid and Jerusalem over the Palestinian question. This step concluded intensive behind-the-scenes Israeli efforts--begun upon the death of President Francisco Franco in 1975--to achieve normal relations with Spain. Prior to establishing diplomatic relations, the two countries discreetly collaborated in antiterrorism efforts, and there were close ties between Labor and Spain's Socialist Party.

Although in 1947 Turkey voted against the UN resolution to establish the Jewish state, in 1948 it became the first Muslim country to establish full diplomatic relations with Israel. The two countries subsequently maintained normal relations.

US ASSISTANCE TO ISRAEL - STRATEGIC INFORMATION[2]

Israel is the largest cumulative recipient of U.S. foreign assistance since World War II. To date, the United States has provided Israel $134.7 billion (current, or noninflation-adjusted, dollars) in bilateral assistance and missile defense funding. Almost all U.S. bilateral aid to Israel is in the form of military assistance, although in the past Israel also received significant economic assistance.

At a signing ceremony at the State Department on September 14, 2016, representatives of the U.S. and Israeli governments signed a new 10-year Memorandum of Understanding (MOU) on military aid covering FY2019 to FY2028. Under the terms of the MOU, the United States pledges to provide $38 billion in military aid ($33 billion in Foreign Military Financing grants plus $5 billion in missile defense appropriations) to Israel. This MOU replaces a previous $30 billion 10-year agreement, which runs through FY2018.

Israel is the first international operator of the F-35 Joint Strike Fighter, the Department of Defense's fifth-generation stealth aircraft, considered to be the most technologically advanced fighter jet ever made. To date, Israel has purchased 50 F-35s in three separate contracts.

P.L. 115-141, the FY2018 Consolidated Appropriations Act, provides the following for Israel:

· $3.1 billion in Foreign Military Financing, of which $815.3 million is for off-shore procurement;

· $705.8 million for joint U.S.-Israeli missile defense projects, including $92 million for Iron Dome, $221.5 million for David's Sling, $310 million for Arrow 3, and $82.3 million for Arrow 2;

· $47.5 million for the U.S.-Israeli anti-tunnel cooperation program;

· $7.5 million in Migration and Refugee Assistance;

· $4 million for the establishment of a U.S.-Israel Center of Excellence in energy and water technologies;

· $2 million for the Israel-U.S. Binational Research & Development Foundation (BIRD) Energy program; and

· The reauthorization of War Reserves Stock Allies-Israel (WRSA-I) program through fiscal year 2019.

For FY2019, the Trump Administration is requesting $3.3 billion in Foreign Military Financing for Israel and $500 million in missile defense aid to mark the first year of the new MOU. The Administration also is seeking $5.5 million in Migration and Refugee Assistance (MRA) funding for humanitarian migrants to Israel.

BACKGROUND

For decades, the United States and Israel have maintained strong bilateral relations based on a number of factors, including robust domestic U.S. support for Israel and its security; shared

[2] U.S. Foreign Aid to Israel Jeremy M. Sharp Specialist in Middle Eastern Affairs April 10, 2018 Congressional Research Service

strategic goals in the Middle East; a mutual commitment to democratic values; and historical ties dating from U.S. support for the creation of Israel in 1948. U.S. foreign aid has been a major component in cementing and reinforcing these ties. Although successive Administrations have disapproved of some Israeli policies, including settlement construction in the West Bank, U.S. officials and many lawmakers have long considered Israel to be a vital partner in the region, and U.S. aid packages for Israel have reflected this calculation. Some observers, including opponents of U.S. aid to Israel, argue that U.S. assistance to Israel supports Israeli arms purchases without providing sufficient scrutiny of controversial Israeli military actions that—these observers assert—contravene various laws and international norms, particularly regarding treatment of Palestinians.

Table 1. Total U.S. Foreign Aid Obligations to Israel: 1946-2017current, or noninflation-adjusted, dollars in millions

Fiscal Year	Military	Economic	Missile Defense	Total
1946-2016	91,617.786	34,265.675	5,104.874	130,988.340
2017	3,175.000	-	600.735	3,775.740
2018	-	-	-	-
2019 Request	3,300.000		500.000	3,800.000
Total	94,792.790	34,265.675	5,705.61	134,764.080

Sources: U.S. Overseas Loans and Grants (Greenbook) and the U.S. State Department.
Notes: The Greenbook figures do not include missile defense funding provided by the Department of Defense. As of February 2018, Congress has not appropriated FY2018 funds.

While overall U.S. public support for Israel remains strong, American public attitudes toward Israel are growing more polarized. In January 2018, the Pew Research Center released poll results about the dispute between Israel and the Palestinians. Among other findings, Pew reported that "46% of Americans say they sympathize more with the Israelis, 16% say they sympathize more with the Palestinians and about four-in-ten (38%) either volunteer that their sympathies are with both (5%), neither (14%) or that they do not know (19%)."1 Pew also highlighted a widening partisan divide between Republicans and Democrats over their support for Israel, noting that 79% of Republicans sympathize more with Israel than the Palestinians, compared with 27% of Democrats.

1 "Republicans and Democrats Grow Even Further Apart in Views of Israel, Palestinians," *Pew Research Center*, January 23, 2018. Some observers have criticized this poll, asserting that it conflates American attitudes toward Israel with public opinion of the Israeli-Palestinian conflict. See, "How Not to Measure Americans' Support for Israel," *The Atlantic*, January 26, 2018.

QUALITATIVE MILITARY EDGE (QME)

Almost all current U.S. aid to Israel is in the form of military assistance.2 U.S. military aid has helped transform Israel's armed forces into one of the most technologically sophisticated militaries in the world. U.S. military aid for Israel has been designed to maintain Israel's "qualitative military edge" (QME) over neighboring militaries.3 The rationale for QME is that Israel must rely on better equipment and training to compensate for being much smaller in land area and population than its potential adversaries. U.S. military aid also has helped Israel build its domestic defense industry, which ranks as one of the top global suppliers of arms.4

2 For many years, U.S. economic aid helped subsidize a lackluster Israeli economy, but since the rapid expansion of Israel's high-tech sector and overall economy in the 1990s (sparked partially by U.S.-Israeli scientific cooperation), Israel has been considered a fully industrialized nation. Consequently, Israel and the United States agreed to gradually phase out economic grant aid to Israel. In FY2008, Israel stopped receiving bilateral Economic Support Fund (ESF) grants. It had been a large-scale recipient of grant ESF assistance since 1971.

3 The concept of QME (independent of its application to Israel) dates back to the Cold War. In assessing the balance of power in Europe, U.S. war planners would often stress to lawmakers that because countries of the Warsaw Pact had a numerical advantage over U.S. and allied forces stationed in Europe, the United States must maintain a "qualitative edge" in defense systems. For example, see, Written Statement of General William O. Gribble, Jr., Hearings on Research, Development, Test, and Evaluation Program for Fiscal Year 1973, Before Subcommittee No. 1 of Committee on Armed Services, House of Representatives, Ninety-Second Congress, Second Session. February 2, 3, 7, 9, 22, 23, 24, March 6, 7, and 8, 1972. The concept was subsequently applied to Israel in relation to its Arab adversaries. In 1981, then-U.S. Secretary of State Alexander Haig testified before Congress, saying, "A central aspect of US policy since the October 1973 war has been to ensure that Israel maintains a qualitative military edge." Secretary of State Al Haig, Statement for the Record submitted in response to Question from Hon. Clarence Long, House Appropriations Subcommittee on Foreign Operations Appropriations, April 28, 1981.

4 See, CRS Report R44716, *Conventional Arms Transfers to Developing Nations, 2008-2015*, by Catherine A. Theohary. Also, according to the Stockholm International Peace Research Institute (SIPRI), from 2012 to 2016, Israel was the 10th largest arms exporter worldwide, accounting for 2.3% of world deliveries. See, "Trends in International Arms Transfers, 2016," SIPRI Fact Sheet, February 2017.

5 William Wunderle and Andre Briere, *U.S. Foreign Policy and Israel's Qualitative Military Edge: The Need for a Common Vision*, Washington Institute for Near East Policy, Policy Focus #80, January 2008.

Successive Administrations have routinely affirmed the U.S. commitment to strengthening Israel's QME. However, for years, no official or public U.S. definition of QME existed.5 In order to clarify U.S. policy on preserving Israel's QME, Congress has passed several pieces of legislation addressing the issue. For example, in 2008, Congress passed legislation (P.L. 110-429, the Naval Vessel Transfer Act of 2008) that defined QME as

the ability to counter and defeat any credible conventional military threat from any individual state or possible coalition of states or from non-state actors, while sustaining minimal damage and casualties, through the use of superior military means, possessed in sufficient quantity, including weapons, command, control, communication, intelligence, surveillance, and reconnaissance capabilities that in their technical characteristics are superior in capability to those of such other individual or possible coalition of states or non-state actors.

Section 201 of P.L. 110-429 required the President to carry out an "empirical and qualitative assessment on an ongoing basis of the extent to which Israel possesses a qualitative military edge over military threats to Israel." The 2008 law also amended Section 36 of the Arms Export Control Act (AECA) to require certifications for proposed arms sales "to any country in the

Middle East other than Israel" to include "a determination that the sale or export of the defense articles or defense services will not adversely affect Israel's qualitative military edge over military threats to Israel." What might constitute a legally defined adverse effect to QME is not clarified in U.S. legislation.

Congress has passed additional legislation addressing Israel's QME. In 2012, Congress passed the United States-Israel Enhanced Security Cooperation Act (P.L. 112-150), which, among other things, reiterated that it is the policy of the United States to "to help the Government of Israel preserve its qualitative military edge amid rapid and uncertain regional political transformation." In 2014, Congress passed The U.S.-Israel Strategic Partnership Act (P.L. 113-296). This act amended Section 36 of the AECA to require that the Administration explain, in cases of sales or exports of major U.S. defense equipment to other Middle Eastern states, what is "Israel's capacity to address the improved capabilities provided by such sale or export."6 The act also requires the Administration to

6 Upon signing P.L. 113-296 into law, President Obama issued a signing statement noting: "Sections 11(b) and 12(c)(2) of this bill purport to require me to provide to the Congress certain diplomatic communications and direct the Secretary of State to undertake certain diplomatic initiatives. Consistent with longstanding constitutional practice, my administration will interpret and implement these sections in a manner that does not interfere with my constitutional authority to conduct diplomacy and to protect the confidentiality of diplomatic communications." See Barack Obama: "Statement on Signing the United States-Israel Strategic Partnership Act of 2014," December 19, 2014. Online by Gerhard Peters and John T. Woolley, The American Presidency Project.

7 QME reports to Congress are reportedly classified.

· Evaluate "how such sale or export alters the strategic and tactical balance in the region, including relative capabilities; and Israel's capacity to respond to the improved regional capabilities provided by such sale or export."

· Include "an identification of any specific new capacity, capabilities, or training that Israel may require to address the regional or country-specific capabilities provided by such sale or export; and a description of any additional United States security assurances to Israel made, or requested to be made, in connection with, or as a result of, such sale or export."

Finally, P.L. 113-296 amends Section 201(c) of the Naval Vessel Transfer Act of 2008 (22 U.S.C. 2776) by requiring Administration reports on QME every two years rather than (as previously required) every four.7

QME AND U.S. ARMS SALES TO THE GULF

Israeli officials periodically express concern over U.S. sales of sophisticated weaponry, particularly aircraft, airborne radar systems, and precision-guided munitions, to Arab Gulf countries. As the United States has been one of the principal suppliers of defense equipment and training to both Israel and the Arab Gulf states, U.S. policymakers and defense officials have sought to carefully navigate U.S. defense commitments, while following the legal requirement to maintain Israel's QME.

Although at times Israel and the Arab Gulf states have coalesced against a commonly perceived Iranian threat, U.S. arms sales to states such as Saudi Arabia still periodically raise Israeli QME concerns. In May 2017, the Trump Administration announced that the United States and Saudi Arabia had completed and proposed defense sales with a potential value of more than $110 billion. While most Israeli government officials refrained from publicly objecting to the deal, several did express concern over whether new U.S. arms sales to Saudi Arabia would erode

Israel's QME.8 According to Israeli Minister of Energy Yuval Steinitz, "We have also to make sure that those hundreds of billions of dollars of weapons to Saudi Arabia will not, by any means, erode Israel's qualitative edge, because Saudi Arabia is still a hostile country without any diplomatic relations and nobody knows what the future will be."9 The American Israel Public Affairs Committee (AIPAC) also called for the preservation of Israel's QME in light of proposed U.S. arms sales to Saudi Arabia, specifically warning that the U.S. sale to Saudi Arabia of the Terminal High Altitude Area Defense (THAAD) system (notified to Congress in October 2017) could "negatively impact Israel's QME" and would "also improve the kingdom's ability to track Israeli F-15 and F-16 fighters."10 Some experts note that even after a sale of U.S. major defense systems to Saudi Arabia, U.S. personnel are often involved in the operation, maintenance, and end-use monitoring of equipment, thereby serving as a possible bulwark against client misuse.11

8 "Israeli Defence Minister says Uneasy over US-Saudi Arms Deal, *Agence France Presse*, May 24, 2017.
9 "Israeli Minister Expresses Concern over U.S.-Saudi Arms Deal, *Reuters*, May 21, 2017.
10 "Congress Must Examine Impact of Saudi Arms Sale," American Israel Public Affairs Committee, Near East Report, June 2017.
11 "Congress OK with Saudi Missile Defense Sale amid warming Israel-Gulf Ties, *Al Monitor*, May 11, 2017.
12 "Trump could let the UAE buy F-35 jets," *Defense News*, November 4, 2017.
13 "To Seal F-35 Deal, UAE Must Agree To Protect Sensitive Information," *Aerospace Daily & Defense Report*, November 14, 2017.

United Arab Emirates (UAE) interest in becoming the first Arab state operator of the F-35 Joint Strike Fighter also may raise Israeli QME concerns. The Trump Administration reportedly has agreed to enter into preliminary talks with the UAE on procurement of the F-35.12 Previously, U.S. officials had said that the United States would not sell the aircraft to the UAE before Israel receives the weapon. In addition to satisfying QME concerns before considering a F-35 sale to the UAE, the United States may also require the UAE to improve its protection of data security due to the sensitive technologies in the F-35's hardware and software.13 To date, no specific decision has been announced to begin preliminary U.S.-UAE talks on the subject.

U.S. BILATERAL MILITARY AID TO ISRAEL

Since 1999, overall U.S. assistance to Israel has been outlined in 10-year government-to-government Memoranda of Understanding (MOUs). MOUs are not legally binding agreements like treaties, and thus do not require Senate concurrence. Also, Congress may accept or change year-to-year assistance levels for Israel, or provide supplemental appropriations. Nevertheless, past MOUs have significantly influenced the terms of U.S. aid to Israel; Congress has appropriated foreign aid to Israel largely according to the terms of the current MOU.

Brief History of MOUs on U.S. Aid to Israel

The first 10-year MOU (FY1999-FY2008), agreed to under the Clinton Administration, was known as the "Glide Path Agreement" and represented a political commitment to provide Israel with at least $26.7 billion in total economic and military aid over its duration (of which $21.3 billion was in military aid).14 This MOU provided the template for the gradual phase-out of all economic assistance to Israel.

In 2007, the Bush Administration and the Israeli government agreed to the current $30 billion military aid package for the 10-year period from FY2009 to FY2018. Under the terms of the agreement, Israel was explicitly permitted to continue spending up to 26.3% of U.S. assistance on Israeli-manufactured equipment (known as Off-Shore Procurement or OSP - discussed below). The agreement states that "Both sides acknowledge that these funding levels assume continuation of adequate levels for U.S. foreign assistance overall, and are subject to the appropriation and availability of funds for these purposes."15

14 See, Joint Statement by President Clinton and Prime Minister Ehud Barak, July 19, 1999. According to the statement, "The United States and Israel will sign a Memorandum of Understanding (MOU) which will express their joint intention to restructure U.S. bilateral assistance to Israel. The MOU will state the United States' intention to sustain its annual military assistance to Israel, and incrementally increase its level by one-third over the next decade to a level of $2.4 billion subject to Congressional consultations and approval. At the same time, the MOU will provide for a gradual phase-out of U.S. economic aid to Israel, over a comparable period, as the Israeli economy grows more robust, less dependent on foreign aid, and more integrated in world markets."
15 United States-Israel Memorandum of Understanding, Signed by then U.S. Under Secretary of State R. Nicholas Burns and Israeli Ministry of Foreign Affairs Director General Aaron Abramovich, August 16, 2007.
16 Memorandum of Understanding between the United States and Israel, September 14, 2016.
17 Ibid.
18 Congress also separately appropriated $3.984 billion in missile defense funds during that period, not including FY2018.

THE CURRENT 10-YEAR SECURITY ASSISTANCE MEMORANDUM OF UNDERSTANDING (MOU)

At a signing ceremony at the State Department on September 14, 2016, representatives of the U.S. and Israeli governments signed a new 10-year Memorandum of Understanding (MOU) on military aid covering FY2019 to FY2028. Under the terms of this MOU, the United States pledges to provide $38 billion in military aid ($33 billion in FMF grants, plus $5 billion in defense appropriations for missile defense programs) to Israel. According to the terms of the MOU, "Both the United States and Israel jointly commit to respect the FMF levels specified in this MOU, and not to seek changes to the FMF levels for the duration of this understanding."16 The agreement also acknowledges that "the funding levels in this understanding assume continuation of adequate funding levels for U.S. foreign assistance and missile defense overall, and are subject to the appropriation and availability of funds for these purposes."17 The new MOU will replace the current $30 billion, 10-year agreement, which runs through FY2018.18

The terms of the 2019-2028 MOU differ from previous agreements on such issues as

· Phasing out Off-Shore Procurement (OSP). Under the terms of the new MOU, OSP will remain until FY2024, but will then be gradually phased out, ending entirely in FY2028. The MOU calls on Israel to provide the United States with "detailed programmatic information related to the use of all U.S. funding, including funds used for OSP." In response to the planned phase-out of OSP, some Israeli defense contractors may be seeking to merge with U.S. companies or open U.S. subsidiaries in order to continue their eligibility for defense contracts financed through FMF.19

· **Missile Defense.** Under the terms of the new MOU, the Administration pledges to request $500 million in annual combined funding for missile defense programs with joint U.S.-Israeli elements—such as Iron Dome, Arrow II and Arrow III, and David's Sling. Previous MOUs did not include missile defense funding, which has traditionally been appropriated via separate interactions between successive Administrations and Congresses. While the MOU commits both the United States and Israel to a $500 million annual U.S. missile defense contribution, it does stipulate that under exceptional circumstances (major armed conflict involving Israel), both sides may agree on U.S. support above the $500 million annual cap.

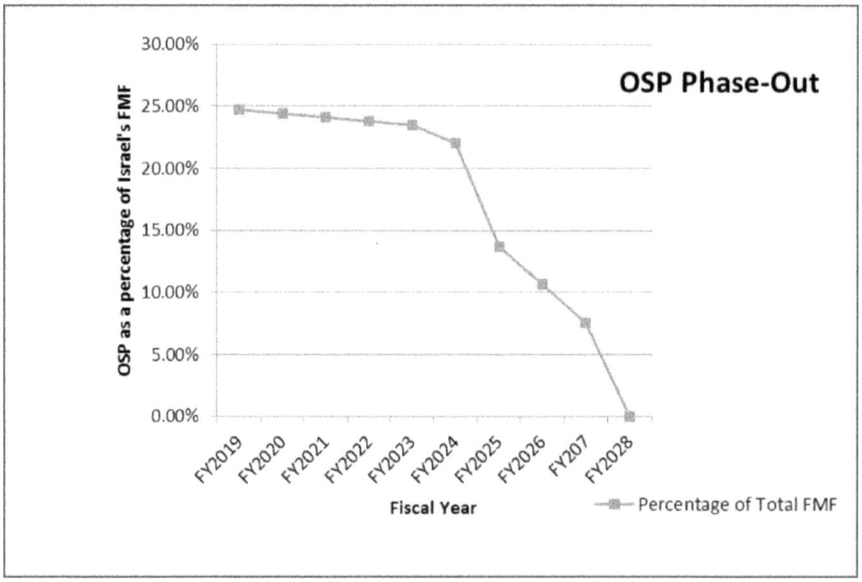

19 "Israeli UAV Firm agrees deal for Unnamed US Company," *Jane's Defence Weekly*, July 18, 2017.

· **No FMF for Fuel.** According to the new MOU, Israel will no longer be permitted to use a portion of its FMF to purchase fuel ("or other consumables") from the United States. Under the previous MOU, Israel had budgeted an estimated $400 million a year in FMF to purchase jet fuel from the United States."20

· **No "extra FMF" for 2017/2018.** Prime Minister Netanyahu, in a letter to Secretary of State John Kerry accompanying the MOU, pledged to reimburse the U.S. government if Israel receives more congressional assistance than specified ($3.1 billion a year) in the last years (FY2017 and FY2018) of the current 2009-2018 MOU. 21 Some lawmakers criticized this addendum to the

MOU, asserting that appropriations are the prerogative of the legislative branch. According to Senator Lindsey Graham, Chairman of the Senate Appropriations Subcommittee on State, Foreign Operations, and Related Programs, the MOU is "not a treaty, and we're not a party to this."22 Section 7041(d) of P.L. 115-31, the Consolidated Appropriations Act, 2017, provided $75 million in FMF-Overseas Contingency Operations (OCO) for FY2017, which was in addition to the $3.1 billion in regular FMF provided in Title IV in the same Act. In fall 2017, news reports surfaced questioning whether Israel would receive the $75 million of "extra FMF" appropriated in P.L. 115-31. In response, State Department spokesperson Heather Nauert remarked that Israel is "going to get the money."23

20 The White House, Office of the Press Secretary, Fact Sheet: Memorandum of Understanding Reached with Israel, September 14, 2016.
21 "Caveats of 2016 US-Israel Aid Deal Come into Focus," *Defense News*, January 10, 2017.
22 "Obama, Lawmakers at Odds over Israel Aid Deal," *Defense News*, September 16, 2016. Senator Graham also filed an amendment to the Senate version of H.R. 2810, the National Defense Authorization Act for Fiscal Year 2018 (P.L. 115-91 as passed). That amendment (S.Amdt. 813) was not adopted. If it had been, it would have maintained the percentage of FMF to Israel designated for OSP at "not less than 26.3 percent from fiscal years 2019 through 2028."
23 U.S. State Department, Department Press Briefing, September 12, 2017.

Figure 2. U.S. Military Aid to Israel over Decades

FOREIGN MILITARY FINANCING (FMF) AND ARMS SALES

Israel is the largest recipient of U.S. Foreign Military Financing. For FY2019, the President's request for Israel would encompass approximately 61% of total requested FMF funding worldwide. Annual FMF grants to Israel represent approximately 19% of the overall Israeli defense budget.24 Israel's defense expenditure as a percentage of its Gross Domestic Product (5.8% in 2016) is one of the highest in the world.25

24 The Israeli Ministry of Defense provides funding figures for its domestic defense budget but excludes some procurement spending and spending on civil defense. The estimate referenced above is based on figures published by *Jane's Defence Budgets, Israel,* IHS Global Insight, January 29, 2018.
25 Stockholm International Peace Research Institute (SIPRI), Military expenditure by country as percentage of gross domestic product, 2003-2016, SIPRI Military Expenditure Database, 2017.
26 For more background, see CRS Report R44060, *Ending Cash Flow Financing to Egypt: Issues for Congress*, by Jeremy M. Sharp.

27 The United States initially began authorizing installment-style sales to Israel to help it rebuild its military capabilities after the 1973 war with Egypt. Congress appropriated $2.2 billion for Israel in P.L. 93-199, the Emergency Security Assistance Act of 1973. Section 3 of that act stated that "Foreign military sales credits [loans or grants] extended to installment payments, rather than having to pay the full amount of such purchases up front. Known as "cash flow financing," this benefit enables Israel to negotiate major arms purchases with U.S. defense suppliers with payments scheduled over a longer time horizon.28

CASH FLOW FINANCING26

Section 23 of the Arms Export Control Act (22 U.S.C. §276351) authorizes the President to finance the "procurement of defense articles, defense services, and design and construction services by friendly foreign countries and international organizations, on such terms and conditions as he may determine consistent with the requirements of this section." Successive Administrations have used this authority to permit Israel27 to finance multiyear purchases through

Israel out of such funds shall be provided on such terms and conditions as the President may determine and without regard to the provisions of the Foreign Military Sales Act as amended." At the time, the Foreign Military Sales Act of 1968 (amended in 1971 and the precursor to the Arms Export Control Act of 1976), capped the annual amount of foreign military sales credit that could be extended to a recipient at no more than $250 million per year. Under the authorities contained in P.L. 93-199, President Nixon, in two separate determinations (April & July 1974), allocated the

$2.2 billion to Israel as $1.5 billion in grant military aid, the largest U.S. grant aid package ever for Israel at the time. The remaining $700 million was designated as a military loan.

A year and a half later, the Ford Administration reached a new arms sales agreement with Israel providing that, according to the *New York Times*, "the cost of the new military equipment would be met through the large amount of aid approved by the just-completed session of Congress as well as the aid that will be approved by future Congresses." See, "U.S. Decides to Sell Some Arms to Israel that it had Blocked in the Past," *New York Times*, October 12, 1976.

28 Cash flow financing is defined in Section 25(d) of the Arms Export Control Act and Section 503(a)(3) of the Foreign Assistance Act.
29 When government operations are funded by a continuing appropriations resolution, Congress may at times include provisions in such resolutions that would prevent the early transfer of FMF to Israel (presumably until a final year appropriations bill is passed). For example, see Section 109 of P.L. 113-46, the Continuing Appropriations Act, 2014.
30 According to the Defense Security Cooperation Agency (DSCA), "Some countries may establish an account with the federal reserve bank (FRB), New York, for their FMS [Foreign Military Sales] deposits. An agreement between the FMS purchaser's defense organization, the purchaser's central bank, FRB New York and DSCA identifies the terms, conditions, and mechanics of the account's operation. Countries receiving FMFP funds must maintain their interest bearing account in the FRB." See, Defense Institute of Security Assistance Management (DISAM), "The Management of Security Cooperation (Green Book)," 34th Edition, April 2015.
31 Foreign Credit Reporting System (FCRS), Amounts Due the U.S. Government from Sovereign and Other Foreign Official Obligors as of 12/31/2015, United States Department of the Treasury, Office of International Debt Policy.
32 Defense Security Cooperation Agency, Transmittal No. 08-83, Israel - F-35 Joint Strike Fighter Aircraft, September 29, 2008.

Early Transfer and Interest Bearing Account

Since FY1991 (P.L. 101-513), Congress has mandated that Israel receive its FMF aid in a lump sum during the first month of the fiscal year.29 The FY2017 Consolidated Appropriations Act (P.L. 115-31) states that "the funds appropriated under this heading for assistance for Israel shall be disbursed within 30 days of enactment of this Act." Once disbursed, Israel's military aid is transferred to an interest bearing account with the U.S. Federal Reserve Bank.30 Israel has used interest collected on its military aid to pay down its bilateral debt (nonguaranteed) to U.S. government agencies, which, according to the U.S. Department of the Treasury, stood at $148.8 million as of December 2015.31 Israel cannot use accrued interest for defense procurement inside Israel.

F-35 Joint Strike Fighter

Israel is the first international operator of the F-35 Joint Strike Fighter, the Department of Defense's fifth-generation stealth aircraft considered to be the most technologically advanced fighter jet ever made. In September 2008, the Defense Security Cooperation Agency (DSCA) notified Congress of a possible Foreign Military Sale of up to 75 F-35s to Israel in a deal with a possible total value of $15.2 billion.32 Since then, Israel has purchased 50 F-35s in three separate contracts (see table below) using FMF grants. Israel is to install Israeli-made C4 (command, control, communications, computers) systems in the F-35s it receives, and call these customized F-35s "*Adirs.*"33

33 "After F-35 makes Aliyah, it will get new Israeli Identity," *Israel Hayom*, May 2, 2016. "Adir" is a Hebrew expression for "mighty" or "powerful."
34 "Israeli F-35 Buy-Back Surpasses $1 Billion," *Defense News*, February 12, 2017.

Table 2. Israel's Purchases of the F-35

Year	# of Planes Purchased	Total Cost	# of Planes in Service
2010	19	$2.75 billion	7
2015	14	$2.82 billion	n/a

2016	17	unspecified	n/a

Source: Jane's World Air Forces, Israel, February 12, 2018.

As part of the F-35 deal, the United States agreed to make reciprocal purchases of equipment (known as "offsets") from Israeli defense companies. If Israel elects to purchase all 75 F-35s, it is estimated that its business offsets could be as high as $4 billion. As of 2017, Israeli firms had received more than one billion dollars' worth of business from Lockheed Martin in building components for the F-35. 34

EXCESS DEFENSE ARTICLES

The Excess Defense Articles (EDA) program provides a means by which the United States can advance foreign policy objectives—assisting friendly and allied nations through provision of equipment in excess of the requirements of its own defense forces. This program, managed by DSCA, enables the United States to reduce its inventory of outdated equipment by providing friendly countries with necessary supplies at either reduced rates or no charge.35

35 To access DSCA's Excess Defense Articles database, see http://www.dsca.mil/programs/eda.
36 On November 4, 1986, President Reagan signed into law P.L. 99-661, the National Defense Authorization Act for FY1987. In Section 1105 of that act, Congress called for greater defense cooperation between the United States and countries that the Secretary of Defense could designate as a "major non-NATO ally" (MNNA). Such cooperation could entail U.S. funding for joint research and development and production of U.S. defense equipment. In February 1987, the United States granted Israel MNNA status along with several other countries (Egypt, Japan, South Korea, and Australia). According to press reports at the time, in the absence of a U.S.-Israeli mutual defense agreement, supporters of Israel had been advocating for Israel to receive "equal treatment" with regard to certain special military benefits (such as the ability to bid on U.S. defense contracts) that NATO allies received from the United States. See, "Israel seeks to obtain the kind of Financial Aid that NATO Members get from U.S. Government," *Wall Street Journal*, February 3, 1987. Nearly a decade later, Congress passed additional legislation that further solidified Israel's MNNA status. In 1996, Section 147 of P.L. 104-164 amended the Foreign Assistance Act of 1961 by requiring the President to notify Congress 30 days before designating a country as a MNNA. According to the act, Israel, along with several other countries, "shall be deemed to have been so designated by the President as of the effective date of this section, and the President is not required to notify the Congress of such designation of those countries." See, 22 U.S.C. §2321j.
37 Excess Defense Articles Database Tool, Defense Security Cooperation Agency.

As a designated "major non-NATO ally,"36 Israel is eligible to receive EDA under Section 516(a) of the Foreign Assistance Act and Section 23(a) of the Arms Export Control Act. According to DSCA, from 2007 to 2017, Israel received $374.399 million in EDA deliveries (current value only).37

DEFENSE BUDGET APPROPRIATIONS FOR U.S.-ISRAELI MISSILE DEFENSE PROGRAMS

Congress and successive Administrations have demonstrated strong support for joint U.S.-Israeli missile defense projects designed to thwart a diverse range of threats. The range spans from short-range missiles and rockets fired by nonstate actors, such as Hamas and Hezbollah, to mid- and longer-range ballistic missiles in Syria's and Iran's arsenals. Congress provides regular U.S. funding for Israeli and U.S.-Israeli missile defense programs in defense authorization and appropriations bills. Israel and the United States each contribute financially to several weapons systems and engage in codevelopment, coproduction, and/or technology sharing in connection with them.

The following section provides background on Israel's four-layered active defense network: Iron Dome (short range), David's Sling (low to mid-range), Arrow II (upper-atmospheric), and Arrow III (exo-atmospheric).

IRON DOME

Iron Dome is a short-range antirocket system developed by Israel's Rafael Advanced Defense Systems and originally produced in Israel. Iron Dome's targeting system and radar are designed to fire its Tamir interceptors only at incoming projectiles that pose threats to the area being protected (generally, strategically important sites, including population centers); it is not configured to fire on rockets headed toward unpopulated areas. Israel can move Iron Dome batteries as threats change. Israel recently developed a naval version of Iron Dome, which it will install on its corvettes to protect off-shore natural gas facilities.38

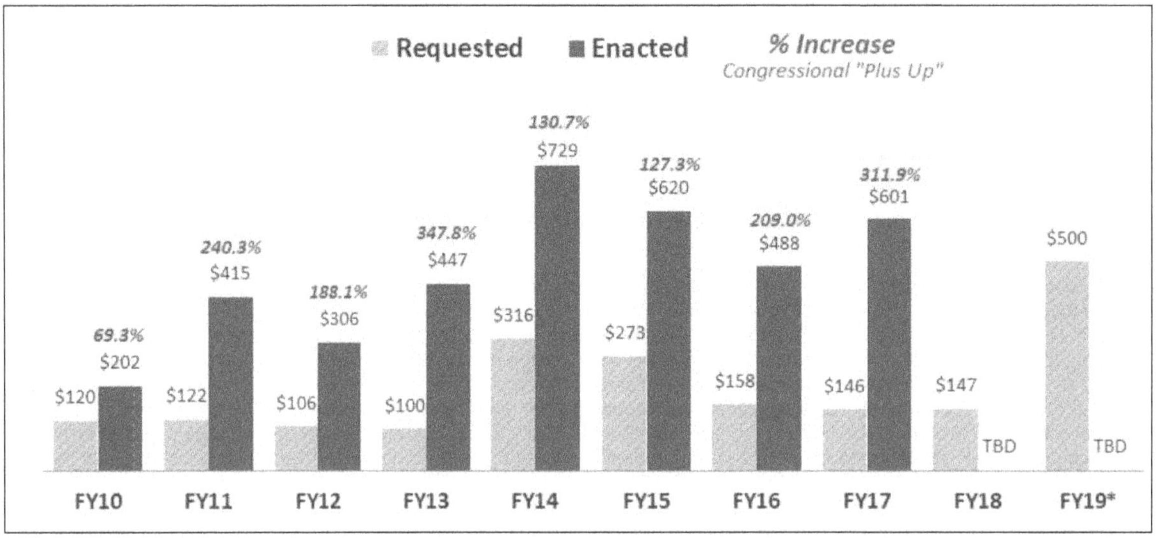

38 "With high-tech warships, Navy readies to guard gas fields from Hezbollah, Hamas," *Times of Israel*, February 5, 2018.

IRON DOME'S PERFORMANCE

Iron Dome was declared operational in early 2011. Its first major test came in November 2012 during a weeklong Israel-Hamas conflict (termed "Operation Pillar of Cloud/Defense" by Israel). Israeli officials claim that Iron Dome intercepted 85% of the more than 400 rockets fired by Gaza-based militants.

Between 2012 and 2014, Israel upgraded Iron Dome's various tracking and firing mechanisms and expanded the number of batteries deployed from five to nine. During Israel's 2014 conflict with Hamas and other Palestinian militants, media reports (generally based on Israeli claims) seem to indicate that Iron Dome had a successful interception rate close to 90%.

According to statistics reported by the Israeli Defense Forces (IDF), Gaza-based terrorist groups fired 35 projectiles into Israel in 2017, of which the vast majority landed in open territory and an estimated 10 struck in residential areas or were intercepted by Iron Dome.39

39 "More Rockets Fired at Israel in 2017 than Previous Two Years," *Jerusalem Post*, January 8, 2018.
40 In conference report language accompanying P.L. 112-239, the National Defense Authorization Act for FY2013, conferees agreed: "The Department of Defense needs to obtain appropriate data rights to Iron Dome technology to ensure us the ability to use that data for U.S. defense purposes and to explore potential co-production opportunities. The conferees support this policy and expect the Department to keep the congressional defense committees informed of developments and progress on this issue."

COPRODUCTION AND U.S. FUNDING

To date, the United States has provided $1.397 billion to Israel for Iron Dome batteries, interceptors, coproduction costs, and general maintenance. Because Iron Dome was developed by Israel alone, Israel initially retained proprietary technology rights to it. The United States and Israel have had a decades-long partnership in the development and coproduction of other missile defense systems (such as the Arrow). As the United States began financially supporting Israel's development of Iron Dome in FY2011, U.S. interest in ultimately becoming a partner in its coproduction grew. Congress then called for Iron Dome technology sharing and coproduction with the United States.40

In March 2014, the United States and Israeli governments signed a coproduction agreement to enable components of the Iron Dome system to be manufactured in the United States, while also providing the U.S. Missile Defense Agency (MDA) with full access to what had been proprietary Iron Dome technology.41 U.S.-based Raytheon is Rafael's U.S. partner in the coproduction of Iron Dome.

41 The co-production agreement is formally titled, "'Agreement Between the Department of Defense of the United States of America and the Ministry of Defense of the State of Israel Concerning Iron Dome Defense System Procurement.''
42 This joint agreement is a Research, Development, Test and Evaluation (RDT&E) Framework agreement between the U.S. and Israel. The joint program to implement the agreement is known as the Short Range Ballistic Missile Defense (SRBMD) David's Sling Weapon System (DSWS) Project. The Department of Defense/ U.S.-Israeli Cooperative Program Office manages the SRBMD/DSWS program, which is equitably funded between the U.S. and Israel.

On September 30, 2014, Raytheon received a $149 million contract from Rafael to provide parts for the Tamir interceptor. The FY2014 Emergency Supplemental Appropriations Resolution, P.L. 113-145, exempted $225 million in Iron Dome funding—requested by Israel on an expedited basis during the summer 2014 Israel-Gaza conflict—from the coproduction requirements agreed upon in March 2014.

Section 1684 of P.L. 115-91, the National Defense Authorization Act (NDAA) for Fiscal Year 2018, authorizes "not more than" $92 million to Israel for the procurement of Tamir interceptors for Iron Dome. It also requires U.S. defense officials to certify that before the United States provides funds to Israel, both the United States and Israel are properly implementing their coproduction agreement for Tamir interceptors.

Table 3. NDAA 2018 Authorized Missile Defense Funding for Israel

dollars in millions

System	Title XLII Research, Development, Test, and Evaluation (P.L. 115-91)	Title XLI Procurement (P.L. 115-91)	Total
Iron Dome	-	92.000	92.000
David's Sling	63.848	120.000	183.848
Arrow II	71.459	-	71.459
Arrow III	133.139	120.000	253.139
Unspecified Israel Coop	105.354	-	105.354
Total	373.800	332.000	705.800

DAVID'S SLING

In August 2008, Israel and the United States officially signed a "project agreement" to codevelop the David's Sling system.42 David's Sling (aka Magic Wand) is a short/medium-

range system designed to counter long-range rockets and slower-flying cruise missiles fired at ranges from 40 km to 300 km, such as those possessed by Iran, Syria, and Hezbollah in Lebanon. David's Sling is designed to intercept missiles with ranges and trajectories for which Iron Dome and/or Arrow interceptors are not optimally configured. It is being developed jointly by Rafael Advanced Defense Systems and Raytheon. David's Sling uses Raytheon's Stunner missile for interception, and each launcher can hold up to 16 missiles. Once the United States and Israel reach a coproduction agreement for the Stunner, the interceptors may be built in Tucson, Arizona by Raytheon. In April 2017, Israel declared David's Sling operational and, according to one analysis, "two David's Sling batteries are sufficient to cover the whole of Israel."43

43 "IDF officially declares David's Sling Operational," *Jane's Defence Weekly*, April 3, 2017.
44 Shortly after the start of the Strategic Defense Initiative (SDI) in 1985, the Reagan Administration sought allied political support through various cooperative technology agreements on ballistic missile defense (BMD). Israeli interest in BMD was strengthened by the missile war between Iran and Iraq in the later 1980s, and the experience of being attacked by Scud missiles from Iraq during Operation Desert Storm in 1991. A memorandum of understanding was signed with Israel on May 6, 1986, to jointly develop an indigenous Israeli capability to defend against ballistic missiles. Subsequently, a number of additional agreements were signed, including, for example, an April 1989 Memorandum of Agreement (MOA) to develop an Israeli computer facility as part of the Arrow BMD program, a June 1991 agreement to develop a second generation Arrow BMD capability, and a September 2008 agreement to develop a short-range BMD system to defend against very short-range missiles and rockets.

Coproduction and U.S. Funding

Since FY2006, the United States has contributed over $1.39 billion to the development of David's Sling. The United States and Israel are negotiating a coproduction agreement to jointly manufacture the Stunner interceptor.

Section 1684 of P.L.115-91, the National Defense Authorization Act (NDAA) for Fiscal Year 2018, authorizes a total of $183.848 million for David's Sling in two tranches ($63.848 million in Title XLII and $120 million in Title XLI). For the $120 million in procurement funds, the act requires a certification regarding coproduction of components. The act also specifies that prior to the transfer of funds, the Under Secretary of Defense for Acquisition and Sustainment must certify that, among other things, Israel has successfully demonstrated production readiness reviews required by bilateral agreements.

The Arrow and Arrow II

Since 1988, Israel and the United States have been jointly developing the Arrow Anti-Missile System.44 The Arrow is designed to counter short-range ballistic missiles. The United States has funded just under half of the annual costs of the development of the Arrow Weapon System, with Israel supplying the remainder. The Arrow II program (officially referred to as the Arrow System Improvement Program or ASIP), a joint effort of Boeing and Israel Aerospace Industries (IAI), is designed to defeat longer-range ballistic missiles. One Arrow II battery is designed to protect large swaths of Israeli territory. In March 2017, media sources reported the first known use of the Arrow II, when it successfully intercepted

a Syrian surface-to-air missile (SAM) that had been fired on an Israeli jet returning to Israel from an operation inside Syria.

Table 4. U.S. Contributions to the Arrow Program (Arrow, Arrow II, and Arrow III) dollars in millions

Fiscal Year	Total	Fiscal Year	Total
1990	52.000	2004	144.803

1991	42.000	2005	155.290
1992	54.400	2006	122.866
1993	57.776	2007	117.494
1994	56.424	2008	118.572
1995	47.400	2009	104.342
1996	59.352	2010	122.342
1997	35.000	2011	125.393
1998	98.874	2012	125.175
1999	46.924	2013	115.500
2000	81.650	2014	119.070
2001	95.214	2015	130.908
2002	131.700	2016	146.069
2003	135.749	2017	272.224
		Total	2,914.511

Source: U.S. Missile Defense Agency.

Under the 1986 agreement (see footnote 44) allowing Israel to participate in the Strategic Defense Initiative (SDI), the United States and Israel have codeveloped different versions of the Arrow anti-ballistic missile. The total U.S. financial contribution exceeds $2.9 billion. The system became operational in 2000 in Israel and has been tested successfully. Since 2001, Israel and the United States have conducted a joint biennial exercise, called Juniper Cobra, to work on integrating their weapons, radars, and other systems.

HIGH ALTITUDE MISSILE DEFENSE SYSTEM (ARROW III)

Citing a potential nuclear threat from Iran, Israel has sought a missile interceptor that operates at a higher altitude and greater range than the original Arrow systems. In October 2007, the United States and Israel agreed to establish a committee to evaluate Israel's proposed "Arrow III," an upper-tier system designed to intercept medium-range ballistic missiles. The Arrow III is a more advanced version—in terms of speed, range and altitude—of the current Arrow II interceptor. In 2008, Israel decided to begin development of the Arrow III and the United States agreed to co-fund its development despite an initial proposal by Lockheed Martin and the Department of Defense (DOD) urging Israel to purchase the Terminal High-Altitude Area Defense (THAAD) missile defense system instead.

The Arrow III, made (like the Arrow II) by Israel Aerospace Industries (IAI) and Boeing, has been operational since January 2017. In July 2010, the United States and Israel signed a bilateral agreement (The Upper-Tier Interceptor Project Agreement) to extend their cooperation in developing and producing the Arrow III, including an equitable U.S.-Israeli cost share. In 2018, the Israel Missile Defense Organization plans to hold a series of Arrow III interception tests conducted from Alaska.45

45 "Israeli Arrow 3 Interceptor Test Previews Upcoming Trials in Alaska," *Jane's Defence Weekly*, February 20, 2018.
46 "Congress Generous, Again, With U.S. Funds for Israel's Defense" *CQ News*, November 13, 2017.
47 "Senate Diluted Tough Oversight of Israeli Antimissile Program," *CQ News*, October 4, 2017.

COPRODUCTION AND U.S. FUNDING

Since codevelopment began in 2008, Congress has appropriated $743.7 million for Arrow III. Section 1684 of P.L.115-91, the National Defense Authorization Act (NDAA) for Fiscal Year

2018, authorizes a total of $253.139 million for Arrow III in two tranches ($133.139 in Title XLII and $120 million in Title XLI). For the $120 million in procurement funds, the act requires a certification regarding coproduction of components. The act also specifies that prior to the transfer of funds, the Under Secretary of Defense for Acquisition and Sustainment must certify that, among other things, Israel has "demonstrated the successful completion of the knowledge points, technical milestones, and production readiness reviews required by the research, development, and technology agreements for the Arrow 3 Upper Tier Development Program." The certification also requires that missile defense funds for Israel will be provided "on the basis of a one-for-one cash match made by Israel or in another matching amount that otherwise meets best efforts (as mutually agreed to by the United States and Israel)." One observer has identified some congressional concern about whether the United States has sufficient data to determine Israeli contributions relative to U.S. contributions in funding missile defense systems.46

The FY2018 NDAA did include a waiver, allowing the Under Secretary to waive the certification requirement if the United States receives sufficient data from Israel demonstrating that, among other things, U.S. contributions are provided to Israel "solely for funding the procurement of long-lead components and critical hardware in accordance with a production plan, including a funding profile detailing Israeli contributions for production, including long-lead production, of the Arrow 3 Upper Tier Interceptor Program." An earlier Senate version of the FY2018 NDAA (S. 1519) included a provision that would have withheld funding for Arrow III until "after the successful completion of two flight tests at a test range in the United States to validate Arrow Weapon System capabilities and interoperability with ballistic missile system components of the United States." According to one account, some lawmakers sought further testing of the Arrow III since "the Israeli military tends to deploy its systems with only limited testing, which is essentially the opposite of the U.S. government's general approach." 47

Table 5. Defense Budget Appropriations for U.S.-Israeli Missile Defense: FY2006-FY2019 Request current dollars in millions

Fiscal Year	Arrow II	Arrow III (High Altitude)	David's Sling (Short-Range)	Iron Dome	Total
FY2006	122.866	—	10.0	—	132.866
FY2007	117.494	—	20.4	—	137.894
FY2008	98.572	20.0	37.0	—	155.572
FY2009	74.342	30.0	72.895	—	177.237
FY2010	72.306	50.036	80.092	—	202.434
FY2011	66.427	58.966	84.722	205.000	415.115
FY2012	58.955	66.220	110.525	70.000 a	305.700
FY2013 After Sequestration	40.800	74.700	137.500	194.000	447.000
FY2014	44.363	74.707	149.712	460.309 (includes supp)	729.091
FY2015	56.201	74.707	137.934	350.972	619.814
FY2016	56.519	89.550	286.526	55.000	487.595
FY2017	67.331	204.893	266.511	62.000	600.735
FY2018	TBD	TBD	TBD	TBD	TBD
FY2019 Request	TBD	TBD	TBD	TBD	500.000
Total	876.176	743.779	1,393.817	1,397.281	4,411.053

a. These funds were not appropriated by Congress but reprogrammed by the Obama Administration from other Department of Defense accounts.

EMERGENCY U.S. STOCKPILE IN ISRAEL

In the early 1980s, Israeli leaders sought to expand what they called their "strategic collaboration" with the U.S. military by inviting the United States to stockpile arms and equipment at Israeli bases for use in wartime.48 In 1989,49 the United States agreed to establish munitions stockpiles in Israel for use by the United States and, with U.S. permission, by Israel in emergency situations. Section 514 of the Foreign Assistance Act of 1961 (22 U.S.C. §2321h) enables U.S. defense articles stored in war reserve stocks to be transferred to a foreign government through Foreign Military Sales or through grant military assistance, such as FMF.

48 "U.S.- Israel Strategic Link: Both Sides Take Stock," *New York Times*, October 2, 1981.
49 In October 1989, the United States and Israel agreed to pre-position $100 million worth of dual-use defense equipment in Israel.
50 The government of Israel, using both its national funds and FMF, pays for the construction, maintenance and
The United States European Command (EUCOM) manages the War Reserves Stock Allies-Israel (WRSA-I) program. The United States stores missiles, armored vehicles, and artillery ammunition in Israel.50 According to one Israeli officer, "Officially, all of this equipment belongs refurbishment costs of WRSA ammunition storage facilities. It also pays for the packaging, crating, handling and transportation of armaments to and from the stockpile.
51 "US may give Israel Iraq Ammo," *Jerusalem Post*, February 11, 2010.
52 "Best Friends Don't Have to Ask," *Politico Magazine*, August 14, 2014.
53 "U.S. Defends Supplying Israel Ammunition during Gaza Conflict," *Reuters*, July 31, 2014.
54 The authorization extension states that (A) Section 12001(d) of the Department of Defense Appropriations Act, 2005 (P.L. 109-108–287; 118 Stat. 1011) is amended by striking "more than 11 years after the date of enactment of this Act" and inserting "after September 30, 2017".
55 This increase for each fiscal year is based on legislative language contained in Section 12002 of P.L. 108-287, the Department of Defense Appropriations Act, 2005.

If however, there is a conflict, the IDF [Israel Defense Forces] can ask for permission to use some of the equipment."51 According to one analyst, "WRSA-I is a strategic boon to Israel. The process is streamlined: No 60-day congressional notification is required, and there's no waiting on delivery."52 During the 2006 war against Hezbollah in Lebanon, the United States granted Israel access to the stockpile. In July 2014, during Israeli military operations against Hamas in the Gaza Strip, the Defense Department permitted Israel to draw from the stockpile, paid with FMF, to replenish 120 mm tank rounds and 40 mm illumination rounds fired from grenade launchers.53

Section 7034(k)(11)(A) of P.L. 114-113, the FY2016 Consolidated Appropriations Act, extended the authorization of WRSA-I through FY2017.54

At times, Congress has passed legislation that has authorized EUCOM to increase the value of materiel stored in Israel. If EUCOM contributed the maximum amount legally permitted in each applicable fiscal year, then the noninflation adjusted value of materiel stored in Israel would currently stand at $2.2 billion. The following legislation authorized increases in value to the stockpile:

· FY1991: P.L. 101-513, the Foreign Operations, Export Financing, and Related Programs Appropriations Act for FY1991, authorized additions to defense articles in Israel up to $200 million in value for FY1991.

· FY1993: P.L. 102-391, the Foreign Operations, Export Financing, and Related Programs Appropriations Act for FY1993, authorized additions to defense articles in Israel up to $100 million in value for FY1993.

· FY1994: P.L. 103-87, the Foreign Operations, Export Financing, and Related Programs Appropriations Act for FY1994, authorized additions to defense articles in Israel up to $200 million in value for FY1994.

· FY1995: P.L. 103-306, the Foreign Operations, Export Financing, and Related Programs Appropriations Act for FY1995, authorized additions to defense articles in Israel up to $100 million for FY1995.

· FY2007-FY2008: Section 13(a)(2)(A)(i) of the Department of State Authorities Act of 2006 (P.L. 109-472) amended Section 514 of the Foreign Assistance Act of 1961, as amended (P.L. 87-195; 22 U.S.C. §2321h) to authorize additions to defense articles in Israel of up to $200 million in value for each of FY2007 and FY2008.55

· FY2011-FY2012: P.L. 111-266, the Security Cooperation Act of 2010, authorized additions to defense articles in Israel up to $200 million in value for each of FY2011 and FY2012.

· FY2014-FY2015: P.L. 113-296, the United States-Israel Strategic Partnership Act of 2014, authorized additions to defense articles in Israel up to $200 million in value for each of FY2014 and FY2015.

· FY2016-FY2017: Section 7034(k)(11)(B) of.P.L.114-113, the FY2016 Consolidated Appropriations Act, authorized additions to defense articles in Israel up to $200 million in value for each of FY2016 and FY2017.

DEFENSE BUDGET APPROPRIATIONS/AUTHORIZATION FOR ANTI-TUNNEL DEFENSE

In 2016, the Israeli and U.S. governments began collaborating on a new system to detect underground smuggling tunnels and counter cross-border tunnels used (most prominently by Hamas in the summer 2014 conflict) to infiltrate Israel. Reportedly, this new technology uses acoustic or seismic sensors and software to detect the sounds of digging by monitoring vibrations underground.56

56 "Israel's Underground War—Technology and Specialist Troops deployed in face of Subterranean Threat," *Wall Street Journal*, March 2, 2016.

Section 1279 of P.L. 114-92, the FY2016 National Defense Authorization Act, authorized the establishment of a U.S.-Israeli anti-tunnel cooperation program. This authorization allowed funds from the research, development, test, and evaluation defense-wide account to be used (in combination with Israeli funds) to establish anti-tunnel capabilities that detect, map, and neutralize underground tunnels that threaten the United States or Israel. The authorization requires the Secretary of Defense to report to Congress on, among other things, the sharing of research and development costs between the United States and Israel. Section 1278 of P.L.115-91, the FY2018 National Defense Authorization Act, extended the authority of the anti-tunnel cooperation program through December 31, 2020. It also required that not less than 50% of U.S. contributions to the program should be used for "research, development, test, and evaluation activities in the United States in connection with such support."

Table 6. U.S.-Israeli Anti-Tunnel Cooperation **dollars in millions**

Fiscal Year	Appropriation
FY2016	40.0
FY2017	42.5
FY2018	TBD

Source: Joint Explanatory Statement accompanying Consolidated Appropriations Acts for FY2016-2017.

AID RESTRICTIONS AND POSSIBLE VIOLATIONS

U.S. aid and arms sales to Israel, like those to other foreign recipients, are subject to U.S. law. Some U.S. citizens and interest groups periodically call upon Congress to ensure that U.S. military assistance to Israel is conditioned on the Israeli government's compliance with applicable U.S. laws and policies and with international humanitarian law.57

57 In November 2017, Representative Betty McCollum introduced a bill, H.R. 4391Promoting Human Rights by Ending Israeli Military Detention of Palestinian Children Act, that would, among other things, prohibit U.S. assistance to Israel (notwithstanding any other provision of law) from being used to support the military detention, interrogation, or ill-treatment of Palestinian children in violation of international humanitarian law.
58 U.S. State Department, *Treaties in Force*, Agreement relating to mutual defense assistance, Entered into force July 23, 1952; TIAS 2675.
59 Nevertheless, in 22 U.S.C. 2753, the AECA also states that the consent of the President shall not be required for the transfer by a foreign country or international organization of defense articles sold by the United States if the recipient is the government of a member country of the North Atlantic Treaty Organization, the Government of Australia, the Government of Japan, the Government of the Republic of Korea, the Government of Israel, or the Government of New Zealand.
60 For example, see (among other sections), Section 502B, Human Rights (22 U.S.C. 2304), Section 505, Conditions of Eligibility (22 U.S.C. §2314), and Section 511, Considerations in Furnishing Military Assistance (22 U.S.C. §2321d).
61 "U.S. Says Israel May Have Violated Agreement on Cluster Bomb Use," *Reuters*, January 29, 2007.
62 For background on the Leahy Law, see CRS Report R43361, *"Leahy Law" Human Rights Provisions and Security Assistance: Issue Overview*, coordinated by Nina M. Serafino.

Arms Sales and Use of U.S.-Supplied Equipment

The 1952 Mutual Defense Assistance Agreement and subsequent arms agreements between Israel and the United States limit Israel's use of U.S. military equipment to defensive purposes.58 The Arms Export Control Act (AECA, 22 U.S.C. §2754) authorizes the sale of U.S. defense articles and services for specific purposes, including "legitimate self-defense." The AECA (22 U.S.C. §2753) states that recipients may not use such articles "for purposes other than those for which [they have been] furnished" without prior presidential consent.59 The act stipulates that sale agreements entered into after November 29, 1999, must grant the U.S. government the right to verify "credible reports" that articles have been used for unauthorized purposes. The Foreign Assistance Act of 1961, as amended, also contains general provisions on the use of U.S.-supplied military equipment.60

In the late 1970s and early to mid-1980s, the Carter and Reagan administrations questioned Israel's use of U.S.-supplied equipment during various military operations in the region. After Israel's 2006 war in Lebanon, the State Department issued a preliminary report to Congress concluding that Israel may have violated the terms of agreements with the United States that restrict Israel's use of U.S.-supplied cluster munitions to certain military targets in noncivilian areas.61

Human Rights Vetting (Leahy Law)62

Section 620M of the Foreign Assistance Act of 1961 (FAA), as amended, prohibits the furnishing of assistance authorized by the FAA and the AECA to any foreign security force unit where there is credible information that the unit has committed a gross violation of human rights. The State Department and U.S. embassies overseas implement Leahy vetting to determine which foreign security individuals and units are eligible to receive U.S. assistance or training.

In February 2016, Senator Leahy and 10 other Members of Congress sent a letter to Secretary of State John Kerry asking the State Department to determine whether alleged extrajudicial killings or torture by Israeli military and police (and Egypt separately) should trigger Leahy law restrictions.63 In its response to Congress, the State Department stated that no Israeli individual or unit potentially involved in the letter's alleged incidents had been submitted to receive U.S. assistance.64

63 The letter's text is available at http://www.politico.com/f/?id=00000153-c56c-d662-a75b-cfecc6be0000.
64 See the text of then Assistant Secretary of State for Legislative Affairs Julia Frifield's April 18, 2016, response letter to Representative Henry C. Johnson at http://www.politico.com/f/?id=00000154-7c2f-d905-a357-7c7f04750000.
65 This stipulation is found in grant agreements between the U.S. State Department's Bureau of Population, Refugees, and Migration (PRM) and United Israel Appeal (clause 8. F. 2 – Use in Territories Subject to the Administration of the State of Israel Prior to June 1967). The FY2013 agreement (S-PRMCO-13-GR-1041 – March 13, 2013) is for $15 million. CRS Correspondence with U.S. State Department, March 2014.
66 http://www.bsf.org.il/BSFPublic/DefaultPage1.aspx?PageId=221&innerTextID=221.
67 The MRA account is authorized as part of the State Department's institutional budget, with funds for the account appropriated through the foreign operations appropriations bill.
68 The Jewish Agency for Israel's website is available at http://www.jafi.org.il/.

Use of U.S. Funds within Israel's Pre-June 1967 Borders

In some instances, U.S. assistance to Israel may be used only in areas subject to the administration of Israel prior to June 1967 (see "Loan Guarantees"). For example, U.S. State Department-provided Migration and Refugee (MRA) assistance (see below), per agreement between the State Department and United Israel Appeal, may only be used for absorption centers, *ulpanim* (intensive Hebrew-language schools with particular focus on immigrants to Israel), or youth *aliyah* (relocation to Israel) institutions located within Israel's pre-June 1967 area of control.65 In addition, according to agreements between the U.S. and Israeli governments, programs funded by certain U.S.-Israeli binational foundations, such as the U.S.-Israel Binational Science Foundation (see below), "may not be conducted in geographic areas which came under the administration of the Government of Israel after June 5, 1967 and may not relate to subjects primarily pertinent to such areas."66

OTHER ONGOING ASSISTANCE AND COOPERATIVE PROGRAMS

Migration & Refugee Assistance

Since 1973, Israel has received grants from the State Department's Migration and Refugee Assistance account (MRA)67 to assist in the resettlement of migrants to Israel. Funds are paid to the United Israel Appeal, a private philanthropic organization in the United States, which in turn transfers the funds to the Jewish Agency for Israel.68 Between 1973 and 1991, the United States gave about $460 million for resettling Jewish refugees in Israel. Annual amounts have varied from a low of $12 million to a high of $80 million, based at least partly on the number of Jews leaving the former Soviet Union and other areas for **Israel.**

Table 7. Migration and Refugee Assistance Funding Levels for Israel

FY2000-FY2012	$519.3 million total
FY2013	$15 million
FY2014	$15 million
FY2015	$10 million
FY2016	$10 million
FY2017	$7.5 million
FY2018	TBD
FY2019 Request	$5.0 million

Source: U.S. State Department.

Congress has changed the earmark language since the first refugee resettlement funds were appropriated in 1973. At first, the congressional language said the funds were for "resettlement in Israel of refugees from the Union of Soviet Socialist Republics and from Communist countries in

Eastern Europe." But starting in 1985, the language was simplified to "refugees resettling in Israel" to ensure that Ethiopian Jews would be covered by the funding. Technically, the legislative language designates funds for refugee resettlement, but in Israel little differentiation is made between Jewish "refugees" and other Jewish immigrants, and the funds are used to support the absorption of all immigrants.

LOAN GUARANTEES

Since 1972, the United States has extended loan guarantees to Israel to assist with housing shortages, Israel's absorption of new immigrants from the former Soviet Union and Ethiopia, and its economic recovery following the 2000-2003 recession, which was probably caused in part by the Israeli-Palestinian conflict known as the second intifada. Loan guarantees are a form of indirect U.S. assistance to Israel, since they enable Israel to borrow from commercial sources at lower rates. Congress directs that subsidies be set aside in a U.S. Treasury account in case of a possible Israeli default. These subsidies, which are a percentage of the total loan (based in part on the credit rating of the borrowing country), have come from the U.S. or the Israeli government. Israel has never defaulted on a U.S.-backed loan guarantee.

LOAN GUARANTEES FOR ECONOMIC RECOVERY

In 2003, then-Prime Minister Ariel Sharon requested an additional $8 billion in loan guarantees to help Israel's ailing economy. The loan guarantee request accompanied a request for an additional $4 billion in military grants to help Israel prepare for possible attacks during an anticipated U.S. war with Iraq. P.L. 108-11, the FY2003 Emergency Wartime Supplemental Appropriations Act, authorized $9 billion in loan guarantees over three years for Israel's economic recovery and $1 billion in military grants. P.L. 108-11 stated that the proceeds from the loan guarantees could be used only within Israel's pre-June 5, 1967, area of control; that the annual loan guarantees could be reduced by an amount equal to the amount Israel spends on settlements outside of Israel's pre-June 1967 area of control; that Israel would pay all fees and subsidies; and that the President would consider Israel's economic reforms when determining terms and conditions for the loan guarantees.69

69 According to P.L. 108-11, "[Loan] guarantees may be issued under this section only to support activities in the geographic areas which were subject to the administration of the Government of Israel before June 5, 1967: Provided further, That the amount of guarantees that may be issued shall be reduced by an amount equal to the amount extended or estimated to have been extended by the Government of Israel during the period from March 1, 2003, to the date of issue of the guarantee, for activities which the President determines are inconsistent with the objectives and understandings reached between the United States and the Government of Israel regarding the implementation of the loan guarantee program: Provided further, That the President shall submit a report to Congress no later than September 30 of each fiscal year during the pendency of the program specifying the amount calculated under the preceding proviso and that will be deducted from the amount of guarantees authorized to be issued in the next fiscal year."
70 CRS correspondence with the U.S. Department of the Treasury's Office of International Affairs, October 2009.
71 This includes $1.6 billion in FY2003; $1.75 billion in FY2004; and $750 million in FY2005.
72 P.L. 108-447, the FY2005 Consolidated Appropriations Act, first extended the authority of the loan guarantees from FY2005 to FY2007. P.L. 109-472, the 2006 Department of State Authorities Act, extended the authority to provide loan guarantees through FY2011. Under that legislation, the loan guarantee program had a stated end of September 30, 2011; however, there was also a "carryover" provision in the statute under which Israel could draw on unused U.S. guarantees until September 30, 2012. In the summer of 2012, Congress passed and the President signed into law P.L. 112-150, the United States-Israel Enhanced Security Cooperation Act of 2012. Section 5(b) of the law extended the loan guarantee authority until September 30, 2015. Section 7034(k)(10) of P.L. 114-113, the FY2016 Consolidated Appropriations Act, further extended the program until September 30, 2019, allowing unused amounts to be carried over into FY2020.
73 "U.S. to Grant Three-year Extension of Loan Guarantees to Israel," *Ha'aretz*, January 24, 2012.

On November 26, 2003, the Department of State announced that the $3 billion in loan guarantees for FY2003 were reduced by $289.5 million because Israel continued to build settlements in the occupied territories and continued construction of a security barrier separating key Israeli and

Palestinian population centers. In FY2005, the U.S. government reduced the amount available for Israel to borrow by an additional $795.8 million. Since then, Israel has not borrowed any funds.

According to the U.S. Department of the Treasury, Israel is legally obligated to use the proceeds of guaranteed loans for refinancing its government debt and also has agreed that proceeds shall not be used for military purposes or to support activities in areas outside its pre-June 5, 1967, areas of control (the West Bank—including East Jerusalem—and Gaza and the Golan Heights). However, U.S. officials have noted that since Israel's national budget is fungible, proceeds from the issuance of U.S.-guaranteed debt that are used to refinance Israeli government debt free up domestic Israeli funds for other uses.70

As of 2018, Israel has issued $4.1 billion in U.S.-backed bonds.71 After deducting the amounts mentioned above, Israel might still be authorized to issue up to $3.814 billion in U.S.-backed bonds. However, if the Israeli government sought to issue new U.S.-backed bonds, it is unclear whether the loan guarantees available to Israel might be subject to reduction based on Israel's estimated expenditures for settlements in the occupied territories. Since the original loan guarantee program authorization for Israel in 2003, Congress has extended the program four times.72 The program is currently authorized through the end of FY2019.

In general, Israel may view U.S. loan guarantees as a "last resort" option, which its treasury could use if unguaranteed local and international bond issuances become too expensive. According to one Israeli official in 2012, "We consider the loan guarantees as preparation for a rainy day.... This is a safety net for war, natural disaster and economic crisis, which allows Israel to maintain economic stability in unstable surroundings."73 Israeli officials may believe that although they have not used the loan guarantees in the last 13 years, maintaining the program boosts the country's fiscal standing among international creditors in capital markets.

Table 8. U.S. Loan Guarantees to Israel: FY2003-FY2018

current dollars in millions

Fiscal Year	Deductions for Settlement Activity	Amount Borrowed by Israel	Amount Available for Israel to Borrow
FY2003	289.5	1,600.0	1,110.5
FY2004	—	1,750.0	1,250.0
FY2005	795.8	750.0	1,454.2
FY2006	—	—	3,814.7
FY2007	—	—	3,814.7
FY2008	—	—	3,814.7
FY2009	—	—	3,814.7
FY2010	—	—	3,814.7
FY2011	—	—	3,814.7
FY2012	—	—	3,814.7
FY2013	—	—	3,814.7
FY2014	—	—	3,814.7
FY2015	—	—	3,814.7
FY2016	—	—	3,814.7
FY2017	—	—	3,814.7
FY2018	—	—	3,814.7

Source: U.S. Department of the Treasury and U.S. State Department.

Note: For FY2003-FY2005, the U.S. Treasury Department authorized Israel to borrow up to **$3 billion per year of the total $9 billion authorized for the Loan Guarantee program.**

AMERICAN SCHOOLS AND HOSPITALS ABROAD PROGRAM (ASHA)74

74 According to USAID, recipients of ASHA grants on behalf of overseas institutions must be private U.S. organizations, headquartered in the United States, and tax-exempt. The U.S. organization must also serve as the founder and/or sponsor of the overseas institution. Schools must be for secondary or higher education and hospital centers must conduct medical education and research outside the United States. Grants are made to U.S. sponsors for the exclusive benefit of institutions abroad. See http://www.usaid.gov/our_work/cross-cutting_programs/asha/.

Through foreign operations appropriations legislation, Congress has funded the ASHA program as part of the overall Development Assistance (DA) appropriation to the United States Agency for International Development (USAID). According to USAID, ASHA is designed to strengthen self-sustaining schools, libraries, and medical centers that best demonstrate American ideals and practices abroad. ASHA has been providing support to institutions in the Middle East since 1957, and a number of universities and hospitals in Israel have been recipients of ASHA grants. In FY2015 (the most recent year for which data are available), ASHA grant recipients in Israel included Shaare Zedek Medical Center in Jerusalem, St. John Eye Hospital Group, Nazareth Hospital, and the Hadassah Medical Organization. According to USAID, institutions based in Israel have received the most program funding in the Middle East region.

Table 9. ASHA Program Grants from Israel Account, FY2000-FY2015

Fiscal Year	Amount
FY2000	$2.75 million
FY2001	$2.25 million
FY2002	$2.65 million
FY2003	$3.05 million
FY2004	$3.15 million
FY2005	$2.95 million
FY2006	$3.35 million
FY2007	$2.95 million
FY2008	$3.90 million
FY2009	$3.90 million
FY2010	$3.80 million
FY2011	$4.225 million
FY2012	$3.00 million
FY2013	$3.800 million
FY2014	$3.052 million
FY2015	$3.075 million
Total	$45.000 million

U.S.-ISRAELI SCIENTIFIC & BUSINESS COOPERATION

In the early 1970s, Israeli academics and businessmen began looking for ways to expand investment in Israel's nascent technology sector. The sector, which would later become the driving force in the country's economy, was in need of private capital for research and development at the time. The United States and Israel launched several programs to stimulate Israeli industrial and scientific research, and Congress has on several occasions authorized and appropriated75 funds for this purpose to the following organizations:

75 With the exception of recent funding for U.S.-Israeli energy cooperation (see " U.S.-Israeli Energy Cooperation " section below), Congress has not appropriated funding for binational foundations since the mid-1980s. At this point, the foundations are able to sustain grant making with interest earned from their respective endowments and fees collected from companies who successfully profited after receiving research support from the foundations.
76 See http://www.birdf.com/default.asp. Congress helped establish BIRD's endowment with appropriations of $30 million and $15 million in 1977 and 1985, respectively. These grants were matched by the Israeli government for a total endowment of $90 million.

· **The BIRD Foundation** (Israel-U.S. Binational Research & Development Foundation).76 BIRD, which was established in 1977, provides matchmaking services between Israeli and American companies in research and development with the goal of expanding cooperation between U.S. and Israeli private high-tech industries. The mission of the Foundation is "to stimulate, promote and support joint (nondefense) industrial R&D of mutual benefit to..." the two

countries.77 Projects are supported in the areas of homeland security, communications, electronics, electro-optics, software, life sciences, and renewable and alternative energy, among others.78 According to the Foundation, $339 million in grants have been awarded to almost a thousand projects. Awards typically range from $700,000 to $900,000. The award size varies based on total project budget and other considerations. The recipients must provide at least 50% of the total project budget. While support for military projects are not a part of the program, several of the completed ventures have yielded products that might be useful in a military setting, including the Aircraft Enhanced Vision System (EVS) camera, "which is designed to provide day/night improved orientation during taxiing or flying. It allows visual landing in reduced visibility conditions, such as fog, haze, dust, smog etc." The Foundation also funded the creation of a Through-Wall Location and Sensing System that is portable and "detects whether people are present behind walls, how many, and where they are situated."79

· **The BSF Foundation** (U.S.-Israel Binational Science Foundation).80 BSF, which was started in 1972, promotes cooperation in scientific and technological research.

· **The BARD Foundation** (Binational Agriculture and Research and Development Fund). BARD was created in 1978 and supports U.S.-Israeli cooperation in agricultural research.81

· In 1995, the United States and Israel established **The U.S.-Israel Science and Technology Foundation (USISTF) to fund and administer projects mandated by the U.S.**-Israel Science and Technology Commission (USISTC),82 a bilateral entity jointly established by the United States Department of Commerce and the Israel Ministry of Industry, Trade, and Labor in 1994 to foster scientific, technological, and economic cooperation between the two countries.

77 Eitan Ydilevich, "Building U.S.-Israel Economic Partnerships, The BIRD Model," Washington, DC. June 10, 2010, p. 2.
78 BIRD Foundation, What is BIRD?, available at http://www.birdf.com/Index.asp?CategoryID=22&ArticleID=79.
79 Information from the BIRD Foundation website, http://www.birdf.com.
80 See http://www.bsf.org.il/Gateway4/. Congress helped establish BSF's endowment with appropriations of $30 million and $20 million in 1972 and 1984, respectively. These grants were matched by Israel for a total endowment of $100 million. According to the treaty establishing the Foundation, the Foundation shall use the interest, as well as any funds derived from its activities, for the operations of the Foundation.
81 See http://www.bard-isus.com/. Congress helped establish BARD's endowment with appropriations of $40 million and $15 million in 1979 and 1985, respectively. These grants were matched by the State of Israel for a total endowment of $110 million. In recent years, Congress has provided funds for BARD in annual Agriculture Appropriations legislation at approximately $500,000 a year.
82 The U.S.-Israel Science and Technology Commission (USISTC) was established in 1993 to facilitate cooperative ventures between high tech industries in the two countries. The goal of the program is to "to maximize the contribution of technology to economic growth." While the collaborative work may be somewhat similar to that supported by the BIRD Foundation, "the Science and Technology Commission assists in the commercialization of new technologies with longer lead times to market. These projects involve higher risk and require substantial capital commitments." The ventures are funded and administered by the U.S.-Israel Science and Technology Foundation. The U.S. and Israeli governments each committed $15 million to the effort over three years for a total of $30 million.

U.S.-ISRAELI ENERGY COOPERATION (BIRD ENERGY)

In 2005, Congress began to consider legislation to expand U.S.-Israeli scientific cooperation in the field of renewable energy. Lawmakers reviewed legislation in the House and the Senate entitled, "The United States-Israel Energy Cooperation Act." Various forms of the bill would have authorized the Department of Energy to establish a joint U.S.-Israeli grant program to fund research in solar, biomass, and wind energy, among other directives. Section 917 of P.L. 110-140, the Renewable Fuels, Consumer Protection, and Energy Efficiency Act of 2007, contains the original language of the U.S.-Israel Energy Cooperation Act (H.R. 1838). Although it did not appropriate any funds for joint research and development, it did establish a grant program to support research, development, and commercialization of renewable energy or energy efficiency. The law also authorized the Secretary of Energy to provide funds for the grant program as needed. Congress authorized the program for seven years from the time of enactment, which was on December 19, 2007. Then, in December 2014, the President signed into law P.L. 113-296, the United States-Israel Strategic Partnership Act of 2014, which reauthorized the U.S.-Israeli Energy Cooperation program for an additional 10 years until September 30, 2024.

To date, Congress and the Administration have provided a total of **$15.7 million** for the grant program, known as BIRD Energy. As of 2017, total combined U.S. and Israeli investment in BIRD Energy for 37 approved projects stands at $30 million.83

83 U.S. Department of Energy, Department of Energy Announces Five New Projects Through BIRD Energy Partnership with Israel, November 1, 2017.

U.S.-ISRAELI WATER COOPERATION

As one of the world's leaders in water reuse and desalination technology, Israel has expanded its cooperation with various U.S. states to export water reuse technology. At the federal level, Congress has supported U.S.-Israeli cooperation through legislation. P.L.114-322, the WIIN Act (Water Infrastructure Improvements for the Nation Act), calls on the White House Office of Science and Technology Policy to develop a coordinated strategic plan that, among other things, strengthens "research and development cooperation with international partners, such as the State of Israel, in the area of desalination technology."

U.S.-ISRAELI CYBERSECURITY COOPERATION

In 2016, Congress passed P.L.114-304, the United States-Israel Advanced Research Partnership Act of 2016, a law that permanently authorized the expansion of an existing joint research-and-development program at the U.S. Department of Homeland Security and expanded it to include cybersecurity technologies. In January 2017, the House passed H.R. 612, the United States-Israel Cybersecurity Cooperation Enhancement Act of 2017. If enacted, the bill would "establish a grant program to support cybersecurity research and development in accordance with existing bilateral agreements between the United States and Israel."

EU ISRAEL COOPERATION

1. POLITICAL BACKGROUND

Israel is a **parliamentary democracy**, with governmental powers divided among separate legislative, executive and judicial branches. Israel has no formal written constitution. The legislative power of the State resides in the Knesset, a unicameral parliament that consists of 120 members elected by universal suffrage under a system of proportional representation. The Prime Minister is the head of Israel's government and appoints a cabinet to assist in governing the country.

2. ECONOMIC BACKGROUND

Israel's per capita GDP (€15.600 in 2002) places it among the 25 most affluent economies world-wide. With a population of roughly 6,5 million, Israel is known for its great achievements in agriculture, irrigation, and various high-tech industries. It depends on imports of crude oil, grains, raw materials, and military equipment. Despite limited natural resources, Israel has intensively developed its agricultural and industrial sectors over the past 20 years. Cut diamonds, high-technology equipment, and agricultural products (fruits and vegetables) are the leading exports.

The influx of immigrants from the former USSR during the period 1989-99 coupled with the opening of new markets at the end of the Cold War energised Israel's economy. In addition free trade agreements with the European Union and with the United States facilitate Israel's exports of goods and services. Investments in new technologies and participation in international business enterprises contributed to the country's accelerated growth during the 1990s.

But growth began moderating in 1996 when the government imposed tighter fiscal and monetary policies and the immigration bonus petered out. Growth was a strong 6.4% in 2000. But the outbreak of Palestinian unrest in late September 2000 with a worsening security situation and the declines in the tourist sector was further aggravated by the global high-tech crisis. GDP declined in 2001 and 2002. Prospects for the Israeli economy have improved in 2003. Economic growth has somewhat recovered, but with about 1% it remains well below average growth rates of 5% during the 1990s and a further deterioration of per capita incomes is expected. In addition to that Israel's unemployment shows an upward trend. Its balance of payment deficit has grown, and growing expenditures on security put pressure on the budget. Additional information on Israel's economic situation can be found on the DG ECFIN site.

3. THE ASSOCIATION AGREEMENT

The EU-Israel Association Agreement is the main agreement governing relations between Israel and the EU. It is much more than just a free trade agreement and enables ongoing dialogue and cooperation between Israel and the EU in a wide variety of fields. The Association Agreement was signed in Brussels, on 20 November 1995, and entered into force on 1 June 2000, following ratification by the 15 Member States parliaments, the European Parliament and the Knesset. It replaces the earlier Co-operation Agreement of 1975.

In line with the new generation of Association Agreements between the EU and its Mediterranean partners, the **preamble** emphasises the importance of the principles of the United Nations Charter, in particular the observance of human rights, democratic principles and economic freedom. The respect for human rights and democratic principles guides the internal and international policy of both Israel and the Community and constitutes an essential and positive element of the Agreement.

It also stresses the need to strengthen political stability and economic development of the region through the encouragement of regional co-operation; to open a regular political dialogue in bilateral and international contexts on issues of common interest; to maintain a dialogue on scientific, technological, cultural, audio-visual and social matters to the benefit of both parties.

The **main text** refers to regular **political dialogue** at ministerial and senior official levels, and at parliamentary level through contacts between the European Parliament and the Knesset. Emphasis is placed on peace, security and regional co-operation and on the need to contribute to the stability and prosperity of the Mediterranean region, to promote understanding and tolerance. Furthermore the agreement includes provisions on **freedom of establishment and liberalisation of services**, free movement of capital and competition rules, the strengthening of **economic** co-operation on the widest possible basis and the co-operation on **social** matters, supplemented by **cultural co-operation**.

The Agreement confirms the existence of **free trade in manufactured goods** and it reinforces the arrangements for free trade in industrial products, which have been in force since the late 1970s. Arrangements for importing Israeli products are more flexible in the new agreement than there were under the 1975 Co-operation Agreement. It also calls for **progressive and reciprocal liberalisation of trade for agricultural products** and indeed a new agreement was reached in July 2003.

A **Joint Declaration** attached to the agreement stresses the importance which both parties attach to the **struggle against xenophobia, anti-Semitism and racism**.

The Association Agreement established two main bodies for the EU-Israel dialogue. The EU-Israel **Association Council** (held at ministerial level) and the EU-Israel **Association Committee** (held at the level of Senior officials) meet at regular intervals (see list below), to discuss political and economic issues as well as bilateral or regional co-operation.

The **second Association Committee** (8 October 2002), devoted time to discuss a number of political issues, among which were the fight against terrorism, the Middle East conflict and the situation in the Palestinian territories, non-proliferation, disarmament and arms control as well as the Euro-Mediterranean Partnership. A number of economic issues of mutual interest to the EU and Israel were also discussed and work is underway on developing these. They include: transport and energy, education, competition, science and technology. Dialogues between the EU and Israel at expert level are scheduled to take place in the fields of: customer protection, social matters, EU enlargement implications, financial services, legal matters and cultural matters.

At the **Economic Dialogue** (17 October 2002), Economic Co-operation issues were discussed in depth. Among others: Israel's economical slowdown and the government's strategy for fiscal consolidation, aiming at bringing down the central government deficit. Israel gave an overview of the structure and development of the financial markets in Israel, as well as of plans for further liberalisation.

The Commission services described the evolution of the international role of the Euro, which is gradually rising. It also described the progress in implementing the Financial Services Action Plan, aiming at removing remaining sources of fragmentation in EU financial markets. The Commission further presented the rules and procedures applied in the EU to ensure sound and sustainable fiscal positions in the context of the Stability and Growth Pact.

The Israeli government assessed the merits of putting in place better infrastructure and communication networks from the periphery to the centre. The EU approach to the reduction of regional disparities was also described, together with its initiatives to promote cross-border co-operation. Future issues, such as labour migration, the high-tech sector and the reform of pension systems will be included in upcoming economic dialogues.

The **third Association Council** (21 October 2002) was held shortly after the last meeting of the Association Committee in Jerusalem. It provided an opportunity to review the two partners' relationship and to take note of progress on points in their common interest, be it in educational and cultural matters, transport and telecommunications or scientific and technological co-operation. An action plan has been adopted on trade and investment facilitation, with the improvement of customs procedure as a first priority. Concerns remained on the EU side about the situation in the Palestinian Territories, and implementation by Israel of the rules of origin provisions of the Association Agreement with respect of import of goods originating in the territories annexed by Israel after the 1967 war and from Israeli settlements. The EU Commission issued a notice to importers in November 2001, in order to preserve the legal and financial responsibility of the EU.

The **third Association Committee** (9 July 2003, Brussels) started with an extensive dialogue on political issues of common interest, including a review of developments in the Peace Process, fight against terrorism and the spread of weapons of mass destruction, ratification of non-proliferation Treaties, and regional issues. Israel announced that a Senior Officials' working group had been set up to prepare a response to the EU's 'Wider Europe' Initiative.

The economic aspects of the Association were discussed in detail, and the Committee noted that considerable work had been accomplished during the past year in several areas. Israel and the EU have renewed their Scientific Co-operation Agreement, and just concluded negotiations for further liberalisation of agricultural trade. Substantial progress has also been achieved on legislative approximation, participation of Israel in the GALILEO Project, common rules for ensuring fair competition within the private sector, and co-operation between Statistical Offices. Further talks have yet to be held on products from Israeli settlements. The Committee identified a number of areas on which follow-up actions will focus in the coming months among them trade facilitation, the environment, social issues, intellectual property, and energy.

In the field of education, the European Commission spelled out the opportunities presented to Israel by the extension of the TEMPUS Programme to the Mediterranean Region, and the new Erasmus Mundus Programme to be adopted next year. Both sides noted the useful and thorough character of their discussions, and their common determination to strengthen bilateral co-operation.

The **fourth Association Council** (17 and 18 November 2003, Brussels) was chaired by Israel. A frank and constructive discussion took place on a whole range of issues of common interest, including the Middle East Peace Process and the Road Map, the humanitarian situation in the Palestinian Territories, Iran, and Iraq. On Wider Europe, the Israeli side welcomed the EU initiative and indicated that a high level task force had been created by the Israeli authorities to work with the European Commission. The EU stressed that the initiative's full potential would be achieved in a context of peace. Various economic and trade issues were discussed in the context of the EU-Israel Association Agreement. Among these were rules of origin where further talks between the European Commission and the Israeli authorities are envisaged. Both sides mentioned the good participation of Israeli enterprises in the first call for proposals launched under the sixth EU Framework Programme for Research. The Israeli government expressed their interest in developing co-operation on Energy, Environment, Justice and Home Affairs.

TRADE RELATIONS

Trade between the EU and Israel is conducted on the basis of the Association Agreement. It has flourished in the last decade. The **EU is Israel's major trading partner**. About 40% of Israeli imports come from the EU, and about 30% of Israeli exports are directed to the EU. It occupies rank number 1 in Israel's imports and rank number 2 in its exports. Israel is the EU's 21st largest export market, and occupies rank number 28 in the EU's imports.

EU imports from Israel in 1990 (€3,626 million) have approximately tripled in 2001 (€9,568 million) as well as EU exports to Israel from 1990 (€5,456 million) to 2001 (€14,449 million). Total trade between the EU and Israel has constantly increased from 1997 to 2000, to reach a record of € 26 billion in 2000. Then a downward trend has developed. Total trade between the EU and Israel decreased, by 7% in 2001 and 8.7% in 2002. Nevertheless in 2002 it reached a level of € 22 billion.

It is due in a large part to a restructuring in diamond trade which represents around 20-25% of EU-Israel trade and to a dramatic reduction in trade in high tech products, the global economic slowdown, a weaker Shekel and a decline of demand. These downward trends have continued during the first semester of 2003.

Agricultural products account for a significant proportion (8.4%) of the community's total imports from Israel, and 2.4% of its total exports there. In 2002, the Community imported agricultural products from Israel for a value of over € 753 million and exported € 326 million worth of agricultural goods.

Under the Euro-Mediterranean Agreement, the two sides granted each other significant trade concessions for certain agricultural products, consisting of tariff reductions or elimination, either within quotas, or for unlimited quantities.

In accordance with Article 14 of the Agreement, which provides for the further reciprocal liberalisation of agricultural trade, negotiations for a package of new concessions have been concluded.

EU-Israeli trade flows (excluding diamonds):

(in millions €)	2001	2002	09/2003
Israeli exports to the EU	6,294	5,638	3,837
Share of EU in total Israeli exports	31 %	29.5 %	31%
Israeli imports from the EU	11,352	10,408	6,486
Share of EU in total Israeli imports	40 %	40 %	40%

CO-OPERATION

Agreements on Scientific and Technical Co-operation between the European Community and the State of Israel

Israel was the first non-European country to be associated to the European Community's Framework Programme for Research and Technical Development (RTD). Israel's special status is the result of its very high level of scientific competence and the dense network of longstanding relations in scientific and technical co-operation between Israel and the EU.

Israel first entered the Fourth Framework programme in August 1996. On 8 March 1999, the "Second Agreement for Scientific and Technical Co-operation between the European Community and Israel" came into force. This agreement fully associated Israel with the 5th Framework Programme for Community RTD (1999-2002). During this period, Israeli universities, research institutes and companies participated in almost 600 research projects with their European counterparts.

The agreement associating Israel to the 6th Framework Programme (FP6 2003-2006) was signed in Brussels on 10 June 2003. FP6 is a key part of the EU's strategy to create a true European Research Area, an Internal Market for science and knowledge in which Israel will play a full role. FP6 is set to play an instrumental part in the Barcelona European Council's target to raise average EU research spending to 3% of European GDP

Agreements on Procurement by Telecommunications Operators and on Government Procurement

The EC and Israel were participants in the negotiations, which led to the WTO's new Government Procurement Agreement (GPA). As part of the negotiations toward an EU-Israel Association Agreement, both parties affirmed their commitment to mutually open their respective procurement markets. It represents real progress in the EU's goal to continue to open up public procurement markets beyond what has already been achieved in the GPA and Israel will be committed to further market opening in urban transport, services, medical equipment and sub-central government procurement, such as municipal and state agencies.

The Agreement on Telecommunications procurement is purely bilateral.

It provides for a mutual opening of procurement by telecommunications operators through granting an exchange of national treatment. The two Agreements build on the close political and economic relationship established between Israel and the EU under the Association Agreement thus making a concrete contribution to the region's economic development and political stabilisation.

The full text of the agreements can be found in the Official Journal of the European Communities L202 of 30 July 1997.

Agreement on Good Laboratory Practice

The agreement provides for the reciprocal acceptance, under certain conditions, of safety studies on chemicals and related data provided by the test facilities of the other party. These studies and data are used for the administrative procedures required to authorise the placing on the market of cosmetics, industrial chemicals, pharmaceuticals, food additives, animal feed additives and pesticides. The agreement therefore reduces the cost and time involved in experiments on chemicals and facilitates market access. The agreement was signed on 26 July 1999 and came into force on 1 May 2000.

Future Cooperation Agreement on Galileo

The European Commission has initiated negotiations with Israel, following the EU Council adoption of relevant directives, with a view to conclude a Cooperation Agreement on Galileo (EU project for a Global Navigation Satellite System) by mid-2004. Galileo is the name of the EU project for a Global Navigation Satellite System to be used in civil telecommunications.

Did you know that ...

- the EU is Israel's major trading partner;

- the European Commission and Israel recently initialled an agreement liberalising most of their agricultural trade (preferential treatment with or without quotas);

- on 30 October 2003, the Palestinian Authority and Israel signed an agreement under EU auspices, aimed at regulating electricity sale and purchase agreements between the Palestinian Distribution Companies and the Israeli Electricity Corporation. The purpose of the commercial agreements is to lower the price and ensure continuity of supply of electricity for Palestinian consumers. Furthermore, the European Commission intends to promote funding of emergency electricity infrastructure projects of common interest;

- Israel was the first and only non-European country to be fully associated to the European Community's Framework Programme for Research and Technical Development;

- in the FP5, which ended in 2002, Israeli organisations participated in 623 cooperative projects with EU partners, representing an estimated total funding of around 165 million €;

- the agreement associating Israel to the 6th Framework Programme (FP6 2003-2006) was signed in Brussels on 10 June 2003, and that first results show that Israel continues to play a very active role with some 140 proposals selected involving Israeli partners;

- the European Commission initiated negotiations with Israel with a view to conclude a Cooperation Agreement on Galileo (EU project for a Global Navigation Satellite System) by mid-2004;

- an Israeli company - InSightec – was among the three winners of the European 2003 IST Grand Prize awarded in Milan, on 2 October 2003, at the IST 2003 conference 'The opportunities Ahead'. This prize is an award for groundbreaking products that represent the best of European innovation in information technology;

- Israel can participate in Tempus projects, aimed at the development of Universities' networks and restructuring of higher education;

- the new Erasmus Mundus programme (scholarships to third country students), which becomes operational in the course of 2004, will involve Israel.

EURO-MEDITERRANEAN PARTNERSHIP

The EU's relations with Israel are managed through different frameworks, bilateral and multilateral, such as the Euro-Mediterranean Partnership.

The South and East Mediterranean and the Middle East is an area of vital strategic importance and a key external relations priority for the EU.

The EU's proximity policy towards the Mediterranean region is governed by the global and comprehensive Euro-Mediterranean Partnership launched at the 1995 Barcelona Conference between the European Union and it's 12 Mediterranean Partners: Israel, Morocco, Algeria, Tunisia, Egypt, Jordan, the Palestinian Authority, Lebanon, Syria; Turkey, Cyprus and Malta. Libya currently has observer status at certain meetings.

The aim of the Euro-Mediterranean Partnership is to turn the Mediterranean basin into an area of dialogue, exchange and co-operation guaranteeing peace, stability and prosperity; to strengthen political dialogue, the development of economic and financial cooperation, the social, cultural and human dimension, and by 2010 establish a free-trade area. It makes economic transition and free trade the central issue of the EU financial co-operation with the Mediterranean region.

Main principles of the Barcelona Declaration

- Establish a common Euro-Mediterranean area of peace and stability based on fundamental principles including respect for human rights and democracy (political and security partnership).

- Create an area of shared prosperity through the progressive establishment of a free-trade area between the EU and its Partners and among the Mediterranean Partners themselves, accompanied by substantial EU financial support for economic transition in the Partners and for the social and economic consequences of this reform process (economic and financial partnership).

- Develop human resources; promote understanding between cultures and rapprochement of the peoples in the Euro-Mediterranean region as well as to develop free and flourishing civil societies (social, cultural and human partnership).

The MEDA programme is the principal financial instrument of the EU for the implementation of the Barcelona process. The programme may apply to States, their local and regional authorities as well as actors of their civil society and has a double vocation: bilateral and regional.

Regional co-operation is an innovative approach of the Barcelona Process. The general aim of this form of co-operation is to promote closer integration between the 27 partners, between the 15 and the 12, but also between the 12 themselves. Regional MEDA programmes complement and reinforce bilateral programmes. Regional cooperation is implemented by multilateral conferences and regional programmes and covers all three baskets of the Barcelona Process. In addition, a number of institutional contacts have been established between Parliaments, Economic and Social Council and Civil Society agents. The fundamental aim is to build trust among the people of the region by engaging them in regular professional co-operation. After enlargement, in May 2004, the co-operation will cover 35 countries, the EU of 25, including Cyprus and Malta and the 10 Mediterranean Partners.

Bilateral co-operation is governed by the Euro-Mediterranean Association Agreements. The EU-Israel Association Agreement was signed on 20 November 1995, and entered into force on 1

June 2000. The ultimate aim of this bilateral dimension is to establish a Euro-Mediterranean Free Trade Area by 2010.

Israel because of its high standard of living and economic development is not eligible for bilateral funding under MEDA. It has however been involved in a wide variety of Euro-Med regional programmes funded under MEDA.

- Young Israelis participate in youth exchange programmes with their European and Mediterranean counterparts under the Euro-Med Youth Action Programme.
- Israeli filmmakers have benefited from funding and training under the Euro-Med Audiovisual Programme.
- Israeli universities participate in the FEMISE forum of economic institutes while chambers of commerce and employers associations have participated in programmes like UNIMED and ArchiMedes.
- Bodies like the Israel Antiquities Authority participate in Euromed Cultural Heritage.

In addition, MEDA is used to support cultural activities in Israel such as the Cinema Europa and DanceEuropa festivals and to encourage cultural cooperation between Israel and the other Mediterranean Partners.
For more information, see Euro-Mediterranean Partnership

SUPPORT TO THE MIDDLE EAST PEACE PROCESS

The European Union attaches great importance to the finding of a just and final settlement to the Arab-Israeli conflict and supports therefore initiatives to further the peace process, in particular through civil society and people to people contacts.

History

The Oslo Accords recommended Israelis and Arabs to launch a series of peace projects – people to people projects in order to build confidence between the communities. In support of the Accords, the Community adopted a new budget line: the Peace process, that covered Community actions connected with the peace agreement concluded between Israel and the PLO. Since the adoption of the Barcelona Declaration in 1995, the European Commission allocated € 88.8 million to the Middle East Peace Projects, an initiative under MEDA. Its main objective was to support the Middle East Peace Process and to increase regional co-operation between Israelis and Arabs in integrated cross-border development, such as environment, health, legal matters, economics, education, media and civil society issues.

PEACE AND TOLERANCE

The EU currently supports the MEPP through local and international initiatives which promote peace and tolerance. The European Commission has allocated € 10 million to the following components:

- EU Partnership for Peace Programme: support to local and international civil society initiatives which promote peace, tolerance and non-violence. The objective of this support is to contribute to the rebuilding of confidence within each society and between societies. An important new strand of this programme aims to bring some of our current individual activities together in a more comprehensive and visible initiative against violence and in support of victims of violence, on both sides of the conflict.

In this framework the EU is making a substantial financial contribution to a Israeli-Palestinian co-operation project – 'Building Business Bridges', based on a unique model developed over the past four years by the Center for Jewish-Arab Economic Development (CJAED) and the Palestinian Media & Development Institute (PMDI).

The overall objective is to prepare Israeli and Palestinian participants both professionally and personally to work together in a multi-cultural environment and enhance their vision as to the possibilities of promoting cooperative ventures in the future. It will be a crucial asset both to the future development of economic and business initiatives in the region and to provide an ongoing platform for dialogue and understanding.

The programme consists of several components. The academic component: a fully accredited MBA program taught by the Graduate School of Business of Haifa University; the Middle Eastern enrichment curriculum: covering a wide range of political, social and economic Middle Eastern and Israeli Palestinian issues; local, regional and international study missions; and a final project, providing the opportunity of working with local and international companies in assessing the feasibility of new business activities in the region.

The current cycle of the 'Building Business Bridges' MBA consists of 19 students: Israelis (Jews and Arabs) and Palestinians (from the West Bank and East Jerusalem). The next cycle is due to begin on 6 May 2004.

- Contribution to the development of ideas for resolving final status issues (in particular refugees and water) by providing factual/technical information and assistance to politicians and negotiators in developing solutions and strategies both on the European side and the parties in the region.
- Support to the verification mechanism for the road map: The roadmap refers to the establishment of a formal monitoring/verification mechanism for its implementation. The roadmap's performance-based approach will require monitoring of compliance with its objectives. The EU, as an active member of the Quartet, has signalled its willingness to contribute to an implementation/verification mechanism by offering technical and/or logistical support.
- In addition to the programme in support of the Middle East peace process, funding for civil society initiatives in support of human rights and democracy is also provided by the European Initiative for democracy and human rights for which Israel and West Bank/Gaza are focus areas.

BASIC LAWS AND REGULATIONS DETERMINIGN THE FUNCTIONS OF THE STATE OF ISRAEL

ISRAEL AS THE NATION-STATE OF THE JEWISH PEOPLE

The Basic Law comprises eleven clauses, as follows:

1 — Basic Principles

A. The land of Israel is the historical homeland of the Jewish people, in which the State of Israel was established.

B. The State of Israel is the national home of the Jewish people, in which it fulfills its natural, cultural, religious and historical right to self-determination.

C. The right to exercise national self-determination in the State of Israel is unique to the Jewish people.

2 — Symbols of the State

A. The name of the state is "Israel."

B. The state flag is white with two blue stripes near the edges and a blue Star of David in the center.

C. The state emblem is a seven-branched menorah with olive leaves on both sides and the word "Israel" beneath it.

D. The state anthem is "Hatikvah."

E. Details regarding state symbols will be determined by the law.

3 — Capital of the State

Jerusalem, complete and united, is the capital of Israel.

4 — Language

A. The state's language is Hebrew.

B. The Arabic language has a special status in the state; Regulating the use of Arabic in state institutions or by them will be set in law.

C. This clause does not harm the status given to the Arabic language before this law came into effect.

5 — Ingathering of the Exiles

The state will be open for Jewish immigration and the ingathering of exiles.

6 — Connection to the Jewish people

A. The state will strive to ensure the safety of the members of the Jewish people in trouble or in captivity due to the fact of their Jewishness or their citizenship.

B. The state shall act within the Diaspora to strengthen the affinity between the state and members of the Jewish people.

C. The state shall act to preserve the cultural, historical and religious heritage of the Jewish people among Jews in the Diaspora.

7 — Jewish Settlement

A. The state views the development of Jewish settlement as a national value and will act to encourage and promote its establishment and consolidation.

8 — Official Calendar

The Hebrew calendar is the official calendar of the state and alongside it the Gregorian calendar will be used as an official calendar. Use of the Hebrew calendar and the Gregorian calendar will be determined by law.

9 — Independence Day and Memorial Days

A. Independence Day is the official national holiday of the state.

B. Memorial Day for the Fallen in Israel's Wars and Holocaust and Heroism Remembrance Day are official memorial days of the State.

10 — Days of Rest and Sabbath

The Sabbath and the festivals of Israel are the established days of rest in the state; Non-Jews have a right to maintain days of rest on their Sabbaths and festivals; Details of this issue will be determined by law.

11 — Immutability

This Basic Law shall not be amended, unless by another Basic Law passed by a majority of Knesset members

THE GOVERNMENT

What the Government is.	1. The Government is the executive authority of the State.
Seat of Government.	2. The seat of the Government is Jerusalem.
Confidence of the Knesset.	3. The Government holds office by virtue of the confidence of the Knesset.
Responsibility.	4. The Government is collectively responsible to the Knesset; each Minister is responsible to the Prime Minister for the field of

	responsibility with which the Minister has been charged.
Composition.	5. (a) The Government is composed of a Prime Minister and other Ministers. (b) The Prime Minister shall be a member of the Knesset. A Minister need not be a member of the Knesset. (c) A Minister shall be in charge of a Ministry; there may be Ministers without Portfolio. (d) One of the Ministers who is a member of Knesset may be designated as Acting Prime Minister. (e) A Minister may be Deputy Prime Minister.
Eligibility of Ministers.	6. (a) A Minister must be an Israeli citizen and a resident of Israel. (b) A person shall not be appointed Minister if he is serving in a position or role as specified in section 7 of The Basic Law: The Knesset, unless he ceased functioning in the said position or role upon or prior to his appointment, as prescribed by law. (c) (1) If a person was convicted of an offense and sentenced to prison and if seven years have not yet passed since the day he on which he finished serving his period of punishment, or since the handing down of his sentence - whichever was later - shall not be appointed Minister, unless the Chairman of the Central Election Committee states that the circumstances of the offense do not involve moral turpitude. (2) The Chairman of the Central Election Committee shall not so rule if the court determined that the offense involved moral turpitude. (d) If a person holds a citizenship other than Israeli, and if the law of the country of which he is a citizen allows him to be released from such citizenship, he shall be appointed Minister only after he has taken all measures necessary to be released from such citizenship. (e) A Knesset member seceding from his faction and failing to tender his resignation as a Knesset member may not be appointed as a Minister during the period of service of that Knesset. This does not apply to the splitting of a faction as defined by law. "Secession from a faction" is defined in section 6(a) of The Basic Law: The Knesset.
Assignment of task of forming Government.	7. (a) When a new Government has to be constituted, the President of the State shall, after consultation with representatives of party groups in the Knesset, assign the task of forming a

	Government to a Knesset Member who has notified him that he is prepared to accept the task; the President shall do so within seven days of the publication of the election results, or should the need arise to form a new government; and in the case of the death of the Prime Minister, within 14 days of his death. (b) Should these consultation take place before the new Knesset is convened, the President will consult the representatives of the lists of candidates to be represented in the new Knesset. (c) This section shall not apply to the formation of a Government following a no confidence vote according to section 28; in the event of an application to the President under section 29(b), the provisions specified in those sections shall apply.
Periods for formation of Government.	8. The Knesset Member to whom the President has assigned the task of forming a Government under section 7 shall have a period of 28 days for the fulfilment of such task. The President of the State may extend the period by additional periods not exceeding in the aggregate 14 days.
Re-assignment of task.	9. (a) Where the periods referred to in section 8 have passed and the Knesset Member has not notified the President of the State that he has formed a Government, or where he has notified him before then that he is unable to form a Government, or where he presented a Government and the Knesset rejected his request for confidence under section 13(d), the President may assign the task of forming a Government to another Knesset Member who has notified him that he is prepared to accept the task, or may inform the Speaker of the Knesset that he sees no possibility of forming a Government - all within three days from the end of the period, or from the day of the Knesset member's statement that he cannot form a government, or from the rejection of confidence in the Government, as applicable. (b) Before assigning the task of forming a Government under this section, or before he informm the Speaker of the Knesset that he sees no possibility of forming a Government, the President may again consult with representatives of factions in the Knesset. (c) A Knesset Member to whom the task of forming a Government has been assigned under this section shall have 28 days in which to do so.
Assignment of task at the request of party groups.	10. (a) Where the President of the State has informed the Speaker of the Knesset, under section 9(a) that he sees no possibility of forming a Government, or where he has assigned the task of forming a Government to a Knesset Member under the same section and the Knesset Member has not notified him within 28 days that he has formed a Government, or has notified him before then that he is unable to form a Government, or presented a

	Government and the Knesset rejected his request for confidence under section 13(d), a majority of the members of the Knesset may request, in writing, that the President of the State assign the task to a particular member of the Knesset, who so agreed in writing, all within 21 days of the President's announcement, or from the end of the period designated in section 9(c), or from the statement by the Knesset Member that he cannot form a Government, or from the rejection of confidence in the Government, as relevant. (b) Where a request as aforesaid has been submitted to the President, the President shall assign the task of forming a Government to that Knesset Member within two days. (c) A Knesset Member to whom the task of forming a Government has been assigned under this section shall have a period of fourteen days for its fulfilment.
Early elections in the event of failure to form a government.	11. (a) Should no request be submitted under section 10(a), or should a Knesset Member fail to form a Government within the period defined in section 10(c), or if he should prior to that time inform the President that he cannot form a Government, the President shall so inform the Knesset Speaker. (b) Should the President so inform the Knesset Speaker, or should a Knesset Member charged with forming a Government under section 10(a) present a Government and fail to win the confidence of the Knesset under section 13(d), then the Knesset shall be deemed to have decided to disperse prior to the completion of its period of service, and elections for the Knesset will be held on the last Tuesday before the end of 90 days of the President's announcement, or of the rejection of the request for confidence in the Government, as relevant.
Discontinuance of proceedings for formation of Government.	12. When a Law for the dissolution of the Knesset has been adopted, the proceedings for the formation of a Government shall cease.
Formation of Government.	13. (a) Where the President of the State has assigned to a Knesset Member the task of forming a Government, he shall notify the Speaker of the Knesset to such effect, and the Speaker of the Knesset shall notify the Knesset. (b) Where the Knesset Member has formed a Government, he shall notify the President of the State and the Speaker of the Knesset to such effect, and the Speaker of the Knesset shall notify the Knesset and set a date for the presentation of the Government to the Knesset within seven days of such notification. (c) The Knesset Member who has formed a Government shall

	head it. (d) When a Government has been formed, it shall present itself to the Knesset, shall announce the basic lines of its policy, its composition and the distribution of functions among the Ministers, and shall ask for an expression of confidence. The Government is constituted when the Knesset has expressed confidence in it, and the Ministers shall thereupon assume office.
Declaration of allegiance.	14. As soon as, or as soon as possible after, the Knesset has expressed confidence in the Government, the Prime Minister shall make before the Knesset the following declaration of allegiance: "I (name) as Prime Minister undertake to uphold the State of Israel and its laws, to faithfully fulfil my role as the Prime Minister and to comply with the decisions of the Knesset"; and each of the other Ministers shall make the following declaration of allegiance: "I (name) as a member of the Government, undertake to uphold the State of Israel and its laws, to faithfully fulfil my role as a member of the Government, and to comply with the decisions of the Knesset."
Cooption of a Minister.	15. The Government may, upon the proposal of the Prime Minister, coopt an additional Minister to the Government. When the Government has decided to coopt a Minister, it shall notify such fact and the function of the additional Minister to the Knesset. Upon the approval of the notification by the Knesset, the additional Minister shall assume office, and as soon as possible after the approval he shall make his declaration of allegiance.
Acting Prime Minister.	16. (a) Should the Prime Minister be absent from Israel, meetings of the Government will be convened and conducted by the designated Acting Prime Minister. (b) Should the Prime Minister be temporarily unable to discharge his duties, his place will be filled by the Acting Prime Minister. After the passage of 100 days upon which the Prime Minister does not resume his duties, the Prime Minister will be deemed permanently unable to exercise his office. (c) Failing the appointment of a designated Acting Prime Minister, or should the Acting Prime Minister be prevented from fulfilling his duties under sections (a) and (b) above, the Government shall designate another Minister to exercise that office.
Interrogation and impeachment of the Prime Minister	17. (a) Criminal proceedings shall not be commenced against the Prime Minister save with the agreement of the Attorney General. (b) Criminal proceedings shall not be commenced against

	someone who served as Prime Minister on suspicion of an offense committed while in office or within a year after serving in office, save with the consent of the Attorney General. (b) An indictment against the Prime Minister will be filed and presided over in the Jerusalem District Court, in a presidium of three judges; proceedings regarding an indictment filed before the Prime Minister begins his term of office shall be prescribed by law. (c) Should the Court convict the Prime Minister of an offense, it will state in its decision whether the offense involved moral turpitude.
Removal from office pursuant to an offense	18. (a) Should the Prime Minister be convicted of an offense which the court defined as involving moral turpitude, the Knesset may remove him from office, pursuant to a decision of a majority of the Knesset members. Should the Knesset so decide, the Government shall be deemed to have resigned. (b) Within 30 days of the verdict becoming final, the Knesset Committee of the Knesset will render its decision regarding its recommendation pertaining to the removal of the Prime Minister from office, and shall present its recommendation to the Knesset plenum; should the committee fail to bring its recommendation to the plenum during the prescribed period, the Speaker will raise the issue in the Knesset plenum. (c) No decision shall be made by either the Knesset or the Knesset Committee regarding the removal of the Prime Minister from office, before the Prime Minister has been given an opportunity to state his case before them. (d) Should the Knesset decide not to remove the Prime Minister from office, and should the verdict as per section (a) above become final, the Prime Minister will cease to serve in office and the Government shall be deemed to have resigned. (e) The provisions of sections 42(a) and 42(b) of the Basic Law: the Knesset, shall not apply to the Prime Minister.
Resignation of Prime Minister.	19. The Prime Minister may, after notifying the Government of his intention to do so, resign by submitting a letter of resignation to the President of the State. The resignation of the Prime Minister shall be deemed to be the resignation of the Government.
Death or permanent incapacity of Prime Minister.	20. (a) If the Prime Minister dies, the Government shall be deemed to have resigned on the day of his death. (b) Should the Prime Minister be permanently incapacitated, the Government shall be deemed to have resigned on the 101st day during which the Acting Prime Minister served in his place.
Prime Minister or	21. (a) Should the Prime Minister cease to function as a member

Acting Prime Minister ceasing to function as member of Knesset.	of the Knesset, he will be deemed to have resigned; the Government shall be deemed to have resigned the same day. (b) Should an Acting Prime Minister cease to be a Knesset Member, he shall cease to serve as Acting Prime Minister.
Termination of tenure of Minister.	22. (a) A Minister may resign from the Government by submitting a letter of resignation to the Prime Minister. His service in the Government will be terminated upon the passage of 48 hours from the time the letter of resignation reached the Prime Minister, unless he retracts prior to such time. (b) The Prime Minister may, by way of written notification, remove a Minister from his post; the removal of Minister will take effect 48 hours after the letter notifying thereof was given to the Minister, unless the Prime Minister retracts prior to such time. (c) The tenure of a Minister in the Government ceases upon his election or appointment to one of the function the holders of which are debarred from being candidates for the Knesset.
Termination of tenure of Minister pursuant to an offense.	23. (a) An indictment against a Minister, except for offenses to be determined by law, will be presented and judged in a district court; procedures regarding indictments filed before a Minister assumed tenure will be determined by law. (b) Should a Minister be convicted by the court, it shall state in its verdict whether the offense involves moral turpitude; should the court so state, the Minister's tenure shall cease on the day of such verdict. (c) This section does not apply to the Prime Minister.
Acting Minister.	24. (a) Should a Minister, except for the Prime Minister, be absent from the country, the Government can charge another Minister to take his place. The Acting Minister will discharge the Minister's duties, in all or in part, as determined by the Government. (b) Should a Minister be temporarily incapable of discharging his duties, the Prime Minister or another Minister appointed by the Government will discharge his duties. (c) The period of tenure of an Acting Minister under subsection (b) will not exceed three months.
Deputy Ministers	25. (a) The Minister in charge of an office, may, with the consent of the Prime Minister and the approval of the Government, appoint one Deputy Minister for the office from among the Knesset members. A Deputy Minister shall assume his role after notice of his appointment has been given by the Government to the Knesset; a Deputy Minister appointed by the Prime Minister shall be entitled "a Deputy Minister in the Prime Minister's office".

	(b) The Deputy Minister shall act both in the Knesset and in the ministry, on behalf of the Knesset member who appointed him and within the parameters allocated to him. (c) A Knesset member seceding from his faction may not be appointed to the position of Deputy Minister during the period of service of the same Knesset. This provision does not apply to the splitting of a faction under the conditions prescribed by law; for the purposes of this subsection, "secession from a faction" is defined by section 6(a) of The Basic Law: The Knesset.
Termination of service of a Deputy Minister	26. The service of a Deputy Minister will be terminated in any of the following cases: (1) The Deputy Minister resigned by submitting a letter of resignation to the Minister who appointed him; (2) The same Minister ceased being a Minister or being in charge of the same office. (3) The Prime Minister, the Government or the appointing Minister decide to terminate the service of the Deputy Minister; however, the Prime Minister will not dismiss a Deputy Minister without first informing both the Government and the appointing Minister of his intention to do so. (4) A new Government was formed. (5) The Deputy Minister ceased being a Knesset member.
Termination of tenure of Deputy Minister pursuant to an offense.	27. Should a Deputy Minister be convicted by the court, it shall state in its judgment whether the offense involves moral turpitude; should the court so state, the Deputy Minister's tenure shall cease on the day of the judgment.
Expression of no confidence in the Government.	28. (a) The Knesset may adopt an expression of no confidence in the Government. (b) An expression of no confidence in the Government will be by a decision adopted by the majority of the Members of Knesset to request that the President assign the task of forming a Government to a certain Knesset member who gave his written consent thereto. (c) If the Knesset has expressed no confidence in the Government, the Government shall be deemed to have resigned on the day of the expression of no confidence. The President will, within two days, charge the Knesset Member so named with the task of forming a Government.

	(d) A Knesset Member to whom the task of forming a Government has been assigned under this section shall have a period of 28 days for its fulfilment. The President of the State may extend the period by additional periods not in the aggregate exceeding 14 days. (e) Where the periods referred to in subsection (d) have passed and the Knesset Member has not notified the President of the State that he has formed a Government, or where he has notified him before then that he is unable to form a Government, the President will so notify the Speaker of the Knesset. (f) If the President so informed the Speaker of the Knesset as per subsection (e) or where he presented a Government and the Knesset rejected his request for confidence under section 13(d), it will be deemed to be a Knesset decision to disperse prior to the completion of its period of service, and elections to the Knesset will be held on the last Tuesday before the end of 90 days of the President's announcement, or of the rejection of the request for confidence in the Government, as relevant.
Authority to disperse the Knesset.	29. (a) Should the Prime Minister ascertain that a majority of the Knesset opposes the Government, and that the effective functioning of the Government is prevented as a result, he may, with the approval of the President of the State, disperse the Knesset by way of an order to be published in Reshumot. The order will enter into feffect 21 days after its publication, unless a request is submitted under subsection (c), and the Government will be deemed to have resigned on the day of the order's publication. (b) Within 21 days of the publication of the order, a majority of the Knesset Members may request that the President charge one of its members, who has so agreed in writing and who is not the Prime Minister, with the task of forming a government. (c) Where a request as aforesaid has been submitted to the President, the President shall inform the Speaker of the Knesset. The President shall assign the task of forming a Government to the Knesset Member named in the request within two days. (d) A Knesset Member to whom the task of forming a Government has been assigned under this section shall have a period of 28 days for its fulfilment. The President of the State may extend the period by additional periods not in the aggregate exceeding 14 days. (e) Should no such request be submitted under subsection (b), or if the period defined in subsection (d) passed, and the Knesset

	Member did not inform the President that he formed a government or where he presented a Government and the Knesset rejected his request for confidence under section 13(d), it will be deemed to be a Knesset decision to disperse prior to the completion of its period of service, and elections to the Knesset will be held on the last Tuesday before the end of 90 days of the President's announcement, or of the rejection of the request for confidence in the government, as relevant. (f) If the President gave notice under subsection (3) or if the Knesset member presented a Government and the Knesset rejected the request that it express confidence in it under section 13(d), then the Knesset is deemed to have decided to disperse before the end of its term of office, and elections to the Knesset will be held on the last Tuesday before the end of 90 days of the President's announcement, or of the rejection of the request for confidence in the government, as relevant. (g) The Prime Minister may not exercise his authority according to this section - (1) From the beginning of the period of service of the incoming Knesset and until the establishment of the new Government. (2) After the Knesset has expressed no confidence in the Government under section 28. (3) After the resignation of the Prime Minister, or from the day on which the Knesset committee of the Knesset decided to recommend that he be removed from service and until the day the Knesset plenum renders its decision in the matter in accordance with the provisions of section 18(a). (h) An Acting Prime Minister shall not be entitled to exercise the authority of the Prime Minister under this section.
Continuity of Government.	30. (a) When a new Knesset has been elected or the Government has resigned under sections 18, 19, 20, 21 or 29, or if a request is submitted under section 29(b), the President of the State shall begin proceedings for the formation of a new Government, as laid out in this Basic Law. (b) When a new Knesset has been elected or the Government has resigned (sections 18, 19, 20, 21 or 29), the outgoing Government shall continue to carry out its functions until the new Government is constituted. (c) A Prime Minister who has resigned shall continue to carry out his functions pending the constitution of the new Government. If

	the Prime Minister has died, or is permanently incapacitated, from carrying out his duties, or if his tenure was ended because of an offense, the Government shall designate another of the Ministers who is a member of the Knesset and of the Prime Minister's faction to be Interim Prime Minister pending the constitution of the new Government. (d) A Government that serves under subsection (b) may appoint a Knesset Member as a Minister in place of a Minister who has ceased to serve; the appointment of a Minister under this subsection does not require the approval of the Knesset.
Functioning of the Government	31. (a) The Government may, with the approval of the Knesset, change the division of roles among the Ministers, with the exception of the role of the Prime Minister. (b) The Government may, with the approval of the Knesset, transfer authorities and duties legally belonging to one Minister, in all or in part, to another Minister. (c) The Government may, with the approval of the Knesset, unite or divide Government ministries, abolish or establish new ministries. (d) The Government may transfer areas of actions from one ministry to another. (e) The Government may establish permanent or temporary Ministerial committees , or for particular matters; after the appointment of a committee the Government may conduct its operations through it. (f) The Government will set work and debate procedures, and decision-making processes in the Government, whether permanent or for a specific matter.
Residual powers of Government	32. The Government is authorized to perform in the name of the State and subject to any law, all actions which are not legally incumbent on another authority.
Delegation of powers	33. (a) Powers granted by law to the Government may be delegated to one of the Ministers; this does not apply to powers granted in accordance with this Basic Law, except for powers under section 32. (b) Powers granted to a Minister by law, transferred to him under the provisions of section 31(b), with the exclusion of the authority to make regulations, may be delegated by the Minister either totally or partially or subject to conditions to a civil servant. (c) Powers delegated by the Government to a Minister, with the exception of the power to make regulations, may be delegated by the Minister either totally or partially or subject to conditions to a civil servant provided that the Government empowered him to do so. (d) For the purposes of this section and section, the power granted to the Government or a Minister also refers to duties incumbent upon them. (e) The provisions of this section will apply provided no other intention is evidenced by the law conferring the power or imposing

	the obligation.
Assumption of powers	34. A Minister charged the implementation of the law, may assume any power, with the exception of powers of a judicial nature, granted by law to a civil servant, provided that no other intention is evidenced by the law; the Minister may do the above for a particular matter or for a specific period.
Secrecy	35. (a) The debates and decisions of the Government and those of the Ministerial committees regarding the following matters are secret and their disclosure and publication is prohibited: (1) State security; (2) Foreign relations of the State; (3) Matters regarding which the Government deems secrecy to be essential to the State, a notification thereof having been declared in an order, for the purposes of this law; (4) A matter that the Government has decided to keep secret; the disclosure and publication of such matters is forbidden only to persons who were aware of the decision. (b) The provisions of subsection (a) shall not apply to matters regarding which the Government or the Prime Minister, or such persons that the Government or the Prime Minister have specifically authorized, have permitted their publication or matters the publication of which is legally mandatory.
Salaries and pensions	36. The salaries of the Ministers and the Deputy Ministers and other payments paid to them during their period of service or thereafter, or to their next of kin after their deaths, will be specified by law, or by virtue of a decision of the Knesset, or a public committee appointed by the Knesset for that purpose.
Regulations	37. (a) The Minister charged with the implementation of a law, is empowered to make regulations for its implementation. (b) A law may empower the Prime Minister or a Minister to make regulations in a matter decided by agreement.
Declaration of a state of emergency	38. (a) Should the Knesset ascertain that the State is in a state of emergency, it may, of its own initiative or, pursuant to a Government proposal, declare that a state of emergency exists. (b) The declaration will remain in force for the period prescribed therein, but may not exceed one year; the Knesset may make a renewed declaration of a state of emergency as stated. (c) Should the Government ascertain that a state of emergency exists in the State and that its urgency necessitates the declaration of a state of emergency, even before it becomes possible to convene the Knesset, it may declare a state of

	emergency. The declaration's validity shall expire upon 7 days from its proclamation, if not previously approved or revoked by the Knesset, pursuant to a decision by a majority of its members; should the Knesset fail to convene, the Government may make a renewed declaration of a state of emergency as stated in this subsection. (d) The Knesset and Governmental declarations of a state of emergency will be published in Reshumot; should publication in Reshumot not be possible, another appropriate manner will be adopted, provided that notification thereof be published in Reshumot at the earliest possible date. (e) The Knesset may at all times revoke the declaration of the state of emergency; notification of its revocation will be published in Reshumot.
State of emergency	39. (a) During a state of emergency the Government may make emergency regulations for the defense of the State, public security and the maintenance of supplies and essential services; emergency regulations will be submitted to the Foreign Affairs and Security Committee at the earliest possible date after their enactment. (b) Should the Prime Minister deem it impossible to convene the Knesset, given the existence of an immediate and critical need to make emergency regulations, he may make such regulations or empower a Minister to make them. (c) Emergency regulations may alter any law temporarily suspend its effect or introduce conditions, and may also impose or increase taxes or other compulsory payments unless there be another provision by law. (d) Emergency regulations may not prevent recourse to legal action, or prescribe retroactive punishment or allow infringement upon human dignity. (e) Emergency regulations shall not be enacted, nor shall arrangements, measures and powers be implemented in their wake, except to the extent warranted by the state of emergency. (f) The force of emergency regulations shall expire three months after the day of their enactment unless their force is extended by law, or they are revoked by the Knesset by law, or pursuant to a decision of a majority of the members of Knesset. (g) Emergency regulations shall come into force on the day of their publication in Reshumot; should publication in Reshumot not be possible another appropriate means of publication will be adopted provided that they be published in Reshumot as soon as possible. (h) Should the state of emergency cease to exist, the regulations enacted will remain in force for the duration of the prescribed period, however not longer than for 60 days after the termination of the state of emergency; state of emergency regulations whose force was lengthened by law shall remain in force.
Declaration of war	40. (a) The state may only begin a war pursuant to a Government decision.

	(b) Nothing in the provisions of this section will prevent the adoption of military actions necessary for the the defence of the state and public security. (c) Notification of a Government decision to begin a war under the provision of subsection (a) will be submitted to the Knesset Foreign Affairs and Security Committee as soon as possible; the Prime Minister also will give notice to the Knesset plenum as soon as possible; notification regarding military actions as stated in subsection (b) will be given to the Knesset Foreign Affairs and Security Committee as soon as possible.
Inapplicability of emergency laws	41. Notwithstanding the provisions of any law, emergency regulations cannot change this Basic Law, temporarily suspend it, or make it subject to conditions.
The Government and Knesset committees	42. (a) The Government will provide the Knesset and its committees with information upon request and will assist them in the discharging of their roles; special provisions will be prescribed by law for the classification of information when the same is required for the protection of state security and foreign relations or international trade connections or the protection of a legally mandated privilege. (b) The Knesset may, at the request of at least forty of its members, conduct a session with the participation of the Prime Minister, pertaining to a topic decided upon; requests as stated may be submitted no more than once a month. (c) The Knesset may obligate a Minister to appear before it, similar authority is granted to any of the Knesset committees within the framework of their tasks. (d) Any of the Knesset committees may within the framework of the discharging of their duties, and under the auspices of the relevant Minister and with his knowledge, require a civil servant or any other person prescribed in the law, to appear before them. (e) Any Minister may speak before the Knesset and its committees. (f) Details regarding the implementation of this section may be prescribed by law or in the Knesset articles.
Change in election date.	43. When a the date for elections to the Knesset has been set under sections 11, 28, and 29, the Knesset may - by a majority vote adopted within five days after grounds for holding the elections arose - decide that because of the proximity of the date of elections to a holiday or memorial day, the elections will be postponed to a date no later than 100 days after the day on which such grounds arose .
Permanence of the Law.	44. (a) This Basic Law can only be changed by a majority of the Knesset members; the majority under this subsection will be required for decisions of the Knesset plenum in the first, second and third readings; for purposes of this subsection, "change" is either explicit or by implication. (b) The provisions of this subsection will not apply to sections 45

	and 46.
Amendment of Basic Law: The Knesset - No. 30	45. In the Basic Law: The Knesset - (1) The following will be added after section 21: "Knesset supervision of secondary legislation 21(a). (a) Regulations enacted by a Minister whose violation entails criminal punishment shall not enter into force until they have been approved by a responsible Knesset committee; should the committee fail to approve or reject the regulations within 45 days of receiving the regulations, the regulations will be deemed approved. (b) The provisions of this subsection do not prejudice the provisions of any Basic Law or other law regarding regulations." (2) Section 35 shall conclude "not later than five months from the adoption of the law." (3) The following will be added after section 36: 36(a). "Dispersion due to failure to adopt budget" (a) Non-adoption of the Budget Law within three months subsequent to the beginning of the fiscal year will be considered to be a Knesset decision on its dispersion, prior to the completion of its term of service, on the day following the end of this period (hereafter: the determining date), and early elections will be held on the last Tuesday before the end of 90 days of the determining date, unless the Knesset decides, within five days of the determining date, may decide that because of the proximity of the date of elections to a holiday or memorial day, to postpone the elections to a date no later than 100 days from the determining date. (b) Notwithstanding the provisions of subsection (a), should the President begin procedures to form a new Government under section 30 of The Basic Law: The Government, or should a law be adopted to disperse the Knesset, or should elections to the Knesset be held after the submission of the Draft Budget under section 3 of The Basic Law: The State Economy, and before the passage of three months from the beginning of the fiscal year, the

	determining day under subsection (a), shall be "three months from the beginning of the fiscal year or 45 days from the constitution of the Government, whichever is later."
Repeal of The Basic Law: The Government.	46. The Basic Law: The Government (1992) is repealed.
Effect and applicability.	47. (a) The provisions of this Basic Law shall apply to elections and to formation of the Government, beginning with elections to the 16th Knesset. (b) Subject to the provisions of subsection (a), this Law shall go into effect on the day the Government is formed as said in subsection (a). (c) Notwithstanding the provisions of subsection (b), section 44 shall go into effect on the day on which this Law is published.

THE PRESIDENT OF THE STATE

Status	1. A President shall stand at the head of the State.
Place of residence.	2. The place of residence of the President of the State shall be Jerusalem.
Election and period of tenure	3. (a) The President of the State shall be elected by the Knesset for seven years. (b) The President will serve for one term only.
Eligibility	4. Every Israel national who is a resident of Israel is qualified to be a candidate for the office of President of the State.
Date of election	5. The election of the President of the State shall be held not earlier than ninety days and not later than thirty days before the expiration of the period of tenure of the President in office. If the place of the President of the State falls vacant before the expiration of his period of tenure, the election shall be held within forty-five days from the day on which such place falls vacant. The Speaker of the Knesset, in consultation with the Deputy Speaker, shall fix the day of the election and shall notify it to all the Members of the Knesset in writing at least twenty days in advance. If the day of the election does not fall in one of the session terms of the Knesset, the Speaker of the Knesset shall convene the Knesset for the election of the President of the State.
Proposal of candidates	6. (a) When the day of the election has been fixed, any ten or more Members of the Knesset may propose a candidate. The proposal shall be in writing and shall be delivered to the Speaker of the Knesset, together with the consent of the candidate in writing or by telegram, not later than ten days before the day of the election. A member of the Knesset shall not sponsor the proposal of more than one candidate. (b) The Speaker of the Knesset shall notify all the members of the Knesset, in writing, not later than seven days before the day of the election, of every candidate proposed and of the names of the Members of the Knesset who have proposed him, and shall announce the candidates at the opening of the meeting at which the election is held.

Voting	7. The election of the President of the State shall be by secret ballot at a meeting of the Knesset assigned only for that purpose.
Election by majority of votes	8. The candidate who has received the votes of a majority of the Members of the Knesset is elected. If no candidate receives such a majority, a second ballot shall be held. If there is no majority as aforesaid at the second ballot, either, voting shall be continued. At the third and every subsequent ballot, the candidate who at the preceding ballot received the smallest number of votes shall no longer stand for election. The candidate who at the third or any subsequent ballot receives a majority of the votes of the Members of the Knesset who take part in the voting and vote for one of the candidates is elected. If two candidates receive the same number of votes, voting shall be repeated.
Declaration of allegiance	9. The President-Elect shall make and sign before the Knesset the following declaration of allegiance: "I pledge myself to bear allegiance to the State of Israel and to its laws and faithfully to carry out my functions as President of the State.".
Making of declaration and commencement of period of tenure	10. The President-Elect shall make his declaration of allegiance and begin to hold office upon the expiration of the period of tenure of the preceding President of the State. If the place of the preceding President of the State falls vacant before the expiration of his period of tenure, the President-Elect shall make his declaration of allegiance as soon as possible after his election and shall begin to hold office upon making his declaration of allegiance.
Functions and powers	11. (a) The President of the State - (1) shall sign every Law, other than a Law relating to its powers; (2) shall take action to achieve the formation of a Government and shall receive the resignation of the Government in accordance with Law; (3) shall receive from the Government a report on its meetings; (4) shall accredit the diplomatic representatives of the State, shall receive the credentials of diplomatic representatives sent to Israel by foreign states, shall empower the consular representatives of the State and shall confirm the appointments of consular representatives sent to Israel by foreign states; (5) shall sign such conventions with foreign states as have been ratified by the Knesset; (6) shall carry out every function assigned to him by Law in connection with the appointment and removal from office of judges and other office-holders. (b) The President of the State shall have power to pardon offenders and to lighten penalties by the reduction or commutation thereof. (c) The President of the State shall carry out every other function and have every other power assigned to him by Law.

Counter-signature	12. The signature of the President of State on an official document, other than a document connected with the formation of a Government, shall require the countersignature of the Prime Minister or of such other Minister as the Government may decide.
Immunity with regard to discharge of functions	13. (a) The President of the State shall not be amenable to any court or tribunal, and shall be immune from any legal act, in respect of anything connected with his functions or powers. (b) The President of the State shall not, in giving evidence, have to disclose anything which came to his knowledge in the discharge of his functions as President of the State. (c) The immunity of the President of the State under this section shall continue after he has ceased to be President of the State.
Immunity from criminal proceedings	14. The President of the State shall not be criminally prosecuted. The period during which, by virtue of this section, the President of the State cannot be prosecuted for an offence shall not be counted in calculating the period of prescription of that offense.
Evidence	15. If the President of the State is required to give evidence, his evidence shall be taken at such place and time as shall be determined with his sanction.
Salary and other payments	16. The salary of the President of the State, and other payments to be made to him during or after his period of tenure, including payments to be made to his survivors, shall be fixed by resolution of the Knesset, which may empower the Finance Committee in that behalf. Resolutions under this section shall be published in Reshumot.
President to hold no other office	17. (a) Save with the sanction of the House Committee of the Knesset, the President of the State shall not hold any post, or exercise any function, other than the post and functions of President of the State. (b) The President of the State shall be exempt from all compulsory service.
Departure for abroad	18. The President of the State shall not leave the territory of the State save with the sanction of the Government.
Resignation	19. The President of the State may resign his office by submitting a letter of resignation to the Speaker of the Knesset. The letter of resignation shall not require a countersignature. The place of the President of the State shall become vacant forty-eight hours after the letter of resignation reaches the Speaker of the Knesset.
Removal of President from office	20. (a) The Knesset may, by resolution, remove the President of the State from office if it finds that he is unworthy of his office owing to conduct unbecoming his status as President of the State. (b) The Knesset shall not remove the President of the State from office, save following a complaint brought before the House Committee by at least twenty members of the Knesset and upon the proposal of the House Committee passed by a three-quarters majority of the members of the Committee. A resolution by the Knesset to remove the President from office shall require a three-quarters majority of the Members of the Knesset.

	(c) The House Committee shall not propose the removal of the President of the State from office before he has been given an opportunity to refute the complaint in accordance with procedure prescribed by the Committee with the approval of the Knesset, and the Knesset shall not resolve to remove the President of the State from office before he has been given an opportunity to be heard in accordance with procedure prescribed by the House Committee with the approval of the Knesset. (d) The President of the State may be represented before the House Committee and before the Knesset by an authorised representative. A Member of the Knesset shall not act as the representative of the President. The House Committee and the Knesset may summon the President of the State to be present at proceedings under this section. (e) Proceedings of the Knesset under this section shall be taken at a meeting, or successive meetings, assigned solely for that purpose. The proceedings shall begin not later than twenty days after the resolution of the House Committee. The time of their beginning shall be notified by the Speaker of the Knesset to all the Members of the Knesset, in writing, at least ten days in advance. If the beginning of the proceedings does not fall in one of the session terms of the Knesset, the Speaker of the Knesset shall convene the Knesset for the proceedings.
Vacation of post for reasons of health	21. (a) The Knesset may, by resolution passed by a majority of its members, declare that for reasons of health the President of the State is permanently unable to carry out his functions. (b) The Knesset shall not pass a resolution as aforesaid save upon the proposal of the House Committee passed by a two-thirds majority of its members on the strength of a medical opinion given in accordance with rules prescribed by the Committee. (c) If the Knesset resolves as aforesaid, the place of the President of the State shall become vacant on the day of the resolution.
Temporary cessation of exercise of office	22. (a) The President of the State shall temporarily cease to carry out his functions and exercise his powers - (1) if he leaves the territory of the State - from the time of his leaving until his return (2) if he notifies the House Committee that for reasons of health he is temporarily unable to carry out his functions and the Knesset Committee approves his notification by a majority of votes -- from the time of the approval of the notification until the expiration of the period fixed by the Committee in its resolution or until the President of the State notifies the House Committee that he is no longer unable to carry out his functions, whichever is the earlier date; (3) if the House Committee, by a two-thirds majority of its members, on the strength of a medical opinion given in accordance with rules prescribed by the Committee, resolves that for reasons of health the President of the State is temporarily unable to carry out his functions -- from the passing of the resolution until the expiration of the period fixed

	by the House Committee in the resolution or until the House Committee resolves that the President is no longer unable to carry out his functions. (b) The House Committee shall not, under subsection (a)(2) or (3), fix a period exceeding three months. It may extend the period, without a break, up to a maximum of three additional months. Any further extension shall require a resolution of the Knesset passed by a majority of the Members of the Knesset upon the proposal of the House Committee.
Interim President and Acting President	23. (a) If the place of the President of the State has fallen vacant, and so long as the new President has not yet begun to hold office, the Speaker of the Knesset shall hold office as Interim President of the State. (b) During a period in which the President of the State has temporarily ceased to carry out his functions and exercise his powers, the Speaker of the Knesset shall hold office as Acting President of the State. (c) While holding office as Interim President of the State or Acting President of the State, the Speaker of the Knesset shall carry out the functions assigned to the President of the State by Law and shall exercise the powers vested in the President of the State by Law.
Notices in Reshumot	24. (a) The Speaker of the Knesset shall publish a notice in Reshumot as to - (1) the commencement of the tenure of the President of the State; (2) the vacancy of the place of the President of the State; (3) the commencement and termination of the tenure of the Speaker of the Knesset as Acting President of the State under section 22(a)(2) and (3). (b) The Prime Minister shall publish a notice in Reshumot as to the President's leaving the territory of the State and as to his return.
Law not to be affected by emergency regulations	25. Notwithstanding the provisions of any other law, this Law cannot be varied, suspended, or made subject to conditions, by emergency regulations.
Repeal	26. (a) There are hereby repealed - (1) sections 2(c), 6 and 7 of the Transition Law, 5709-1949(1); (2) the State President (Tenure) Law, 5712-1951(2); (b) The State President, Government Members and Chief Rabbis of Israel (Fixing of Salaries) Law, 5711-1950(3), shall no longer apply to the salary of the President of the State or to payments due to him or his survivors.
Transitional provision	27. The President of the State who was elected by the Knesset on the 27th Iyar, 5723 (21st May, 1963) shall be deemed to have been elected, and to hold office, under this Law.

- Basic Law: The Knesset

THE JUDICIARY

BASIC PROVISIONS

Judicial power	1. (a) Judicial power is vested in the following courts**: (1) the Supreme Court; (2) a District Court; (3) a Magistrate's Court; (4) another court designated by Law as a court. In this Law, "judge" means a judge of a court as aforesaid. (b) Judicial power is vested also in the following: (1) a religious court (beit din); (2) any other court (beit din): (3) another authority all as prescribed by Law. (c) No court or court (beit din) shall be established for a particular case.
Independence	2. A person vested with judicial power shall not, in judicial matters, be subject to any authority but that of the Law.
Publicity of proceedings	3. A court shall sit in public unless otherwise provided by Law or unless the court otherwise directs under Law.

JUDGES

Appointment of judges	4. (a) A judge shall be appointed by the President of the State upon election by a Judges' Election Committee. (b) The Committee shall consist of nine members, namely, the President of the Supreme Court, two other judges of the Supreme Court elected by the body of judges thereof, the Minister of Justice and another Minister designated by the Government, two members of the Knesset elected by the Knesset and two representatives of the Chamber of Advocates elected by the National Council of the Chamber. The Minister of Justice shall be the chairman of the Committee. (c) The Committee may act even if the number of its members has decreased, so long as it is not less than seven.
Nationality	5. Only an Israeli national shall be appointed judge.
Declaration of allegiance	6. A person appointed judge shall make a declaration of allegiance before the President of the State. The declaration shall be as follows: "I pledge myself to be in allegiance to the State of Israel and to its laws, to dispense justice fairly, not to pervert the law and to show no favour.".
Period of tenure	7. The tenure of a judge shall begin upon his declaration of allegiance and shall end only -

	(1) upon his retirement on pension; or (2) upon his resignation; or (3) upon his being elected or appointed to one of the positions the holders of which are debarred from being candidates for the Knesset; or (4) upon a decision of the Judges' Election Committee prepared by the chairman of the Committee or the President of the Supreme Court and passed by a majority of at least seven members; or (5) upon a decision of the Court of Discipline.
Retired judge	8. A judge who has retired on pension may be appointed to the position of a judge for such time, in such manner and on such conditions as may be prescribed by Law.
Restriction on re-posting	9. (a) A judge shall not be permanently transferred from the locality where he is serving to a court in another locality save with the consent of the President of the Supreme Court or pursuant to a decision of the Court of Discipline. (b) A judge shall not without his consent be appointed to an acting position at a lower court.
Salary and benefits	10. (a) The salaries of judges and other payments to be made to them during or after their period of tenure or to their survivors after their death shall be prescribed by Law or by a decision of the Knesset or of a Knesset committee empowered by the Knesset in that behalf. (b) No decision shall be passed reducing the salaries of judges only.
Judge not to engage in additional occupation, etc.	11. A judge shall not engage in an additional occupation, and shall not carry out any public function save with the consent of the President of the Supreme Court and the Minister of Justice.
Criminal proceedings	12. (a) No criminal investigation shall be opened against a judge save with the consent of the Attorney-General, and no information shall be filed against a judge save by the Attorney-General. (b) A criminal charge against a judge shall not be tried save before a District Court consisting of three judges unless the judge has consented that the charge be tried in the ordinary manner. (c) The provisions of this section shall not apply to categories of offences designated by Law.
Disciplinary proceedings	13. (a) A judge shall be subject to the jurisdiction of a Court of Discipline. (b) A Court of Discipline shall consist of judges and judges retired on pension appointed by the President of the Supreme Court. (c) Provisions as to the grounds for instituting disciplinary proceedings, the modes of filing complaints, the composition of the bench, the powers of the Court of Discipline and the disciplinary measures it shall be authorised to impose shall be prescribed by Law. The rules of procedure shall be in accordance with Law.
Suspension	14. Where a complaint or information is filed against a judge, the President of the Supreme Court may suspend him from office for such period as he may prescribe.

THE COURTS

Supreme Court	15. (a) The seat of the Supreme Court is Jerusalem. (b) The Supreme Court shall hear appeals against judgments and other decisions of the District Courts. (c) The Supreme Court shall sit also as a High Court of Justice. When so sitting, it shall hear matters in which it deems it necessary to grant relief for the sake of justice and which are not within the jurisdiction of another court (beit mishpat or beit din). (d) Without prejudice to the generality of the provisions of subsection (c), the Supreme Court sitting as a High Court of Justice shall be competent - (1) to make orders for the release of persons unlawfully detained or imprisoned. (2) to order State and local authorities and the officials and bodies thereof, and other persons carrying out public functions under law, to do or refrain from doing any act in the lawful exercise of their functions or, if they were improperly elected or appointed, to refrain from acting; (3) to order courts (batei mishpat and batei din) and bodies and persons having judicial or quasi-judicial powers under law, other than courts dealt with by this Law and other than religious courts (batei din), to hear, refrain from hearing, or continue hearing a particular matter or to void a proceeding improperly taken or a decision improperly given; (4) to order religious courts (batei din) to hear a particular matter within their jurisdiction or to refrain from hearing or continue hearing a particular matter not within their jurisdiction, provided that the court shall not entertain an application under this paragraph is the applicant did not raise the question of jurisdiction at the earliest opportunity; and if he had no measurable opportunity to raise the question of jurisdiction until a decision had been given by a religious court (beit din), the court may quash a proceeding taken or a decision given by the religious court (beit din) without authority. (e) Other powers of the Supreme Court shall be prescribed by Law.
Other courts	16. The establishment, powers, places of sitting and areas of jurisdiction of the District Courts, the Magistrates' Courts and other courts shall be in accordance with Law.
Appeal	17. A judgment of a court of first instance, other than a judgment of the Supreme Court, shall be appealable as of right.
Further hearing	18. In a matter adjudged by the Supreme Court by a bench of three, a further hearing may be held by a bench of five on such grounds and in such manner as shall be prescribed by Law.
Retrial	19. In a criminal matter adjudged finally, a retrial may be held on such grounds

	and in such manner as shall be prescribed by Law.
Established rule	20. (a) A rule laid down by a court shall guide any lower court. (b) A rule laid down by the Supreme Court shall bind any court other than the Supreme Court.
Registrar	21. A court may have a registrar, who may or may not be a judge.

MISCELLANEOUS PROVISIONS

Law not to be affected by emergency regulations	22. This Law cannot be varied, suspended, or made subject to conditions by emergency regulations.
Provisions to be prescribed by Law	23. Provisions as to the following matters shall be prescribed by Law: (1) the manner of electing, and duration of the tenure of, the members of the Judges' Election Committee; (2) qualifications for the posts of judges of the various grades; (3) the manner of appointing the President of the Supreme Court, the Deputy President of the Supreme Court and the President and Vice-president of a District Court and a Magistrate's Court; (4) the conditions and procedures for terminating the tenure of a judge; (5) the manner of appointing a judge to an acting assignment at another court and of transferring a judge, temporarily or permanently, from the locality where he is serving to a court in another locality; (6) proceedings for the suspension of a judge from office, and review of the suspension; (7) the matters which the courts of the different grades are to hear by a single judge or by three or more judges; (8) the manner of designating the judge or judges who is or are to hear a particular matter.
Provisions to be prescribed under Law	24. Provisions as to the following matters shall be prescribed under Law: (1) rules as to the administration of the courts, the making thereof and responsibility for their implementing; (2) the rules of procedure of the Judges' Election Committee; (3) procedure for the resignation of a judge; (4) procedure for the appointment and the powers of the

	registrar of a court; (5) the number of judges who are to serve in the courts of the different grades and location.

THE STATE COMPTROLLER

Essence	1. The State Audit shall be implemented by the State Comptroller.
State Audit	2. (a) The Comptroller will audit the economy, the property, the finances, the obligations and the administration of the State, of Government Ministries, of all enterprises, institutions, or corporations of the State, of Local Authorities, and of bodies or other institutions which were defined by law as subject to audit by the State Comptroller. (b) The State Comptroller shall inspect the legality, integrity, managerial norms, efficiency and economy of the audited bodies, as well as any other matter which he deems necessary.
Duty to provide information	3. A body subject to State Audit will upon request, immediately provide the State Comptroller with information, documents, explanations, or any other material which the Comptroller deems necessary for audit purposes.
Comptroller as Commissioner for Complaints	4. The State Comptroller will investigate complaints from the public about bodies and persons, as provided by law: in this capacity the State Comptroller shall bear the title 'Commissioner for Complaints from the Public'.
Additional tasks	5. The State Comptroller shall undertake additional tasks as provided by law.
Accountability to the Knesset	6. In carrying out his functions, the State Comptroller shall be accountable only to the Knesset and not to the Cabinet.
Election	7. (a) The State Comptroller shall be chosen by the Knesset in a secret ballot; the exact arrangements shall be set by law.
Term of office	(b) The term of office of the State Comptroller shall be seven years. (c) The State Comptroller will serve for one term only.
Qualifications	8. Any Israeli citizen, residing in Israel, shall be eligible to serve as State Comptroller; any additional qualifications may be determined by law.
Pledge of allegiance	9. The State Comptroller-elect shall make and sign before the Knesset the following declaration: 'I pledge allegiance to the State of Israel and to its laws, and will faithfully carry out my duties as State Comptroller'.
Budget	10. The budget of the State Comptroller's Office shall be determined by the Appropriations Committee of the Knesset, upon the recommendation of the State Comptroller, and will be published together with the State Budget.

Salary and emoluments	11. The salary of the State Comptroller and other payments made to him during his term of office or subsequently, or to his survivors upon his demise, shall be determined by law or by a Knesset Resolution or by a duly authorized committee of the Knesset.
Contact with Knesset and issuance of reports	12. (a) The State Comptroller shall maintain contact with the Knesset, as determined by law. (b) The State Comptroller shall issue reports and opinions within the scope of his duties and shall publish them, subject to any restrictions determined by law.
Removal from office	13. The State Comptroller shall not be removed from office except by a two-thirds majority of those Knesset members voting; arrangements for impeachment shall be determined by law. 14. If the State Comptroller is not able to fulfill his functions, an acting Comptroller shall be appointed, in a manner and for a period as determined by law.

THE ARMY

Defence Army of Israel	1. The Defence Army of Israel is the army of the State.
Subordination to civil authority	2. (a) The Army is subject to the authority of the Government. (b) The Minister in charge of the Army on behalf of the Government is the Minister of Defence.
Chief of the General Staff	3. (a) The supreme command level in the Army is the Chief of the General Staff. (b) The Chief of the General Staff is subject to the authority of the Government and subordinate to the Minister of Defence. (c) The Chief of the General Staff shall be appointed by the Government upon the recommendation of the Minister of Defence.
Duty to serve and recruitment	4. The duty of serving in the Army and recruitment for the Army shall be as prescribed by or by virtue of Law.
Instructions and orders in the Army	5. The power to issue instructions and orders binding in the Army shall be prescribed by or by virtue of Law.
<i	6. No armed force other than the Defence Army of Israel shall be established or maintained except under Law.

JERUSALEM, CAPITAL OF ISRAEL

Jerusalem, Capital of Israel	1. Jerusalem, complete and united, is the capital of Israel.
Seat of the President, the Knesset, the Government and the Supreme Court	2. Jerusalem is the seat of the President of the State, the Knesset, the Government and the Supreme Court.
Protection of Holy	3. The Holy Places shall be protected from desecration and any other

Places	violation and from anything likely to violate the freedom of access of the members of the different religions to the places sacred to them or their feelings towards those places.
Development of Jerusalem	4. (a) The Government shall provide for the development and prosperity of Jerusalem and the well-being of its inhabitants by allocating special funds, including a special annual grant to the Municipality of Jerusalem (Capital City Grant) with the approval of the Finance Committee of the Knesset. (b) Jerusalem shall be given special priority in the activities of the authorities of the State so as to further its development in economic and other matters. (c) The Government shall set up a special body or special bodies for the implementation of this section.

ISRAEL LANDS

Prohibition of transfer of ownership	1. The ownership of Israel lands, being the lands in Israel of the State, the Development Authority or the Keren Kayemet Le-Israel, shall not be transferred either by sale or in any other manner.
Permission by Law	2. Section 1 shall not apply to classes of lands and classes of transactions determined for that purpose by Law.
Definition	3. In this Law, "lands" means land, houses, buildings and anything permanently fixed to land.

THE STATE ECONOMY

Taxes, compulsory loans, and fees	1. (a) Taxes, compulsory loans and other compulsory payment shall not be imposed, and their amounts shall not be varied, save by or under Law; the same shall apply with regard to fees. (b) Where the amounts of any taxes, compulsory loans or other compulsory payments, or fees, payable to the Treasury are not prescribed in the Law itself, the amounts prescribed therefor by regulations shall require approval - in advance or within the period prescribed by the Law - by a decision of the Knesset or of a committee of the Knesset empowered by it in that behalf.
State property	2. Transactions in State property and the acquisition of rights and assumption of liabilities on behalf of the State shall be effected by a person empowered in that behalf by or under Law.
The State Budget	3. (a) (1) The State Budget shall be prescribed by Law. (2) The Budget shall be for one year and shall set out the expected and planned expenditure of the Government. (b) (1) The Government shall lay the Budget Bill on the table of the Knesset at the time prescribed by the Knesset or by a committee of the Knesset empowered by it in that behalf. (2) The Budget Bill shall be accompanied by an estimate of the sources

	for financing the Budget. (c) In case of necessity, the Government may bring in an Additional Budget Bill during the financial year. (d) Where it appears to the Government that the Budget Law will not be adopted before the beginning of the financial year, it may bring in an Interim Budget Bill. (e) The Minister of Finance shall submit to the Knesset every year a report on the implementation of the State Budget. Particulars shall be prescribed by Law.
Currency notes and coins	4. The printing of legal tender currency notes and the minting of legal tender coins, and the issue thereof, shall be done under Law.
Inspection	5. The State economy shall be subject to the inspection of the State Comptroller. Particulars shall be prescribed by Law.

* Passed by the Knesset on the 13th of Av, 5735 (21st July, 1975) and published in Sefer Ha-Chukkim No. 777 of the 23rd Av, 5735 (31st July, 1975), p. 206; the Bill and an Explanatory Note were published in Hatza'ot Chok No. 1039 of 5733, p. 147.

THE STATE ECONOMY (AMENDMENT)

Amendment of section 1	1. In section 1(b) of the Basic Law: The State Economy**, after the words "are not prescribed in the Law itself", there shall be inserted the words "and the Law does not provide that the amounts prescribed therefor by regulations shall require approval by the Knesset or by a committee of the Knesset".
Amendment of section 3	2. In section 3 of the Basic Law: The State Economy, at the end of subsection (b)(1), there shall be added the words "but not later than sixty days before the beginning of the financial year".

HUMAN DIGNITY AND LIBERTY*

Purpose	1. The purpose of this Basic Law is to protect human dignity and liberty, in order to establish in a Basic Law the values of the State of Israel as a Jewish and democratic state.
Preservation of life, body and dignity	2. There shall be no violation of the life, body or dignity of any person as such.
Protection of property	3. There shall be no violation of the property of a person.
Protection of life, body and dignity	4. All persons are entitled to protection of their life, body and dignity.
Personal liberty	5. There shall be no deprivation or restriction of the liberty of a person by imprisonment, arrest, extradition or otherwise.
Leaving and entering Israel	6. (a) All persons are free to leave Israel. (b) Every Israel national has the right of entry into Israel from abroad.
Privacy	7. (a) All persons have the right to privacy and to intimacy. (b) There shall be no entry into the private premises of a person who has

	not consented thereto. (c) No search shall be conducted on the private premises of a person, nor in the body or personal effects. (d) There shall be no violation of the confidentiality of conversation, or of the writings or records of a person.
Violation of rights	8. There shall be no violation of rights under this Basic Law except by a law befitting the values of the State of Israel, enacted for a proper purpose, and to an extent no greater than is required.
Reservation regarding security forces	9. There shall be no restriction of rights under this Basic Law held by persons serving in the Israel Defence Forces, the Israel Police, the Prisons Service and other security organizations of the State, nor shall such rights be subject to conditions, except by virtue of a law, or by regulation enacted by virtue of a law, and to an extent no greater than is required by the nature and character of the service.
Validity of laws	10. This Basic Law shall not affect the validity of any law (din) in force prior to the commencement of the Basic Law.
Application	11. All governmental authorities are bound to respect the rights under this Basic Law.
Stability	12. This Basic Law cannot be varied, suspended or made subject to conditions by emergency regulations; notwithstanding, when a state of emergency exists, by virtue of a declaration under section 9 of the Law and Administration Ordinance, 5708-1948, emergency regulations may be enacted by virtue of said section to deny or restrict rights under this Basic Law, provided the denial or restriction shall be for a proper purpose and for a period and extent no greater than is required.

FREEDOM OF OCCUPATION*

Basic principles	1. Fundamental human rights in Israel are founded upon recognition of the value of the human being, the sanctity of human life, and the principle that all persons are free; these rights shall be upheld in the spirit of the principles set forth in the Declaration of the Establishment of the State of Israel.
Purpose	2. The purpose of this Basic Law if to protect freedom of occupation, in order to establish in a Basic Law the values of the State of Israel as a Jewish and democratic state.
Freedom of occupation.	3. Every Israel national or resident has the right to engage in any occupation, profession or trade.
Violation of freedom of occupation	4. There shall be no violation of freedom of occupation except by a law befitting the values of the State of Israel, enacted for a proper purpose, and to an extent no greater than is required, or by regulation enacted by virtue of express autorisation in such law.
Application	5. All governmental authorities are bound to respect the freedom of occupation of all Israel nationals and residents.
Stability	6. This Basic Law shall not be varied, suspended or made subject to conditions by emergency regulations.
Entrenchment	7. This Basic Law shall not be varied except by a Basic Law passed by a majority of the members of the Knesset.
Effect of nonconforming law	8. A provision of a law that violates freedom of occupation shall be of effect, even though not in accordance with section 4, if it has been

	included in a law passed by a majority of the members of the Knesset, which expressly states that it shall be of effect, notwithstanding the provisions of this Basic Law; such law shall expire four years from its commencement unless a shorter duration has been stated therein.
Repeal	9. Basic Law: Freedom of Occupation** is is hereby repealed.
Provisional	10. The provisions of any enactment which, immediately prior to this Basic Law would have been of effect but for this Basic Law or the Basic Law repealed in section 9, shall remain in effect two years from the commencement of this Basic Law, unless repealed earlier; however, such provisions shall be construed in the spirit of the provisions of this Basic Law.
Amendment of Basic Law: Human Dignity and Liberty	In Basic Law: Human Dignity and Liberty - (1) Section 1 shall be designated 1(a) and shall be preceded by the following section: Basic principles 1. Fundamental human rights in Israel are founded upon recognition of the value of the human being, the sanctity of human life, and the principle that all persons are free; these rights shall be upheld in the spirit of the principles set forth in the Declaration of the Establishment of the State of Israel. (2) At the end of section 8, the following shall be added: "or by regulation enacted by virtue of express authorization in such law."

ISRAEL MILITARY AND NATIONAL SECURITY STRATEGY

The creation of the State of Israel in 1948 was preceded by more than 50 years of efforts by Zionist leaders to establish a sovereign nation as a homeland for Jews. The desire of Jews to return to what they consider their rightful homeland was first expressed during the Babylonian exile and became a universal Jewish theme after the destruction of Jerusalem by the Romans in 70 A.D. and the dispersal that followed. After the end of World War II, and the near-extermination of European Jewry by the Nazis, international support for Jews seeking to settle in Palestine overcame British efforts to restrict immigration, and laid the foundation for establishing a Jewish state. On 14 May 1948 the State of Israel was proclaimed. The following day, armies from neighboring Arab nations entered the former Mandate of Palestine to engage Israeli military forces.

The State of Israel has always had a single defense goal - to ensure the existence of Israel and the security of its citizens. Israel is tiny (smaller than New Jersey) when compared to its Arab neighbors. More pointedly, it lacks strategic depth. A hostile fighter could fly across all of Israel (40 nautical miles wide from the Jordan River to the Mediterranean Sea) within four minutes, while traveling at "only" subsonic speed. Israel is unable to field a large standing force compared with those it faces and must rely on its reserves. Israel's small population also increases its sensitivity to civilian and military losses. To make up for quantitative disadvantages, Israel maintains as large a qualitative lead as possible. The IDF makes up for its lack of size by superior maneuverability and firepower, and by relying on intelligence.

Israeli national security strategy is founded on the premise that Israel cannot afford to lose a single war. Because the best way to avoid losing a war is to not fight it in the first place, Israeli strategy begins with the maintenance of a credible deterrent posture, which includes the willingness to carry out preemptive strikes. Should deterrence fail, Israel would seek to prevent escalation, and determine the outcome of war quickly and decisively. Since it lacks strategic depth, Israel must prevent the enemy from entering its territory, and must try to quickly transfer the battle to enemy territory.

Israel applies its nuclear weapons to all levels of this formula. The total Israeli nuclear stockpile consists of several hundred weapons of various types, including boosted fission and enhanced radiation weapons ("neutron bombs"), as well as nuclear artillery shells. Strategically, Israel uses its long-range missiles and nuclear-capable aircraft (and, some say, submarines with nuclear-armed cruise missiles) to deter both conventional and unconventional attacks, or to launch "the Samson Option", an all-out attack against an adversary should defenses fail and population centers be threatened. In addition, despite Israel's insistence that it "will not be the first to introduce nuclear weapons into the Middle East," these systems represent an effective preemptive strike force. At the same time, Israel deploys tactical systems designed to rapidly reduce an invading force. Following the 1973 war, Israel fielded at least three batteries of atomic-capable self-propelled 175mm cannons equipped with a total of no less than 108 warheads, and placed atomic land mines in the Golan Heights during the early 1980s.

Nuclear weapons need not be detonated to be used as weapons. Early in the 1973 war, Israel went on a nuclear alert, partly in the knowledge that it would be detected by the United States and the Soviet Union. The Soviets, Israel assumed, would restrain their Arab allies while the Americans would speed up resupply efforts. While the USSR did inform Egypt that Israel had armed three nuclear weapons, the extent to which Israel's nuclear alert affected the timing of Washington's subsequent decision to rearm Israel is not clear.

Israel does not have an overt nuclear doctrine beyond its insistence that it will not introduce nuclear weapons into the region. Instead, it follows a policy of what Avner Cohen calls "nuclear opacity" - visibly possessing nuclear weapons while denying their existence. This has allowed Israel to enjoy the benefits of being a nuclear weapons state in terms of deterrence without having to suffer the international repercussions of acknowledging their arsenal. Israel also has a strong commitment to preventing its potential adversaries in the region from becoming declared nuclear weapon states, as evidenced by Israel's 1981 raid on Iraq Osirak nuclear installation.

Given the very long range of the Jericho-2 missile, some analysts have speculated that this system was developed to deter Soviet intervention in the region. The USSR has always been one of the primary targets of Israel's nuclear force, as Israeli assumptions hold that no Arab nation would attack Israel without Soviet support. The purchase of fifty F-4 fighters from the US in 1968 provided Israel with a platform capable of delivering a nuclear payload as far as Moscow, and it has actively pursued imagery and other information necessary for targeting weapons against the USSR. In 1979, the US agreed to provide Israel with access to high-resolution images of its neighbors taken by the KH-11 satellite. Israel was able to use this agreement to view targets of interest in western Russia (as well as to obtain targeting information for the attack on the Osirak reactor). Israel received more such data during the mid-1980s through the espionage activities of Jonathan Pollard.

Although commonly viewed as the ultimate guarantor of its security, the nuclear option has not led Israel to be complacent about national security. On the contrary, it has impelled Israel to seek unquestioned superiority in conventional capability over the Arab armies to forestall use of nuclear weapons as a last resort - as early as 1962-63, prime minister David Ben-Gurion eschewed restructuring the IDF to base it on nuclear weapons. Instead, IDF doctrine and tactics stress quality of weapons versus quantity; integration of the combined firepower of the three branches of the armed forces; effective battlefield command, communications, and real-time intelligence; use of precision-guided munitions and stand-off firepower; and high mobility.

As of 2004, Israel had not acceded to the Treaty on the Non-Proliferation of Nuclear Weapons (1968). It was, however, a party to the Treaty Banning Nuclear Weapons Tests in the Atmosphere, in Outer Space, and Under Water (1963).

During the IAEA Director General's visit to Israel in June 2004, the Israeli officials stated that they would consider the application of Agency safeguards only in the context of a nuclear-weapon-free zone in the region which they would consider favourably in the context of the peace process and as part of phase II of the "road map to the solution of the Israeli-Palestinian conflict", developed by the Quartet Group (of the European Union, the Russian Federation, the United Nations and the USA which foresees a "revival of multilateral engagement on issues including... arms control". The other States of the region maintain that there is no automatic sequence which links the application of comprehensive safeguards to all nuclear facilities in the Middle East, or the establishment of a nuclear-weapon-free zone, to the prior conclusion of a peace settlement, and that the former would contribute to the latter.

INTERNATIONAL AND DOMESTIC SECURITY

As of 1988, experts considered the IDF superior to any combination of Arab forces that was likely to be massed against it in a future conflict. The total manpower and firepower that could be directed against Israel far outweighed the battlefield resources that Israel could muster, yet Israel's dynamic military leadership, troop proficiency, and sophisticated weaponry still promised to be decisive, as they had been in previous wars.

The Arab nations remained deeply divided over a host of issues in mid-1988, including their postures toward Israel. Although the Camp David peace process between Egypt and Israel failed to achieve normalization of relations, Israel no longer considered Egypt part of the circle of hostile states. Nevertheless, Israeli planners did not rule out an upheaval in Egyptian politics that would renew the risk of military confrontation. With the Sinai region effectively demilitarized, the element of surprise that had initially worked in Egypt's favor in the October 1973 War would not be available. In any future conflict, Egyptian forces would have to cross 130 kilometers of desert exposed to Israeli air power. Jordan's military weakness vis-à-vis Israel and its exposure to Israeli retaliation seemed to rule out military action except as a reluctant ally in a larger Arab coalition. The modernization of Jordan's army and air force was continuing, however, with the help of the United States and France. Many important Israeli targets were within the range of Jordanian artillery and rockets.

Syria posed the paramount threat. The Syrian armed forces had pursued a massive build-up of offensive and defensive manpower and equipment in an effort to maintain parity with Israel. Although the inflexibility of their military strategy had resulted in crushing defeats in engagements with the IDF, the Syrians had proved to be skillful and stubborn fighters during the Lebanon conflict. The concentrations of Syrian troops facing the Golan Heights probably could make initial gains in a thrust against the IDF, but would absorb heavy punishment once the Israelis mobilized for a counterattack.

Like other Arab states, Saudi Arabia had upgraded its naval and air arms, improving its capability to defend its air space and control activities in the Red Sea area. Saudi Arabia's outlook and strategic doctrine were primarily defensive, and its primary objective was stability in the Middle East to minimize the danger to its oil facilities and other vital installations. Nevertheless, from Israel's perspective, that country had the potential to undertake offensive air operations in conjunction with other Arab air forces. In the eyes of Israeli strategists, Saudi Arabia's 1988 purchase of long-range missiles from China and its acquisition of Tornado fighter-bombers from Britain enhanced its role in a future conflict.

The Iraqi army had not played a decisive role in previous wars. During the October 1973 fighting, two Iraqi brigades were quickly overcome in the IDF drive toward Damascus. If Iraq again attempted to advance its forces to support Syria and Jordan, they would, like those of Egypt, be vulnerable to Israeli air strikes. Nevertheless, as of late 1988, Israeli officers were less confident of their ability to neutralize Iraq's armed potential. During the war with Iran, the Iraqi army had expanded to more than twenty divisions and had acquired combat experience and skill in the use of sophisticated weaponry. Iraq also had demonstrated the capacity and willingness to resort to chemical weapons. On the other hand, Iraq was economically drained and presumably tired of fighting after the eight-year struggle with Iran. Israeli military analysts felt, moreover, that tensions would persist in the Persian Gulf and that Iraq's armed forces would be unlikely to welcome military involvement elsewhere.

The buildup of the Arab armies between the October 1973 War and the mid-1980s was both qualitative and quantitative. Egypt, Syria, and Jordan had expanded the total of their divisions from twenty to twenty-five during this period. Of these, the number of armored and mechanized divisions rose from ten to twenty-two. Israeli planners estimated that Iraq could contribute another ten divisions, increasing the Arab disparity over Israel even more

The lifting of restrictions on arms sales by the Western powers, combined with the increased resources at the disposal of oil-exporting countries, enabled the Arab powers vastly to expand their sophisticated weaponry between 1973 and 1988. The tank inventories of Egypt, Jordan, and Syria rose by 60 percent, while their stocks of aircraft, helicopters, and armored personnel carriers roughly doubled. Both Syria and Iraq had acquired high performance aircraft of Soviet design. To the Arab countries' primary land weapons had been added more self-propelled artillery, guided antitank missiles, new munitions--including cluster and homing shells--improved fire-control systems, and laser rangefinders. Previously vulnerable air defenses now could be shielded using advanced mobile missile systems acquired from both East and West. Most of the strategic sites in Israel were exposed to Syrian striking power in the form of Soviet-supplied SS-21 SSMs, with a range of 120 kilometers and far greater accuracy than the earlier generation FROG-7 (70 kilometers) and Scud-B (300 kilometers).

Israel could draw only tentative conclusions regarding the improvement in Arab military leadership and manpower resources. Arab field commanders had not yet demonstrated the successful adaptation of modern command and control systems to battlefield situations. Arab forces had in the past shown greater effectiveness in static defense than in mobile offensive operations.

The paucity of qualified technical personnel in the Arab armies, attributed to deficiencies in education and training, continued to detract from the ability of the Arab armed forces to employ modern weaponry with full efficiency. The superior skills of Israeli pilots had been decisive in the 1982 invasion of Lebanon and in earlier engagements. Although the rising level of weapons technology presented more of a problem to the Arab nations than to Israel, the Arabs' Soviet systems were simpler to use and maintain than their more sophisticated United States counterparts. The improved performance of the Iraqi air force against Iran after 1985 offered some evidence that the disparity in pilot skills and experience might be narrowing.

NATIONAL SECURITY

IN FEW COUNTRIES of the world have matters of national security played as pervasive a role in society as in Israel. The Israel Defense Forces (IDF--commonly known in Israel as Zahal, the Hebrew acronym for Zvah Haganah Le Yisrael) was organized to be the ultimate guarantor of national security. Israeli policy makers, however, have believed that strong armed forces alone were not enough to protect the state. All of the state's resources were to be marshalled and applied to national security. In 1960 David Ben-Gurion stated that Israeli security also depended on the integration of immigrants, the settlement and peopling of "empty areas," the dispersal of the population and establishment of industries throughout the country, the development of agriculture, the "conquest of the sea and air," economic independence, and the fostering of research and scientific skill at the highest level of technology in all branches of science. Israel's quest for national security has been a prime motivating factor behind the state's rapid development.

The quest for national security also has imposed great costs on the state and its citizens. Defense expenditures on a per capita basis, and as a percentage of gross national product (GNP--see Glossary), have been consistently higher in Israel than in almost any other country in the world. Moreover, the IDF has diverted scarce manpower from the civilian economy, and Israeli industry has been compelled to manufacture military matériel instead of the consumer items that would raise the standard of living. Defense spending has also fueled double digit inflation for protracted periods and created a large national debt.

The prominence given national security by Israeli society stems from the perceived massive security threat posed by Israel's Arab neighbors. Having founded the State of Israel in the wake of the Holocaust, in which Diaspora (see Glossary) Jews were defenseless against an enemy bent on their destruction, Israeli Jews were determined to devote considerable resources to defend their young nation. In 1988 most outside observers agreed that the IDF was stronger than ever and clearly superior to the armies of its Arab enemies. Unlike the years after the June 1967 War, however, Israelis in the late 1980s did not display overconfidence in their defense capability. The surprise Arab offensive in October 1973 had renewed Israel's fears of defeat at the hands of its Arab enemies. Israel's 1982 invasion of Lebanon restored confidence in the tactical superiority of the IDF, but it also engendered controversy. The invasion was opposed from its inception by many Israeli politicians and IDF officers, who referred to it as Israel's first imperial war. Moreover, the IDF's victory on the battlefield was not matched by strategic accomplishments. In 1988 the IDF confronted a new problem--sustained protest by Palestinians in the occupied territories.

Many observers in the late 1980s described Israel as a democratic garrison state and a praetorian society. Indeed, in many respects Israel resembled an armed camp, and a wide range of government policies, particularly in foreign affairs, was dictated by security considerations as advised by IDF commanders. Unlike many garrison states, however, in Israel the armed forces played an indirect role in politics, and the IDF was unlikely to abandon its tradition of strict subordination to civilian authority.

Nevertheless, national defense policy was a major component of civilian politics during 1988. The Palestinian uprising in the occupied territories, known as the *intifadah*, created a new threat to Israel's security. Although the army seemed able to contain the violence militarily, its resources were strained by the dual role of policing the territories while maintaining strong border defenses. A nationwide debate centered on the question of whether Israeli concessions were strategically preferable to further Jewish settlement in the occupied territories. With the growing sophistication and deadliness of modern armaments in the Middle East, the alternative to peace with Israel's neighbors was the specter of increasingly costly wars. Since Israel's birth forty years earlier, such conflicts already had cost nearly 12,000 Israeli lives.

HISTORICAL BACKGROUND

Ancient Jewish military tradition is deeply rooted in biblical history and begins with Abraham, who led an ad hoc military force. Joshua, who conquered Canaan, is an early hero, and David, who captured Jerusalem, is regarded by Israeli Jews as their greatest king and warrior. Solomon organized and maintained the first standing Jewish army

Little in the way of military tradition arose out of the nearly 2,000 years of the Diaspora. In fact, the lack of military prowess in the Jewish communities of the Diaspora was commonly viewed as a cause of their hardships and became a major motivation for building a strong defense establishment within Israel. As a result of the Russian pogroms of the 1880s, a small number of Jews began settling in the area of Palestine and, determined to end the centuries of persecution, created self-defense units called Shomrim, or Guardsmen, to protect the early settlements. In 1909 the Shomrim were formally organized throughout the area of Jewish settlement in Palestine and renamed HaShomer, or the Watchmen. Although HaShomer numbered fewer than 100 men at the organization's peak, these armed militias became extremely important to Israeli military tradition. Many members of HaShomer joined the Jewish Legion, which fought with the British against imperial Germany during World War I. They also established a precedent of armed self-defense of the Zionist movement, which during the War of Independence in 1948 would flower into the IDF.

Increasing tensions between the Arab communities and the growing Jewish communities of Palestine brought the need to expand the capacity of the Yishuv (see Glossary) for self-defense. In 1920, after serious Arab disturbances in Jerusalem and in northern Palestine, HaShomer militias were disbanded and replaced by the Haganah (abbreviation for Irgun HaHaganah, Defense Organization), which was intended to be a larger and more wide-ranging organization for the defense of all Palestinian Jewry. By 1948, when it was disbanded so that the IDF would be the sole Israeli military organization, the Haganah was a force of about 30,000.

The Haganah, financed originally through the Zionist General Federation of Laborers in the Land of Israel (HaHistadrut HaKlalit shel HaOvdim B'Eretz Yisrael, known as Histadrut) and later through the Jewish Agency (see Glossary), operated clandestinely under the British Mandate, which declared the bearing of unauthorized arms by Palestinian Jews to be illegal. Arms and ammunition were smuggled into the country, and training was conducted in secret. In addition to guarding settlements, the Haganah manufactured arms, built a series of roads and stockades throughout Palestine to facilitate defense, and organized and defended groups of Jewish immigrants during periods under the Mandate when immigration was illegal or restricted.

Arab attacks on Jewish communities in 1921 and 1929 found the Haganah ill-equipped and ineffective: more than 100 Jews were killed in 1929 alone. When renewed Arab rioting broke out in Jaffa (Yafo) in 1936 and soon spread throughout Palestine, the Mandate authorities--realizing that they could not defend every Jewish settlement--authorized the creation of the Jewish Settlement Police, also known as Notrim, who were trained, armed, and paid by the British. In 1938 a British intelligence officer, Captain Orde Charles Wingate, organized three counterguerrilla units, called special night squads, manned by British and Jewish personnel. As both of these organizations contained a large number of Haganah members, their formation greatly increased the assets of the Haganah while providing a legal basis for much of their activities. Although these nearly continuous disturbances from 1936 to 1939 cost the lives of nearly 600 Jews and more than 5,000 Arabs, Israeli observers have pointed out that Jewish casualties would have been far greater were it not for the increasing effectiveness of these paramilitary units

During these disturbances, the Haganah's policy of *havlaga*, or self-restraint, under which retaliation against the Arab community at large was strictly forbidden, was not aggressive enough for some. Under Vladimir (Zeev) Jabotinsky and later Menachem Begin, these dissidents in 1937 established the National Military Organization (Irgun Zvai Leumi, known both as the Irgun and by the acronym Etzel). Initially the Irgun waged a campaign of terror, sabotage, and reprisal against the Arabs. After the British government issued a white paper in May 1939 extending the Mandate for ten years and placing limits on Jewish immigration, however, the Irgun turned its terrorist activities against the British troops in Palestine in an all-out struggle against the Mandate authority.

With the outbreak of World War II, Irgun leaders settled on a policy of cooperation with the British in the war effort; but a hard core within the organization opposed the policy and accordingly split off from the larger body. This group, led by Avraham Stern, formed the Fighters for Israel's Freedom (Lohamei Herut Israel--Lehi), known as the Stern Gang. The Stern Gang, which included Begin and later Yitzhak Shamir, specialized in the assassination of British and other officials. At their peaks, the Irgun contained about 4,000 men; the Stern Gang, 200 to 300. Defeat of Nazi Germany in 1945 precipitated a resumption of anti-British activities by both Haganah and Irgun in pursuance of their common ultimate goal, the establishment of a national home and the creation of a sovereign Jewish state.

During World War II, about 32,000 Palestinian Jews, both men and women, volunteered for the British army. In 1944 about 5,000 of these were formed into the Jewish Brigade, which fought successfully in Italy in 1945. With so many of its members serving abroad, the ranks of the Haganah were depleted, and in 1941 its leaders decided to raise a mobile force--the Palmach (abbreviation of Pelugot Mahatz--Shock Forces--see Glossary)--of approximately 3,000 full-time soldiers, whose mission was to defend the Yishuv. Trained with the aid of the British, the Palmach was the first full-time standing Jewish army in more than 2,000 years and is considered the direct forerunner to the IDF. For many years, the vast majority of IDF officers were veterans of either the Palmach or the Jewish Brigade.

CONCEPTS OF NATIONAL SECURITY

The need for a strong military posture in the face of the perceived Arab threats to Israel's survival has been endorsed with near unanimity by Israeli policy makers and citizens. Nevertheless, the question of which strategies best ensure national defense has often caused acrimonious national, as well as international, controversy. Events subsequent to Ben-Gurion's initial concepts of national security laid down when Israel was founded in 1948, particularly Israel's occupation of Arab territories since the June 1967 War, have modified the foundations for Israel's concepts of national security.

THE DAHIYAH DOCTRINE

The Dahiyah Doctrine arose in the aftermath of the Second Lebanon War and the perceived failure of the IDF to utilize its military advantage against heavily armed non-state members of the Resistance Network (primarily Hizbullah and Hamas.)

The IDF's traditional 'use of force' doctrine was perceived to have been unsuccessful in preventing rocket fire on Israeli civilian areas as well as resulting in IDF casualties.[1]

The Dahiyah Doctrine developed out of the realization that the IDF was fighting against a new type of enemy which required new tactics. In this context, the heavy bombardment inflicted on the South-Beirut Dahiyah neighborhood during the Second Lebanon war seen as a relevant model for fighting against non-state terror or guerilla organizations.

DOCTRINE CHARACTERISTICS

According to the Doctrine, the targets against which the IDF should focus disproportionate force may vary between villages from which rockets are fired, the political, social or religious strongholds of the Resistance Network,[3] or the civilian infrastructure of the political entity within which the Resistance Network operates.

Moreover, the military response envisaged by the Dahiyah Doctrine marks a departure from previous military IDF strategy.

- Rather than use of firepower and quick maneuverability on the ground, the Doctrine adopts a strategy of massive firepower, primarily from the air.
- Rather than hunting down individual missile launchers, the Doctrine focuses on punitively destroying the entire area from which rockets are fired.
- Rather than seeking to achieve decisive victory, the Doctrine focuses on deterring the enemy via considerations of cost effectiveness, and hopes the threat of massive economic and physical destruction to infrastructure will drive a wedge between members of the Resistance Network and the local population.

The Dahiya Doctrine is therefore worthless as an actual military strategy. As a publicly made threat it only serves to make Israel look monstrous. If Israel really intends to bomb Lebanese targets, it could make its intention known quietly to the Lebanese government through the usual channels. So what is the purpose of these warnings other than to exhibit the self importance of generals?

The Dahiya Doctrine is a declaration of strategic and tactical bankruptcy. In any war with Hezbollah and to a lesser extent Hamas, Israel faces a number of threats for which it has not found solutions:
* Rockets of varying range that can be launched from mobile platforms or remote-launched from hardened silos.

* Anti-tank rockets.

* Huge explosive charges that can blow up tanks from below, used very effectively in Gaza.

* An enemy that has implanted itself in civilian population and has no concern for civilian casualties.

* An enemy that is dug in in underground bunkers. These fortifications are very advanced in Lebanon, and are apparently located beneath population centers.

* A home population that has become totally undisciplined and has no tolerance for casualties.

* A basically hostile international environment.

Most of the above threats remain without solutions, in part because nobody sought solutions, in part because the solutions are not ready yet, partly because international political considerations prevent a solution, and partly because there might not be any solutions.

For the enemy, casualties are a strategic asset, as they are used to put pressure on Israel and delegitimize it, which is the strategic objective of the enemy. For Israel, our casualties, however light, are an increasingly a limiting liability with overwhelming force. Two people were lightly injured in rocket barrages in the Negev in the last few days, causing a huge swelling of political pressure, in part artificially generated, to stop the rockets at any cost. Two Israelis with nose bleeds after a rocket attack have a greater demoralizing effect on Israelis than a hundred dead Palestinians have in Palestinian society.

The absence of resolution causes erratic solutions. The government flip-flops between ill considered and pointless military adventures and shameful capitulation. Because of PR gimmicks and political pressure, the Israeli government made a disastrous and humiliating deal to swap Lebanese prisoners for the bodies of two soldiers, giving Hezbollah a huge and bloodless victory. Now there is pressure to make an even more one-sided and dangerous deal for the return of captive Gilad Shalit. A deal that must ultimately result in the kidnapping of many more soldiers. It is absurd that the military planning for a Gaza operation, which would necessarily involve numerous Israeli dead and wounded, takes into account the captivity of one lone soldier as a serious strategic consideration. None of this has any objective basis - it is all psychological and irrational.

The "Dahiya Doctrine" proposes a huge and barbarous Israeli reaction to what is objectively a fairly minimal enemy threat. Of course, that is exactly what the enemy wants to accomplish.

Objectively, the simplest problem to solve is that of the home population. During the Second Lebanon war, the Hezbollah rockets killed about 50 Israelis. The attempts to stop the rockets by military force and to recover two captive soldiers killed an additional 100 Israelis approximately. The arithmetic has obvious implications. Objective observers pointed out that Israeli civilian casualties were relatively low because of a relatively good civil defense infrastructure. By Middle Eastern standards our provision of shelters and warning are excellent. By Israeli standards we know they are poor. A relatively small investment in shelters and reorganization of civil defense in the north and near Gaza would yield a great dividend in saved lives, but it is not being done. The cabinet vetoed Defense Minister Ehud Barak's request for more shelters in the Western Negev. The vote was not based on objective criteria. Ehud Barak is from the wrong political party and elections are only a few months away. Politically, it is much better to withhold the funds, since as defense minister, Barak will be blamed for the resulting casualties, whereas if the shelters were built, the Labor party and Barak would gain support at the expense of the Kadima party. So you see, it really doesn't pay to build shelters.

Israel's biggest asset in previous wars, especially the Israel War of Independencewas a population that was fairly inured to casualties. Unlike the Palestinian Arabs, Israelis did not run away and did not panic. The British guns of the Jordan Legion pounded Jerusalem and the Egyptian air force dropped bombs on Tel Aviv with impunity in the first days of the war, yet there was no real pressure either to end the war by capitulation or to replace the government with one that would "do something" about the threat. Noncombatants were routinely evacuated for long periods from threatened areas.

The same was true during the years preceding the Six Day War, when Syrian artillery terrorized Israeli Kibbutzim and towns along the northern border. There wasn't really a great and constant outcry in any of these cases by politicians calling for surrender or by politicians calling for aggressive action. The same was true again during Desert Storm, when an uncomplaining population suffered the inconvenience and danger of Iraqi Scud missiles which could not be stopped by the Likud government.

The Hezbollah and the Hamas can pose an existential threat to Israel only if we let them do so. Objectively, their ability to inflict casualties is small. If we are serious about beating the terrorists, Israeli society has to prepare a resolute population and give the home population confidence in the measures taken to protect it. Tactical solutions to the threats posted by the enemy are important too, but without an orderly and determined population and a united political leadership, tactical solutions will never be enough, as there will always be some casualties. That, and not barbarous and impractical plans for mass bombings ought to be the focus of Israeli strategy.

IDF PRINCIPLES OF WAR

(1) Mission and Aim -- Adherence to the missing by being guided by the aim (understanding the force's mission within the framework of the aim -- and acting according)

(2) Optimal utilization of forces (achieving the maximum with what is available while correctly combining capabilities)

(3) Initiative and offensive (the commander in the field determines action; he must aim for contact and engagement with the enemy)

(4) Statagem (achieving surprise, but more importantly, identifying, targeting, and exploiting weak points of the enemy)

(5) Concentration of efforts (every effort, action, and effect are made to attain the principal mission and aim)

(6) Continuity of action (unswerving pressure to prevent the enemy from reorganizing; exploiting our forces' successes)

(7) Depth and reserves (to distance threats in order to enable continuity of action in crises)

(8) Security (to avoid exposure of the flanks and weakness following a concerted effort)

(9) Maintenance of morale and fighting spirit (impels the soldier forward and preserves the unit's vitality under pressure; essential for a small army to compensate for its materiel weakness)

(10) Simplicity (each element of the stratagem must be simple to execute even if the broader plan and mission are complicated)

parenthetical explanations are the author's

Source: Maj. Gen (res.) Yaakov Amidror, "Winning Counterinsurgency War: The Israeli Experience, " The Jerusalem Center for Public Affairs, p. 30.

ISRAEL DEFENSE FORCES

Founded	1948
Service branches	Israeli Army Israeli Air Force Israeli Navy
Leadership	
Prime Minister Defense Minister	Benjamin Netanyahu Moshe Ya'alon
Chief of General Staff	Rav Aluf Benny Gantz
Manpower	
Military age	18
Conscription	18
Available for military service	1,554,186 males, age 17–49 (2000 est.), 1,514,063 females, age 17–49 (2000 est.)
Fit for military service	1,499,998 males, age 17–49 (2000 est.), 1,392,319 females, age 17–49 (2000 est.)
Reaching military age annually	54,148 males (2000 est.), 47,996 females (2000 est.)
Active personnel	176,500 (ranked 34th)
Reserve personnel	445,000
Expenditures	
Budget	50.6₪ billion (~$14.5 billion) (2012)
Percent of GDP	6.9% (2011)
Industry	
Domestic suppliers	Israel Aerospace Industries Israel Military Industries Israel Weapon Industries Elbit Systems Elisra Elta Rafael Advanced Defense Systems Soltam Systems Plasan Automotive Industries Hatehof Israel Shipyards SimiGon BUL Transmark Aeronautics Defense Systems Israel Ordnance Corps Meprolight
Foreign suppliers	United States (1968–present) Czechoslovakia (1948) Germany

	France (1955–1966)
Related articles	
History	War of Independence (1948–1949) Retribution operations (1950s–1960s) Sinai War (1956) War over Water (1964–1967) Six-Day War (1967) War of Attrition (1967–1970) Battle of Karameh (1968) Operation Spring of Youth (1973) Yom Kippur War (1973) Operation Entebbe (1976) Litani (1978) First Lebanon War (1982) South Lebanon conflict (1982–2000) First Intifada (1987–1993) Second Intifada (2000–2005) Operation Defensive Shield (2002) Second Lebanon War (2006) Gaza War (2008–2009) Operation Pillar of Defense (2012) Other

The IDF traces its roots to Jewish paramilitary organizations in the New Yishuv, starting with the Second Aliyah (1904 to 1914). The first such organization was Bar-Giora, founded in September 1907. It was converted to Hashomer in April 1909, which operated until the British Mandate of Palestine came into being in 1920. Hashomer was an elitist organization with narrow scope, and was mainly created to protect against criminal gangs seeking to steal property. During World War I the forerunners of the Haganah/IDF were the Zion Mule Corps and the Jewish Legion, both of which were part of the British Army. After the Arab riots against Jews in April 1920, the Yishuv's leadership saw the need to create a nationwide underground defense organization, and the Haganah was founded in June of the same year. The Haganah became a full-scale defense force after the 1936–1939 Arab revolt in Palestine with an organized structure, consisting of three main units—the Field Corps, Guard Corps, and the Palmach. During World War II the successor to the Jewish Legion of World War I was the Jewish Brigade.

The IDF was founded following the establishment of the State of Israel, after Defense Minister and Prime Minister David Ben-Gurion issued an order on 26 May 1948. The order called for the establishment of the Israel Defense Forces, and the abolishment of all other Jewish armed forces. Although Ben-Gurion had no legal authority to issue such an order, the order was made legal by the cabinet on 31 May.

The two other Jewish underground organizations, Irgun and Lehi, agreed to join the IDF if they would be able to form independent units and agreed not to make independent arms purchases. This was the background for the dispute which led to the Altalena Affair, when following a confrontation regarding the weapons it brought resulted in a battle between Irgun members and the newly created IDF. It ended when the ship was shelled. Following the affair, all independent Irgun and Lehi units were either disbanded or merged into the IDF. The Palmach, a strong lobby within the Haganah, also joined the IDF with provisions, and Ben Gurion responded by disbanding its staff in 1949, after which many senior Palmach officers retired, notably its first commander, Yitzhak Sadeh.

The new army organized itself during the 1948 Arab–Israeli War when neighbouring Arab states attacked Israel. Twelve infantry and armored brigades formed: Golani, Carmeli, Alexandroni, Kiryati, Givati, Etzioni, the 7th, and 8th armored brigades, Oded, Harel, Yiftach, and Negev. After the war, some of the brigades were converted to reserve units, and others were disbanded. Directorates and corps were created from corps and services in the Haganah, and this basic structure in the IDF still exists today.

Immediately after the 1948 war, the Israel Defense Forces shifted to low intensity conflict against Arab Palestinian guerrillas. In the 1956 Suez Crisis, the IDF's first test of strength after 1949, the new army proved itself by capturing the Sinai Peninsula from Egypt, which was later returned. In the 1967 Six-Day War, Israel conquered the Sinai Peninsula, Gaza Strip, West Bank (including East Jerusalem) and Golan Heights from the surrounding Arab states, changing the balance of power in the region as well as the role of the IDF. In the following years leading up to the Yom Kippur War, the IDF fought a war of attrition against Egypt in the Sinai and a border war against the PLO in Jordan, culminating in the Battle of Karameh.

The surprise of the Yom Kippur War and its aftermath completely changed the IDF's procedures and approach to warfare. Organizational changes were made and more time was dedicated to training for conventional warfare. However, in the following years the army's role slowly shifted again to low-intensity conflict, urban warfare and counter-terrorism. It was involved in the Lebanese Civil War, initiating Operation Litani and later the 1982 Lebanon War, where the IDF ousted Palestinian guerilla organizations from Lebanon. Palestinian militancy has been the main focus of the IDF ever since, especially during the First and Second Intifadas, Operation Defensive Shield, and the Gaza War, causing the IDF to change many of its values and publish the IDF Spirit. The Islamic Shia organization Hezbollah has also been a growing threat, against which the IDF fought an asymmetric conflict between 1982 and 2000, as well as a full-scale war in 2006.

ISRAEL'S NUCLEAR WEAPONS

The Israeli nuclear weapons program grew out of the conviction that the Holocaust justified any measures Israel took to ensure its survival. Consequently, Israel has been actively investigating the nuclear option from its earliest days. In 1949, HEMED GIMMEL a special unit of the IDF's Science Corps, began a two-year geological survey of the Negev desert with an eye toward the discovery of uranium reserves. Although no significant sources of uranium were found, recoverable amounts were located in phosphate deposits.

The program took another step forward with the creation of the Israel Atomic Energy Commission (IAEC) in 1952. Its chairman, Ernst David Bergmann, had long advocated an Israeli bomb as the best way to ensure "that we shall never again be led as lambs to the slaughter." Bergmann was also head of the Ministry of Defense's Research and Infrastructure Division (known by its Hebrew acronym, EMET), which had taken over the HEMED research centers (HEMED GIMMEL among them, now renamed Machon 4) as part of a reorganization. Under Bergmann, the line between the IAEC and EMET blurred to the point that Machon 4 functioned essentially as the chief laboratory for the IAEC. By 1953, Machon 4 had not only perfected a process for extracting the uranium found in the Negev, but had also developed a new method of producing heavy water, providing Israel with an indigenous capability to produce some of the most important nuclear materials.

For reactor design and construction, Israel sought the assistance of France. Nuclear cooperation between the two nations dates back as far as early 1950's, when construction began on France's 40MWt heavy water reactor and a chemical reprocessing plant at Marcoule. France was a natural partner for Israel and both governments saw an independent nuclear option as a means by which they could maintain a degree of autonomy in the bipolar environment of the cold war.

THE SINAI CRISIS

In the fall of 1956, France agreed to provide Israel with an 18 MWt research reactor. However, the onset of the Suez Crisis a few weeks later changed the situation dramatically. Following Egypt's closure of the Suez Canal in July, France and Britain had agreed with Israel that the latter should provoke a war with Egypt to provide the European nations with the pretext to send in their troops as peacekeepers to occupy and reopen the canal zone. In the wake of the Suez Crisis, the Soviet Union made a thinly veiled threat against the three nations. This episode not only enhanced the Israeli view that an independent nuclear capability was needed to prevent reliance on potentially unreliable allies, but also led to a sense of debt among French leaders that they had failed to fulfill commitments made to a partner. French premier Guy Mollet is even quoted as saying privately that France "owed" the bomb to Israel.

On 3 October 1957, France and Israel signed a revised agreement calling for France to build a 24 MWt reactor (although the cooling systems and waste facilities were designed to handle three times that power) and, in protocols that were not committed to paper, a chemical reprocessing plant. This complex was constructed in secret, and outside the IAEA inspection regime, by French and Israeli technicians at Dimona, in the Negev desert under the leadership of Col. Manes Pratt of the IDF Ordinance Corps.

Both the scale of the project and the secrecy involved made the construction of Dimona a massive undertaking. A new intelligence agency, the Office of Science Liasons,(LEKEM) was created to provide security and intelligence for the project. At the height construction, some 1,500 Israelis some French workers were employed building Dimona. To maintain secrecy, French customs officials were told that the largest of the reactor components, such as the reactor tank, were part of a desalinization plant bound for Latin America. In addition, after buying heavy water from Norway on the condition that it not be transferred to a third country, the French Air Force secretly flew as much as four tons of the substance to Israel.

Trouble arose in May 1960, when France began to pressure Israel to make the project public and to submit to international inspections of the site, threatening to withhold the reactor fuel unless they did. President de Gaulle was concerned that the inevitable scandal following any revelations about French assistance with the project, especially the chemical reprocessing plant, would have negative repercussions for France's international position, already on shaky ground because of its war in Algeria.

At a subsequent meeting with Ben-Gurion, de Gaulle offered to sell Israel fighter aircraft in exchange for stopping work on the reprocessing plant, and came away from the meeting convinced that the matter was closed. It was not. Over the next few months, Israel worked out a compromise. France would supply the uranium and components already placed on order and would not insist on international inspections. In return, Israel would assure France that they had no intention of making atomic weapons, would not reprocess any plutonium, and would reveal the existence of the reactor, which would be completed without French assistance. In reality, not much changed - French contractors finished work on the reactor and reprocessing plant, uranium fuel was delivered and the reactor went critical in 1964.

U.S. SPIES ON DIMONA

The United States first became aware of Dimona's existence after U-2 overflights in 1958 captured the facility's construction, but it was not identified as a nuclear site until two years later. The complex was variously explained as a textile plant, an agricultural station, and a metallurgical research facility, until David Ben-Gurion stated in December 1960 that Dimona complex was a nuclear research center built for "peaceful purposes."

There followed two decades in which the United States, through a combination of benign neglect, erroneous analysis, and successful Israeli deception, failed to discern first the details of Israel's nuclear program. As early as 8 December 1960, the CIA issued a report outlining Dimona's implications for nuclear proliferation, and the CIA station in Tel Aviv had determined by the mid-1960s that the Israeli nuclear weapons program was an established and irreversible fact.

United States inspectors visited Dimona seven times during the 1960s, but they were unable to obtain an accurate picture of the activities carried out there, largely due to tight Israeli control over the timing and agenda of the visits. The Israelis went so far as to install false control room panels and to brick over elevators and hallways that accessed certain areas of the facility. The inspectors were able to report that there was no clear scientific research or civilian nuclear power program justifying such a large reactor - circumstantial evidence of the Israeli bomb program - but found no evidence of "weapons related activities" such as the existence of a plutonium reprocessing plant.

Although the United States government did not encourage or approve of the Israeli nuclear program, it also did nothing to stop it. Walworth Barbour, US ambassador to Israel from 1961-73, the bomb program's crucial years, primarily saw his job as being to insulate the President from facts which might compel him to act on the nuclear issue, alledgedly saying at one point that "The President did not send me there to give him problems. He does not want to be told any bad news." After the 1967 war, Barbour even put a stop to military attachés' intelligence collection efforts around Dimona. Even when Barbour did authorize forwarding information, as he did in 1966 when embassy staff learned that Israel was beginning to put nuclear warheads in missiles, the message seemed to disappear into the bureaucracy and was never acted upon.

ISRAEL'S FIRST BOMB

In early 1968, the CIA issued a report concluding that Israel had successfully started production of uclear weapons. This estimate, however, was based on an informal conversation between Carl Duckett, head of the CIA's Office of Science and Technology, and Edward Teller, father of the hydrogen bomb. Teller said that, based on conversations with friends in the Israeli scientific and defense establishment, he had concluded that Israel was capable of building the bomb, and that the CIA should not wait for an Israeli test to make a final assessment because that test would never be carried out.

CIA estimates of the Israeli arsenal's size did not improve with time. In 1974, Duckett estimated that Israel had between ten and twenty nuclear weapons. The upper bound was derived from CIA speculation regarding the number of possible Israeli targets, and not from any specific intelligence. Because this target list was presumed to be relatively static, this remained the official American estimate until the early 1980s.

The actual size and composition of Israel's nuclear stockpile is uncertain, and is the subject of various estimates and reports. It is widely reported that Israel had two bombs in 1967, and that Prime Minister Eshkol ordered them armed in Israel's first nuclear alert during the Six-Day War. It is also reported that, fearing defeat in the October 1973 Yom Kippur War, the Israelis assembled 13 twenty-kiloton atomic bombs.

VANUNU REVEALS SECRETS

Israel could potentially have produced a few dozen nuclear warheads in the period 1970-1980, and might have possessed 100 to 200 warheads by the mid-1990s. In 1986 descriptions and photographs of Israeli nuclear warheads were published in the *London Sunday Times* of a purported underground bomb factory. The photographs were taken by Mordechai Vanunu, a dismissed Israeli nuclear technician. His information led some experts to conclude that Israel had a stockpile of 100 to 200 nuclear devices at that time.

By the late 1990s the U.S. Intelligence Community estimated that Israel possessed between 75-130 weapons, based on production estimates. The stockpile would certainly include warheads for mobile Jericho-1 and Jericho-2 missiles, as well as bombs for Israeli aircraft, and may include other tactical nuclear weapons of various types. Some published estimates even claimed that Israel might have as many as 400 nuclear weapons by the late 1990s. We believe these numbers are exaggerated.

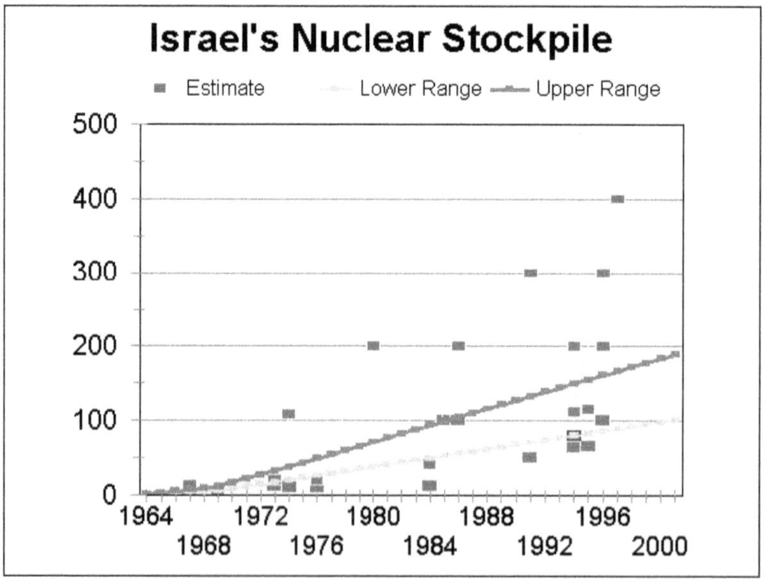

The Dimona nuclear reactor is the source of plutonium for Israeli nuclear weapons, and the number of nuclear weapons that could have been produced by Israel can be estimated on the basis of the power level of this reactor. Information made public in 1986 by Mordechai Vanunu indicated that at that time, weapons grade plutonium was being produced at a rate of about 40 kilograms annually. If this figure corresponded with the steady-state capacity of the entire Dimona facility, analysts suggested that the reactor might have a power level of at least 150 megawatts, about twice the power level at which is was believed to be operating around 1970.

To accomodate this higher power level, analysts had suggested that Israel had constructed an enlarged cooling system. An alternative interpretation of the information supplied by Vanunu was that the reactor's power level had remained at about 75 megawatts, and that the production rate of plutonium in the early 1980s reflected a backlog of previously generated material.

The upper and lower plausible limits on Israel's stockpile may be bounded by considering several variables, several of which are generic to any nuclear weapons program. The reactor may have operated an average of between 200 and 300 days annually, and produced approximately 0.9 to 1.0 grams of plutonium for each thermal megawatt day. Israel may use between 4 and 5 kilograms of plutonium per weapon [5 kilograms is a conservative estimate, and Vanunu reported that Israeli weapons used 4 kg].

The key variable that is specific to Israel is the power level of the reactor, which is variously reported to be at least 75 MWt and possibly as high as 200 MWt. New high-resolution satellite imagery provides important insight this matter. The imagery of the Dimona nuclear reactor was acquired by the Public Eye Project of the Federation of American Scientists from Space Imaging Corporation's IKONOS satellite. The cooling towers associated with the Dimona reactor are clearly visible and identifiable in satellite imagery. Comparison of recently acquired commercial IKONOS imagery with declassified American CORONA reconnaissance satellite imagery indicates that no new cooling towers were constructed in the years between 1971 and 2000. This strongly suggests that the reactor's power level has not been increased significantly during this period. This would suggest an annual production rate of plutonium of about 20 kilograms.

Based on plausible upper and lower bounds of the operating practices at the reactor, Israel could have thus produced enough plutonium for at least 100 nuclear weapons, but probably not significantly more than 200 weapons.

Some type of non-nuclear test, perhaps a zero yield or implosion test, occurred on 2 November 1966 [possibly at Al-Naqab in the Negev]. There is no evidence that Israel has ever carried out a nuclear test, although many observers speculated that a suspected nuclear explosion in the southern Indian Ocean in 1979 was a joint South African-Israeli test.

SOURCES AND RESOURCES

- The Third Temple's Holy Of Holies: Israel's Nuclear Weapons Warner D. Farr, LTC, U.S. Army, September 1999

- The Bomb That Never Is by Avner Cohen, Bulletin of the Atomic Scientists, May/June 2000, Vol 56, No. 3 pp.22-23
- Israel and the Bomb. Avner Cohen has provides a detailed account of of the political aspects of Israel's nuclear history that draws on thousands of American and Israeli government documents-most of them recently declassified and never before cited-and more than one hundred interviews with key individuals who played important roles in this story.
- Obsessive secrecy undermines democracy By Reuven Pedatzur Ha'aretz. Tuesday, August 8, 2000 -- Cohen published "Israel and the Bomb" in the United States, and a Hebrew translation of the book has appeared here. In the eyes of the defense establishment, Cohen has committed a double sin.
- Fighting to preserve the tattered veil of secrecy *By Ronen Bergman* The publication of Dr. Avner Cohen's book and of the Vanunu trial transcripts set off alarm bells for the Defense Ministry's chief of security, who is striving to protect the traditional opacity regarding Israel's nuclear affairs.
- Blast, from the past to the present By Yirmiyahu Yovel Ha'aretz. 28 July 2000 -- If, in the context of the peace agreements and talks with the United States, Israel were to confirm its nuclear capability - while committing itself to no nuclear testing and pledging to build its defense system on conventional weapons as in the past - maybe then it might achieve at least de facto recognition, if not international legitimacy, for its nuclear weaponry, to be used only as a "last resort" and a tool for safeguarding peace after Israel withdraws.
- Israel **The Nuclear Potential of Individual Countries Treaty on Nonproliferation of Nuclear Weapons Problems of Extension** Appendix 2 *Russian Federation Foreign Intelligence Service* 6 April 1995
- Israel's Nuclear Weapons - A Case Study by Elizabeth Stevens
- The Samson Option. Israel's Nuclear Arsenal and American Foreign Policy Seymour M Hersh, [New York: Random House, 1991]
- Israel's Nuclear Development & Strategy: Future Ramifications for the Middle East Regional Balance By Laura Drake
- Israeli Nuclear Strategy by Air Marshal Sir Timothy Garden
- Israel: Plutonium Production The Risk Report Volume 2 Number 4 (July-August 1996).
- Israel: Uranium Processing and Enrichment The Risk Report Volume 2 Number 4 (July-August 1996).

ISRAEL'S SECURITY DOCTRINE

BASIC POINTS

- Israel cannot afford to lose a single war
- Defensive on the strategic level, no territorial ambitions.
- Desire to avoid war by political means and a credible deterrent posture.
- Preventing escalation.
- Determine the outcome of war quickly and decisively.
- Combating terrorism.

THE OPERATIONAL LEVEL

DEFENSIVE STRATEGY - OFFENSIVE TACTICS

- Prepare for Defense
- A small standing army with an early warning capability, regular air force and navy.
- An efficient reserve mobilization and transportation system.
- Move to CounterAttack
- Multiarm coordination.
- Transferring the battle to enemy's territory quickly.
- Quick attainment of war objectives.

CAPABILITIES

- Intelligence
- High capability to destroy mobile targets.
- Longrange capabilities.
- Antimissile defense.
- Allweather and lowvisibility capabilities.
- Advanced training systems.

MAIN AREAS OF ACTIVITY

- Continuous high state of readiness for war.
- Antiterrorist warfare.
- Combating terrorism by Palestinian rejectionist groups.
- Building the armed forces for the future battlefield.

ISRAELI CASUALTIES IN BATTLE

A total of 22,570 men and women have been killed defending the land of Israel since 1860, the year that the first Jewish settlers left the secure walls of Jerusalem to build new Jewish neighborhoods. Over the course of the year between Remembrance Day 2008 and Remembrance Day 2009, another 133 members of the security forces - police, IDF, Border Police, Israel Security Agency and other organizations - were killed in the service of the state.

War Of Independence (1947-49)	6,373
1956 War	231
1967 War	776
War of Attrition (1968-70)	1,424
1973 War	2,688
Lebanon War (1982-85)	1,216
Palestinian War (2000-2005)	328
Hizballah War (2006)	117
Operation Cast Lead (2008-2009)	10
Miscellaneous engagements and terrorist attacks (through April 2009)	9,407
Total	22,570*

*This number includes disabled IDF veterans who later died from their wounds and non- IDF personnel who fell in the line of duty.

There are 17,967 members of bereaved families, as follows:

3,285 widows

4,457 single bereaved parents

4,029 bereaved parents (couples) - 8,058 individuals

2,167 orphans

There are 79,239 disabled veterans.

The total population of bereaved families and disabled IDF veterans cared for by the Defense Ministry Rehabilitation department numbers is currently 97,206.

THE ISRAELI DEFENSE INDUSTRY

Israel produces a wide range of products from ammunition, small arms and artillery pieces to sophisticated electronic systems and the world's most advanced tank.

Having to fight five major wars in its first four decades, Israel built a comprehensive standing army – the Israel Defense Forces (IDF) - and furnished it with an arsenal of highly advanced military hardware. The government, which owns three major defense firms, also encouraged the formation of private companies to equip the IDF. The development of a sophisticated defense industry inevitably led to exports, which today account for a majority of its revenues and allows the country's defense industry to compete against some of the largest companies in the world for foreign contracts, in addition to producing many of the arms needed for Israel's own defense.

Faced with a shrinking market for military hardware over the last decade and a half, Israeli defense concerns have made a concerted effort to employ their research and development teams in devising products for non-military markets and, more frequently, in adapting defense technology for civilian applications. Indeed, many of the most innovative products developed by Israel's civilian high tech industry, especially in the field of telecommunications, trace their origins to military technology.

BORN OF NECESSITY

The modern defense industry in Israel was set in motion in the early 1920s. Faced by an increasingly hostile Arab population, the Jewish community began to manufacture homemade hand grenades and explosives. In the early 1930s, members of the Haganah (the pre-state Jewish underground defense organization) set up clandestine small arms factories, which became the Israel Military Industries (IMI) in 1948. In the first two decades after independence, IMI produced many of the basic weapons used by the IDF, including the Uzi sub-machine gun. The more costly aircraft and other advanced weapons were procured from foreign suppliers, principally France.

The major catalyst for Israel's metamorphosis from a small-arms manufacturer to a producer of sophisticated military systems came after the 1967 Six-Day War. During the war, France imposed an embargo on arms sales to Israel, including the Mirage planes already on order from the

Dassault aircraft factory. When the United States became the primary supplier of combat aircraft, Israel began to develop its own production capability. The government-owned Israel Aircraft Industries (IAI), founded as a maintenance facility in 1953, soon began developing and assembling a variety of its own aircraft, including the Kfir - a replacement for the Mirage - as well as the Arava and Nesher planes. At the same time, IAI's contacts with US suppliers advanced from subcontracting jobs to joint ventures with Boeing and Lockheed-Martin. As a result, employment at IAI grew rapidly from 4,000 to a peak of 14,000 in the late 1980s.

The growing sophistication of Israel's defense industry gave it the confidence to develop an all-Israeli military aircraft, the Lavi. Over the first half of the 1980s, IAI developed avionics, electronics and weapons systems for the aircraft, and by 1986 the first prototype had taken to the air. However, the government concluded that it was unable to finance such an ambitious undertaking, and the project was canceled a year later. Shorn of the Lavi, IAI began to develop a variety of products in the military and civilian spheres - such as advanced radar systems, precision weapon systems, unmanned air vehicles (UAVs) and commercial and military aircraft conversion - many of which were based on the technology developed during the Lavi project.

INDUSTRY PLAYERS

There are approximately 150 defense firms in Israel, with combined revenues of an estimated $3.5 billion. The three largest entities are the government-owned IAI, IMI and the Rafael Arms Development Authority, all of which produce a wide range of conventional arms and advanced defense electronics. The medium-sized privately owned companies include Elbit Systems and the Tadiran Group, which focus mainly on defense electronics. The smaller firms produce a narrower range of products. In all, the industry employs close to 50,000 people, all of whom share a commitment to high levels of research and development and the ability to make use of the IDF's combat experience.

Israel's defense exports are coordinated and regulated through SIBAT - the Foreign Defense Assistance and Defense Export Organization - which is run by the Ministry of Defense. SIBAT's tasks include licensing all defense exports as well as marketing products developed for the IDF, from electronic components to missile boats and tanks. Each year, SIBAT publishes a defense sales directory, an authoritative guide to what the industry has to offer.

Despite their far-reaching client base, even the biggest local firms are relatively small players in the global defense market. With increasing competition from the major world aerospace players, Israeli companies tend to specialize in niche markets, or have sought to combine forces through mergers or joint marketing efforts. In addition, declining global defense spending has provided them with new opportunities as foreign governments seek to upgrade their existing arsenal rather than buy new equipment. This policy is typified by the Phantom 2000, a sweeping modernization of the F-4 aircraft that Israel acquired from the US in the early 1970s.

THE GOVERNMENT SECTOR

In the wake of the Lavi's cancellation, IAI diversified and expanded with funding from the United States, developing the Amos and Ofeq satellites and the world's first operational anti-missile missile system, the Arrow. IAI's unmanned air vehicles (UAV or pilotless aircraft) systems, including the Hunter, have now become standard for military establishments in many countries around world. The company is also engaged in the repair and maintenance of aircraft and helicopters, and in upgrading aircraft with state-of-the-art avionics. It also designs, develops and manufacturers naval and ground systems, electronic warfare and radar equipment and missiles. Company sales in 2000 amounted to $2.18 billion, of which exports accounted for $1.7 billion. In the same year, IAI signed some 1,600 new contracts worth approximately $2.6 billion.

Israel Military Industries (IMI) was founded in 1933, as a secret small-arms plant. After the establishment of the State in 1948, it was operated by the Ministry of Defense, developing and manufacturing assault weapons - from the classic Uzi sub-machine gun to the Tavor assault rifle - heavy ammunition, aircraft and rocket systems, armored vehicles like the Merkava tank, and integrated security systems. In 1990, IMI was converted into a government-owned company. Altogether IMI manufactures some 350 products and employs over 4,000 people. In addition to Israel and the US, IMI has distributors in a number of countries, including Norway, Belgium, the Philippines and Greece. Some 60% of its revenues, worth approximately $550 million, come from exports.

The third government-owned defense firm, the Rafael Arms Development Authority, developed and now manufactures Python and Popeye "smart" airborne missiles, both of which have co-production agreements with major US aerospace companies. In addition, its products include such varied categories as passive armor, naval decoys, observation balloon systems, acoustic torpedo countermeasures, ceramic armor, air-breathing propulsion, and air-to-air, air-to-surface and surface-to-surface missiles.

THE PRIVATE SECTOR

Elbit Systems, based in Haifa, develops, manufactures and integrates advanced, high-performance defense electronics systems, focusing on upgrade programs for aircraft and armored vehicles. The company also manufactures command, control and communication (C3) systems, and upgrades in weapons platforms and electronic systems and products for both Western and former Eastern bloc countries. In 2000, Elbit Systems merged with another major private-sector defense concern, El-Op Electro-Optics Industries Ltd, and combined sales reached $591 million, up from $436 million the previous year.

The second major private sector defense firm is the Tadiran-Elisra Group, whose subsidiaries specialize in defense electronics. The group's Elisra Electronics offers a range of electronic warfare systems for the military, including radar warning systems, active countermeasure systems, comprehensive self-protection systems, ESM and ELINT systems, and sophisticated communication links complemented by extremely lightweight components and super components. It employs a staff of over 800, two thirds of whom are engineers. Tadiran Electronic Systems designs and produces a wide range of military applications, including intelligence, reconnaissance and electronic warfare and specialized naval communication systems, all tailored to customer specifications. Tadiran Spectralink specializes in pilot-rescue electronic equipment while BVR Systems develops innovative flight simulators for fighter pilots. The group, which is controlled by Koor Industries, announced sales of $284 million in 2000.

In addition to Elbit and Tadiran-Elisra, there are scores of smaller, more specialized defense firms in the private sector, including: Cyclone Aviation, which upgrades helicopters and makes aircraft components; Urdan Industries, which through its Associated Steel Foundries makes many of the components of the Merkava tank; Magal Security Systems, whose products include sensors for security perimeter fences and explosive-detection devices for airports and other public facilities; BVR Technologies, which produces airborne collision-avoidance security systems, trainers for pilots and for the use of "smart" weapons, and a variety of simulators for combat training and pilot debriefing; the Elul Group, a complex of companies which specialize in development and coordination of defense business for Israeli firms abroad, and for international firms in Israel; RSL Electronics, which produces both airborne electronics systems for airplanes and helicopters and muzzle-velocity radar for field artillery; and Soltam, which makes both mortars and heavy artillery pieces as well as Israel's most popular line of stainless steel kitchen equipment.

CIVILIAN MARKETS

Since the end of the Cold War, the global defense industry, including the IDF, has had to cope with declining military spending. In response, many private companies have either merged or reduced staff, or diversified into civilian markets, with some companies fully spinning off their civilian activities into separate businesses. Many of the high technology products designed by Israeli companies for such areas as the Internet, medical electronics and robotics, are based on technology originally developed by the IDF or the defense industries. Friendly Robotics is one notable high-tech start-up that traces its origins to the army. Its top executives worked in army technology units and the company's robot lawnmowers are based on advanced missile guidance technology, providing accurate positioning and navigation functions to perform its tasks. Among the few private sector defense firms with civilian activities, Elisra designs, develops and produces electronic and microwave applications for the commercial market.

In 1968, IAI acquired the rights to manufacture the Jet Commander executive aircraft from the US company Rockwell, which eventually evolved into the IAI's Astra. In the 1990s, IAI began producing the Galaxy executive jet in partnership with the Pritzker family of Chicago. In April 2001, the international aerospace firm General Dynamics contracted to purchase the Galaxy firm for approximately $600 million. In addition, in the late 1970s Bedek, a division of IAI specializing in aircraft maintenance, began overhauling and refitting Boeing 707 airliners, and today the upgrade of commercial aircraft has become a major business for IAI. The civilian content of the new contracts signed in 2000 was worth $1.1 billion, or 42% of total new contracts. IMI has fewer civilian businesses but has developed technology for electronic wallets and computerized payment systems.

Rafael develops military technologies for civilian use through its Rafael Development Corp., a joint venture with the private sector Discount Investment Group. One of these projects used miniaturization and guidance techniques to produce a transmitter and camera the size of a vitamin capsule. The capsule is swallowed by a patient and pictures of the gastrointestinal tract are then taken by the camera for use by diagnosticians, substituting for invasive diagnostic procedures. The system, which was developed by Given Imaging, was the brainchild of a missile guidance expert.

CHARIOT OF FIRE

During the 1973 Yom Kippur War, Israeli armor suffered heavy losses from Egyptian and Syrian wire-guided anti-tank missiles. The high casualty rate spurred the IDF, which had previously depended on US-made Patton and Sherman tanks and British Centurion tanks, to develop the Merkava (Heb., chariot), considered one of the world's most effective and safest battle tanks.

Development of the Merkava was headed by Gen. Israel Tal, a former Armored Corps commander. Tal's team sought to design a tank that provided maximum protection to the tanks crew. One element of that defense is the placement of the tank's engine at the front of the vehicle, where it serves as a shield for the personnel compartment.

This in turn provided more space in the vehicle's rear, which can be used to carry up to six extra soldiers. In addition, a special "canopy" protects the commander from indirect fire; the turret and the hull are fitted with a modular armor system that can be changed in the field; and the forward section of the turret is fitted with additional blocks of armor that provide extra protection against the latest generation of anti-tank missiles. A "skirt" of chains with ball weights is attached to the lower half of the turret, causing incoming projectiles to detonate on impact with the chains instead of penetrating the turret ring.

The tank became operative in 1979, and was first employed in the 1982 Operation "Peace for Galilee". The Mark I model was succeeded by the Mark II in 1983, which was replaced by the Mark III in 1990. Among the features of the Mark III are a new suspension system, a 1200-horsepower engine and new transmission, a more powerful main gun, and ballistic protection provided by special armor modules. The main 120-mm gun, developed by Israel Military Industries, is enclosed in a thermal sleeve that increases accuracy by preventing heat distortion.

Mark II and Mark III tanks are currently in service in the IDF; a Mark IV model, with additional safety and fire-control features, is currently being developed. It will include a new compressed-gas recoil system and thermal sleeve for the 120-mm gun, to enable the firing of enhanced kinetic energy ammunition. With the exception of the engine, all systems and assemblies of the Merkava tanks are of Israeli design and manufacture.

ISRAEL HAS 17TH LARGEST DEFENSE BUDGET

“Defense News” ranked Israel 17th in a list of the world’s top 25 defense spenders based on absolute numbers, not as a percentage of GDP. The list is based on updated information from the CIA’s “World Fact Book” and from the Stockholm International Peace Research Institute (SIPRI). Most of the figures in the list, including those for Israel, refer to the 2005 fiscal year. The numbers are mostly consistent with official data from the relevant countries. Only one Arab country, Saudi Arabia, made the list, although Iran, with $4.3 billion in military spending in 2005, just lost the 25th place to Argentina.

World's Top Defense Spenders		
1.	United States	$518.1 billion
2.	China	$81.47 billion
3.	France	$45 billion

4.	Japan	$44.31 billion
5.	United Kingdom	$42.84 billion
6.	Germany	$35.06 billion
7.	Italy	$28.18 billion
8.	South Korea	$21.05 billion
9.	Russia	$21 billion
10.	India	$19.04 billion
11.	Saudi Arabia	$18 billion
17.	Israel	$9.44 billion

THE ISRAELI NAVY

The Israeli Navy is neither famous nor large. Long overshadowed by its more glamorous counterparts in the Tank Corps and the Israel Air Force, the Sea Corps has nevertheless built up an impressive record for itself and managed to make good use of its indigenous weapon technology and ship design. The Sea Corps first won acclaim in the Yom Kippur War of 1973 when it sank eight Arab FFLs without a the loss of a single Israeli vessel; the crews of the Israeli Navy successfully destroying or otherwise evading over seventy Arab Soviet-supplied SS-N-2 Styx missiles. Although the size of the Egyptian Navy in 1988 was twice that of Israel's, observers felt that the tactical and technological superiority of the Sea Corps offset any Egyptian quantitative advantage.

Operating in two unconnected bodies of water, the Sea Corps is based in the Mediterranean Sea by way of ports at Ashdod and Haifa and in the Red Sea from the port of Eilat. Although Israel does not maintain a Marine Corps per se, it does make use of an elite group of underwater commandos (Flotilla 13) who have proven themselves to be highly successful in amphibious and sabotage operations.

MISSION

The Israeli Sea Corps' main objective lies in defending the Israeli coastline. The heart of the fleet is the Sa'ar class of Fast Attack Craft, who with their exceptional offensive capability and high speed make excellent tools in the navy's overall scheme. The air wing of the navy is made up of maritime reconnaissance aircraft and helicopters used for search and rescue, generally with minimal armament.

Engagements with terrorists and other low-intensity conflicts neglected the need for larger ships such as cruisers or destroyers. The Navy makes full use of its smaller missile craft and interdiction vessels to keep the Eastern Mediterranean and Red Seas clean. However, during the 1982 Peace for Galilee war with Lebanon the Israeli navy proved to be capable of missions beyond policing its waters and landed troops and armor on the beaches near Sidon using their small flotilla of amphibious craft with relative success; and during the 1996 Operation Grapes of Wrath Israeli missile craft shelled the coastal roads of Lebanon. Even still, this defensive role has not relegated the Israeli Navy to a coast guard mission. The Israeli Navy, while strategically defensive, is highly offensive tactically and conducts its mission dynamically and with a high degree of elan.

MODERNIZATION

With the added capabilities of the new *Dolphin* submarines and *Eilat/Sa'ar V* missile corvettes the Israeli Navy possesses the power to operate off of the coast of Libya or any other potential threat with a good deal of strength. In addition, the Israeli Air Force operates some of its AH-1 *Cobra* gunships to patrol the Israeli coastline in conjunction with Naval *Sea Scan* search aircraft and an extensive land-based radar network.

The Israeli Sea Corps has always been keen to modernize and one such program is in place today. New systems and techniques are being developed to meet the unsettling and quickly changing realities of modern naval warfare, from thrust vectored propulsion on the *Super Dvora MkII* patrol craft to the new Elisra ECM/ESM electronic warfare suite on the *Sa'ar V*s. The well established Israeli high-tech in

dustry has been well prepared to meet the needs of the ever-mightier fleet of fast attack craft and this mutual cooperation is ever so visible in the new look and equipment of the *T'sva Hagana L'Yisrael HeylHa'Yam*.

The Israeli Navy has begun incorporating the Israeli-designed Typhoon naval gun system into its operational scheme. The gun, manufactured by El-Op and Rafael, is targeted thermally and will employ either a 25mm cannon or a .50 cal-triple barrel Phalanx gun. It is intended to be used on patrol boats and operated by remote control, thus reducing the risk to the sailors manning it.

WOMEN OF THE IDF

WOMEN IN ISRAELI COMBAT UNITS

In 1999, Israel announced that women would begin serving as combat soldiers in the year 2000. According to a plan prepared by the Israel Defense Forces, female units would serve along the Egyptian and Jordanian borders and, eventually, take on the vast majority of border patrol duty. The Carcal company, for example, is being trained to patrol the border for drug smugglers and terrorist infiltrators. This is a coed unit whose 200 female soldiers outnumber the men by 2-to-1.

In early 2000, the IDF decided to also deploy women in the artillery corps, followed by infantry units, armored divisions and elite combat units. The Navy has also decided to place women in its diving repair unit. Altogether, at the beginning of 2004, about 450 women were in combat units.

Female soldiers are supposed to be trained and responsible for the same duties as their male counterparts. Those recruited for combat units have to serve for 30 months instead of the current mandatory period for women of 21 months.

"CHEN"-THE WOMEN'S CORPS

The Defense Service Law of 1959 defines and regulates the obligation of service in the Israel Defense Forces. According to the Law, all citizens and permanent residents of the State of Israel are required to perform military service. All women between the ages of 18 and 26, who are physically fit, unmarried, have not borne children, and have not objected on religious grounds or grounds of conscience must fulfill their military obligation.

Women currently perform compulsory military service in the IDF for a period of one year and nine months (as compared with the three years required of male conscripts). In 2001, eligibility for women reserve soldierswas extended until the age of 38, with an exemption for pregnant women or mothers. To promote equal opportunity for women, the IDF plan calls for expanding the types of roles for women during reserve duty.

HISTORY

The role of women in Israel's defense has a long tradition reaching back to the biblical days of Yael and Deborah. Women played a vital role in the underground struggle for Israel's independence, including participation in signals and combat roles in the prestate military cadres: Haganah, Irgun, and Lehi.

In 1948, the IDF began to reorganize its frontline brigades, and the issue was raised as to whether women should be integrated into men's units, or whether separate battalions of women should be formed that would serve in the brigade while remaining independent of it.

The second option was decided upon, and the Women's Corps was thus founded on May 16, 1948. Within a year, however, the Women's Corps was restructured, and female soldiers were dispersed throughout various units. From then and until today, servicewomen come under the direct command of the commander of the unit to which they are assigned, but the Women's Corps constitutes a professional support system for women in the IDF.

Though women can serve in support and combat support roles in the IDF, they have, until recently, been prohibited from engaging in actual combat. The rationale for this policy was that should a woman be captured by the enemy, the effect on national morale would be devastating. This situation has changed following a recent Supreme Court ruling.

WOMEN'S SERVICE IN THE IDF

All young women with Israeli citizenship are sent their first draft notice at age 17. During the year preceding their induction, they are classified and processed. The initial selection process includes the preparation of a medical profile, a psychotechnical examination and verification of formal education and personal background.

As a result of improvements in the selection process, a large percentage of female candidates for military service are assigned postings before their actual conscription. A considerable number of women volunteer for premilitary courses, taken on their own time (as civilians) before their induction. These courses prepare candidates for military service in specific military occupational specialties. These options are important to both the needs of the IDF, which is interested in making maximum use of the ability of its recruits, and to the recruit, who is personally involved in establishing the course that her military service will take.

The first stage of IDF service is basic training. During this period, which lasts two and a half weeks for female conscripts (or a week and a half for women who are preposted), recruits gain basic knowledge of the IDF organizational structure, weapons handling, first aid and more.

Over the course of the years, the number of military occupational specialties open to women in the IDF has expanded and today most jobs are open to women. Women have long served in technological positions, intelligence, operations and training. Likewise, women can be found servicing IDF computerized systems, working as computer programmers, smart weapons systems operators and electronics technicians.

Following a recent Supreme Court ruling, which upheld the petition of a servicewoman (Alice Miller) to be allowed to apply for Flight School, the Defense Service Law was amended in 1995 to enable servicewomen to attend Flight School, and woman recruits to serve in units outside the IDF ORBAT (women may thus serve in the police force and in the border police). In 2001, the first female fighter pilot graduated the Israel Air Force flight school. In 2003, the first female combat helicopter pilot was due to graduate.

All women have the opportunity to participate in an officers course, providing they have met stiff criteria and have demonstrated their ability while in the ranks. Becoming an officer is voluntary, and those who successfully complete the officers course must sign up for an additional nine months of career service.

STRUCTURE AND OBJECTIVES

Recognizing the uniqueness of women's service, the IDF established the Women's Corps as a parallel administrative system to the command system. Its main tasks are to formulate policy relating to the service of female recruits, to advise commanders on the issue of women's service, and to command the Women's Corps units. The objectives of the Women's Corps system are:

1. To help realize the potential of women in the IDF, in accordance with the needs of the IDF and policies of General Staff.

2. To advise commanders and servicewomen on specific issues pertaining to the military service of female soldiers.

3. To be responsible for the instruction and training of female recruits, NCOs and officers.

The Women's Corps is commanded by a Brigadier General who has, under her command, professional Women's Corps officers and NCOs.

This network performs a large number of functions ranging from advising at the General Staff level to handling matters of individual servicewomen at the personal level, establishing guiding principles for the service of female soldiers, professional training, terms of service, integration of various professions and duties, intersex tension and women's health issues.

THE CORPS DISBANDS

On August 1, 2001, the existing Women's Corps was incorporated into the General Staff rather than acting as an independent unit. Changes in the IDF are supposed to give female soldiers new opportunities and allow them to be part of all units, including combat units. The Commander of the Women's Corps, Brig.-Gen. Suzy Yogev, was appointed to serve as Advisor on Women's Issues to the Chief of Staff.

WOMAN & SPECIAL FORCES

Over the years there have been many myth and misconceptions regarding the combat status of woman in the Israeli Defense Forces (IDF), most of them incorrect.

The combat history of female soldiers in the IDF can be dividend into three:

- 1948 - War of Independence - women on full combat status
- 1948-Late 1990's - no women are allowed in combat positions
- Late 1990's - women are taking more and more combat positions in the IDF

As an army created during war, when first formed in 1948 the IDF used what ever personnel it had as warriors regardless of gender. After the War of Independence ended and until the late 1990's no women were allowed in combat positions, except for an attempt in the 1950's to accept women to flight school.

However, women did take over almost all field instructing positions in the IDF and, as such, were issued weapons, but they were not, combatants just instructors.

In the mid 1990's following an appeal to the Israeli Supreme Court the IDF was forced to accept women to its famous flight school. Additional Supreme Court appeals as well as political pressure caused the IDF to open more combat positions to women.

Today female soldiers can be found on combat status in the following positions, involving male and female fighting formations:

- Artillery
- Anti Aircraft corps in the Surface to Air Missiles (SAM) elements.
- Combat Engineering corps in the Atomic Biological Chemical (ABC) unit.
- Light infantry (Karakal) - positioned in the peaceful border with Egypt.
- Military Police (Sachlav) - stationed in the Occupied Territories, usually in Hebron.
- MAGAV - SAMAG - a special patrol unit.
- Israeli Police - YASAM - a special patrol unit akin to the MAGAV SAMAG.
- Air Crew including fighter pilots.

- Naval officers
- Unit 869 - in peacetime borders, mainly along the peaceful border with Egypt.

Helicopter airborne mechanics - there are currently three female airborne mechanics in the Israeli Air Force (IAF). Two are assigned to UH60 Blackhawk and one to CH53.

There are also few female operators in various roles in Special Forces units:

- Unit YAMAG - the female operators here are combatants similar to the male ones.
- Unit 669 - the woman in the unit are airborne paramedics replacing reserve personnel. During mission they will deploy from the helicopter and make the actual rescue as the man, but rather will stay in the helicopter and provide medical assistance.
- Unit YABAN - the woman operators in the unit act as defense divers.
- Unit Oket'z - the unit has two types of female canine handlers
  - Non combatants - belong to the Rescue Palga and participate in civilian Search And Rescue (SAR) missions.
  - Combatants - receive extensive combat training and are placed in borders check points in the Occupied Territories, in order to do weapons and explosives searches in vehicles and on civilians.

ISRAEL AND WEAPONS OF MASS DESTRUCTION

Israel is widely believed to possess **weapons of mass destruction**, and to be one of four nuclear-armed countries not recognized as a Nuclear Weapons State by the Nuclear Non-Proliferation Treaty (NPT). The US Congress Office of Technology Assessment has recorded Israel as a country generally reported as having undeclared chemical warfare capabilities, and an offensive biological warfare program. Officially Israel neither confirms nor denies possessing nuclear weapons.

NUCLEAR WEAPONS

Although no official statistics exist, it has been estimated that Israel possesses up to 400 thermonuclear weapons, believed to be of Teller-Ulam design, including strategic warheads in the megaton-range. Delivery mechanisms include intercontinental ballistic missiles. The Israeli government maintains a policy of deliberate ambiguity on whether it has nuclear weapons, saying only that it would not be the first to "introduce nuclear weapons in the Middle East." Former International Atomic Energy Agency Director General Mohamed ElBaradei regarded Israel as a state possessing nuclear weapons.

Israel has not signed the Nuclear Non-Proliferation Treaty. However, on July 13, 2008, Israel took part in a regional conference of the Union for the Mediterranean which pledged to pursue a Middle East Zone free of weapons of mass destruction.

CHEMICAL WEAPONS

Israel has signed but not ratified the Chemical Weapons Convention (CWC). There are speculations that a chemical weapons program might be located at the Israel Institute for Biological Research (IIBR) in Ness Ziona

190 liters of dimethyl methylphosphonate, a CWC schedule 2 chemical used in the synthesis of Sarin nerve gas, was discovered in the cargo of El Al Flight 1862 after it crashed in 1992 en route to Tel Aviv. Israel insisted the material was non-toxic, was to have been used to test filters that protect against chemical weapons, and that it had been clearly listed on the cargo manifest in accordance with international regulations. The shipment was from a U.S. chemical plant to the IIBR under a U.S. Department of Commerce license.

In 1993, the U.S. Congress Office of Technology Assessment WMD proliferation assessment recorded Israel as a country generally reported as having undeclared offensive chemical warfare capabilities. Former US deputy assistant secretary of defense responsible for chemical and biological defense, Bill Richardson, said in 1998 "I have no doubt that Israel has worked on both chemical and biological offensive things for a long time ... There's no doubt they've had stuff for years."

BIOLOGICAL WEAPONS

Israel is not a signatory to the Biological Weapons Convention (BWC). It is assumed that the Israel Institute for Biological Research in Ness Ziona develops vaccines and antidotes for chemical and biological warfare. While Israel is not known to be producing biological weapons currently, there remains speculation that Israel's ability to start production and dissemination, if necessary, remains active

Israel is widely believed to be the sixth country in the world to develop nuclear weapons and to be one of four nuclear-armed countries not recognized as a Nuclear Weapons State by the Nuclear Non-Proliferation Treaty (NPT), the others being India, Pakistan and North Korea. International Atomic Energy Agency Director General Mohamed ElBaradei regards Israel as a state possessing nuclear weapons, but Israel maintains a policy known as "nuclear ambiguity" (also known as "nuclear opacity"). Israel has never officially admitted to having nuclear weapons, instead repeating over the years that it would not be the first country to "introduce" nuclear weapons to the Middle East, leaving ambiguous whether it means it will not create or will not use the weapons.

Israel began investigating the nuclear field just one year after its 1948 founding and with French support secretly began building a nuclear reactor and reprocessing plant in the late 1950s. Although Israel first built a nuclear weapon in 1967-68, it was not publicly confirmed from the inside until Mordechai Vanunu, a former Israeli nuclear technician, revealed details of the program to the British press in 1986. Israel is currently believed to possess between 75 and 400 nuclear warheads with the ability to deliver them by intercontinental ballistic missile, aircraft, and submarine

DEVELOPMENT HISTORY

PRE-DIMONA 1949-1956

Israel first showed interest in procuring nuclear materials in 1949, when a unit of the Israel Defense Forces Science Corps, known by the Hebrew acronym HEMED GIMMEL, carried out a two year geological survey of the Negev. While a preliminary study was initially prompted by rumors of petroleum fields, one objective of the longer two year survey was to find sources of uranium; some small recoverable amounts were found in phosphate deposits. That same year, HEMED GIMMEL funded six Israeli physics graduate students to study overseas, including one to go to the University of Chicago and study under Enrico Fermi, who had overseen the world's first artificial and self-sustaining nuclear chain reaction.

In early 1952 HEMED GIMMEL was moved from the IDF to the Ministry of Defense and was reorganized as the Division of Research and Infrastructure (EMET). That June, Ernst David Bergmann, the chief of research at the Defense Ministry and Prime Minister David Ben Gurion's scientific advisor, was appointed by Ben-Gurion to be the first chairman of the Israel Atomic Energy Commission (IAEC). HEMED GIMMEL was renamed Machon 4 during the transfer, and was used by Bergmann as the "chief laboratory" of the IAEC; by 1953, Machon 4, working with the Department of Isotope Research at the Weizmann Institute, developed the capability to extract uranium from the phosphate in the Negev and new technique to produce indigenous heavy water. Bergmann, who was interested in increasing nuclear cooperation with the French, sold both patents to the Commissariat à l'énergie atomique (CEA) for 60 million francs. Although they were never commercialized, it was a consequential step for future French-Israeli cooperation. In addition, Israeli scientists probably helped construct the G-1 plutonium production reactor and UP-1 reprocessing plant at Marcoule.

France and Israel had close relations in many areas. France was principal arms supplier for the young Jewish state, and as instability spread through French colonies in North Africa, Israel provided valuable intelligence obtained from contacts with Sephardi Jews in those countries. At the same time Israeli scientists were also observing France's own nuclear program, and were the only foreign scientists allowed to roam "at will" at the nuclear facility at Marcoule.

After US President Dwight Eisenhower announced the Atoms for Peace initiative, Israel became the second country to sign on (following Turkey), and signed a peaceful nuclear cooperation agreement with the United States on 12 July 1955. This culminated in a public signing ceremony on 20 March 1957 to construct a "small swimming-pool research reactor in Nachal Soreq," which would be used to shroud the construction of a much larger facility with the French at Dimona.

NEGEV NUCLEAR RESEARCH CENTER

The **Negev Nuclear Research Center** is an Israeli nuclear installation located in the Negev desert, about thirteen kilometers to the south-east of the city of Dimona.

Its construction commenced in 1958, with French assistance according to the secret Protocol of Sèvres agreements. The complex was constructed in secret, and outside the International Atomic Energy Agency inspection regime. To maintain secrecy, French customs officials were told that the largest of the reactor components, such as the reactor tank, were part of a desalination plant bound for Latin America. The purpose of Dimona is widely assumed to be the manufacturing of nuclear weapons, and the majority of defense experts have concluded that it does in fact do that. An estimate based on the known power of the reactor concluded that enough plutonium for 100 to 200 nuclear bombs could have been produced by the year 2000. However, the Israeli government refuses to confirm or deny this publicly, as part of a policy of deliberate ambiguity.

The Dimona reactor went on-line some time between 1962 and 1964, and with the plutonium produced there the Israel Defence Forces most probably had their first nuclear weapons ready before the Six-Day War.

When the United States intelligence community discovered the purpose of Dimona in the early 1960s, it demanded that Israel agree to international inspections. Israel agreed, but on a condition that US, rather than International Atomic Energy Agency, inspectors were used, and that Israel would receive advance notice of all inspections.

Some claim that because Israel knew the schedule of the inspectors' visits, it was able to hide the alleged purpose of the site (manufacturing of nuclear weapons) from the inspectors, by installing temporary false walls and other devices before each inspection. The inspectors eventually informed the U.S. government that their inspections were useless, due to Israeli restrictions on what areas of the facility they could inspect. By 1969 the U.S. believed that Israel might have a nuclear weapon, and terminated inspections that year.

The Dimona reactor was overflown by unidentified jet aircraft before the Six Day War in 1967. These planes were later determined to be Soviet MiG-25s.

In 1986, Mordechai Vanunu, a former technician at Dimona, revealed to the media some evidence of Israel's nuclear program. Israeli agents abducted him from Italy and transported him to Israel. An Israeli court then tried him in secret on charges of treason and espionage, and sentenced him to eighteen years imprisonment. At the time of Vanunu's arrest, *The Times* reported that Israel had material for approximately 20 hydrogen bombs and 200 fission bombs. In the spring of 2004, Vanunu was released from prison, and placed under several strict restrictions, such as the denial of a passport, freedom of movement limitations and restrictions on communications with the press. Since his release, he has been rearrested and charged multiple times for violations of the terms of his release.

Dimona's reactor was defended by batteries of Patriot missiles in anticipation of strikes from Iraq in 2002 to 2003

Recently safety concerns about this 40-year-old reactor have been reported. In 2004 as a preventive measure Israeli authorities distributed potassium iodide anti-radiation tablets to thousands of residents living nearby.

In 2006 a group of local residents was formed due to concerns regarding health and safety from living near the reactor.

According to a lawsuit filed in Be'er Sheva Labor Tribunal, workers at the center were subjected to human experimentation in 1998. According to Julius Malick, the worker who submitted the lawsuit, they were given drinks with uranium without medical supervision and without obtaining written consent or warning them about risks of side effects

NEGOTIATION

The French decision to help Israel build a nuclear reactor was not without precedent; in September 1955 Canada publicly announced that it would help the Indian government build a heavy-water research reactor for "peaceful purposes." When Egyptian President Gamal Abdel Nasser nationalized the Suez Canal, France asked Israel to cross the Sinai in order to justify its and Britain's invasion of Egypt (see Suez Crisis), and Shimon Peres, sensing the opportunity on the nuclear reactor, accepted. On 17 September 1956, Peres and Bergmann reached a tentative agreement in Paris for the CEA to sell Israel a small research reactor. This was reaffirmed by

Peres at the Protocol of Sèvres conference in late October for the sale of a reactor to be built near Dimona and for a supply of uranium fuel. After the Suez Crisis led to the threat of Soviet intervention and the British and French were being forced to withdraw under pressure from the US, Ben-Gurion sent Peres and Golda Meir to France. During their discussions the groundwork was laid for France to build a larger nuclear reactor and chemical reprocessing plant, and French Prime Minister Guy Mollet, ashamed at having abandoned his commitment to fellow socialists in Israel, supposedly told an aide, "I owe the bomb to them."

This deal was finalized on 3 October 1957 in two agreements: one political that declared the project to be for peaceful purposes and specified other legal obligations, and one technical that described a 24 megawatt EL-102 reactor. The one to actually be built was to be two to three times as large and be able to produce 22 kilograms of plutonium a year.

EXCAVATION

Before construction began it was determined that the scope of the project would be too large for the EMET and IAEC team, so Shimon Peres recruited Colonel Manes Pratt, then Israeli military attaché in Burma, to be the project leader. Building began in late 1957 or early 1958, bringing hundreds of French engineers and technicians to the Beersheba and Dimona area In addition, thousands of newly immigrated Sephardic Jews were recruited to do digging; to circumvent strict labor laws, they were hired in increments of 59 days, separated by one day off.

RUPTURE WITH FRANCE

When Charles de Gaulle became French President in late 1958 he wanted to end French-Israeli nuclear cooperation, and said that he would not supply Israel with uranium unless the plant was opened to international inspectors, declared peaceful, and no plutonium was reprocessed. Through an extended series of negotiations, Shimon Peres finally reached a compromise with Foreign Minister Maurice Couve de Murville over two years later, in which French companies would be able to continue to fulfill their contract obligations and Israel would declare the project peaceful. Because of this, French assistance did not end until 1966.

BRITISH AID

Top secret British documents obtained by BBC *Newsnight* show that Britain made hundreds of secret shipments of restricted materials to Israel in the 1950s and 1960s. These included specialist chemicals for reprocessing and samples of fissile material—uranium-235 in 1959, and plutonium in 1966, as well as highly enriched lithium-6 which is used to boost fission bombs and fuel hydrogen bombs. The investigation also showed that Britain shipped 20 tons of heavy water directly to Israel in 1959 and 1960 to start up the Dimona reactor.

The transaction was made through a Norwegian front company called Noratom which took a 2% commission on the transaction. Britain was challenged about the heavy water deal at the International Atomic Energy Agency after it was exposed on Newsnight in 2005. British Foreign Minister Kim Howells claimed this was a sale to Norway. But a former British intelligence officer who investigated the deal at the time confirmed that this was really a sale to Israel and the Noratom contract was just a charade. The Foreign Office finally admitted in March 2006 that Britain knew the destination was Israel all along. Israel admits running the Dimona reactor with

Norway's heavy water since 1963. French engineers who helped build Dimona say the Israelis were expert operators, so only a relatively small portion of the water were lost during the years past since the first operation of the reactor.

In 1961, the Israeli Prime Minister David Ben-Gurion informed the Canadian Prime Minister John Diefenbaker that a pilot plutonium-separation plant would be built at Dimona. British intelligence concluded from this and other information that this "can only mean that Israel intends to produce nuclear weapons".The nuclear reactor at Dimona went critical in 1962. By 1965 the Israeli reprocessing plant was completed and ready to convert the reactor's fuel rods into weapons grade plutonium.

COSTS

The exact cost for the construction of the Israeli nuclear program are unknown, though Peres later said that the reactor cost $80 million in 1960 dollars, half of which was raised by foreign Jewish donors, including many American Jews. Some of these donors were given a tour of the Dimona complex in 1968.

WEAPONS PRODUCTION 1967-PRESENT

Israel is believed to have begun full scale production of nuclear weapons following the 1967 Six-Day War, although it may have had bomb parts earlier. A CIA report from early 1967 stated that Israel had the materials to construct a bomb in six to eight weeks and some authors suggest that Israel had two crude bombs ready for use during the war. According to US journalist Seymour Hersh, everything was ready for production at this time save an official order to do so. Moshe Dayan, then Defense Minister, convinced the Labor Party's economic boss Pinchas Sapir of the value of commencing the program by giving him a tour of the Dimona site in early 1968, and soon after Dayan decided that he had the authority to order the start of full production of 4 to 5 nuclear warheads a year. Hersh stated that it is widely believed that the words "Never Again" were welded, in English and Hebrew, onto the first warhead.

In order to produce plutonium the Israelis needed a large supply of uranium ore, some of which was procured by the Mossad on the pretense of buying it for an Italian chemical company in Milan. Once the uranium was shipped from Antwerp it was transferred to an Israeli freighter at sea and brought to Israel. The orchestrated disappearance of the uranium, named Operation Plumbat, became the subject of the 1978 book *The Plumbat Affair.*

Estimates as to how many warheads Israel has built since the late 1960s have varied, mainly based on the amount of fissile material that could have been produced and on the revelations of Israeli nuclear technician Mordechai Vanunu.

By 1969, U.S. Defense Secretary Melvin Laird believed that Israel might have a nuclear weapon that year. Later that year, U.S. President Richard Nixon in a meeting with Israeli Prime Minister Golda Meir pressed Israel to "make no visible introduction of nuclear weapons or undertake a nuclear test program", so maintaining a policy of nuclear ambiguity. The US Central Intelligence Agency believed that Israel's first bombs may have been made with highly enriched uranium stolen in the mid-1960s from the US Navy nuclear fuel plant operated by the *Nuclear Materials and Equipment Corporation*, where sloppy material accounting would have masked the theft.

By 1974 US intelligence believed Israel had stockpiled a small number of fission weapons, and by 1979 were perhaps in a position so they could test a more advanced small tactical nuclear weapon or thermonuclear weapon trigger design.

The CIA believed that the number of Israeli nuclear weapons stayed from 10 to 20 from 1974 through the early 1980s. Vanunu's information in October 1986 said that based on a reactor operating at 150 megawatts and a production of 40 kg of plutonium per year, Israel had 100 to 200 nuclear devices. Furthermore, Vanunu revealed that between 1980-1986 Israel attained the ability to build thermonuclear weapons. By the mid 2000s estimates of Israel's arsenal ranged from 75 to 400 nuclear warheads.

Several reports have surfaced claiming that Israel has some uranium enrichment capability at Dimona. Vanunu asserted that gas centrifuges were operating in Machon 8, and that a laser enrichment plant was being operated in Machon 9 (Israel holds a 1973 patent on laser isotope separation). According to Vanunu, the production-scale plant has been operating since 1979-80. The scale of a centrifuge operation would necessarily be limited due to space constraints. Laser isotope separation, however, if developed to operational status, could be quite compact. If highly enriched uranium is being produced in substantial quantities, then Israel's nuclear arsenal could be much larger than estimated solely from plutonium production. Uranium enrichment could also be used to re-enrich reprocessed uranium into reactor fuel to more efficiently use Israel's uranium supply.

In 1991 alone, as the Soviet Union dissolved, nearly 20 Jewish top Soviet scientists reportedly emigrated to Israel, some of whom had been involved in operating nuclear power plants and planning for the next generation of Soviet reactors. In September 1992, German intelligence was quoted in the press as estimating that 40 Soviet nuclear scientists had emigrated to Israel since 1989.

NUCLEAR CAPACITY

Israel's nuclear history in the period from 1973 until the first Gulf War in 1990-91 can be recounted along two distinct themes. First, it was the period in which Israel's policy of nuclear opacity was transformed from a short-lived improvisation to a semi-permanent strategic posture. In retrospect, the period from 1974 to 1990 was the golden age of nuclear opacity. By the end of the period, Israelis came to view the policy as a great strategic success because it provided Israel the benefits of existential deterrence at a very low political cost. Nuclear opacity became an indispensable pillar in its national security doctrine. In particular, the policy of nuclear opacity seemed to have removed the nuclear issue from the U.S.-Israeli agenda, without restricting Israel's freedom of action in this field. For Israeli strategists, opacity was the best of all possible worlds. Even Vanunu's public disclosure of Dimona's secrets in 1986 (see footnote 2 and below) was not politically sufficient to shake Israel's posture of opacity.

Second, it was a period of rapid growth for Israel's nuclear arsenal, with Israel taking advantage of its freedom of action under opacity. It is widely believed (and supported by Vanunu's information) that during this period, Israel's nuclear arsenal made a major transformation. Israel no longer possessed a dozen or so low-yield first-generation bombs; it expanded and modernized its arsenal, which became qualitatively advanced and quantitatively sizable.

It is important to look at the lessons of the 1973 war in order to understand these changes. In the eyes of most Israeli strategists and military historians, Israel almost reached the brink, the moment of "last resort." Had the Syrians been able to cross the Jordan River, this could have called for "last resort" nuclear use. Yet, it appears that Israel's dozen or so bombs did not fit such a use. To stop armor columns moving on the Golan Heights, in the proximity of Israeli troops, Israel needed low-yield weapons for tactical use. But, presumably, Israel lacked such weapons. Also, if some Israeli leaders (such as Dayan) had concerns about the Soviet Union, Israel had no weapons to constitute even a minimum deterrence vis-à-vis the Soviet Union.

According to Vanunu, since the mid-1970s, Israel had expanded and modernized its nuclear infrastructure in Dimona to be able to produce new types of advanced nuclear weaponry, small and large, and in greater quantities. Some sources believe that during that period Israel produced both larger advanced weapons (boosted, and possibly even thermonuclear) as well as advanced tactical weapons (possibly enhanced radiation weapons). In addition, by the mid-to-late 1970s, Israel started the development of the Jericho-II missile, a ballistic missile with an operational range of 1,500 kilometers or more. The Jericho-II was tested in the late 1980s, and it was deployed in 1989-90.

Israel significantly expanded its nuclear capability throughout that period, but it did not move to establish a secured second-strike capability. While apparently there were occasional discussions about this, operational and costly decisions were deferred. The underlying assumption that guided Israel's strategic planning was that Israel's regional nuclear monopoly was still holding, and if and when this situation changed, Israel would have ample time to adjust. This assessment was reinforced by the success of Israel's attack on the Iraqi Osiraq reactor in 1981. Until the late 1980s, Israel assumed that Saddam's nuclear vision was for all practical purposes dead. But this assumption came under scrutiny by the late 1980s. As the Iran-Iraq War came to a close, Iraq emerged as a regional Arab power with strong nuclear aspirations. In 1990, before Iraq invaded Kuwait, Israeli strategists believed that Israel and Iraq were on a path to conflict within a few years.

During the buildup of the first Gulf War, and as a reaction to Iraqi missile threats, Prime Minister Yitzhak Shamir issued an unveiled threat to Iraq without directly referring to the Israeli nuclear arsenal: "all those who threaten us should know that whoever dares strike Israel will be struck hard and in the most severe way," adding that "...Israel has a very strong deterrent capability." Defense Minister Moshe Ayan went even further by warning Saddam Hussein about Israeli weapons, "which the world does not yet know about." During an Arrow anti-missile test in August 1990, intended to underscore Israeli missile capabilities, military officials spoke of "other responses" to potential Iraqi chemical attacks on Israeli territory.

The post-Gulf War nuclear developments, both in Iraq and Iran, compounded by the international community's intelligence failure in detecting Iraq's nuclear program, were critical in Israel's strategic decision to establish its own sea-based strategic force. The Israeli Navy had been pushing for a small fleet of modern diesel submarines for "strategic purposes" since the early 1980s, and after long negotiations with Germany, the Thyssen-Nordseewerke shipyard in Emden, and the Howaldtswerke-Deutsche Werft AG shipyard in Kiel were chosen as the contractors to build three modern diesel-electric 1900-ton Dolphin-class submarines, equipped with ten 21-inch multipurpose tubes capable of launching torpedoes, mines, and cruise missiles.

In June 2000, the Sunday Times broke a story about an alleged Israeli test-launch of a nuclear capable submarine-launched-cruise-missile (SLCM) in the Indian ocean, using the newly commissioned Dolphin submarines. According to unconfirmed reports the missile hit its target at a range of around 1500km. It is believed that the alleged test missile was based on the Israeli Popeye, an ALCM with a range of 250-300kms. Israel has categorically denied the allegations about the missile tests in the Indian Ocean.

In 2003, in an interview with the Los Angeles Times, Israeli and American officials announced that Israel had deployed U.S. supplied Harpoon ASCMs on its Dolphin submarines and modified the missiles to carry nuclear warheads. Prominent missile experts believe this to be a real possibility, though the range of the Harpoon armed with an Israeli nuclear warhead would probably be decreased to around 90kms due to the added weight. In November 2005, Israel signed a contract worth $1.17 billion with Germany for the construction of two more attack submarines, the first of which is planned to be completed by 2012. These factors underline that having secured a sea launch capability, Israel has, or is well on its way to having its own nuclear triad with sea, land, and air launched options.

On 21 April 2004, after 18 years in an Israeli prison, nuclear whistleblower Mordechai Vanunu was released. However, in July 2007, Vanunu was sentenced to an additional six months in prison after violating a gag order that had been placed on him that forbade him from further disclosing details about the nuclear program. The Israeli government also set severe restrictions on his movements and conduct after his initial release from prison in 2004. In July of the same year, the Israeli Atomic Energy Commission launched an official website providing only general details about Israel's civilian nuclear program. Later that month International Atomic Energy Agency director Mohammed El-Baradei visited Israel to meet with government officials. Despite El-Baradei's visit, Israel continues to assert that it will not discuss disarmament issues until after a comprehensive Middle Eastern peace agreement has been reached.

In an interesting development in early 2007, following the progress of the U.S.-India nuclear deal, Israeli officials lobbied their American counterparts to convince the NSG to allow Israel to conduct nuclear trade without being subjected to full-scope safeguards. Even though the U.S. declined this request, Israel nonetheless presented a plan to the NSG suggesting an objective set of criteria to judge whether to allow nuclear trade with non-NPT states. The proposal was greeted unenthusiastically; and the Bush administration only reiterated its stance that the India deal could not be seen as a precedent for other non-NPT states. These efforts by Israel to lobby the NSG have come at a time when the Israeli government has expressed an active interest in nuclear energy generation. This has been confirmed by the Israeli Atomic Energy Commission in an official statement, citing an increasing shortage in indigenous electricity production capacity and the government's wish to reduce dependency on imported energy sources.

In August 2007, National Infrastructure Minister, Ben-Eliezer told a gathering of engineers of the Israel Electric Corporation (ICE), that he would soon submit a proposal to the government that suggests building a nuclear power plant at Shivta, on the border with Egypt in the South of Israel. According to Ben-Eliezer, the plan calls for the construction of a 1,200 to 1,500MW plant over nine years. So far there have been no discussions with any foreign vendors about reactor exports, but it is understood that Israel will be looking to U.S. supplied reactor technology. Furthermore, it is believed that the plan would entail similar provisions as those in the U.S.-India nuclear deal, i.e., that the supplied reactor would be put under safeguards, with other Israeli nuclear facilities being exempt. Presently, all cooperation with Israel in the nuclear field is limited to safety and it remains to be seen what steps Israel takes in moving forward on its plans for civilian nuclear power generation.

NUCLEAR TESTING

On 2 November 1966, Israel may have carried out a non-nuclear test, speculated to be zero yield or implosion in nature. The only suspected nuclear test conducted by Israel has become known as the Vela Incident. On 22 September 1979, a US Vela satellite, built in the 1960s to detect nuclear tests, reported a flash resembling a nuclear detonation in the southern Indian Ocean. In response the Carter administration set up a panel led by MIT professor Jack Ruina to analyze the reliability of the Vela detection; they concluded in July 1980 that the flash "was probably not from a nuclear explosion," although the original intelligence community estimate was that it was 90% likely to be a nuclear test and a secret study by the Nuclear Intelligence Panel agreed with that initial finding. According to journalist Seymour Hersh, the detection was actually the third joint Israeli-South African nuclear test in the Indian Ocean, and the Israelis had sent two IDF ships and "a contingent of Israeli military men and nuclear experts" for the test.

IMPORTANT INFORMATION AND EVALUATIONS

DIMONA

The Israeli nuclear program was first revealed publicly on 13 December 1960 in a small *Time* article, which said that a non-Communist non-NATO country had made an "atomic development." On December 16, the *Daily Express* revealed this country to be Israel, and on December 18, US Atomic Energy Commission chairman John McCone appeared on *Meet the Press* to officially confirm the Israeli construction of a nuclear reactor and announce his resignation. The following day *The New York Times*, with the help of McCone, revealed that France was assisting Israel.

This flurry of media reporting led Ben-Gurion to make the only statement ever by an Israeli Prime Minister about Dimona. On December 21 he announced in front of the Knesset that they were building a 24 megawatt reactor *"which will serve the needs of industry, agriculture, health, and science,"* and that it "is designed exclusively for peaceful purposes." However, Ernst David Bergmann, chairman of the Israel Atomic Energy Commission (from 1954 to 1966), said that *"There is no distinction between nuclear energy for peaceful purposes or warlike ones."* and that "*We shall never again be led as lambs to the slaughter*".

WEAPONS PRODUCTION

The first public revelation of Israel's nuclear capability (as opposed to development program) came from NBC News, which reported in January 1969 that Israel decided "to embark on a crash course program to produce a nuclear weapon" two years previously, and that they possessed or would soon be in possession of such a device. This was initially dismissed by Israeli and US officials, as well as in an article in *The New York Times*. Just one year later on July 18, *The New York Times* made public for the first time that the US government believed Israel to possess nuclear weapons or to have the "capacity to assemble atomic bombs on short notice."

The first extensive details of the weapons program came in the London based *Sunday Times* on 5 October 1986, which printed information provided by Mordechai Vanunu, a technician formerly employed at the Negev Nuclear Research Center near Dimona. For publication of state secrets Vanunu was kidnapped by the Mossad in Rome, brought back to Israel, and sentenced to 18 years in prison for treason and espionage. Although there had been much speculation prior to Vanunu's revelations that the Dimona site was creating nuclear weapons, Vanunu's information indicated that Israel had also built thermonuclear weapons.

STOCKPILE ESTIMATES

The State of Israel has never made public any details of its nuclear capability or arsenal. The following is a history of estimates by many different reputable sources on the size and strength of Israel's nuclear arsenal. Estimates may vary due to the amount of material Israel has on store versus assembled weapons, and estimates as to how much material the weapons actually use, as well as the overall time in which the reactor was operated. Israel nuclear might is commonly estimated as moving between 200 to 400 warheads, equivalent to almost four thousand Hiroshima-type bombs.

- 1967 (Six Day War)- 2 bombs; 13 bombs
- 1969- 5-6 bombs of 19 kilotons yield each
- 1973 (Yom Kippur War)- 13 bombs; 20 nuclear missiles plus developed a suitcase bomb
- 1974- 3 capable artillery battalions each with 12 175 mm tubes and a total of 108 warheads; 10 bombs
- 1976- 10-20 nuclear weapons
- 1980- 100-200 bombs
- 1984- 12-31 atomic bombs; 31 plutonium bombs and 10 uranium bombs
- 1985- at least 100 nuclear bombs
- 1986- 100 to 200 fission bombs and a number of fusion bombs
- 1991- 50-60 to 200-300
- 1992- more than 200 bombs
- 1994- 64-112 bombs (5 kg/warhead); 50 nuclear tipped Jericho missiles, 200 total
- 1995- 66-116 bombs (at 5 kg/warhead); 70-80 bombs; "A complete Repertoire" (neutron bombs, nuclear mines, suitcase bombs, submarine-borne)
- 1996- 60-80 plutonium weapons, maybe more than 100 assembled, ER variants, varitable yields

- 1997- More than 400 deliverable thermonuclear and nuclear weapons (an intentionally high estimate)
- 2002– Between 75 and 200 weapons
- 2004- 82
- 2006- Federation of American Scientists believes that Israel "could have produced enough plutonium for at least 100 nuclear weapons, but probably not significantly more than 200 weapons".
- 2008- 150 or more nuclear weapons.
- 2008- 80 intact warheads, of which 50 are re-entry vehicles for delivery by ballistic missiles and the rest bombs for delivery by aircraft. Total military plutonium stockpile 340–560 kg.
- 2009- 300-400 nuclear weapons with lower limit of 70 -100 weapons.

DELIVERY SYSTEMS

Israeli military forces possess land, air, and sea based methods for deploying their nuclear weapons, thus forming nuclear triad that is mainly medium to long ranged, the backbone of which is submarine launched cruise missiles and medium and intercontinental ballistic missiles, with Israeli Air Force tactical aircraft fulfilling the role normally played by strategic bombers in the Russian and American strategic deterrent. During 2008 the Jericho III ICBM became operational, giving Israel extremely long range nuclear strike abilities.

MISSILES

Israel is believed to have second-strike abilities in the form of its submarines fleet and its nuclear-capable ballistic missiles, which are buried so far underground they would survive a nuclear strike. Ernst David Bergmann was the first to seriously began thinking about a ballistic missile capability and Israel test-fired its first Shavit II missile in July 1961. It was not until 1963 when Israel actually put a large-scale project into motion, spending $100 million to jointly develop and build 25 short-range missiles with the French aerospace company Dassault. The Israeli project, codenamed Project 700, also included the construction of a missile field at Hirbat Zacharia, a site west of Jerusalem. The missiles that were first developed with France became the Jericho I system, first operational in 1971. It is possible that the Jericho I was removed from operational service during the 1990s. In the mid 1980s the Jericho II medium-range missile, which is believed to have a range of 2800–5000 km, entered service. It is believed that Jericho II is capable of delivering nuclear weapons with a superior degree of accuracy. The Shavit three stages solid fuel space launch vehicle produced by Israel to launch many of its satellites into low earth orbit since 1988 is actually a civilian version of the Jericho II. The Jericho III ICBM, became operational in January 2008 and some reports speculate that the missile may be able to carry MIRVed warheads.

The maximum range estimation of the Jericho III is 11,500 km with a payload of 1000–1300 kg (up to six small nuclear warheads of 100 kt each or one 1 megaton nuclear warhead), and its accuracy is considered high. In January 2008 Israel has carried out the successful test launch of a long-range, ballistic missile capable of carrying a nuclear warhead from the reported launch site at the Palmachim air base south of Tel Aviv. Israeli radio identified the missile as a Jericho III and the Hebrew YNet news Web site quoted unnamed defence officials as saying the test had been "dramatic" and that the new missile can reach "extremely long distances," without elaborating. Soon after the successful test launch, Isaac Ben-Israel, a retired army general and Tel Aviv University professor who is now an MP, told Israeli Channel 2 TV:

> *"Everybody can do the math and understand that the significance is that we can reach with a rocket engine to every point in the world"*

he test came two days after Ehud Olmert, then Israel's Prime Minister, warned that "all options were on the table to prevent Tehran from acquiring nuclear weapons" and few months after Israel bombed Syrian facility that was suspected as nuclear plant, built with extensive help from North Korea . At the same time, regional defence experts said that by the beginning of 2008 Israel has already launched a programme to extend the range of its existing Jericho II ground attack missiles. The Jericho-II B missile is capable of sending a one ton nuclear payload 5,000 kilometers. The range of Israels' Jericho II B missiles is reportedly capable of being modified to carry nuclear warheads no heavier than 500 kg over 7,800 km, making it an ICBM.

It is estimated that Israel has between 50 and 100 Jericho II B missiles based at facilities which were built in the 1980s. However, the number of Jericho III missiles that Israel possess is unknown.

AIRCRAFT

Israel lacks strategic bombers to deliver nuclear weapons over a long-range, although its F-16 fighter aircraft have been cited as possible nuclear delivery systems The U.S. Air Force F-15 has tactical nuclear weapon capability.

The Israeli Air Force possesses the following types of fighter aircraft:

- Lockheed Martin F-16I Sufa ("Storm")
- McDonnell Douglas/Boeing F-15 Eagle Baz 2000 (A/B/C/D/E)

future:

- Lockheed Martin F-35 Lightning II JSF; the US Defense Department notified Congress of plans to sell up to 75 jets to Israel in a $ 5 to 15.2 billion deal for the aircraft. A contract is expected to be signed by Israel before 2009 will end (Israel will begin receiving the aircraft in 2013-2014), after the Pentagon agreed to an integration of Israeli electronic warfare systems into the plane as well as integration of Israeli communication systems, and ability to independently maintain the plane in the event of a technical or structural problem The deal includes 50 Short-Take-Off and Vertical-Landing jets. Modifications of the JSF could provide the aircraft with nuclear strike capabilities.

Unmanned:

IAI Eitan (איתן)(Heron TP)- the world's largest unmanned aircraft (UCAV), has a wing span of 35 metres (110 feet) — similar to that of a Boeing 737 passenger plane, was developed by the IAI for a very long-range high-altitude operations and destroying ballistic missiles as they are being launched, in response to the Iranian nuclear program. According to *Janes Defence Weekly* the weapons payload is 1800 kg, more than enough to carry nuclear weapons, and can fly for 50 hours at 50,000 feet, above anti-aircraft defences, and must have a range of thousands of kilometers.

MARINE

Israel is operating five modern German-built *Dolphin*-class submarines. First three Dolphins were delivered to Israel in 1999. Various reports indicate that these submarines are equipped with cruise missiles that can deliver the lethal nuclear warheads with extremely high accuracy. The proven effectiveness of cruise missiles of its own production may have been behind Israel's recent acquisition of these submarines which are equipped with torpedo tubes suitable for launching long-range (1500–2400 km) nuclear-capable cruise missiles that would offer Israel a second strike capability.

Israel is reported to possess a 200 kg nuclear warhead, containing 6 kg of plutonium, that could be mounted on cruise missiles. The missiles were reportedly test launched in the Indian Ocean near Sri Lanka in June 2000, and are reported to have hit their target at a range of 1500 km.In June 2002, former State Department and Pentagon officials confirmed that the U.S. Navy observed Israeli missile tests in the Indian Ocean in 2000, and that the Dolphin-class vessels have been fitted with nuclear-capable cruise missiles of a new design.It is believed by some to be a version of Rafael Israels' Armament Development Authority's Popeye turbo cruise missile while some believe that the missile may be a version of the Gabriel 4LR that is produced by Israel Aircraft Industries. However, others claim that such a range implies an entirely new type of missile.

During the 1990s second half, Israel asked the United States to sell it 50 Tomahawk land-attack cruise missiles to enhance its deep-strike capabilities under its wide-ranging strategic defense program. Washington rejected Israel's request in March 1998, since such a sale would have violated the Missile Technology Control Regime which prohibits the transfer of missiles with a range exceeding 300 km, prompting concern that Israel may develop its own indigenous long-range cruise missile. Shortly after the rejection, an Israeli official told Defense News, "History has taught us that we cannot wait indefinitely for Washington to satisfy our military requirements. If this weapon system is denied to us, we will have little choice but to activate our own defense industry in pursuit of this needed capability." Indeed, Air Intelligence Center warned the U.S. Congress in July 1998 that Israel was developing a cruise missile of new type.

According to Israeli defence sources, in June 2009 Israeli Dolphin-class submarine sailed from the Mediterranean to the Red Sea via Suez Canal during a drill that showed that Israel can far more easily access the Indian Ocean, and the Gulf, than before. IDF sources said the decision to allow navy vessels to sail through the canal was made recently and was a definite "change of policy" within the service. Israeli officials said the sub passed through the canal above water. In the event of a conflict with Iran, and if Israel decided to involve its Dolphin-class submarines, the quickest route would be to send them through the Suez Canal.

The Israeli fleet was extended after Israel has signed 1.3 billion euros contract to purchase two additional submarines from ThyssenKrupp's subsidiary HDW in 2006. These two U212s were delivered to the Israeli sea corps during September 2009 and are "Dolphin II" class sumarines Although when it confirmed the sale in 2006 the German government said the two vessels were not equipped to carry nuclear weapons, the submarines are believed to be competent for launching cruise missiles carrying nuclear warheads, . The two new boats are an upgraded version of the old Dolphins, and equipped with an Air-independent propulsion system, that allow them to remain submerged for longer periods of time than the three nuclear arms-capable submarines that are in Israel's fleet since 1999.

In advance, on October 2009 it was reported that the Israeli navy seeks to buy a sixth Dolphin class submarine.

OTHER

It has been reported that Israel has several other nuclear weapons capabilities:

- Suitcase bomb: Seymour Hersh reports that Israel developed the ability to miniaturize warheads small enough to fit in a suitcase by the year 1973.
- Tactical nuclear weapon: Israel may also have 175 mm and 203 mm self-propelled artillery pieces, capable of firing nuclear shells. There are three battalions of the 175mm artillery (36 tubes), reportedly with 108 nuclear shells and more for the 203mm tubes. If true, these low yield, tactical nuclear artillery rounds could reach at least 25 miles (40 km), while by some sources it is possible that the range was extended to 45 miles (72 km) during the 1990s.
- EMP strike capabilities: Israel allegedly possesses several 1 megaton bombs which give it a very large EMP attack abilities. For example, if a megaton class weapon were to be detonated 400 kilometers above Omaha, nearly the entire contiguous 48 States would be affected with potentially damaging EMP experience from Boston to Los Angeles, from Chicago to New Orleans. Similarly, a high altitude airburst could cause serious damage to electrical systems in most of Iran.
- Enhanced Radiation Weapon (ERW): Israel also is reported to have an unknown number of neutron bombs.

POLICY AND DEVELOPMENTS

Israel's refusal to admit it has nuclear weapons or to state its policy on use of them make it necessary to gather details from other sources, including unauthorized statements by its political and military leaders.

POSSESSION

Although Israel has officially acknowledged the existence of Dimona since Ben-Gurion's speech to the Knesset in December 1960, Israel has never officially acknowledged its construction or possession of nuclear weapons. In addition to this policy, on 18 May 1966 Prime Minister Levi Eshkol told the Knesset that "Israel has no atomic weapons and will not be the first to introduce them into our region," a policy first articulated by Shimon Peres to US President John F. Kennedy in April 1963. In the late 1960s, Israeli Ambassador to the US Yitzhak Rabin informed the United States State Department that its understanding of "introducing" such weapons meant that they would be tested and publicly declared, while merely possessing the weapons did not constitute "introducing" them. Avner Cohen defines this initial posture as "nuclear ambiguity," but he defines the stage after it became clear by 1970 that Israel possessed nuclear weapons as a policy of "nuclear opacity."

In 1998, former Prime Minister Shimon Peres said that Israel "built a nuclear option, not in order to have a Hiroshima but an Oslo".The "nuclear option" may refer to a nuclear weapon or to the nuclear reactor near Dimona, which Israel claims is used for scientific research. Peres, in his capacity as the Director General of the Ministry of Defense in the early 1950s, was responsible for building Israel's nuclear capability.

In a December 2006 interview, Israeli Prime Minister Ehud Olmert came close to breaking with Israel's policy of nuclear opacity, saying that Iran aspires "to have a nuclear weapon as America, France, Israel and Russia." Olmert's office later said that the quote was taken out of context; in other parts of the interview, Olmert refused to confirm or deny Israel's nuclear weapon status.

DOCTRINE

Israel's nuclear doctrine is shaped by its lack of strategic depth: a subsonic fighter jet could cross in four minutes the 40 nautical miles (74 km) from the Jordan River to the Mediterranean Sea. It additionally relies on a reservist-based military which magnifies civilian and military losses in its small population. Israel tries to compensate for these weaknesses by emphasising intelligence, maneuverability and firepower.

As a result, its strategy is based on the premise that it cannot afford to lose a single war, and thus must prevent them by maintaining deterrence, including the option of preemption. If these steps are insufficient, it seeks to prevent escalation and determine a quick and decisive war outside of its borders.

Strategically, Israel's long-range missiles, nuclear capable aircraft, and possibly its submarines present an effective second strike deterrence against unconventional and conventional attack, and if Israel's defences fail and its population centres be threatened, the Samson Option, an all out attack against an adversary, would be employed. Its nuclear arsenal can also be used tactically.

Although nuclear weapons are viewed as the ultimate guarantor of Israeli security, as early as the 1960s the country has avoided building its military around them, instead pursuing absolute conventional superiority so as to forestall a last resort nuclear engagement.

According to historian Avner Cohen, Israel first articulated an official policy on the use of nuclear weapons in 1966, which revolved around four "red lines" that could lead to a nuclear response:

1. A successful Arab military penetration into populated areas within Israel's post-1949 (pre-1967) borders.
2. The destruction of the Israeli Air Force.
3. The exposure of Israeli cities to massive and devastating air attacks or to possible chemical or biological attacks.
4. The use of nuclear weapons against Israeli territory.

USE

On 8 October 1973 just after the start of the Yom Kippur War, Golda Meir and her closest aides decided to put eight nuclear armed F-4s at Tel Nof Airbase on 24 hour alert and as many nuclear missile launchers at Sedot Mikha Airbase operational as possible. Seymour Hersh adds that the initial target list that night "included the Egyptian and Syrian military headquarters near Cairo and Damascus." This nuclear alert was meant not only as a means of precaution, but to push the Soviets to restrain the Arab offensive and to convince the US to begin sending supplies. One later report said that a Soviet intelligence officer did warn the Egyptian chief of staff, and colleagues of US National Security Advisor Henry Kissinger said that the threat of a nuclear exchange caused him to urge for a massive Israeli resupply. Hersh points out that before Israel obtained its own satellite capability, it engaged in espionage against the United States to obtain nuclear targeting information on Soviet targets.

Israeli military and nuclear doctrine increasingly focused on preemptive war against any possible attack with conventional, chemical, biological or nuclear weapons, or even a potential conventional attack on Israel's weapons of mass destruction.

Louis René Beres, who contributed to Project Daniel, urges that Israel continue and improve these policies, in concert with the increasingly preemptive nuclear policies of the United States, as revealed in the Doctrine for Joint Nuclear Operations.

After Iraq attacked Israel with Scud missiles during the 1991 Gulf War, Israel went on full-scale nuclear alert and mobile nuclear missile launchers were deployed. In the build up to the United States 2003 invasion of Iraq, there were concerns that Iraq would launch an unconventional weapons attack on Israel. After discussions with President George W. Bush then Israeli Prime Minister Ariel Sharon warned "If our citizens are attacked seriously - by a weapon of mass destruction, chemical, biological or by some mega-terror attack act - and suffer casualties, then Israel will respond." Israeli officials interpreted President Bush's stance as allowing a nuclear Israeli retaliation on Iraq, but only if Iraq struck before the US military invasion.

MAINTAINING NUCLEAR SUPERIORITY

Alone or with other nations, Israel has used diplomatic and military efforts as well as covert action to prevent other Middle Eastern countries from acquiring nuclear weapons.

For example, it is believed that Israel filed a false laser patent in the late 1970s to mislead Arab nuclear research. Mossad agents triggered explosions in April 1979 at a French production plant near Toulouse, damaging the two reactor cores destined for the Iraqi reactors. Mossad agents may also have been behind the assassinations of an Egyptian nuclear engineer in Paris as well as two Iraqi engineers, all working for the Iraqi nuclear program.

On 7 June 1981, Israel launched a preemptive air strike against Saddam Hussein's breeder reactor in Osirak, Iraq, in Operation Opera. The Mossad is also said to have assassinated professor Gerald Bull, an artillery expert, who was allegedly building a massive cannon or "super gun" for Saddam Hussein in the 1980s, which was capable of delivering a tactical nuclear payload.

On 6 September 2007, Israel launched an air strike dubbed Operation Orchard against a target in the Deir ez-Zor region of Syria. While Israel refused to comment, unnamed US officials said Israel had shared intelligence with them that North Korea was cooperating with Syria on some sort of nuclear facility. Both Syria and North Korea denied the allegation and Syria filed a formal complaint with the United Nations. Journalist Seymour Hersh speculates that this air strike may have been intended as a trial run for striking alleged Iranian nuclear weapons facilities. On January 7, 2007 *The Sunday Times* reported that Israel had drawn up plans to destroy three Iranian nuclear facilities with low-yield nuclear bunker-busters that would be launched by aircraft through "tunnels" created by conventional laser-guided bombs. These tactical nuclear weapons would then explode underground to reduce radioactive fallout. Israel denied the specific allegation. However, its military leaders admit that it rules out no option. The death of the Iranian physicist Ardeshir Hassanpour, who may have been involved in the nuclear program, has been reported by the intelligence group Stratfor to have been a Mossad assassination. Iran is currently conducting atomic research that Israel fears is aimed at building a nuclear weapon. Israel has pressed for United Nations economic sanctions against Iran, and has repeatedly threatened to launch a military strike on Iran if the United States does not do so first.

NUCLEAR NON-PROLIFERATION TREATY AND UNITED NATIONS' RESOLUTIONS

Israel was originally expected to sign the 1968 Nuclear Non-Proliferation Treaty (NPT) and on 12 June 1968 Israel voted in favor of the treaty in the UN General Assembly. But when the invasion of Czechoslovakia in August by the Soviet Union delayed ratification around the world, Israel's internal division and hesitation over the treaty became public. The Johnson administration attempted to use the sale of 50 F-4 Phantoms to pressure Israel to sign the treaty that fall, culminating in a personal letter from Lyndon Johnson to Israeli PM Levi Eshkol. But by November Johnson had backed away from tying the F-4 sale with the NPT after a stalemate in negotiations, and Israel would neither sign nor ratify the treaty. After the series of negotiations, US assistant secretary of defense for international security Paul Warnke was convinced that Israel already possessed nuclear weapons. In 2007 Israel sought an exemption to non-proliferation rules in order to import atomic material legally.

In 1996 the United Nations General Assembly passed a resolution calling for the establishment of a nuclear-weapon-free zone in the region of the Middle East. Arab nations and annual conferences of the International Atomic Energy Agency (IAEA) repeatedly have called for application of IAEA safeguards and the creation of a nuclear-free Middle East. Arab nations have expressed their disgust that the United States practices a double standard in criticizing Iran's nuclear program while ignoring Israel's possession of nuclear weapons. According to a statement by the Arab League, Arab states will withdraw from the NPT if Israel acknowledges having nuclear weapons and then does not open its facilities to international inspection and destroy its arsenal.

In a statement to the May 2009 preparatory meeting for the 2010 NPT Review Conference, the U.S. delegation reiterated the longstanding U.S. support for "universal adherence to the NPT," but uncharacteristically named Israel among the four countries that have not done so. An unnamed Israeli official dismissed the suggestion that it would join the NPT and questioned the effectiveness of the treaty. The *Washington Times* reported that this statement threatened to derail the 40-year-old secret agreement between the US and Israel to shield Israel's nuclear weapons program from international scrutiny, while Avner Cohen, author of *Israel and the Bomb*, argued that acknowledging its nuclear program would allow Israel to take part constructively in efforts to control nuclear weapons

ECONOMY AND ECONOMIC DEVELOPMENTS

ECONOMY: BASIC INFORMATION

Rank	50th (PPP) / 39th (nominal)
Currency	Israeli new shekel (NIS; ₪)
Fiscal year	Calendar year
Trade organisations	BIS, CLS, EBRD, IADB, ICC, ISO, ITUC, OECD, UN, WCO, WFTU, WTO.
Statistics	
GDP	$235.446 billion (PPP; 2011 est.) $245.266 billion (nominal; 2011 est.)
GDP growth	4.8% (2011 est.; 81st)
GDP per capita	$31,005 (PPP; 2011 est.; 26th) $32,298 (nominal; 2011 est.; 27th)
GDP by sector	agriculture: 2.5%, industry: 31.2%, services: 64.7% (2011 est.)
Inflation (CPI)	3.2% (2011 est.; 59th)
Population below poverty line	22.5% (2012)
Gini coefficient	39.2 (2008; 69th)
Labour force	3.227 million (2011 est.; 100th)
Labour force by occupation	agriculture: 2%, industry: 16%, services: 82% (September 2008)
Unemployment	5.6% (2011 est.; 56th)
Main industries	high-technology products (including aviation, communications, telecommunications equipment, computer hardware and software, computer-aided design and manufacturing, medical electronics, fiber optics), pharmaceuticals, potash and phosphates, metals products, chemical products, plastics, diamond cutting, petroleum refining, textiles.
Ease of Doing Business Rank	38th (2013)
External	
Exports	$62.5 billion FOB (2011 est.; 54th)
Export goods	high technology products, telecommunications equipment, military equipment, pharmaceuticals, mechanical machinery and machinery based equipment, cut diamonds and jewelry, agricultural products and foodstuffs, chemicals, textiles and apparel.
Main export partners	China 17.1%, Russia 11.6%, United States 11.1%, Norway 5.5% , Switzerland 5.3% (2011)
Imports	$70.62 billion FOB (2011 est.; 47th)
Import goods	raw materials, military and defense equipment, aircraft parts, motor vehicles, consumer electronics, investment goods, mechanical machinery and related parts, rough diamonds, petroleum, fuels, grain and wheat, consumer goods.
Main import partners	United States 16.9%, Switzerland 9.0%, China 8.7%, Russia 7.0%, Turkey 4.7% (2011)
FDI stock	$82.82 billion (2011 est.; 43rd)
Gross external debt	$112 billion (31 December 2011 est.; 40th)
Public finances	
Public debt	74% of GDP (2011 est.; 28th)
Budget deficit	−3% of GDP (2011 est.; 105th)
Revenues	$68.29 billion (2011 est.)
Expenses	$75.65 billion (2011 est.)
Credit rating	Standard & Poor's: AA− (Domestic) A+ (Foreign) AA (T&C Assessment) Outlook: Stable Moody's: A1 Outlook: Stable

	Fitch: A Outlook: Stable
Foreign reserves	$78.93 billion (31 December 2011 est.; 26th)

Israel is considered one of the most advanced countries in Southwest Asia in economic and industrial development. In 2010, it joined the OECD. The country is ranked 3rd in the region and 38th worldwide on the World Bank's Ease of Doing Business Index as well as in the World Economic Forum's Global Competitiveness Report. It has the second-largest number of startup companies in the world (after the United States) and the largest number of NASDAQ-listed companies outside North America.

In 2010, Israel ranked 17th among the world's most economically developed nations, according to IMD's World Competitiveness Yearbook. The Israeli economy was ranked as the world's most durable economy in the face of crises, and was also ranked first in the rate of research and development center investments.

The Bank of Israel was ranked first among central banks for its efficient functioning, up from 8th place in 2009. Israel was also ranked as the worldwide leader in its supply of skilled manpower. The Bank of Israel holds $78 billion of foreign-exchange reserves.

Despite limited natural resources, intensive development of the agricultural and industrial sectors over the past decades has made Israel largely self-sufficient in food production, apart from grains and beef. Imports to Israel, totaling $77.59 billion in 2012, include raw materials, military equipment, investment goods, rough diamonds, fuels, grain, consumer goods. Leading exports include electronics, software, computerized systems, communications technology, medical equipment, pharmaceuticals, fruits, chemicals, military technology, and cut diamonds; in 2012, Israeli exports reached $64.74 billion.

Israel is a leading country in the development of solar energy.

Israel is a global leader in water conservation and geothermal energy, and its development of cutting-edge technologies in software, communications and the life sciences have evoked comparisons with Silicon Valley. According to the OECD, Israel is also ranked 1st in the world in expenditure on Research and Development (R&D) as a percentage of GDP. Intel and Microsoft built their first overseas research and development centers in Israel, and other high-tech multi-national corporations, such as IBM, Google, Apple, HP, Cisco Systems, and Motorola, have opened R&D facilities in the country. In July 2007, American billionaire Warren Buffett's Berkshire Hathaway bought an Israeli company, Iscar, its first non-U.S. acquisition, for $4 billion. Since the 1970s, Israel has received military aid from the United States, as well as economic assistance in the form of loan guarantees, which now account for roughly half of Israel's external debt. Israel has one of the lowest external debts in the developed world, and is a net lender in terms of net external debt (the total value of assets vs. liabilities in debt instruments owed abroad), which as of June 2012 stood at a surplus of US$60 billion.

Days of working time in Israel are Sunday through Thursday (for a five-day workweek), or Friday (for a six-day workweek). In observance of *Shabbat*, in places where Friday is a work day and the majority of population is Jewish, Friday is a "short day", usually lasting till 14:00 in the winter, or 16:00 in the summer. Several proposals have been raised to adjust the work week with the majority of the world, and make Sunday a non-working day, while extending working time of other days, and/or replacing Friday with Sunday as a work day

The **economy of Israel** is a technologically advanced market economy, including rapidly developing high-tech, agricultural, financial and service sectors. As of 2012 Israel ranks 16th among 187 world nations on the UN's Human Development Index, which places it in the category of "Very Highly Developed".

The major industrial sectors include high-technology products, metal products, electronic and biomedical equipment, agricultural products, processed foods, chemicals, and transport equipment; the Israeli diamond industry is one of the world's centers for diamond cutting and polishing. Relatively poor in natural resources, Israel depends on imports of petroleum, raw materials, wheat, motor vehicles, uncut diamonds and production inputs, though the country's nearly total reliance on energy imports may change with recent discoveries of large natural gas reserves off its coast. Israel is a world leader in software, telecommunication and semiconductors development. The high concentration of high-tech industries in Israel, which are backed by a strong venture capital industry, gave it the nickname "Silicon Wadi", which is considered second in importance only to its Californian counterpart. Numerous Israeli companies have been acquired by global corporations for its reliable and quality corporate personnel. The country was the destination for Berkshire Hathaway's first investment outside the US when it purchased ISCAR Metalworking, and the first research and development centers outside the USA for companies including Intel, Microsoft, and Apple. Israel is also a major tourist destination, with 3.5 million foreign tourists visiting in 2012.

In September 2010, Israel was invited to join the OECD. Israel has also signed free trade agreements with the European Union, the United States, the European Free Trade Association, Turkey, Mexico, Canada, Jordan, Egypt, and on 18 December 2007, became the first non-Latin-American country to sign a free trade agreement with the Mercosur trade bloc.

After statehood, Israel faced a deep economic crisis. As well as having to recover from the devastating effects of the 1948 Arab-Israeli War, it also had to absorb hundreds of thousands of Jewish refugees from Europe and the Arab world. Israel was financially overwhelmed and faced a deep economic crisis, which led to a policy of austerity from 1949 to 1959. Unemployment was high, and foreign currency reserves were scarce.

In 1952, Israel and West Germany signed an agreement stipulating that West Germany was to pay Israel for the persecution of Jews during the Holocaust, and compensate for Jewish property stolen by the Nazis. Over the next 14 years, West Germany paid Israel 3 billion marks. The reparations became a decisive part of Israel's income, comprising as high as 87.5% of Israel's income in 1956. In 1950, the Israeli government launched Israel Bonds for American and Canadian Jews to buy. In 1951, the final results of the bonds program exceeded $52 million. Additionally, many American Jews made private donations to Israel, which in 1956 were thought to amount to $100 million a year. In 1957, bond sales amounted to 35% of Israel's special development budget. Later in the century Israel became significantly reliant on economic aid from the United States, a country which also became Israel's most important source of political support internationally.

The proceeds from these sources was invested in industrial and agricultural development projects, which allowed Israel to become economically self-sufficient. Among the projects made possible by the aid was the Hadera power plant, the Dead Sea Works, the National Water Carrier, port development in Haifa, Ashdod, and Eilat, desalination plants, and national infrastructure projects.

After statehood, priority was given to establishing industries in areas slated for development, among them Lachish, Ashkelon, the Negev and Galilee. The expansion of Israel's textile industry was a consequence of the development of cotton growing as a profitable agricultural branch. By the late 1960s, textiles were one of the largest industrial branches in Israel, second only to the foodstuff industry. Textiles constituted about 12% of industrial exports, becoming the second-largest export branch after polished diamonds. In the 1990s, cheap East Asian labor decreased the profitability of the sector. Much of the work was subcontracted to 400 Israeli Arab sewing shops. As these closed down, Israeli firms, among them Delta, Polgat, Argeman and Kitan, began doing their sewing work in Jordan and Egypt, usually under the QIZ arrangement. In the early 2000s, Israeli companies had 30 plants in Jordan. Israeli exports reached $370 million a year, supplying such retailers and designers as Marks & Spencer, The Gap, Victoria's Secret, Wal-Mart, Sears, Ralph Lauren, Calvin Klein, and Donna Karan.

In its first two decades of existence, Israel's strong commitment to development led to economic growth rates that exceeded 10% annually. Average living standards steadily rose, with the expenditure of an average wage-earner's family rising in real terms by 97.% between 1950 and 1963. The years after the 1973 Yom Kippur War were a lost decade economically, as growth stalled, inflation soared and government expenditures rose significantly. Also worthy of mention is the 1983 Bank stock crisis. By 1984, the economic situation became almost catastrophic with inflation reaching an annual rate close to 450% and projected to reach over 1000% by the end of the following year. However, the successful economic stabilization plan implemented in 1985 and the subsequent introduction of market-oriented structural reforms reinvigorated the economy and paved the way for its rapid growth in the 1990s and became a model for other countries facing similar economic crises

Two developments have helped to transform Israel's economy since the beginning of the 1990s. The first is waves of Jewish immigration, predominantly from the countries of the former USSR, that has brought over one million new citizens to Israel. These new immigrants, many of them highly educated, now constitute some 16% of Israel's 7.5 million population. The second development benefiting the Israeli economy is the peace process begun at the Madrid conference of October 1991, which led to the signing of accords and later to a peace treaty between Israel and Jordan (1994).

Despite the Second Intifada, which cost Israel billions of dollars in economic terms, Israel managed to open up new markets to Israeli exporters farther afield, such as in the rapidly growing countries of East Asia.

In the past few years there has been an unprecedented inflow of foreign investment in Israel, as companies that formerly shunned the Israeli market now see its potential contribution to their global strategies. In 2006, foreign investment in Israel totaled $13 billion, according to the Manufacturers Association of Israel. The Financial Times said that 'bombs drop, yet Israel's economy grows'. Moreover, while Israel's total gross external debt is US$95 billion, or approximately 41.6% of GDP, since 2001 it has become a net lender nation in terms of net external debt (the total value of assets vs. liabilities in debt instruments owed abroad), which as of June 2012 stood at a significant surplus of US$60 billion. The country also maintains a current account surplus in an amount equivalent to about 3% of its gross domestic product in 2010.

The Israeli economy withstood the late-2000s recession, registering positive GDP growth in 2009 and ending the decade with an unemployment rate lower than that of many western countries. There are several reasons behind this economic resilience, for example, the fact, as stated above, that the country is a net lender rather than a borrower nation and the government and the Bank of Israel's generally conservative macro-economic policies.

Two policies in particular can be cited, one is the refusal of the government to succumb to pressure by the banks to appropriate large sums of public money to aid them early in the crisis, thus limiting their risky behavior. The second is the implementation of the recommendations of the Bach'ar commission in the early to mid-2000s which recommended decoupling the banks' depository and investment banking activities, contrary to the then-opposite trend, particularly in the United States, of easing such restrictions which had the effect of encouraging more risk-taking in the financial systems of those countries

OECD MEMBERSHIP

In May 2007, Israel was invited to open accession discussions with the OECD. In May 2010, the OECD voted unanimously to invite Israel to join, despite Palestinian objections. It became a full member on 7 September 2010. The OECD praised Israel's scientific and technological progress and described it as having "produced outstanding outcomes on a world scale."

CHALLENGES

Israel economy faces many challenges, some are short term and some are long term challenges. On the short term its inability to duplicate its success in the telecommunication industry into other growing industries hampers its economic outlooks. Its inability to foster large multinational companies in the last decade also calls into question its ability to employ large numbers of people in advanced industries. On the long term, Israel is facing challenges of high dependency of the growing number of Ultra-Orthodox Jews who have a low level of official labor force participation amongst men, and this situation could lead to a materially lower employment-to-population ratio and a higher dependency ratio in the future. The governor of the Bank of Israel, Stanley Fischer, stated that the growing poverty amongst the Ultra-Orthodox is hurting the Israeli economy. According to the data published by Ian Fursman, 60% of the poor households in Israel are of the Haredi Jews and the Israeli Arabs. Both groups together represent 25–28% of the Israeli population.

MAFOR SECTORS

AGRICULTURE

The Kibbutzim, collective communities in Israel traditionally based on agriculture, played an important role in Israel's economy until the late 1970s.

2.8% of the country's GDP is derived from agriculture. Of a total labor force of 2.7 million, 2.6% are employed in agricultural production while 6.3% in services for agriculture. While Israel imports substantial quantities of grain (approximately 80% of local consumption), it is largely self-sufficient in other agricultural products and food stuffs. For centuries, farmers of the region have grown varieties of citrus fruits, such as grapefruit, oranges and lemons. Citrus fruits are still Israel's major agricultural export. In addition, Israel is one of the world's leading greenhouse-food-exporting countries. The country exports more than $1.3 billion worth of agricultural products every year, including farm produce as well as $1.2 billion worth of agricultural inputs and technology.

FINANCIAL SECTOR

Israel has over 100 active funds operating throughout the country with $10 billion under management. In 2004, international foreign funds from various nations around the world committed over 50% of the total dollars invested exemplifying the country's strong and sound reputation as an internationally sought after foreign investment by many countries. Israel's venture capital sector has rapidly developed from the early 1990s, and has about 70 active venture capital funds (VC), of which 14 international VCs have Israeli offices. Israel's thriving venture-capital and business-incubator industry played an important role in the booming high-tech sector. In 2008, venture capital investment in Israel, rose 19 percent to $1.9 billion

Between 1991 and 2000, Israel's annual venture-capital outlays, nearly all private, rose nearly 60-fold, from $58 million to $3.3 billion; companies launched by Israeli venture funds rose from 100 to 800; and Israel's information-technology revenues rose from $1.6 billion to $12.5 billion. By 1999, Israel ranked second only to the United States in invested private-equity capital as a share of GDP. Israel led the world in the share of its growth attributable to high-tech ventures: 70 percent."

Israel's thriving venture capital industry has played an important role in the booming high-tech sector, the financial crisis of 2007-2010 also affected the availability of venture capital locally. In 2009, there were 63 mergers and acquisitions in the Israeli market worth a total of $2.54 billion; 7% below 2008 levels ($2.74 billion), when 82 Israeli companies were merged or acquired, and 33% lower than 2007 proceeds ($3.79 billion) when 87 Israeli companies were merged or acquired.

Numerous Israeli high tech companies have been acquired by global corporations for its reliable and quality corporate personnel. In addition to venture capital funds, many of the worlds leading investment banks, pension funds, and insurance companies have a strong presence in Israel to financially back Israeli high-tech firms and benefit from its burgeoning high tech sector. These companies include Goldman Sachs, Bear Stearns, Deutsche Bank, JP Morgan, Credit Swiss First Boston, Merrill Lynch, CalPERS, Ontario Teachers Pension Plan, and AIG.

Israel also has a small but fast growing hedge fund industry. Within the last five years between 2007 to 2012, the number of active hedge funds have doubled to 60 while the total asset values that the funds control have quadrupled since 2006. Israel based hedge funds have registered an increase of 162% since 2006 and currently manage a total of $2 billion (NIS 8 billion) as well as employing about 300 people. The ever growing hedge fund industry in Israel is also attracting a myriad of investors from around the world, particularly from the United States

TECHNOLOGY SECTOR

Science and technology in Israel is one of the country's most highly developed and industrialized sectors. The percentage of Israelis engaged in scientific and technological inquiry, and the amount spent on research and development (R&D) in relation to gross domestic product (GDP), is amongst the highest in the world. Israel ranks fourth in the world in scientific activity, as measured by the number of scientific publications per million citizens. Israel's percentage of the total number of scientific articles published worldwide is almost 10 times higher than its percentage of the world's population.

Despite its small population relative to other industrialized nations around the world, Israel has the highest number of scientists, technicians, and engineers per capita in the world with 140 scientists, technicians, and engineers per 10,000 employees. In comparison, the same is 85 per 10,000 in the United States and 83 per 10,000 in Japan.

Israeli scientists have contributed to the advancement of the natural sciences, agricultural sciences, computer sciences, electronics, genetics, medicine, optics, solar energy and various fields of engineering. Israel is home to major players in the high-tech industry and has one of the world's technologically most literate populations. In 1998, Tel Aviv was named by *Newsweek* as one of the ten technologically most influential cities in the world. In 2012, the city was also named one of the best places for high-tech startup companies, placed second behind its California counterpart. Israel also remains of the largest centers in the world for technology start-up enterprises. 200 start-ups are created annually and more than 2500 start-up companies are operating throughout the country.

ENERGY

Historically, Israel relied on external imports for meeting most of its energy needs, spending an amount equivalent to over 5% of its GDP per year in 2009 on imports of energy products. The transportation sector relies mainly on gasoline and diesel fuel, while the majority of electricity production is generated using imported coal. The country possesses negligible reserves of crude oil but does have abundant domestic natural gas resources which were discovered in large quantities starting in 2009, after many decades of previously unsuccessful exploration.

NATURAL GAS

Until the early 2000s, natural gas use in Israel was minimal. In the late 1990s, the government of Israel decided to encourage the usage of natural gas because of environmental, cost, and resource diversification reasons. At the time however, there were no domestic sources of natural gas and the expectation was that gas would be supplied from overseas in the form of LNG and by a future pipeline from Egypt (which eventually became the Arish–Ashkelon pipeline). Plans were made for the Israel Electric Corporation to construct several gas-driven power plants, for erecting a national gas distribution grid, and for an LNG import terminal. Soon thereafter, gas began to be located within Israeli territory, first in modest amounts and a decade later in very large quantities located in deep water off the Israeli coastline. This has greatly intensified the utilization of natural gas within the Israeli economy, especially in the electrical generation and industrial sectors.

Natural Gas Usage in Israel

2004	2005	2006	2007	2008	2009	2010	2014*	2016*	2018*	2020*	2022*	2024*	2026*	2028*	2030*
1.2	1.6	2.3	2.7	3.7	4.2	5.2	8.1	9.5	10.1	11.1	11.7	13	14.3	15.3	16.8

Figures are in Billion Cubic Meters (BCM) per year. *Estimated.

GAS DISCOVERIES

In 2000, a modest discovery was made when a 33-billion-cubic-metre (BCM), or 1,200-billion-cubic-foot, natural-gas field was located offshore Ashkelon, with commercial production starting in 2004. As of 2012 however, this field is nearly exhausted—earlier than expected to due increased pumping to partially compensate for the loss of Egyptian gas in the wake of unrest associated with the fall of the Mubarak regime in 2011. In 2009, a significant gas find named Tamar, with proven reserves of 188 BCM or 6.6×10^{12} cu ft (283 BCM probable) was located in deep water approximately 90 km (60 mi) west of Haifa, as well as a smaller 15 BCM (530×10^{9} cu ft) field situated nearer the coastline. Furthermore, results of 3D seismic surveys and test drilling conducted since 2010 have confirmed that an estimated 535 BCM (18.9×10^{12} cu ft) natural-gas deposit exists in a large underwater geological formation nearby the large gas field already discovered in 2009.

The Tamar field began commercial production on 30 March 2013 after four years of extensive development works.

The supply of gas from Tamar is expected to provide a boost to the Israeli economy, which has suffered losses of approximately NIS15 billion since 2011 resulting from the disruption of gas supplies from nearby Egypt (and which are not expected to resume due to Egypt's decision to indefinitely suspend its gas supply agreement to Israel).

As a result Israel, as well as its neighbor Jordan, which also suffered from disruption of gas deliveries from Egypt, had to resort to importing significantly more expensive and polluting liquid heavy fuels as substitute sources of energy. While Egyptian gas supplies to Jordan were partially restored in 2013, supplies from Tamar, and in the future from the Leviathan field, are expected to satisfy all Israeli domestic natural gas needs for decades to come.

The large gas discoveries so far have confirmed that the Levant basin of the Eastern Mediterranean contains significant quantities of natural gas and, potentially, crude oil. Consequently, additional exploration for oil and gas off Israel's coastline is continuing. A source close to Prime Minister Benjamin Netanyahu has valued Israel's natural gas reserves at $130 billion, while in 2012 BusinessWeek estimated the reserves' value at $240 billion. The businesses involved in exploration aim to export a share of future production, but others argue that it would be preferable, on geopolitical grounds, to use the gas within the country instead of other energy sources. In early 2012 the Israeli cabinet announced plans to set up a sovereign wealth fund that would allocate part of the royalties from energy exploration to education, defense and overseas investments.

Field	Discovered	Production	Estimated size
Noa North	1999	2012	50 billion cubic feet
Mari-B	2000	2004	1 trillion cubic feet
Tamar	2009	2013	10 trillion cubic feet
Dalit	2009	Not in production	700 billion cubic feet
Leviathan	2010	Not in production	19 trillion cubic feet
Dolphin	2011	Not in production	81.3 billion cubic feet
Tanin	2012	Not in production	1.2–1.3 trillion cubic feet

ELECTRICITY

Israel Electric Corporation (IEC), a state-owned enterprise, produced nearly all of the electricity generated in Israel. The IEC has an aggregate installed generating capacity of 11,690 MW, virtually all of it produced from fossil fuels. The company sold 52,037 GWh of electricity in 2010. The IEC is in the midst of adding several thousand megawatts of generating capacity due to increased demand and a low operating reserve, though a debate is currently raging with respect to how much should be generated from new coal-fired versus gas-fired plants, a determination complicated by the fact that some of the company's capital investment decisions predate the recent discoveries of significant reserves of natural gas offshore. In addition, in order to encourage competition in the electricity market, the government of Israel is currently (mid-2010) considering proposals from four private companies to generate up to 3,640 MW of electricity in 11 new sites, most of which would be gas-fired combined cycle power stations.

A chronic problem faced by Israel's electricity market is a persistently low operating reserve, which is mostly the result of Israel being an "electricity island". Most countries have the capability of relying on power drawn from producers in adjacent countries in the event of a power shortage. Israel's grid however, is unconnected to those of neighboring countries. This is mostly due to political reasons but also to the considerably less-developed nature of the power systems of Jordan and Egypt, whose per-capita electric generation is one quarter to one fifth that of Israel's. That said, rolling blackouts, even at periods of extreme demand in Israel are rare. However, to help alleviate the low reserve situation and to enable the potential of electricity exports when surplus electricity is available, Israel and Cyprus are considering implementing the proposed EuroAsia Interconnector project, which involves laying a 2000MW HVDC undersea power cable between them and between Cyprus and Greece, thus connecting Israel to the greater European power grid.

Share of Total Electricity Generation Capacity at Full Output by Plant Type and Fuel Types Used by the IEC in 2010				
	Coal	Fuel oil	Natural gas	Diesel
Installed capacity by plant type	39.7%	3.4%	39.8%	18.9%
Total annual generation by fuel source	61.0%	0.9%	36.6%	1.5%

SOLAR POWER

Solar power in Israel and the Israeli solar energy industry has a history that dates to the founding of the country. In the 1950s, Levi Yissar developed a solar water heater to help assuage an energy shortage in the new country. By 1967 around one in twenty households heated their water with the sun and 50,000 solar heaters had been sold.

With the 1970s oil crisis, Harry Zvi Tabor, the father of Israel's solar industry, developed the prototype solar water heater that is now used in over 90% of Israeli homes. Israeli engineers are on the cutting edge of solar energy technology, and its solar companies work on projects around the world.

INDUSTRIAL SECTOR

Israel has a well-developed chemical industry with many of its products aimed at the export market. Most of the chemical plants are located in Ramat Hovav, the Haifa Bay area and near the Dead Sea. Israel Chemicals is one of largest fertilizer and chemical companies in Israel and its subsidiary, the Dead Sea Works in Sdom is the world's fourth largest producer and supplier of potash products. The company also produces other products such as magnesium chloride, industrial salts, de-icers, bath salts, table salt, and raw materials for the cosmetic industry. One of the country's largest employers is Israel Aerospace Industries which produces mainly aviation and defense products. Another large employer is Teva Pharmaceutical Industries, one of the world's largest pharmaceutical companies, currently employing 40,000 people as of 2011. It specializes in generic and proprietary pharmaceuticals and active pharmaceutical ingredients. It is the largest generic drug manufacturer in the world and one of the 15 largest pharmaceutical companies worldwide.

DIAMOND INDUSTRY

Israel is one of the world's three major centers for polished diamonds, alongside Belgium and India. Israel's net polished diamond exports dropped slid 22.8 percent in 2012 as polished diamond exports fell to $5.56 billion from $7.2 billion in 2011. Net exports of rough diamonds dropped 20.1 percent to $2.8 billion and net exports of polished diamonds slipped 24.9 percent to $4.3 billion, while net rough diamond imports dropped 12.9 percent to $3.8 billion. Net exports and imports have dropped to due to the ongoing Global financial crisis, particularly within the Eurzone and the United States. The United States is the largest market accounting for 36% of overall export market for polished diamonds while Hong Kong remains at second with 28 percent and Belgium at 8 percent coming in third.

DEFENSE INDUSTRY

Israel is one of the world's major exporters of military equipment, accounting for 10% of the world total in 2007. Three Israeli companies were listed on the 2010 Stockholm International Peace Research Institute index of the world's top 100 arms-producing and military service companies: Elbit Systems, Israel Aerospace Industries and RAFAEL. The Defense industry in Israel is a strategically important sector and a large employer within the country. It is also a major player in the global arms market and is the 11th largest arms exporter in the world as of 2012. Total arms transfer agreements topped 12.9 billion between 2004 to 2011.

There are over 150 active defense companies based in the country with combined revenues of more than 3.5 billion USD annually. Israeli defense equipment exports have reached 7 billion U.S. dollars in 2012, making it a 20 percent increase from the amount of defense-related exports in 2011. Much of the exports are sold to the United States and Europe. Other major regions that purchase Israeli defense equipment include Southeast Asia and Latin America. India is also major country for Israeli arms exports and has remained Israel's largest arms market in the world. Israel is considered to be the leading UAV exporter in the world. According to the Stockholm International Peace Research Institute, Israeli defense companies were behind 41% of all drones exported in 2001-2011.

TOURISM

Tourism is one of Israel's major sources of income and economic growth engine in the country, attracting 3.5 million foreign tourists in 2012, representing a 4 percent increase since 2011 making it an all-time high. Israel offers a plethora of historical and religious sites, beach resorts, archaeological tourism, heritage tourism and ecotourism. Israel has the highest number of museums per capita in the world. The most popular paid site is Masada

EXTERNAL TRADE

EXPORT
$64.74 billion (2012 est.)
country comparison to the world: 54
$64.19 billion (2011 est.)

Exports - commodities:
machinery and equipment, software, cut diamonds, agricultural products, chemicals, textiles and apparel

Exports - partners:
US 28.8%, Hong Kong 7.9%, Belgium 5.6%, UK 5%, India 4.5%, China 4% (2011)

Imports:
$77.59 billion (2012 est.)
country comparison to the world: 40
$72.03 billion (2011 est.)

Imports - commodities:
raw materials, military equipment, investment goods, rough diamonds, fuels, grain, consumer goods

Imports - partners:
US 11.8%, China 7.4%, Germany 6.2%, Belgium 6.1%, Switzerland 5.4%, Italy 4.2% (2011)

Reserves of foreign exchange and gold:
$75.24 billion (31 December 2012 est.)
country comparison to the world: 28
$74.87 billion (31 December 2011 est.)

Debt - external:
$104.2 billion (31 December 2012 est.)
country comparison to the world: 44

$102.6 billion (31 December 2011 est.)
Stock of direct foreign investment - at home:
$73.07 billion (31 December 2012 est.)
country comparison to the world: 49
$66.57 billion (31 December 2011 est.)
Stock of direct foreign investment - abroad:
$74.53 billion (31 December 2012 est.)
country comparison to the world: 30
$69.83 billion (31 December 2011 est.)

The United States is Israel's largest trading partner; two-way trade totaled some $24.5 billion in 2010, up from $12.7 billion in 1997. The principal U.S. exports to Israel include computers, integrated circuits, aircraft parts and other defense equipment, wheat, and automobiles. Israel's chief exports to the U.S. include cut diamonds, jewelry, integrated circuits, printing machinery, and telecommunications equipment. The two countries signed a free trade agreement (FTA) in 1985 that progressively eliminated tariffs on most goods traded between the two countries over the following ten years. An agricultural trade accord was signed in November 1996, which addressed the remaining goods not covered in the FTA. Some non-tariff barriers and tariffs on goods remain, however. Israel also has trade and cooperation agreements in place with the European Union and Canada, and is seeking to conclude such agreements with a number of other countries, including Turkey, Jordan and several countries in Eastern Europe.

In regional terms, the European Union is the top destination for Israeli exports. In the four-month period between October 2011 and January 2012, Israel exported goods totalling $5 billion to the EU – amounting to 35% of Israel's overall exports. During the same period, Israeli exports to the Far East came to $3.1 billion.

Until 1995, Israel's trade with the Arab world was minimal due to the Arab League boycott, which was begun against the Jewish community of Palestine in 1945. Arab nations not only refused to have direct trade with Israel (the primary boycott), but they also refused to do business with any corporation that operated in Israel (secondary boycott), or any corporation that did business with a corporation that did business with Israel (tertiary boycott).

In 2013, commercial trade between Israel and the Palestinian territories were valued at US$ 20 billion annually.

RANKINGS

As of 2012Israel ranks 26th in Global Competitiveness Report by World Economic Forum, and 17th among 187 world nations on the UN's Human Development Index, which places it in the category of "Very Highly Developed". Israel's economy also ranks 17th among the world's most economically developed nations, according to IMD's World Competitiveness Yearbook rankings. The Israeli economy was ranked as the world's most durable economy in the face of crises, and was also ranked first in the rate research and development center investments. The Bank of Israel was ranked first among central banks for its efficient functioning, up from the 8th place in 2009. Israel was ranked first also in its supply of skilled manpower. Israeli companies, particularly in the high-tech area, have enjoyed considerable success raising money on Wall Street and other world financial markets: Israel ranked second among foreign countries in the number of its companies listed on U.S. stock exchanges.

Having moved away from the socialist economic model since the mid-1980s and early 1990s, Israel has made dramatic moves toward the free-market paradigm. As of 2012 Israel's economic freedom score is 67.8, making its economy the 48th freest in the 2012 Index of Economic

Freedom. Israel's economic competitiveness is helped by strong protection of property rights, relatively low corruption levels, and high openness to global trade and investment. Income and corporate tax rates remain relatively high. As of 2011 Israel ranks 36th out of 182 countries in Transparency International's Corruption Perceptions Index. Bribery and other forms of corruption are illegal in Israel, which is a signatory to the OECD Bribery Convention since 2008

SUPPLEMENTS

MUNICIPAL GOVERNMENT CONTACTS

MUNICIPAL GOVERNMENT : CITIES OF ISRAEL

Cities with a population of at least 20,000.

District	City	Code	Phone
Northern	Afula	106	04.6520355
Northern	Akko	106	04.9956063
Southern	Arad	106	08.9951706
Yosh	Ariel	106	03.9368844
Southern	Ashdod	106	08.8545003
Southern	Ashkelon	106	08.6792380
Tel Aviv	Bat Yam	107	03.5558555
Southern	Beer Sheva	106	08.6463777
Northern	Beit Shean	106	04.6489400
Jerusalem	Beit Shemesh	106	02.9909999
Yosh	Betar Illit	106	02.5888111
Tel Aviv	Bnei Berak	106	03.5776555
Southern	Dimona	106	08.6563111
Southern	Eilat	106	08.6367112
Central	Elad		03.9078100
Tel Aviv	Givatayim	107	03.5722217
Haifa	Hadera	106	04.6303311
Haifa	Haifa	106	04.8356000
Tel Aviv	Herzliya	106	09.9591469
Central	Hod HaSharon	108	09.7418002
Tel Aviv	Holon	106	03.5027222
Jerusalem	Jerusalem	106	02.6296666
Northern	Karmiel	106	04.9085555
Central	Kfar Sava	106	09.7649111
Haifa	Kiryat Ata	109	04.8478478
Haifa	Kiryat Bialik	108	04.8780878
Southern	Kiryat Gat	106	08.6874511
Southern	Kiryat Malachi	106	08.8500888
Haifa	Kiryat Motzkin	107	04.8780202
Tel Aviv	Kiryat Ono	106	03.5311111
Northern	Kiryat Shemone	106	04.6908444
Haifa	Kiryat Yam		04.8789700
Central	Lod	106	08.9279028
Yosh	Maale Adumim	107	02.5418888
Northern	Maalot Tarshiha	106	04.9578888
Northern	Migdal HaEmek	106	04.6507777

District	City	Code	Phone
Central	Modiin	106	08.9726000
Northern	Nahariya		04.9879811
Northern	Nazareth	106	04.6459200
Northern	Nazareth Illit	107	04.6478888
Central	Nes Ziona	106	08.9383838
Haifa	Nesher	106	04.8215111
Central	Netanya	106	09.8603131
Southern	Netivot	106	08.9938701
Southern	Ofakim	106	08.9923911
Haifa	Or Akiva	106	04.6108800
Tel Aviv	Or Yehuda	106	03.5335758
Central	Petah Tikva	106	03.9052272
Central	Raanana	*9107	09.7610610
Southern	Rahat		08.9914811
Tel Aviv	Ramat Hasharon	106	03.5483888
Tel Aviv	Ramat-Gan	109	03.6753555
Central	Ramla	108	08.9771795
Central	Rehovot	106	08.9392222
Central	Rishon Lezion	106	03.9682362
Central	Rosh Ha'ayin	106	03.9385656
Southern	Sderot	*8516	08.6620222
Tel Aviv	Tel Aviv	106	03.5218438
Northern	Tiberias	106	04.6739555
Central	Tira		09.7938432
Haifa	Tirat Carmel	106	04.8547000
Northern	Tsfat (Safed)	106	04.6927402
Central	Yavne	106	08.9433300
Central	Yehud-Monosson	106	03.5391212

REGIONAL COUNCILS IN ISRAEL

A Regional Council includes villages and communities each with a population of less than 2,000.

District	Regional Council	Phone
Haifa	Alona	04.6388561
Southern	Beer Tuvia	08.8507979
Northern	Beit Shean Valley	04.6065850
Yosh	Binyamin	02.9977111
Southern	Bnei Shimon	08.9915811
Central	Brener	08.9399999
Southern	Central Arava	08.6592201
Northern	Daliyat al-Karmel	04.8395333

District	Regional Council	Phone
Central	Drom Hasharon	03.9000500
Northern	Emek Hayarden	04.6757600
Central	Emek Hefer	09.8981666
Northern	Emek Yizrael	04.6520111
Southern	Eshkol	08.9929111
Northern	Galil Elion (Upper Galilee)	04.6816611
Northern	Galil Tachton (Lower Galilee)	04.6767213
Central	Gan Rave	08.9408230
Central	Gderot	08.8592950
Central	Gezer	08.9274040
Northern	Gilboa	04.6533233
Northern	Golan	04.6969777
Yosh	Gush Etzion	02.9939933
Yosh	Har Hevron	02.9969111
Southern	Hevel Eilot	08.6355888
Central	Hevel Yavne	08.8561011
Southern	Hof Ashkelon	08.6775555
Haifa	Hof HaKarmel	04.8136200
Central	Hof HaSharon	09.9596555
Yosh	Jordan Valley	02.9946666
Southern	Lachish	08.6871666
Central	Lev HaSharon	09.7960222
Northern	Maale Yosef	04.9105500
Northern	Mateh Asher	04.9879666
Jerusalem	Mateh Yehuda	02.9900888
Northern	Megido	04.9598444
Yosh	Megilot Yam HaMelah	02.9943222
Haifa	Menashe	04.6177301
Southern	Merhavim	08.9929480
Northern	Merom HaGalil	04.6919800
Northern	Mevoot Hermon	04.6942120
Northern	Misgav	04.9902311
Central	Modiin Region	03.9722888
Central	Nahal Soreq	08.8593180
Southern	Ramat Negev	08.6564111
Central	Sadot Dan	073.2230600
Southern	Sdot Negev	08.9938933
Southern	Shaar HaNegev	08.6806237
Southern	Shafir	08.8508901
Yosh	Shomron	02.9061156
Southern	Tamar	08.6688888
Southern	Yoav	08.8500777

District	Regional Council	Phone
Haifa	Zvulun	04.8478111

EMBASSIES OF ISRAEL

Country	City	Office	Phone	Fax
Albania	Tiran	Non-Resident		
Angola	Luanda	Embassy of Israel	244.222.395295	244.222.396.366
Argentina	Buenos Aires	Embassy of Israel	54.11.43382500	
Armenia	Yerevan	Non-Resident		
Australia	Canberra	Embassy of Israel	61.2.6273.1309	61.2.6273.4273
Austria	Vienna	Embassy of Israel	43.1.4764.6500	43.1.4764.6554
Azerbaijan	Baku	Embassy of Israel	994.12.4907881	
Bahamas	Nassau	Non-Resident		
Belarus	Minsk	Embassy of Israel	375.17.298.4392	
Belgium	Brussels	Embassy of Israel	32.2.373.5500	
Bosnia-Herzegovina	Sarajevo	Non-Resident		
Brazil	Sao Paulo	Consulate General of Israel	55.11.2127.0500	
Brazil	Brasilia	Embassy of Israel	55.61.2105.0500	55.61.244.6129
Bulgaria	Sofia	Embassy of Israel	359.2.951.5044	359.2.952.1101
Cameroon	Yaounde	Embassy of Israel	237.22201644	237.2221.0823
Canada	Toronto	Consulate General of Israel	1.416.640.8500	1.416.640.8555
Canada	Ottawa	Embassy of Israel	1.613.567.6450	1.613.567.9878
Canada	Montreal	Consulate General of Israel	1.514.940.8500	1.514.940.8555
Chile	Santiago	Embassy of Israel	56.2.750.0500	56.2.750.0555
China	Shanghai	Consulate General of Israel	86.21.6209.8008	86.21.6209.8010
China	Hong Kong	Consulate General of Israel	852.2821.7500	852.2865.0220
China	Guangzhou	Embassy of Israel	86.20.8513.0500	
China	Beijing	Embassy of Israel	86.10.8532.0500	
Colombia	Bogota	Embassy of Israel	57.1.327.7500	57.1.327.7555
Congo	Kinshasa	Non-Resident	243.998.7218	
Costa Rica	San Jose	Embassy of Israel	506.2221.6444	506.2254.1000
Croatia	Zagreb	Embassy of Israel	385.1.616.9500	
Cyprus	Nicosia	Embassy of Israel	357.22.369500	357.22.3695555
Czech Rep.	Prague	Embassy of Israel	420.2.3309.7500	420.2.3309.7519
Denmark	Copenhagen	Embassy of Israel	45.8818.5500	45.8818.5555
Dominican Republic	Santo Domingo	Embassy of Israel	809.920.1500	809.472.1785
Ecuador	Quito	Embassy of Israel	593.3971500	593.3971555
Egypt	Cairo	Embassy of Israel	20.2.33321500	

Country	City	Office	Phone	Fax
El Salvador	San Salvador	Embassy of Israel	503.2211.3434	503.2211.3443
Eritrea	Asmara	Embassy of Israel	291.1.188626	291.1.188550
Estonia	Tallinn	Non-Resident		
Ethiopia	Addis Ababa	Embassy of Israel	251.11.6460999	
Finland	Helsinki	Embassy of Israel	358.9.681.2020	358.9.1356959
France	Paris	Embassy of Israel	33.1.4076.5500	33.1.4076.5555
France	Marseille	Consulate General of Israel	33.4.1324.6500	33.4.1324.6536
Georgia	Tbilisi	Embassy of Israel	995.32.556500	995.32.556533
Germany	Munich	Consulate General of Israel	49.895.4348.6500	49.895.4348.6555
Germany	Berlin	Embassy of Israel	49.30.8904.5500	49.30.8904.5309
Ghana	Accra	Embassy of Israel	233.302.743838	233.302.743857
Greece	Athens	Embassy of Israel	30.1.671.9530/1	
Guatemala	Guatemala	Embassy of Israel	502.2363.5665	502.23633.6950
Hungary	Budapest	Embassy of Israel	36.1.392.6200	36.1.200.0783
Iceland	Reykjavik	Non-Resident		
India	Mumbai	Consulate General of Israel	91.22.61600500	91.22.61600599
India	New Delhi	Embassy of Israel	91.11.3041.4500	91.11.3041.4555
Ireland	Dublin	Embassy of Israel	353.1.230.9400	353.1.230.9446
Italy	Rome	Embassy of Israel	39.6.3619.8500	39.6.3619.8555
Ivory Coast	Abidjan	Embassy of Israel	225.2021.3178	225.2021.3178
Japan	Tokyo	Embassy of Israel	81.3.3264.0911	81.3.3264.0792
Jordan	Amman	Embassy of Israel	962.6.552.4680	
Kazakhstan	Astana	Embassy of Israel	7.7172. 688.739	7.7172.688.735
Kenya	Nairobi	Embassy of Israel	254.20.492.7500	254.20.271.5966
Korea-South	Seoul	Embassy of Israel	82.2.564.3448	
Latvia	Riga, also serves Lithuania	Embassy of Israel	371.6763.5574	371.7.830170
Liberia	Monrovia	Non-Resident		
Mauritania	Nouakchott	Embassy of Israel	222.254610	
Mexico	Mexico City	Embassy of Israel	52.555.201.1500	52.555.201.1555
Moldova	Kishinev	Non-Resident		
Mongolia	Ulan Bator	Non-Resident		
Nepal	Kathmandu	Embassy of Israel	977.1.441.3419	977.1.441.3920
Netherlands	The Hague	Embassy of Israel	31.70.376.0500	31.70.376.0555
New Zealand	Wellington	Embassy of Israel	64.4.439.9500	64.4.439.9555
Nigeria	Abuja	Embassy of Israel	233.9.3143170/4	233.9.3143177
Norway	Oslo	Embassy of Israel	47.2.101.9500	47.2101.9530
Panama	Panama	Embassy of Israel	507.208.4700	
Paraguay	Asuncion	Non-Resident	591.2371287/4239	

Country	City	Office	Phone	Fax
Peru	Lima	Embassy of Israel	51.1.418.0500	51.1.418.0555
Philippines	Manila	Embassy of Israel	63.2.894.0441	63.2.894.1027
Poland	Warsaw	Embassy of Israel	48.22.825.0923	48.22.825.1607
Portugal	Lisbon	Embassy of Israel	351.21.045.5500	351.21.355.3658
Puerto Rico	San Juan	Consulate General of Israel	1.305.925.9400	
Qatar	Doha	Israeli Trade Office	974.468.9077	
Romania	Bucharest	Embassy of Israel	40.21.302.8500	40.21.302.8555
Russia	Moscow	Embassy of Israel	7.095.230.6700	7.095.2381346
Senegal	Dakar	Embassy of Israel	221.823.7965	221.823.6490
Sierra Leone	Freetown	Non-Resident		
Singapore	Singapore	Embassy of Israel	65.6834.9200	65.6834.9299
Slovakia	Bratislava	Embassy of Israel	421.2.5441.0556	
Slovenia	Ljubljana	Non-Resident		
South Africa	Pretoria	Embassy of Israel	27.12.470.3500	27.12.470.3555
Spain	Madrid	Embassy of Israel	34.91.782.9500	34.91.782.9555
Sri Lanka	Colombo	Non-Resident		
Sweden	Stockholm	Embassy of Israel	46.8.5280.6500	46.8.5280.6555
Switzerland	Geneva	Israel Mission to the United Nations	41.22.716.0500	41.22.716.0555
Switzerland	Bern	Embassy of Israel	41.31.356.3588	41.31.356.3556
Taiwan	Taipei	Israel Economic and Cultural Office	886.2.2757.9692	
Tajikistan	Dushanbe	Non-Resident		
Tanzania	Dodoma	Non-Resident		
Thailand	Bangkok	Embassy of Israel	66.2.204.9200	
Turkey	Istanbul	Consulate General of Israel	90.212.317.6500	90.212.317.6555
Turkey	Ankara	Embassy of Israel	90.312.4597500	90.312.4597555
Turkmenistan	Ashgabat	Non-Resident		
U.K.	London	Embassy of Israel	44.207.957.9500	44.207.957.9555
USA	Los Angeles	Consulate General of Israel	1.323.852.5500	
USA	Washington	Embassy of Israel	1.202.364.5500	
USA	New York, UN	Israel Mission to the United Nations	1.212.499.5510	1.212.499.5515
USA	San Francisco	Consulate General of Israel	1.415.844.7500	1.415.844.7555
USA	Philadelphia	Consulate General of Israel	1.215. 977.7600	1.215. 977.7611
USA	New York	Consulate General of Israel	1.212.499.5000	1.212.499.5435
USA	Miami	Consulate General of Israel	1.305.925.9400	1.305.925.9455

Country	City	Office	Phone	Fax
USA	Houston	Consulate General of Israel	1.832.301.3560	1.713.627.0149
USA	Chicago	Consulate General of Israel	1.312.380.8800	1.312.380.8855
USA	Boston	Consulate General of Israel	1.617.535.0200	1.617.535.0255
USA	Atlanta	Consulate General of Israel	1.404.487.6500	1.404.487.6555
Uganda	Kampala	Non-Resident		
Ukraine	Kiev	Embassy of Israel	380.44.586.1500	380.44.586.1556
Uruguay	Montevideo	Embassy of Israel	598.2.400.4164	598.2.409.5821
Uzbekistan	Tashkent	Embassy of Israel	998.71.140.7500	
Vatican	Holy See	Embassy of Israel	39.06.3619.8690	39.06.3619.8626
Vietnam	Hanoi	Embassy of Israel	84.4.3843.3140	84.4.3843.5760
Zambia	Lusaka	Non-Resident	27.12.342.2693	
Zimbabwe	Harare	Non-Resident	27.12.342.2693	

ECONOMIC & TRADE REPRESENTATIVES ABROAD

ANGOLA

Mr. Bahig Manzour

Ambassador

Embassy of Israel
Rua Raina Ngina 34
Edificio Siscal Luanda

Tel: (+244.2) 395-295/3
Fax: (+244.2) 396-366

E-mail: info@luanda.mfa.gov.il

ARGENTINA

Mr. Dori Goren
Counsellor - Economic Affairs

Embassy of Israel
Ave. de Mayo 701, 10th floor
C.P. 1084
Buenos Aires

Tel: (+5411) 4338 2519/20
Fax: (+5411) 4338-2617

E-mail: buenosaires@moital.gov.il
Site: www.israeltrade.gov.il/argentina

AUSTRALIA

Mrs. Nili Shalev
Trade Commissioner

Israel Trade Commission
6/37 York St.
Sydney, NSW 2000

Tel: (+61.2) 9262-3943
Fax: (+61.2) 9262-5242

E-mail: sydney@moital.gov.il
Site: www.israeltrade.gov.il/australia

AUSTRIA

Mr. Joseph Peri
Minister Counsellor for Economic Affairs

Embassy of Israel
Anton Frank- Gasse 20
A-1180 Vienna

Tel: (+43.1) 4764-6504
Fax: (+43.1) 4764-6576

E-mail: economy@vienna.mfa.gov.il
Site: www.israeltrade.gov.il/austria

AZERBAIJAN	BELGIUM
H.E. Eitan Na'eh Ambassador Embassy of Israel 1033 Izmir St. Hyatt Tower 3 Baku Tel: (+994.12) 4907-885 Fax: (+994.12) 4907-892 **E-mail:** ambassador@baku.mfa.gov.il	Ms. Rachel Hirshler Minister Counsellor - Economic Affairs Embassy of Israel & Mission of Israel to the EU 40 Avenue. de l'Observatoire, Brussels 1180 Tel: (+32.2) 373-5534/5 Fax: (+32.2) 373-5666 **E-mail:** brusseles@moital.gov.il **Site:** www.israeltrade.gov.il/belgium
BRAZIL	**BULGARIA**
Mrs. Rona Kotler – Ben Aroya First Secretary - Economic Affairs Economic Office Av. Brig. Faria Lima 1713 01452-001 Sao Paulo Tel: (+55.11) 3032-3511 Fax: (+55.11) 3032-9233 **E-mail:** brazil@moital.gov.il **Site:** www.israeltrade.gov.il/brazil	Mr. Michael Khoury First Secretary - Economic Affairs (Resident in Greece) Ms. Zarina Benoun Trade Secretary Embassy of Israel 1 Bulgaria Square N.D.K Administrative Building, 7th Floor Sofia 1463 Tel: (+359.2) 9516-962/5044 Fax: (+359.2) 9521-101 **E-mail:** sofia@moital.gov.il **Site:** www.israeltrade.gov.il/bulgaria
CAMEROON	**CANADA** – Montreal
Mr. Benny Omer Ambassador Mr. David Levy Second Secretary Embassy of Israel P.O.B 5934, Yaoundé Tel: (+237) 2201-644, 2211-291 Fax: (+237) 2210-823 **E-mail:** info@yaounde.mfa.gov.il	Ms. Sandra Winston Deputy Trade Commissioner Embassy of Israel 1155 Blvd. Rene Levesque W., Suite 2620 Montreal, Quebec H3B 4S5 Tel: (+1.514) 940-8518 Fax: (+1.514) 940-8520 **E-mail:** montreal@moital.gov.il
CANADA – Toronto	**CHILE**

Mr. Ephraim Shoham Consul - Economic Affairs Israel Economic Mission 180 Bloor St. West, Suite 700 Toronto, Ontario M5S 2V6 Tel: (+1.416) 6408-540 Fax: (+1.416) 6408-546 **E-mail:** toronto@moital.gov.il **Site:** www.israeltrade.gov.il/canada_toronto	Mr. George Lambeth Head of Commercial Department **E-mail:** glambeth@isracom.cl Mrs. Gili Sharir Second Secretary Embassy of Israel San Sebastian 2812, Piso 5 Las Condes P.O.B. 146 Stgo 35 Santiago Tel: (+562) 7500-518 Fax: (+562) 7500-549 **E-mail:** econ.sec@santiago.mfa.gov.il
CHINA – Beijing	**CHINA** – Hong Kong
Mr. Oded Arbel First Secretary – Economic Affairs Mrs. Iris Tal-Arbel Commercial Attaché Embassy of Israel No. 17 Tian Ze Lu Chaoyang District Beijing 100600 Tel: (+86.10) 6532-0041 Fax: (+86.10) 6532-0048 **E-mail:** beijing@moital.gov.il **Site**: http://www.israeltrade.org.cn	Mrs. Ornit Avidar Head of Commercial Department Consulate General of Israel Admiralty Center 701 Tower 2, P.O.B 245 Hong Kong Tel: (+852) 2821-7508/9 Fax: (+852) 2865-0220 **E-mail:** hongkong@moital.gov.il **Site:** www.israeltrade.gov.il/hongkong
CHINA – Shanghai	**COLOMBIA**
Mr. Ilan Maor Consul General Consulate General of Israel New Town Mansion 55 Loushanguan Ro. Shanghai 200336 Tel: (+86.21) 6209-8008 Fax: (+86.21) 6209-8010 **E-mail:** economy_mashav@shanghai.mfa.gov.il **Site**: http://shanghai.mfa.gov.il	Mr. Edwin Yabo First Secretary Embassy of Israel Edificio Caxdac Calle 35 7-25 Piso 14, Bogota Tel: (+57.1) 288-4637/732 Fax: (+57.1) 287-7783 **E-mail:** dcm@bogota.mfa.gov.il
COSTA RICA	**CYPRUS**

Mr. Gadi Spieler Second Secretary Embassy of Israel Edificio Centro Colon Piso 11, Aprd. 5147-1000 San Jose Tel: (+506) 221-6444 Fax: (+506) 257-0867 **E-mail:** comercioisrael_cr@amnet.co.cr	Mrs. Revital Malca First Secretary Embassy of Israel 4 Grypari St. P.O.B. 25159 Nicosia 1307 Tel: (+357.2) 2369-524 Fax: (+357.2) 2666-338 **E-mail:** deputy@nicosia.mfa.gov.il
CZECH REPUBLIC	**DENMARK**
Mrs. Ethy Levy First Secretary - Economic Affairs (Resident in Budapest) Embassy of Israel Badeniho St. 2 Prague 7, 17000 Tel: (+420.2) 3309-7500/41 Fax: (+420.2) 3309-7549 **E-mail:** prague@moital.gov.il **Site:** www.israeltrade.gov.il/czech-republic	Mr. Ophir Kariv Counsellor Embassy of Israel Lundevangsvej 4 2900 Hellerup Copenhagen Tel: (+45) 8818-5520 Fax: (+45) 8818-5555 **E-mail:** dcm@copenhagen.mfa.gov.il **Site:** www.embassy-of-israel.dk
DOMINICAN REPUBLIC	**ECUADOR**
Mr. Yoav Bar-On Ambassador Embassy of Israel Pedro Henriquez Urena 80 Apartado Postal 1404 Santo Domingo Tel: (+1.809) 4720-774/5 Fax: (+1.809) 4721-785 **E-mail:** emb.israel@codetel.net.do	Mr. Dani Saban Ambassador Embassy of Israel Ave. 12 de Octubre 1059 Y.General Salasar Ed. Plaza 2000 Quito Tel: (+593.2) 2237-474 Fax: (+593.2) 2238-055 **E-mail:** israemb@interactive.net.ec
EGYPT	**EL SALVADOR**
Ambassador Embassy of Israel 6 Ibn El Malek St. Giza Cairo Tel: (+20.2) 7610-528/45 Fax: (+20.2) 761-0414	Mr. Jonathan Peled Ambassador Embassy of Israel Centro Financiero Gigante 63 Ave. Sur Y Alameda Roosevelt Torre B, Piso 11 San Salvador Tel: (+503) 211-3434

E-mail: mofa@menanet.net	Fax: (+503) 211-3443 **E-mail:** ambassador@integra.com.sv
ERITREA	**ETHIOPIA**
Mr. Hanan Goder-Glodberger Ambassador Embassy of Israel 32 ABO St. P.O.B 5600 Asmara Tel: (+29.11) 188-626 Fax: (+29.11) 188-550 **E-mail:** info@asmara.mfa.gov.il	Ms. Shlomit Sufa Second Secretary Embassy of Israel Higher16, Kebele 22 House No. 283 P.O.B 1266 Addis Ababa Tel: (+251.1) 460-999 Fax: (+251.1) 461-961 **E-mail:** embassy@addisababa.mfa.gov.il
FINLAND	**FRANCE**
Mr. Mordechai Ish-Shalom Minister - Economic Affairs (Resident in Stockholm) Mr. Kalevi Von Behr Trade Officer Embassy of Israel Vironkatu 5A 00170 Helsinki Tel: (+358.9) 6812-0226 Fax: (+358.9) 1356-959 **E-mail:** helsinki@moital.gov.il **Site:** www.israeltrade.gov.il/finland	Mr. Inon Elroy First Secretary – Commercial Affairs Embassy of Israel 3 Rue Rabelais 75008 Paris Tel: (+33.1) 4076-5460 Fax: (+33.1) 4076-5329 **E-mail:** paris@moital.gov.il **Site:** www.israeltrade.gov.il/france
GEORGIA	**GERMANY**
Mr. Gary Klaiman Second Secretary Embassy of Israel 61 Achmashenebeli Ave. 380002 Tbilisi Tel: (+995.32) 951-709, 964-457 Fax: (+995.32) 237-133 **E-mail:** isremb@access.sanet.ge	Mr. Eitan Kuperstoch Minister-Counselor – Economic Affairs Embassy of Israel Auguste-Viktoria St. 74 14193 Berlin Tel: (+49.30) 2064-490 Fax: (+49.30) 2064-4955 **E-mail:** berlin@moital.gov.il **Site:** www.israeltrade.gov.il/germany
GREECE	**GUATEMALA**
Mr. Michael Khoury	Ms. Dorit Nachum

First Secretary – Economic Affairs Embassy of Israel 1 Marathonodromou St. Paleo Psychico 15452 Athens Tel: (+30.210) 6727-351 Fax: (+30.210) 6722-025 **E-mail:** athens@moital.gov.il **Site:** www.israeltrade.gov.il/greece	Counsellor Embassy of Israel 13 Avenida 14-07 Zona 10 Colonia Oaklend Guatemala City Tel: (+502) 2333-4624 Fax: (+502) 2333-6950 **E-mail:** consul@guatemala.mfa.gov.il econ@guatemala.mfa.gov.il
HUNGARY	**INDIA** – New Delhi
Mrs. Ethy Levy First Secretary - Economic Affairs Embassy of Israel Fullank 8 1026 Budapest 2 Tel: (+36.1) 3926-283/200 Fax: (+36.1) 2000-787 **E-mail:** budapest@israeltrade.gov.il **Site:** www.israeltrade.gov.il/hungary	Mr. Mouneer Agbariya First Secretary - Economic Affairs Embassy of Israel 3 Aurangzeb Road New Delhi 1100011 Tel: (+91.11) 2301-3238 Fax: (+91.11) 2301-5304 **E-mail:** econ@vsni.com **Site:** www.israeltrade.gov.il/india_delhi
IRELAND	**ITALY** – Milan
Mr. Colin Sheena Head of Commercial Section Embassy of Israel 122 Pembroke Road Ballsbridge Dublin 4 Tel: (+353.1) 2309-415 Fax: (+353.1) 2309-415 **E-mail:** trade@dublin.mfa.gov.il **Site:** www.israeltrade.gov.il/ireland www.embassyofisrael.ie	Mr. Gal Mor Counsellor – Economic Affairs Israel Commercial & Investment Office Corso Europa 12 Milan 20122 Tel: (+390.2) 7601-5545 Fax: (+390.2) 7601-4145 **E-mail:** milan@moital.gov.il **Site:** www.israeltrade.gov.il/italy_milan
ITALY – Rome	**IVORY COAST**

Mr. Mordechay Rodgold Counsellor - Economic Affairs Embassy of Israel Via Michele Mercati 14 00197 Rome Tel: (+39.06) 3619-8673 Fax: (+39.06) 3619-8555 **E-mail:** economico@roma.mfa.gov.il	Ms. Michele Seguev Charge d'Affairs Embassy of Israel Ave. Chardy Immeuble Nur El Hayat, 9e etage 01 B.P. 1877 Abidjan 01 Tel: (+225) 2021-4953 Fax: (+225) 2021-8704 **E-mail:** info@abidjan.mfa.gov.il
JAPAN	**JORDAN**
Mr. Noah Shani Minister - Economic Affairs Embassy of Israel 3 Nibancho Chiyoda-ku Tokyo 102-0084 Tel: (+81.3) 3264-0398/911 Fax: (+81.3) 3264-0829 **E-mail:** tokyo@moital.gov.il **Site:** www.israeltrade.gov.il/japan	Mr. Danny Navo Deputy Head of Mission Embassy of Israel 47 Maysaloun St. Rabiya P.O.B 950866 Amman 111195 Tel: (+962.6) 552-5170/2/3/4/5 Fax: (+962.6) 552-4689 **E-mail:** amman@moital.gov.il
KAZAKHSTAN	**KENYA**
Ms. Noomi Aldouby Deputy Chief of Mission Embassy of Israel Dgeltoxan St. 87 Almaty Tel: (+7.3272) 506-215 /6/7/284 Fax: (+7.3272) 506-283 **E-mail:** cao@almaty.mfa.gov.il	Mr. Gilad Milo Second Secretary Embassy of Israel Fair View Hotel Bishop Road P.O.B. 30354 Nairobi Tel: (+254.20) 2724-021/2, 2722-182/3 Fax: (+254.20) 2715-966 **E-mail:** dcm@nairobi.mfa.gov.il
KOREA (South)	**LATVIA**
Mr. Jonathan Hadar First Secretary - Economic Affairs Embassy of Israel 18th Fl. Cheonggye 11 Bldg. 149 Seorin-dong, Jongro-gu Seoul, 110-726 Tel: (+82.2) 739-8666 Fax: (+82.2) 7399-963	Ms. Clara Vesterman Second Secretary Embassy of Israel to the Baltic States 2 Elizabetes St. Riga LV-1010 Tel: (+371) 7321-092/0980 Fax: (+371) 7830-170

E-mail: seoul@moital.gov.il **Site:** www.israeltrade.gov.il/korea	**E-mail:** zir@rig.mfa.gov.il econ@rig.mfa.gov.il **Site:** www.riga.mfa.gov.il
MEXICO	**MYANMAR** – Burma
Mr. Joshua Peleg First Secretary - Economic Affairs Embassy of Israel Sierra Madre 215 Lomas de Chapultepec 11000 Mexico City Tel: (+52.55) 5201-1582 Fax: (+52.55) 5201-1558 **E-mail:** mexico@moital.gov.il **Site:** www.israeltrade.gov.il/mexico	Ms. Marie France-Majer Counsellor – Economic and Trade Affairs (Resident in Bangkok) Mrs. Ruth Shats Ambassador Embassy of Israel 15, Khbaung St. Hlaing Township Yangon Tel: (+95.1) 515-115 Fax: (+95.1) 515-116 **E-mail:** info@yangon.mfa.gov.il
NEPAL	**NETHERLANDS**
Mr. Dan Ben-Eliezer Ambassador Embassy of Israel Bishramalaya House, Lazimpat St. G.P.O.B. 371 Katmandu Tel: (+977.1) 411-811, 413-419 Fax: (+977.1) 413-920 **E-mail:** israelem@mos.com.np	Mr. Arnon Yosef Minister Counsellor - Economic Affairs Embassy of Israel Buitenhof 47 2513 AH Hague Tel: (+31.70) 3760-514 Fax: (+31.70) 3760-573 **E-mail:** hague@moital.gov.il **Site:** www.israeltrade.gov.il/netherlands
NIGERIA	**NORWAY**
Mr. Meir Dagan Consul Embassy of Israel Plot 1317 A&B Udo Udoma Crescent Zone 4A Asokoro District-Abuja Tel: (+234.9) 3143-170 /4 Fax: (+234.9) 3143-177 **E-mail:** admin@abuja.mfa.gov.il	Mr. Mordechai Ish-Shalom Minister - Economic Affairs (Resident in Stockholm) Mr. Andreas Lorange Trade Officer Embassy of Israel Box 534 Skoyen N-0214 Oslo Tel: (+47) 2101-9513 Fax: (+47) 2101-9530 **E-mail:** oslo@moital.gov.il

	Site: www.israeltrade.gov.il/norway
PERU	**PHILIPPINES**
Mr. Lior Keinan Second Secretary Embassy of Israel Natalio Sanchez 125, Piso 6 Santa Beatriz, Lima Tel: (+51.1) 4334-431 Fax: (+51.1) 4338-925 **E-mail:** dcm@lima.mfa.gov.il	Mr. Guy Feldman Second Secretary Embassy of Israel Trafalgar Plaza, 23 Floor 105 H.V. Dela Costa St. Salcedo Village, Makati City Manila Tel: (+63.2) 8940-441/2/3 Fax: (+63.2) 8941-027 **E-mail:** dcmil@info.com.ph
POLAND	**PORTUGAL**
Mr. Ronen Katz First Secretary - Economic Affairs Embassy of Israel Krzywickiego 24 Warsaw 02-078 Tel: (+48.22) 8252-512 Fax: (+48.22) 8251-410 **E-mail:** warsaw@moital.gov.il **Site:** www.israeltrade.gov.il/poland	Mr. Gil Shaki First Secretary - Economic Affairs (Resident in Madrid) Embassy of Israel Rua Antonio Enes 16-4 Lisbon 1050-025 Tel: (+351.21) 3553-643 Fax: (+351.21) 3553-656 **E-mail:** Lisbon@moital.gov.il **Site:** www.israeltrade.gov.il/portugal
QATAR	**ROMANIA**
Mr. Dov Steinberg Head of Mission Israel Trade Representation Office 18 Razy Rd. P.O.B. 22183 Doha Tel: (974) 4689-077 Fax (974) 4685-258 **E-mail:** doha@moital.gov.il	Mr. Arnon Arbel First Secretary – Economic Affairs Embassy of Israel Blvd. Dimitrie Cantemir. 1 Sitraco Center Bucharest Tel: (+40.21) 3302-355/6 Fax: (+40.21) 3303-917 **E-mail:** Bucharest@israeltrade.gov.il **Site:** www.israeltrade.gov.il/romania
RUSSIAN FEDERATION	**SENEGAL**
Mr. Yehezkel Pollyack Counsellor – Economic, Commercial & Tourism Affairs Embassy of Israel 56 Bolshaya Ordynka St.	Mr. Daniel Pinhasi Ambassador **E-mail:** info@dakar.mfa.gov.il Uri Reznik

Moscow 101000 Tel: (+7095) 2306-700/779 Fax: (+7095) 2301-208 **E-mail:** economy@moscow.mfa.gov.il **Site:** www.israeltrade.gov.il/russia	Second Secretary **E-mail:** dcm@dakar.mfa.gov.il Embassy of Israel 3 Place de l'Independance B.P. 2096, Dakar Tel: (+221) 8233-561/8355/7965 Fax: (+221) 8236-490
SERBIA – MONTENEGRO	**SINGAPORE**
Ms. Hadas Wittenberg Second Secretary Embassy of Israel 47 Bul. Mira (Dedinje) Belgrade Tel: (+381.11) 3672-400 Fax: (+381.11) 3670-304 **E-mail:** dcm@belgrade.mfa.gov.il	Mrs. Anat Katz First Secretary - Economic Affairs Embassy of Israel 24 Steven Close Singapore, 257964 Tel: (+65) 68349-220 Fax: (+65) 67372-502 **E-mail:** singapore@moital.gov.il **Site:** www.israelbiz.org.sg
SPAIN	**SOUTH AFRICA**
Mr. Gil Shaki First Secretary - Economic Affairs Embassy of Israel Velazquez 150, 7th Fl. Madrid 28002 Tel: (+34.91) 7829-577/8 Fax: (+34.91) 5640-002 **E-mail:** comercial@embajada-israel.es **Site:** http://www.israeltrade.gov.il/spain	Mr. Ilan Fluss Counsellor (Deputy Ambassador) Embassy of Israel 428 Kings Highway Lynnwood 0081 Pretoria Tel: (+2712) 3485-204/ 504-4703 Fax: (+2711) 4703-555 **E-mail:** dcm@pretoria.mfa.gov.il
SWEDEN	**SWITZERLAND**
Mr. Mordechai Ish-Shalom Minister - Economic Affairs Embassy of Israel Torstenssonsgatan 4 P.O.B 14006 S-10440 Stockholm Tel: (+46.8) 6639-270/8390 Fax: (+46.8) 6604-406 **E-mail:** Stockholm@moital.gov.il	Mr. Joseph Akerman First Secretary - Economic Affairs Deputy Permanent Representative to the WTO Permanent Mission of Israel to the U.N & International Organisation 1-3, Rue de la Paix 1202 Geneva Tel: (+41.22) 7160-507 Fax: (+41.22) 7160-416

Site: www.israeltrade.gov.il/sweden	**E-mail:** geneva@moital.gov.il **Site:** www.israeltrade.gov.il/switzerland
TAIWAN	**THAILAND**
Mr. Hovav Ref Director of Economic Affairs Israel Economic & Cultural Office ITB, Rm. 2408, 24 Fl. 333 Keelung Rd. Sec 1 Taipei 110 Tel: (+886.2) 2757-7221/2 Fax: (+886.2) 2757-7197 **E-mail:** taipei@moital.gov.il **Site:** www.israeltrade.gov.il/taiwan	Ms. Marie France-Majer Counsellor - Economic and Trade Affairs Embassy of Israel Ocean Tower 2, 25th Fl. 75 Sukhumvit 19 Bangkok 10110 Tel: (+66.2) 2049-240/1 Fax: (+66.2) 2049-245 **E-mail:** bangkok@moital.gov.il **Site:** www.israeltrade.gov.il/thailand
TURKEY	**UKRAINE**
Mr. Arie Cal Consul - Economic Affairs ***Consulate General of Israel*** ***Buyukdere Cad. Yapi Kredi Plaza*** ***C Blok Kat 7*** ***4 Levent 80620*** ***Istanbul*** Tel: (+90.212) 3176-548 Fax: (+90.212) 3176-549 **E-mail:** istra@bnet.net.tr ariecal@israeltrade.gov.il **Site:** www.israeltrade.gov.il/turkey	Mr. Valerie Golodivsky Senior Trade Officer Economic Department Embassy of Israel 34 L. Ukrainki Blvd. Kiev 01901 Tel: (+380.44) 2955-718 Fax: (+380.44) 2949-748 **E-mail:** trade@kiev.mfa.gov.il **Site:** www.israeltrade.gov.il/ukraine
UNITED KINGDOM	**U.S.A** – Atlanta
Mr. Meron Hacohen Minister - Commercial Affairs Embassy of Israel 2 Palace Green, London W8 4QB Tel: (+44.207) 9579-525/6 Fax: (+44.207) 4168-185 **E-mail:** london@moital.gov.il **Site:** www.israeltrade.gov.il/united-kingdom Mr. Moshe Langerman Minister – Economic Affairs Tel: (+44.207) 9579-528/9	Mr. Moshe Z. Shoham Trade Commissioner and Consul to the Midwest and Southeast Regions (Resident in Chicago) Israel Trade and Investment Center 111 E. Wacker Drive, Suit 1230 Chicago, Illinois 60601 Tel: (+1.312) 3322-160 Fax: (+1.312) 3322-163 **E-mail:** chicago1@moital.gov.il

Fax: (+44.207) 9579-593 **E-mail:** isr-econ@dircon.co.uk	
U.S.A – Chicago	**U.S.A** – Houston
Mr. Moshe Z. Shoham Trade Commissioner and Consul to the Midwest and Southeast Regions Israel Trade and Investment Center 111 E. Wacker Drive, Suit 1230 Chicago, Illinois 60601 Tel: (+1.312) 3322-160 Fax: (+1.312) 3322-163 **E-mail:** chicago1@moital.gov.il **Site:** www.israeltrade.gov.il/chicago	Mr. Joseph Abraham Consul - Economic Affairs Consulate General of Israel 24 Greenway Plaza, Suite 1500 Houston, Texas 77046 Tel: (+1.713) 6273-780 Fax: (+1.713) 6270-149 **E-mail:**Joseph.Abraham@mindspring.com
U.S.A – Los Angeles	**U.S.A** – Miami
Mr. Shai Aizin Consul - Economic Affairs Government of Israel 6380 Wilshire Blvd. Suite1700 Los Angeles, California 90048 Tel: (+1.323) 6587-924 Fax: (+1.323) 6510-572 **E-mail:** losangeles@moital.gov.il **Site:** www.israeleconomicla.com	Mr. Assaf Haim Director of Economic Affairs Consulate General of Israel Embassy of Israel 100 N. Biscayne Blvd. 1800 Florida 33132 Tel: (+1.305) 9259-411 Fax: (+1.305) 9259-455 **E-mail:** info@miami.mfa.gov.il
U.S.A – New York	**U.S.A** – Philadelphia
Mr. Zohar Peri Economic Minister for North America Government of Israel Economic Mission 800 Second Av. New York 10017 Tel: (+1.212) 4995-610 Fax: (+1.212) 4995-615 **E-mail:** zohar_peri@emus.gov.il	Mr. Shahar Shelef Consul Consulate General of Israel 230 South 15th St. Philadelphia, Pennsylvania 19102 Tel: (+1.215) 5465-556 Fax: (+1.215) 5453-986 **E-mail:** consul@philadelphia.mfa.gov.il
U.S.A – San Francisco	**U.S.A** – Washington
Mr. Tzach Segal Director Business Development Consulate General 456 Montgomery St. Suite 2100 San Francisco CA 94104	Ms. Liana Foksheniano Economic & Trade Officer Embassy of Israel 3514 International Drive N.W. Washington D.C. 20008

Tel: (+1.415) 8447-500/9 Fax: (+1.415) 8447-555 **E-mail:** economic@sanfrancisco.mfa.gov.il	Tel: (+1.202) 3645-692/5500 Fax: (+1.202) 3645-647 **E-mail:** liana@israelemb.org
URUGUAY	**UZBEKISTAN**
Mr. Joel Salpak Ambassador Embassy of Israel Bulevar Artigas 1585 Montevideo **E-mail:** ambassador@montevideo.mfa.gov.il Mr. Leo Vinovezky Second Secretary Tel: (+598.2) 4004-164 Fax: (+598.2) 4095-821 **E-mail:** dcm@montevideo.mfa.gov.il	Mr. Ofer Moreno Deputy Chief of Mission Embassy of Israel 3 Kahar St. Tashkent Tel: (+998.71) 1205-808/9/10 Fax: (+998.71) 1205-812 **E-mail:** dcm@tashkent.mfa.gov.il
VENEZUELA	**VIETNAM**
Ms. Livia Link Second Secretary Embassy of Israel Avenida Fransisco de Miranda Edif. Centro Empresarial de Miranda Piso 4, Oficina 4D Los Ruices 70081 Caracas Tel: (+58.212) 2394-511 /21 Fax: (+58.212) 2394-320 **E-mail:** info@caracas.mfa.gov.il dcm@caracas.mfa.gov.il	Mr. Avraham Nir Ambassador **E-mail:** ambassador@emisrael-vn.org Embassy of Israel 68 Nguyen Thai-Hoc P.O.B. 003 Hanoi Tel: (+84.4) 8433-140/3/4 Fax: (+84.4) 8435-760 Ms. Marie France-Majer Counsellor - Economic and Trade Affairs (Resident in Bangkok) **E-mail:** eco.sel@emisrael-vn.org

BASIC TITLES ON ISRAEL

IMPORTANT!

All publications are updated annually!

Please contact IBP, Inc. at ibpusa3@gmail.com for the latest ISBNs and additional information

TITLE
Israel A "Spy" Guide - Strategic Information and Developments
Israel A Spy" Guide"
Israel Aerospace Industries Handbook
Israel Aerospace Industries Handbook
Israel Agro and Biotechnology Industry Export-Import Directory
Israel Agro and Biotechnology Industry Export-Import Directory
Israel Air Force Handbook
Israel Air Force Handbook
Israel Army Weapon Systems Handbook
Israel Army Weapon Systems Handbook
Israel Army Weapon Systems Handbook
Israel Army, National Security and Defense Policy Handbook
Israel Army, National Security and Defense Policy Handbook
Israel Aviation and Aerospace Industry Handbook
Israel Aviation and Aerospace Industry Handbook
Israel Banking & Financial Market Handbook
Israel Banking & Financial Market Handbook
Israel Biotechnology Industry Export-Import Directory
Israel Biotechnology Industry Export-Import Directory
Israel Business and Investment Opportunities Yearbook
Israel Business and Investment Opportunities Yearbook
Israel Business and Investment Opportunities Yearbook Volume 1 Strategic Information and Opportunities
Israel Business and Investment Opportunities Yearbook Volume 2 Leading Export-Import, Business, Investment Opportunities and Projects
Israel Business Intelligence Report - Practical Information, Opportunities, Contacts
Israel Business Intelligence Report - Practical Information, Opportunities, Contacts
Israel Business Law Handbook - Strategic Information and Basic Laws
Israel Business Law Handbook - Strategic Information and Basic Laws
Israel Business Law Handbook - Strategic Information and Basic Laws
Israel Business Law Handbook - Strategic Information and Basic Laws
Israel Business Law Handbook Volume 2 Investment and Trade Laws Volume 2 Investment and Trade Laws
Israel Business Success Guide - Basic Practical Information and Contacts
Israel Central Bank & Financial Policy Handbook Volume 1 Strategic Information and Important Regulations
Israel Clothing & Textile Industry Handbook
Israel Clothing & Textile Industry Handbook
Israel Company Laws and Regulations Handbook
Israel Company Laws and Regulations Handbook - Strategic Information and Basic Laws
Israel Constitution and Citizenship Laws Handbook - Strategic Information and Basic Laws
Israel Consumer Goods Export-Import Directory (Arts & Crafts Footwear Furniture Cosmetics Toys))
Israel Consumer Goods Export-Import Directory (Arts & Crafts Footwear Furniture Cosmetics Toys))
Israel Cooperation with the States of the United State Handbook: Programs, organizations and contacts
Israel Cooperation with the States of the United State Handbook: Programs, organizations and contacts
Israel Country Study Guide - Strategic Information and Developments

TITLE
Israel Country Study Guide - Strategic Information and Developments
Israel Country Study Guide - Strategic Information and Developments Volume 1 Strategic Information and Developments
Israel Criminal Laws, Regulations and Procedures Handbook - Strategic Information, Regulations, Procedures
Israel Customs, Trade Regulations and Procedures Handbook
Israel Customs, Trade Regulations and Procedures Handbook
Israel Defense Industry Export-Import Directory (Aviation Airspace Automotive Electronics)
Israel Defense Industry Export-Import Directory (Aviation Airspace Automotive Electronics)
Israel Diplomatic Handbook - Strategic Information and Developments
Israel Diplomatic Handbook - Strategic Information and Developments
Israel Ecology & Nature Protection Handbook
Israel Ecology & Nature Protection Handbook
Israel Ecology & Nature Protection Laws and Regulation Handbook
Israel Economic & Development Strategy Handbook
Israel Economic & Development Strategy Handbook
Israel Education System and Policy Handbook
Israel Electoral, Political Parties Laws and Regulations Handbook - Strategic Information, Regulations, Procedures
Israel Electronics Computer Systems and Software Industry Export-Import Directory
Israel Electronics Computer Systems and Software Industry Export-Import Directory
Israel Energy Policy, Laws and Regulation Handbook
Israel Environmental Technology Industry Export-Import Directory
Israel Environmental Technology Industry Export-Import Directory
Israel Export-Import Trade and Business Directory
Israel Export-Import Trade and Business Directory
Israel Fishing and Aquaculture Industry Handbook - Strategic Information, Regulations, Opportunities
Israel Foreign Policy and Government Guide
Israel Foreign Policy and Government Guide
Israel Government and Business Contacts Handbook
Israel Government and Business Contacts Handbook
Israel Healthcare Sector Organization, Management and Payment Systems Handbook - Strategic Information, Programs and Regulations
Israel Immigration Handbook
Israel Immigration Handbook
Israel Immigration Laws and Regulations Handbook - Strategic Information and Basic Laws
Israel Industrial and Business Directory
Israel Industrial and Business Directory
Israel Insolvency (Bankruptcy) Laws and Regulations Handbook - Strategic Information and Basic Laws
Israel Intelligence & Security Activities & Operations Handbook
Israel Intelligence & Security Activities & Operations Handbook
Israel Internet and E-Commerce Investment and Business Guide - Strategic and Practical Information: Regulations and Opportunities
Israel Internet and E-Commerce Investment and Business Guide - Strategic and Practical Information: Regulations and Opportunities
Israel Investment & Business Guide
Israel Investment & Business Guide
Israel Investment and Business Guide - Strategic and Practical Information
Israel Investment and Business Guide - Strategic and Practical Information
Israel Investment and Business Guide Volume 2 Business, Investment Opportunities and Incentives

TITLE
Israel Investment and Business Profile - Basic Information and Contacts for Succesful investment and Business Activity
Israel Investment and Trade Laws and Regulations Handbook
Israel Investment, Trade Strategy and Agreements Handbook - Strategic Information and Basic Agreements
Israel IT & Telecommunication Industry Export-Import Directory
Israel IT & Telecommunication Industry Export-Import Directory
Israel Jewelry Industry Export-Import Directory
Israel Jewelry Industry Export-Import Directory
Israel Justice System and National Police Handbook
Israel Justice System and National Police Handbook
Israel Labor Laws and Regulations Handbook - Strategic Information and Basic Laws
Israel Land Ownership and Agriculture Laws Handbook
Israel Medical & Pharmaceutical Industry Handbook
Israel Medical & Pharmaceutical Industry Handbook
Israel Mineral & Mining Sector Investment and Business Guide - Strategic and Practical Information
Israel Mineral & Mining Sector Investment and Business Guide - Strategic and Practical Information
Israel Mining Laws and Regulations Handbook
Israel Prime Minister Ariel Sharon Handbook
Israel Prime Minister Ariel Sharon Handbook
Israel Privatization Programs and Regulations Handbook
Israel Privatization Programs and Regulations Handbook
Israel Recent Economic and Political Developments Yearbook
Israel Recent Economic and Political Developments Yearbook
Israel Recent Economic and Political Developments Yearbook
Israel Research & Development Policy Handbook
Israel Research & Development Policy Handbook
Israel Research & Development Policy Handbook
Israel Safety and Security Equipment Producers Export-Import Directory
Israel Safety and Security Equipment Producers Export-Import Directory
Israel Starting Business (Incorporating) in Israel Guide
Israel Starting Business (Incorporating) in....Guide
Israel Tax Guide Volume 1 Strategic Information and Basic Regulations
Israel Taxation Laws and Regulations Handbook
Israel Telecom Laws and Regulations Handbook
Israel Telecommunication Industry Business Opportunities Handbook
Israel Telecommunication Industry Business Opportunities Handbook
Israel Transportation Policy and Regulations Handbook
Israel: How to Invest, Start and Run Profitable Business in Israel Guide - Practical Information, Opportunities, Contacts
Israel: Incentives for Foreign Investors and Companies for Conducting Business In Israel
Israel: Incentives for Foreign Investors and Companies for Conducting Business In Israel Handbook

38.	Cayman Islands - Government System Handbook - Strategic Information and Developments
39.	Central African Republic - Government System Handbook - Strategic Information and Developments
40.	Chad - Government System Handbook - Strategic Information and Developments
41.	Chile - Government System Handbook - Strategic Information and Developments
42.	China - Government System Handbook - Strategic Information and Developments
43.	Colombia - Government System Handbook - Strategic Information and Developments
44.	Comoros - Government System Handbook - Strategic Information and Developments
45.	Congo - Government System Handbook - Strategic Information and Developments
46.	Congo, Democratic Republic - Government System Handbook - Strategic Information and Developments
47.	Cook Islands - Government System Handbook - Strategic Information and Developments
48.	Costa Rica - Government System Handbook - Strategic Information and Developments
49.	Cote d'Ivoire - Government System Handbook - Strategic Information and Developments
50.	Croatia - Government System Handbook - Strategic Information and Developments
51.	Cuba - Government System Handbook - Strategic Information and Developments
52.	Cyprus - Government System Handbook - Strategic Information and Developments
53.	Czech Republic - Government System Handbook - Strategic Information and Developments
54.	Denmark - Government System Handbook - Strategic Information and Developments
55.	Djibouti - Government System Handbook - Strategic Information and Developments
56.	Dominica - Government System Handbook - Strategic Information and Developments
57.	Dominican Republic - Government System Handbook - Strategic Information and Developments
58.	Ecuador - Government System Handbook - Strategic Information and Developments
59.	Egypt - Government System Handbook - Strategic Information and Developments
60.	El Salvador - Government System Handbook - Strategic Information and Developments
61.	Equatorial Guinea - Government System Handbook - Strategic Information and Developments
62.	Eritrea - Government System Handbook - Strategic Information and Developments
63.	Estonia - Government System Handbook - Strategic Information and Developments
64.	Ethiopia - Government System Handbook - Strategic Information and Developments
65.	Falkland Islands - Government System Handbook - Strategic Information and Developments
66.	Faroes Islands - Government System Handbook - Strategic Information and Developments
67.	Fiji - Government System Handbook - Strategic Information and Developments
68.	Finland - Government System Handbook - Strategic Information and Developments
69.	France - Government System Handbook - Strategic Information and Developments
70.	Gabon - Government System Handbook - Strategic Information and Developments
71.	Gambia - Government System Handbook - Strategic Information and Developments
72.	Georgia - Government System Handbook - Strategic Information and Developments
73.	Germany - Government System Handbook - Strategic Information and Developments
74.	Ghana - Government System Handbook - Strategic Information and Developments
75.	Gibraltar - Government System Handbook - Strategic Information and Developments
76.	Greece - Government System Handbook - Strategic Information and Developments
77.	Greenland - Government System Handbook - Strategic Information and Developments
78.	Grenada - Government System Handbook - Strategic Information and Developments
79.	Guam - Government System Handbook - Strategic Information and Developments
80.	Guatemala - Government System Handbook - Strategic Information and Developments
81.	Guernsey - Government System Handbook - Strategic Information and Developments
82.	Guinea - Government System Handbook - Strategic Information and Developments
83.	Guinea-Bissau - Government System Handbook - Strategic Information and Developments
84.	Guyana - Government System Handbook - Strategic Information and Developments
85.	Haiti - Government System Handbook - Strategic Information and Developments
86.	Honduras - Government System Handbook - Strategic Information and Developments
87.	Hungary - Government System Handbook - Strategic Information and Developments
88.	Iceland - Government System Handbook - Strategic Information and Developments
89.	India - Government System Handbook - Strategic Information and Developments

90. Indonesia - Government System Handbook - Strategic Information and Developments
91. Iran - Government System Handbook - Strategic Information and Developments
92. Iraq - Government System Handbook - Strategic Information and Developments
93. Ireland - Government System Handbook - Strategic Information and Developments
94. Israel - Government System Handbook - Strategic Information and Developments
95. Italy - Government System Handbook - Strategic Information and Developments
96. Jamaica - Government System Handbook - Strategic Information and Developments
97. Japan - Government System Handbook - Strategic Information and Developments
98. Jersey - Government System Handbook - Strategic Information and Developments
99. Jordan - Government System Handbook - Strategic Information and Developments
100. Kazakhstan - Government System Handbook - Strategic Information and Developments
101. Kenya - Government System Handbook - Strategic Information and Developments
102. Kiribati - Government System Handbook - Strategic Information and Developments
103. Korea, North - Government System Handbook - Strategic Information and Developments
104. Korea, South - Government System Handbook - Strategic Information and Developments
105. Kosovo - Government System Handbook - Strategic Information and Developments
106. Kurdistan - Government System Handbook - Strategic Information and Developments
107. Kuwait - Government System Handbook - Strategic Information and Developments
108. Kyrgyzstan - Government System Handbook - Strategic Information and Developments
109. Laos - Government System Handbook - Strategic Information and Developments
110. Latvia - Government System Handbook - Strategic Information and Developments
111. Lebanon - Government System Handbook - Strategic Information and Developments
112. Lesotho - Government System Handbook - Strategic Information and Developments
113. Liberia - Government System Handbook - Strategic Information and Developments
114. Libya - Government System Handbook - Strategic Information and Developments
115. Liechtenstein - Government System Handbook - Strategic Information and Developments
116. Lithuania - Government System Handbook - Strategic Information and Developments
117. Luxembourg - Government System Handbook - Strategic Information and Developments
118. Macao - Government System Handbook - Strategic Information and Developments
119. Macedonia,- Government System Handbook - Strategic Information and Developments
120. Madagascar - Government System Handbook - Strategic Information and Developments
121. Madeira- Government System Handbook - Strategic Information and Developments
122. Malawi - Government System Handbook - Strategic Information and Developments
123. Malaysia - Government System Handbook - Strategic Information and Developments
124. Maldives - Government System Handbook - Strategic Information and Developments
125. Mali - Government System Handbook - Strategic Information and Developments
126. Malta - Government System Handbook - Strategic Information and Developments
127. Man - Government System Handbook - Strategic Information and Developments
128. Marshall Islands - Government System Handbook - Strategic Information and Developments
129. Mauritania - Government System Handbook - Strategic Information and Developments
130. Mauritius - Government System Handbook - Strategic Information and Developments
131. Mayotte - Government System Handbook - Strategic Information and Developments
132. Mexico - Government System Handbook - Strategic Information and Developments
133. Micronesia - Government System Handbook - Strategic Information and Developments
134. Moldova - Government System Handbook - Strategic Information and Developments
135. Monaco - Government System Handbook - Strategic Information and Developments
136. Mongolia - Government System Handbook - Strategic Information and Developments
137. Monserrat - Government System Handbook - Strategic Information and Developments
138. Montenegro - Government System Handbook - Strategic Information and Developments
139. Morocco - Government System Handbook - Strategic Information and Developments
140. Mozambique - Government System Handbook - Strategic Information and Developments
141. Myanmar - Government System Handbook - Strategic Information and Developments
142. Nagorno-Karabakh Republic - Government System Handbook - Strategic Information and Developments

143. Namibia - Government System Handbook - Strategic Information and Developments
144. Nauru - Government System Handbook - Strategic Information and Developments
145. Nepal - Government System Handbook - Strategic Information and Developments
146. Netherlands - Government System Handbook - Strategic Information and Developments
147. New Caledonia - Government System Handbook - Strategic Information and Developments
148. New Zealand - Government System Handbook - Strategic Information and Developments
149. Nicaragua - Government System Handbook - Strategic Information and Developments
150. Niger - Government System Handbook - Strategic Information and Developments
151. Nigeria - Government System Handbook - Strategic Information and Developments
152. Niue - Government System Handbook - Strategic Information and Developments
153. Northern Cyprus (Turkish Republic of Northern Cyprus)
154. Northern Mariana Islands - Government System Handbook - Strategic Information and Developments
155. Norway - Government System Handbook - Strategic Information and Developments
156. Oman - Government System Handbook - Strategic Information and Developments
157. Pakistan - Government System Handbook - Strategic Information and Developments
158. Palau - Government System Handbook - Strategic Information and Developments
159. Palestine (West Bank & Gaza) - Government System Handbook - Strategic Information and Developments
160. Panama - Government System Handbook - Strategic Information and Developments
161. Papua New Guinea - Government System Handbook - Strategic Information and Developments
162. Paraguay - Government System Handbook - Strategic Information and Developments
163. Peru - Government System Handbook - Strategic Information and Developments
164. Philippines - Government System Handbook - Strategic Information and Developments
165. Pitcairn Islands - Government System Handbook - Strategic Information and Developments
166. Poland - Government System Handbook - Strategic Information and Developments
167. Polynesia French - Government System Handbook - Strategic Information and Developments
168. Portugal - Government System Handbook - Strategic Information and Developments
169. Qatar - Government System Handbook - Strategic Information and Developments
170. Romania - Government System Handbook - Strategic Information and Developments
171. Russia - Government System Handbook - Strategic Information and Developments
172. Rwanda - Government System Handbook - Strategic Information and Developments
173. Sahrawi Arab Democratic Republic - Government System Handbook - Strategic Information and Developments
174. Saint Kitts and Nevis - Government System Handbook - Strategic Information and Developments
175. Saint Lucia - Government System Handbook - Strategic Information and Developments
176. Saint Vincent and The Grenadines - Government System Handbook - Strategic Information and Developments
177. Samoa (American) A - Government System Handbook - Strategic Information and Developments
178. Samoa (Western) - Government System Handbook - Strategic Information and Developments
179. San Marino - Government System Handbook - Strategic Information and Developments
180. Sao Tome and Principe - Government System Handbook - Strategic Information and Developments
181. Saudi Arabia - Government System Handbook - Strategic Information and Developments
182. Scotland - Government System Handbook - Strategic Information and Developments
183. Senegal - Government System Handbook - Strategic Information and Developments
184. Serbia - Government System Handbook - Strategic Information and Developments
185. Seychelles - Government System Handbook - Strategic Information and Developments
186. Sierra Leone - Government System Handbook - Strategic Information and Developments
187. Singapore - Government System Handbook - Strategic Information and Developments
188. Slovakia - Government System Handbook - Strategic Information and Developments
189. Slovenia - Government System Handbook - Strategic Information and Developments
190. Solomon Islands - Government System Handbook - Strategic Information and Developments
191. Somalia - Government System Handbook - Strategic Information and Developments
192. South Africa - Government System Handbook - Strategic Information and Developments

193. Spain - Government System Handbook - Strategic Information and Developments
194. Sri Lanka - Government System Handbook - Strategic Information and Developments
195. St. Helena - Government System Handbook - Strategic Information and Developments
196. St. Pierre & Miquelon - Government System Handbook - Strategic Information and Developments
197. Sudan (Republic of the Sudan) - Government System Handbook - Strategic Information and Developments
198. Sudan South - Government System Handbook - Strategic Information and Developments
199. Suriname - Government System Handbook - Strategic Information and Developments
200. Swaziland - Government System Handbook - Strategic Information and Developments
201. Sweden - Government System Handbook - Strategic Information and Developments
202. Switzerland - Government System Handbook - Strategic Information and Developments
203. Syria - Government System Handbook - Strategic Information and Developments
204. Taiwan - Government System Handbook - Strategic Information and Developments
205. Tajikistan - Government System Handbook - Strategic Information and Developments
206. Tanzania - Government System Handbook - Strategic Information and Developments
207. Thailand - Government System Handbook - Strategic Information and Developments
208. Timor Leste (Democratic Republic of Timor-Leste) - Government System Handbook - Strategic Information and Developments
209. Togo - Government System Handbook - Strategic Information and Developments
210. Tonga - Government System Handbook - Strategic Information and Developments
211. Trinidad and Tobago - Government System Handbook - Strategic Information and Developments
212. Tunisia - Government System Handbook - Strategic Information and Developments
213. Turkey - Government System Handbook - Strategic Information and Developments
214. Turkmenistan - Government System Handbook - Strategic Information and Developments
215. Turks & Caicos - Government System Handbook - Strategic Information and Developments
216. Tuvalu - Government System Handbook - Strategic Information and Developments
217. Uganda - Government System Handbook - Strategic Information and Developments
218. Ukraine - Government System Handbook - Strategic Information and Developments
219. United Arab Emirates - Government System Handbook - Strategic Information and Developments
220. United Kingdom - Government System Handbook - Strategic Information and Developments
221. United States - Government System Handbook - Strategic Information and Developments
222. Uruguay - Government System Handbook - Strategic Information and Developments
223. Uzbekistan - Government System Handbook - Strategic Information and Developments
224. Vanuatu - Government System Handbook - Strategic Information and Developments
225. Vatican City (Holy See) - Government System Handbook - Strategic Information and Developments
226. Venezuela - Government System Handbook - Strategic Information and Developments
227. Vietnam - Government System Handbook - Strategic Information and Developments
228. Virgin Islands, British - Government System Handbook - Strategic Information and Developments
229. Wake Atoll - Government System Handbook - Strategic Information and Developments
230. Wallis & Futuna - Government System Handbook - Strategic Information and Developments
231. Western Sahara - Government System Handbook - Strategic Information and Developments
232. Yemen - Government System Handbook - Strategic Information and Developments
233. Zambia - Government System Handbook - Strategic Information and Developments
234. Zimbabwe - Government System Handbook - Strategic Information and Developments

WORLD COUNTRY STUDY GUIDES LIBRARY

Strategic political, geographic, economic, business information, contacts and important developments

Price: $99.95 each

1.	Abkhazia (Republic of Abkhazia) Volume 1 Strategic Information and Developments
2.	Afghanistan Country Study Guide Volume 1 Strategic Information and Developments
3.	Aland Country Study Guide Volume 1 Strategic Information and Developments
4.	Albania Country Study Guide Volume 1 Strategic Information and Developments
5.	Algeria Country Study Guide Volume 1 Strategic Information and Developments
6.	Andorra Country Study Guide Volume 1 Strategic Information and Developments
7.	Angola Country Study Guide Volume 1 Strategic Information and Developments
8.	Anguilla Country Study Guide Volume 1 Strategic Information and Developments
9.	Antigua and Barbuda Country Study Guide Volume 1 Strategic Information and Developments
10.	Antilles (Netherlands) Country Study Guide Volume 1 Strategic Information and Developments
11.	Argentina Country Study Guide Volume 1 Strategic Information and Developments
12.	Armenia Country Study Guide Volume 1 Strategic Information and Developments
13.	Aruba Country Study Guide Volume 1 Strategic Information and Developments
14.	Australia Country Study Guide Volume 1 Strategic Information and Developments
15.	Austria Country Study Guide Volume 1 Strategic Information and Developments
16.	Azerbaijan Country Study Guide Volume 1 Strategic Information and Developments
17.	Bahamas Country Study Guide Volume 1 Strategic Information and Developments
18.	Bahrain Country Study Guide Volume 1 Strategic Information and Developments
19.	Bangladesh Country Study Guide Volume 1 Strategic Information and Developments
20.	Barbados Country Study Guide Volume 1 Strategic Information and Developments
21.	Belarus Country Study Guide Volume 1 Strategic Information and Developments
22.	Belgium Country Study Guide Volume 1 Strategic Information and Developments
23.	Belize Country Study Guide Volume 1 Strategic Information and Developments
24.	Benin Country Study Guide Volume 1 Strategic Information and Developments
25.	Bermuda Country Study Guide Volume 1 Strategic Information and Developments
26.	Bhutan Country Study Guide Volume 1 Strategic Information and Developments
27.	Bolivia Country Study Guide Volume 1 Strategic Information and Developments
28.	Bosnia and Herzegovina Country Study Guide Volume 1 Strategic Information and Developments
29.	Botswana Country Study Guide Volume 1 Strategic Information and Developments
30.	Brazil Country Study Guide Volume 1 Strategic Information and Developments
31.	Brunei Country Study Guide Volume 1 Strategic Information and Developments
32.	Bulgaria Country Study Guide Volume 1 Strategic Information and Developments
33.	Burkina Faso Country Study Guide Volume 1 Strategic Information and Developments
34.	Burundi Country Study Guide Volume 1 Strategic Information and Developments
35.	Cambodia Country Study Guide Volume 1 Strategic Information and Developments
36.	Cameroon Country Study Guide Volume 1 Strategic Information and Developments
37.	Canada Country Study Guide Volume 1 Strategic Information and Developments

38.	Cape Verde Country Study Guide Volume 1 Strategic Information and Developments
39.	Cayman Islands Country Study Guide Volume 1 Strategic Information and Developments
40.	Central African Republic Country Study Guide Volume 1 Strategic Information and Developments
41.	Chad Country Study Guide Volume 1 Strategic Information and Developments
42.	Chile Country Study Guide Volume 1 Strategic Information and Developments
43.	China Country Study Guide Volume 1 Strategic Information and Developments
44.	Colombia Country Study Guide Volume 1 Strategic Information and Developments
45.	Comoros Country Study Guide Volume 1 Strategic Information and Developments
46.	Congo Country Study Guide Volume 1 Strategic Information and Developments
47.	Congo, Democratic Republic Country Study Guide Volume 1 Strategic Information and Developments
48.	Cook Islands Country Study Guide Volume 1 Strategic Information and Developments
49.	Costa Rica Country Study Guide Volume 1 Strategic Information and Developments
50.	Cote d'Ivoire Country Study Guide Volume 1 Strategic Information and Developments
51.	Croatia Country Study Guide Volume 1 Strategic Information and Developments
52.	Cuba Country Study Guide Volume 1 Strategic Information and Developments
53.	Cyprus Country Study Guide Volume 1 Strategic Information and Developments
54.	Czech Republic Country Study Guide Volume 1 Strategic Information and Developments
55.	Denmark Country Study Guide Volume 1 Strategic Information and Developments
56.	Djibouti Country Study Guide Volume 1 Strategic Information and Developments
57.	Dominica Country Study Guide Volume 1 Strategic Information and Developments
58.	Dominican Republic Country Study Guide Volume 1 Strategic Information and Developments
59.	Ecuador Country Study Guide Volume 1 Strategic Information and Developments
60.	Egypt Country Study Guide Volume 1 Strategic Information and Developments
61.	El Salvador Country Study Guide Volume 1 Strategic Information and Developments
62.	Equatorial Guinea Country Study Guide Volume 1 Strategic Information and Developments
63.	Eritrea Country Study Guide Volume 1 Strategic Information and Developments
64.	Estonia Country Study Guide Volume 1 Strategic Information and Developments
65.	Ethiopia Country Study Guide Volume 1 Strategic Information and Developments
66.	Falkland Islands Country Study Guide Volume 1 Strategic Information and Developments
67.	Faroes Islands Country Study Guide Volume 1 Strategic Information and Developments
68.	Fiji Country Study Guide Volume 1 Strategic Information and Developments
69.	Finland Country Study Guide Volume 1 Strategic Information and Developments
70.	France Country Study Guide Volume 1 Strategic Information and Developments
71.	Gabon Country Study Guide Volume 1 Strategic Information and Developments
72.	Gambia Country Study Guide Volume 1 Strategic Information and Developments
73.	Georgia Country Study Guide Volume 1 Strategic Information and Developments
74.	Germany Country Study Guide Volume 1 Strategic Information and Developments
75.	Ghana Country Study Guide Volume 1 Strategic Information and Developments
76.	Gibraltar Country Study Guide Volume 1 Strategic Information and Developments
77.	Greece Country Study Guide Volume 1 Strategic Information and Developments
78.	Greenland Country Study Guide Volume 1 Strategic Information and Developments
79.	Grenada Country Study Guide Volume 1 Strategic Information and Developments
80.	Guam Country Study Guide Volume 1 Strategic Information and Developments
81.	Guatemala Country Study Guide Volume 1 Strategic Information and Developments
82.	Guernsey Country Study Guide Volume 1 Strategic Information and Developments
83.	Guinea Country Study Guide Volume 1 Strategic Information and Developments
84.	Guinea-Bissau Country Study Guide Volume 1 Strategic Information and Developments
85.	Guyana Country Study Guide Volume 1 Strategic Information and Developments
86.	Haiti Country Study Guide Volume 1 Strategic Information and Developments
87.	Honduras Country Study Guide Volume 1 Strategic Information and Developments
88.	Hungary Country Study Guide Volume 1 Strategic Information and Developments
89.	Iceland Country Study Guide Volume 1 Strategic Information and Developments
90.	India Country Study Guide Volume 1 Strategic Information and Developments

91. Indonesia Country Study Guide Volume 1 Strategic Information and Developments
92. Iran Country Study Guide Volume 1 Strategic Information and Developments
93. Iraq Country Study Guide Volume 1 Strategic Information and Developments
94. Ireland Country Study Guide Volume 1 Strategic Information and Developments
95. Israel Country Study Guide Volume 1 Strategic Information and Developments
96. Italy Country Study Guide Volume 1 Strategic Information and Developments
97. Jamaica Country Study Guide Volume 1 Strategic Information and Developments
98. Japan Country Study Guide Volume 1 Strategic Information and Developments
99. Jersey Country Study Guide Volume 1 Strategic Information and Developments
100. Jordan Country Study Guide Volume 1 Strategic Information and Developments
101. Kazakhstan Country Study Guide Volume 1 Strategic Information and Developments
102. Kenya Country Study Guide Volume 1 Strategic Information and Developments
103. Kiribati Country Study Guide Volume 1 Strategic Information and Developments
104. Korea, North Country Study Guide Volume 1 Strategic Information and Developments
105. Korea, South Country Study Guide Volume 1 Strategic Information and Developments
106. Kosovo Country Study Guide Volume 1 Strategic Information and Developments
107. Kurdistan Country Study Guide Volume 1 Strategic Information and Developments
108. Kuwait Country Study Guide Volume 1 Strategic Information and Developments
109. Kyrgyzstan Country Study Guide Volume 1 Strategic Information and Developments
110. Laos Country Study Guide Volume 1 Strategic Information and Developments
111. Latvia Country Study Guide Volume 1 Strategic Information and Developments
112. Lebanon Country Study Guide Volume 1 Strategic Information and Developments
113. Lesotho Country Study Guide Volume 1 Strategic Information and Developments
114. Liberia Country Study Guide Volume 1 Strategic Information and Developments
115. Libya Country Study Guide Volume 1 Strategic Information and Developments
116. Liechtenstein Country Study Guide Volume 1 Strategic Information and Developments
117. Lithuania Country Study Guide Volume 1 Strategic Information and Developments
118. Luxembourg Country Study Guide Volume 1 Strategic Information and Developments
119. Macao Country Study Guide Volume 1 Strategic Information and Developments
120. Macedonia,Country Study Guide Volume 1 Strategic Information and Developments
121. Madagascar Country Study Guide Volume 1 Strategic Information and Developments
122. MadeiraCountry Study Guide Volume 1 Strategic Information and Developments
123. Malawi Country Study Guide Volume 1 Strategic Information and Developments
124. Malaysia Country Study Guide Volume 1 Strategic Information and Developments
125. Maldives Country Study Guide Volume 1 Strategic Information and Developments
126. Mali Country Study Guide Volume 1 Strategic Information and Developments
127. Malta Country Study Guide Volume 1 Strategic Information and Developments
128. Man Country Study Guide Volume 1 Strategic Information and Developments
129. Marshall Islands Country Study Guide Volume 1 Strategic Information and Developments
130. Mauritania Country Study Guide Volume 1 Strategic Information and Developments
131. Mauritius Country Study Guide Volume 1 Strategic Information and Developments
132. Mayotte Country Study Guide Volume 1 Strategic Information and Developments
133. Mexico Country Study Guide Volume 1 Strategic Information and Developments
134. Micronesia Country Study Guide Volume 1 Strategic Information and Developments
135. Moldova Country Study Guide Volume 1 Strategic Information and Developments
136. Monaco Country Study Guide Volume 1 Strategic Information and Developments
137. Mongolia Country Study Guide Volume 1 Strategic Information and Developments
138. Monserrat Country Study Guide Volume 1 Strategic Information and Developments
139. Montenegro Country Study Guide Volume 1 Strategic Information and Developments
140. Morocco Country Study Guide Volume 1 Strategic Information and Developments
141. Mozambique Country Study Guide Volume 1 Strategic Information and Developments
142. Myanmar Country Study Guide Volume 1 Strategic Information and Developments
143. Nagorno-Karabakh Republic Country Study Guide Volume 1 Strategic Information and Developments

144. Namibia Country Study Guide Volume 1 Strategic Information and Developments
145. Nauru Country Study Guide Volume 1 Strategic Information and Developments
146. Nepal Country Study Guide Volume 1 Strategic Information and Developments
147. Netherlands Country Study Guide Volume 1 Strategic Information and Developments
148. New Caledonia Country Study Guide Volume 1 Strategic Information and Developments
149. New Zealand Country Study Guide Volume 1 Strategic Information and Developments
150. Nicaragua Country Study Guide Volume 1 Strategic Information and Developments
151. Niger Country Study Guide Volume 1 Strategic Information and Developments
152. Nigeria Country Study Guide Volume 1 Strategic Information and Developments
153. Niue Country Study Guide Volume 1 Strategic Information and Developments
154. Northern Cyprus (Turkish Republic of Northern Cyprus)
155. Northern Mariana Islands Country Study Guide Volume 1 Strategic Information and Developments
156. Norway Country Study Guide Volume 1 Strategic Information and Developments
157. Oman Country Study Guide Volume 1 Strategic Information and Developments
158. Pakistan Country Study Guide Volume 1 Strategic Information and Developments
159. Palau Country Study Guide Volume 1 Strategic Information and Developments
160. Palestine (West Bank & Gaza) Country Study Guide Volume 1 Strategic Information and Developments
161. Panama Country Study Guide Volume 1 Strategic Information and Developments
162. Papua New Guinea Country Study Guide Volume 1 Strategic Information and Developments
163. Paraguay Country Study Guide Volume 1 Strategic Information and Developments
164. Peru Country Study Guide Volume 1 Strategic Information and Developments
165. Philippines Country Study Guide Volume 1 Strategic Information and Developments
166. Pitcairn Islands Country Study Guide Volume 1 Strategic Information and Developments
167. Poland Country Study Guide Volume 1 Strategic Information and Developments
168. Polynesia French Country Study Guide Volume 1 Strategic Information and Developments
169. Portugal Country Study Guide Volume 1 Strategic Information and Developments
170. Qatar Country Study Guide Volume 1 Strategic Information and Developments
171. Romania Country Study Guide Volume 1 Strategic Information and Developments
172. Russia Country Study Guide Volume 1 Strategic Information and Developments
173. Rwanda Country Study Guide Volume 1 Strategic Information and Developments
174. Sahrawi Arab Democratic Republic Volume 1 Strategic Information and Developments
175. Saint Kitts and Nevis Country Study Guide Volume 1 Strategic Information and Developments
176. Saint Lucia Country Study Guide Volume 1 Strategic Information and Developments
177. Saint Vincent and The Grenadines Country Study Guide Volume 1 Strategic Information and Developments
178. Samoa (American) A Country Study Guide Volume 1 Strategic Information and Developments
179. Samoa (Western) Country Study Guide Volume 1 Strategic Information and Developments
180. San Marino Country Study Guide Volume 1 Strategic Information and Developments
181. Sao Tome and Principe Country Study Guide Volume 1 Strategic Information and Developments
182. Saudi Arabia Country Study Guide Volume 1 Strategic Information and Developments
183. Scotland Country Study Guide Volume 1 Strategic Information and Developments
184. Senegal Country Study Guide Volume 1 Strategic Information and Developments
185. Serbia Country Study Guide Volume 1 Strategic Information and Developments
186. Seychelles Country Study Guide Volume 1 Strategic Information and Developments
187. Sierra Leone Country Study Guide Volume 1 Strategic Information and Developments
188. Singapore Country Study Guide Volume 1 Strategic Information and Developments
189. Slovakia Country Study Guide Volume 1 Strategic Information and Developments
190. Slovenia Country Study Guide Volume 1 Strategic Information and Developments
191. Solomon Islands Country Study Guide Volume 1 Strategic Information and Developments
192. Somalia Country Study Guide Volume 1 Strategic Information and Developments
193. South Africa Country Study Guide Volume 1 Strategic Information and Developments
194. Spain Country Study Guide Volume 1 Strategic Information and Developments
195. Sri Lanka Country Study Guide Volume 1 Strategic Information and Developments

196. St. Helena Country Study Guide Volume 1 Strategic Information and Developments
197. St. Pierre & Miquelon Country Study Guide Volume 1 Strategic Information and Developments
198. Sudan (Republic of the Sudan) Country Study Guide Volume 1 Strategic Information and Developments
199. Sudan South Country Study Guide Volume 1 Strategic Information and Developments
200. Suriname Country Study Guide Volume 1 Strategic Information and Developments
201. Swaziland Country Study Guide Volume 1 Strategic Information and Developments
202. Sweden Country Study Guide Volume 1 Strategic Information and Developments
203. Switzerland Country Study Guide Volume 1 Strategic Information and Developments
204. Syria Country Study Guide Volume 1 Strategic Information and Developments
205. Taiwan Country Study Guide Volume 1 Strategic Information and Developments
206. Tajikistan Country Study Guide Volume 1 Strategic Information and Developments
207. Tanzania Country Study Guide Volume 1 Strategic Information and Developments
208. Thailand Country Study Guide Volume 1 Strategic Information and Developments
209. Timor Leste (Democratic Republic of Timor-Leste) Country Study Guide Volume 1 Strategic Information and Developments
210. Togo Country Study Guide Volume 1 Strategic Information and Developments
211. Tonga Country Study Guide Volume 1 Strategic Information and Developments
212. Trinidad and Tobago Country Study Guide Volume 1 Strategic Information and Developments
213. Tunisia Country Study Guide Volume 1 Strategic Information and Developments
214. Turkey Country Study Guide Volume 1 Strategic Information and Developments
215. Turkmenistan Country Study Guide Volume 1 Strategic Information and Developments
216. Turks & Caicos Country Study Guide Volume 1 Strategic Information and Developments
217. Tuvalu Country Study Guide Volume 1 Strategic Information and Developments
218. Uganda Country Study Guide Volume 1 Strategic Information and Developments
219. Ukraine Country Study Guide Volume 1 Strategic Information and Developments
220. United Arab Emirates Country Study Guide Volume 1 Strategic Information and Developments
221. United Kingdom Country Study Guide Volume 1 Strategic Information and Developments
222. United States Country Study Guide Volume 1 Strategic Information and Developments
223. Uruguay Country Study Guide Volume 1 Strategic Information and Developments
224. Uzbekistan Country Study Guide Volume 1 Strategic Information and Developments
225. Vanuatu Country Study Guide Volume 1 Strategic Information and Developments
226. Vatican City (Holy See) Country Study Guide Volume 1 Strategic Information and Developments
227. Venezuela Country Study Guide Volume 1 Strategic Information and Developments
228. Vietnam Country Study Guide Volume 1 Strategic Information and Developments
229. Virgin Islands, British Country Study Guide Volume 1 Strategic Information and Developments
230. Wake Atoll Country Study Guide Volume 1 Strategic Information and Developments
231. Wallis & Futuna Country Study Guide Volume 1 Strategic Information and Developments
232. Western Sahara Country Study Guide Volume 1 Strategic Information and Developments
233. Yemen Country Study Guide Volume 1 Strategic Information and Developments
234. Zambia Country Study Guide Volume 1 Strategic Information and Developments
235. Zimbabwe Country Study Guide Volume 1 Strategic Information and Developments